HANDBOOK OF RESEARCH ON MERGERS AND ACQUISITIONS

Handbook of Research on Mergers and Acquisitions

Edited by

Yaakov Weber

Chair, Department of Strategy and Entrepreneurship, School of Business Administration, College of Management, Israel

Edward Elgar
Cheltenham, UK • Northampton, MA, USA

Published by
Edward Elgar Publishing Limited
The Lypiatts
15 Lansdown Road
Cheltenham
Glos GL50 2JA
UK

Edward Elgar Publishing, Inc.
William Pratt House
9 Dewey Court
Northampton
Massachusetts 01060
USA

A catalogue record for this book
is available from the British Library

Library of Congress Control Number: 2012943743

ISBN 978 1 84844 956 5 (cased)

Typeset by Servis Filmsetting Ltd, Stockport, Cheshire
Printed and bound by MPG Books Group, UK

Contents

Contributors

Mohammad Faisal Ahammad, Division of Accounting and Finance, Nottingham Business School, Nottingham Trent University, United Kingdom.

Neal M. Ashkanasy, University of Queensland, Australia.

Ziva Bachar-Rozen, Department of Political Sciences, The Western Galilee College, Acre, Israel.

Lars Bengtsson, Lund Technical University, Lund, Sweden.

Kimberly M. Ellis, Florida Atlantic University, Barry Kaye College of Business, Florida, USA.

Keith W. Glaister, Management School, The University of Sheffield, United Kingdom.

Pierre-Guy Hourquet, EDHEC Business School, Nice, France.

Paulina Junni, Hanken School of Economics, Helsinki, Finland.

Marie H. Kavanagh, University of Southern Queensland, Australia.

Bruce T. Lamont, The College of Business, Florida State University, USA.

Rikard Larsson, School of Economics and Management, Lund University, Lund, Sweden.

Mitchell Lee Marks, Department of Management, San Francisco State University, USA.

Olimpia Meglio, University of Sannio, Benevento, Italy.

Emmanuel Metais, EDHEC Business School, Nice, France.

Philip H. Mirvis, Center for Corporate Citizenship, Boston College, USA.

Annette L. Ranft, The College of Business, Florida State University, USA.

Taco H. Reus, Erasmus University, Rotterdam School of Management, the Netherlands.

Annette Risberg, Copenhagen Business School, Denmark.

Riikka M. Sarala, Bryan School of Business and Economics, University of North Carolina at Greensboro, USA.

Anne-Marie Søderberg, Copenhagen Business School, Denmark.

Günter K. Stahl, INSEAD, France, and WU ViennaAugasse, Vienna, Austria.

Shlomo Yedidia Tarba, Department of Economics and Management, The Open University, Raanana, Israel.

Eero Vaara, Hanken School of Economics, Helsinki, Finland.

Philippe Very, EDHEC Business School, Nice, France.

Yaakov Weber, School of Business Administration, College of Management, Rishon Lezion, Israel.

Introduction
Yaakov Weber

For the last four decades, researchers in various disciplines have been trying to explain the enduring paradox of the growing activity and volume of mergers and acquisitions (M&A) versus the high failure rate of M&A. Recent meta-analyses that examined the most studied variables (King et al., 2004; Stahl and Voigt, 2008) did not provide clear answers for this paradox or for the high failure rate of M&A. Scholars indicate that the results of many studies including those concerning the predictors of M&A success are inconsistent and confusing. It is clear that existing research on M&A provides limited and insufficient understanding of this important phenomenon.

Possible answers to this paradox may be that research on M&A as well as practice need new directions, some improvements and a different focus. These new directions and focus may include different, maybe new, variables, as well as different relationships among variables in this complex managerial task.

Some scholars (Weber and Fried, 2011a; Weber, 2011b, Weber et al., 2011; 2012) point out that a major drawback of existing literature is that, while the M&A is a multi-stage, multi-leveled, and multidisciplinary phenomenon, most of the research tends to be conducted in a single stage (for example, pre- or post-merger), omitting the stage of negotiation (a recent exception is Weber et al., 2011a), at a single level (for example, macro or micro) and in single disciplinary (for example, strategic management, or organizational behavior). Thus, current literature lacks a systematic framework that combines M&A stages and points at possible relationships between variables within and between all stages.

The goal of this book is to stimulate scholars to focus on such new directions and new relationships among variables in M&A. This complex, widespread and growing phenomenon of M&A will require the incorporation of multidisciplinary, multi-level and multi-stage models and analyses. Therefore, this book also aims to explore how underlying concepts and methodologies can make an important contribution towards understanding M&A process and its performance.

DIFFERENT STREAMS OF RESEARCH: DIFFERENT M&A STAGES

Several possible explanations exist for the lack of consistency that permeates recent studies on the relationship between success factors and M&A performance. For example, Teerikangas and Very (2006) focused on the sources of complexity underlying these relationships. Others suggested that different measures of performance (Zollo and Meier, 2008), national culture of the acquirer (Weber and Tarba, 2010), focus on micro- or macro-levels of analysis only, negotiation (Weber et al., 2011a) or taking into account either pre- or post-merger variables are not sufficient to find consistent relationships (Weber et al., 1996; Weber, 1996; Weber and Fried, 2011a).

The latter explanation relates to lack of connections between M&A stages. For example, the failure of past research to find a consistent relationship between synergy and M&A success may stem from an overemphasis on the pre-merger stage at the expense of the post-merger stage and the mechanisms inherent in processes of firm integration. It is interesting to see that historically, two main independent streams of management research have studied either the *pre*-acquisition or *post*-merger integration stages. One stream that focuses on the pre-acquisition stage examined the relationship between firm-level measures of financial performance and the strategic fit between buying and selling firms (for example, Singh and Montgomery, 1988; Palich et al., 2000), with a focus on the potential synergy and added value of the acquisition to the buying company, in other words, on choosing the right merger. The implicit assumption in these studies is that the activities and actions of the acquiring firm, during the pre-merger stage, are the sole determinants of value. Accordingly, studies either observe how managers in the acquiring firm search for alternatives or probe the content of their strategies, devoting less attention to the actual process of its implementation. For example, strategic theories, especially the "strategic fit" concept, suggest that relatedness between the buying and target firms depends upon synergy potential, and as such, it is the key determinant of value creation. Curiously, though, the empirical evidence drawn from studies of M&A that exhibit relatedness is mixed at best. Furthermore, the finance literature suggests that M&A, on average, do not add value to the acquiring firm, and that more probably, they are seriously detrimental to long-term shareholder value (King et al., 2004). The results of a recent meta-analytical study on the effects of finance and strategy variables on M&A performance by King et al. (2004: 197) led the authors to conclude, "Researchers simply may not be looking at the 'right' set of variables as predictors of post-acquisition performance."

The second stream of research focuses on the post-merger stage and examines the cultural fit of the buying and selling firms, and its impact on the success of the merged company (Chatterjee et al., 1992; Sarala and Vaara, 2010; Stahl and Voigt, 2008; Weber et al., 1996; Weber, 1996; Weber et al., 2011b). But findings are not always conclusive (Stahl and Voigt, 2008). These studies have paid little attention to cross-cultural management, for example, to the role of HR practices, given the effect of cultural differences on the success or failure of domestic and international M&A.

Note that the various bodies of literature on M&A seem to exist in a state of splendid isolation. This issue has been raised by several scholars many years ago (for example, Weber et al., 1996), but the situation has not changed much since then. Although they share some definitions and terms, authors writing about pre-merger and post-merger issues generally refrain from stepping onto each other's territory, thereby missing out on opportunities to fully understand the M&A process and the effects of each stage on M&A performance.

DIFFERENT STREAMS DIFFERENT RESEARCH LEVELS: CONTEXT VERSUS PROCESS

The strategy literature has focused primarily on strategic analysis that identified characteristics of the two firms in a merger in order to determine the best fit between the partners. These characteristics that supposedly suggest the best strategic choice, usually macro level variables, such as identification of industry and relatedness, and relative size of the two organizations, were the contextual factors that aim to predict, for instance, synergy potential, and thus, value creation in M&A.

On the other hand, organizational behavior literature has focused primarily on factors pertaining to the human side during post-merger integration. These include a focus on individual behavior and the processes during integration such as top executives' commitment and turnover as a result of culture clash (Lubatkin et al., 1999; Weber, 1996; Weber et al., 1996; Weber and Drori, 2011), structural changes (Ellis et al., 2012; Weber, Tarba and Rozen-Bachar, 2011c) and HR practices such as different effect of training and communication on M&A success in various countries (Weber et al., 2012).

As before, each stream of research focuses on different variables. These differences lead to a focus on different units of analysis that make comparison and consistency of findings very difficult.

NEGLECTED VARIABLES AND M&A STAGE

The two streams of research highlight one more difference between the types of variables that each stream investigated. This difference is related to the difference between context and process variables. Thus, while much research attention focuses more on context variables at the pre-merger stage, other research focuses on process variables at the post-merger stage. Context variables that have been studied at the pre-merger stages include, among others, relatedness, relative size of buyer to target firm, cultural differences and buyer experience in previous M&A. On the other hand, process variables that have been investigated, usually at the post-merger stages, include level of integration, identity, executive turnover, communication and structural changes.

Another characteristic of these differences between the two streams is that process variables at the pre-merger stage receive much less attention, such as due diligence process. On the other hand, research attention about the post-merger stage focuses on process variables rather than context variables.

Finally, while each stream of research focuses on specific types of variables (context versus process) in a specific merger stage (pre- or post-merger), the negotiation stage by and large has been neglected. There is a dearth of research attention to the negotiation stage, either context or process variables. A recent study (Weber et al., 2011a) pointed out the importance of cultural differences and planning to the result of the negotiation process.

Table I.1 presents examples of variables that receive relatively more attention. This table is divided into three stages, namely, pre-merger, negotiation, and post-merger stages and types (context versus process). Here, variables such as level of integration received much attention.

Table I.1   Variables that received high research attention

	Pre-merger	Negotiation	Post-merger
Context	Relatedness, cultural differences, experience, relative size		
Process			HR practices, level of integration, communication, structural changes

Table I.2   Examples of stages that may receive more research attention

	Pre-merger	Negotiation	Post-merger
Context	Trust	Cultural differences	Trust, identity, new culture
Process	Planning	Negotiation process	Integration approaches, HR practices, cultural changes

However, other variables such as structural changes and communication received attention only recently. Human resources (HR) practices in M&A have recently received much more attention in two special issues of the *Human Resource Management Journal* (2011). A recent article showed the role of cultural differences analysis, such as cultural differences analysis, in all M&A stages (Weber and Tarba, 2012). Yet, these are exceptions and most of the potential relationships are yet to be explored. Table I.2 presents examples for future research.

NEGLECTED CONNECTIONS AMONG M&A STAGES

While researchers agree that M&A are complex phenomena, most of the current research focuses on a few relationships, in many cases only context variables, or only on one stage. The overarching theme of this book is that focus on the pre-merger stage can only predict the potential of M&A performance. In fact, the failure to find a consistent relationship between context variables such as relatedness (synergy) and M&A success may stem from an over-emphasis on one stage, here the pre-merger stage, at the expense of the relationships with variables of the negotiation and post-merger stages.

Past literature, for instance about the pre-merger stage, with few exceptions, has not considered the possibility that management of the acquired firm, as well as interaction between buying and target firms following the merger, play a key role in M&A success. Indeed, the management of the post-merger stage and the integration process is crucial in determining the extent to which synergy potential is realized. However, to this point, only a limited number of management studies about the pre-merger stage have focused on identifying the factors that might contribute to post-merger integration success. It is likely, then, that strategic fit interacts with other systematic variables in the negotiation process and post-merger integration process in order to produce robust performance results.

There are numerous possible research questions and connections among variables within each stage and between different M&A stages. For example, looking at relationships between context and process variables at the pre-merger stages may lead to better understanding of the strategic analysis, the screening process and the recommended merger for executives. Such research questions may focus on the importance of a thorough and longer process of planning to the screening process. Similarly, the involvement of experts in the process of screening, from buying firm and the time and use of consultants, may shed light on what leads to M&A success.

These can be extended to relationships with other M&A stages. For example, does better planning of negotiation steps lead to better negotiation outcomes, as was recently suggested (Weber et al., 2011a). Does inclusion of implementation challenges in the choice of target firm make the post-merger integration process more successful than cases where these challenges were ignored?

In terms of context variables, what information (variables) can best be used in the negotiation process? What information and in what situations (cultural differences level, relatedness, relative size), when (timing), and how should it be used during negotiation steps?

Similarly, what information from the pre-merger stage will be needed for a successful post-merger integration process? And, what information should be used from the negotiation stage during post-merger integration? How does the information from the negotiation stage influence the strategic choice of buying a company? For the process part, how is information from the negotiation stages used in the screening process during the pre-merger stage? Will it influence the inclusion of executives and experts in the negotiation stage and in the pre-merger stage?

Similar research questions can be developed for the relationships between context and process variables in the post-merger stage. For example, Weber et al. (2012) found that the effect of training and communication processes on M&A success varied in different countries. This raises questions about the role of national culture of the acquirers on the effectiveness of various processes such as HR practices during the post-merger integration process.

What is the importance of context variables versus process variables? Are some necessary for success while others are sufficient?

Thus, scholars and executives must understand that to seize the potential of M&A that is usually identified in the pre-merger stage, the steps to be taken in the integration process must be discussed as part of the merger choice. For example, with its breadth of acquisition experience, Teva has structured HR tools for due diligence. Due diligence covers all HR aspects (legal, economic, structural, demographic, and turnover data) as well as other "soft" issues, especially culture (Claus, 2006).

Finally, negotiation is also an essential part of a successful M&A (Weber et al., 2011a).

Although the chapters in this book reflect a wide array of theoretical and empirical perspectives, their thematic focus hones in on three primary issues. First, some of the chapters take on the important task of incorporating both pre- and post-merger stages into their research, while others conduct interdisciplinary research. Second, other chapters consider the status of theory and research in specialized areas of M&A and investigate context variables that are under-explored, such as trust, and knowledge transfer, among others.

The chapters that follow thus focus attention on the connection between M&A stages and context variables, identifying gaps in the current research, presenting new findings, and generating new insights into important issues in M&A and how to manage them. The book is divided into four parts:

Part I: New models and empirical findings on connections between M&A stages
Part II: Research agenda and theoretical development on connection between M&A stages and context variables
Part III: Methodological issues in M&A research
Part IV: New and under-explored context and process variables in various M&A stages.

A brief overview of each part follows.

Part I: New Models and Empirical Findings on Connections between M&A Stages

This part focuses on empirical findings of new models that show the promise of the perspective that aims at connecting M&A stages. In Chapter 1, Günter Stahl combines context and process variables from pre- and post-merger stages to present an integrative model of the antecedents and consequences of trust in M&A, with the target firm members' trustworthiness perceptions as a key mediating process He provides empirical evidence supporting this model.

In the second chapter, Weber, Tarba, Stahl and Bachar-Rozen develop and test a new paradigm that combines pre- and post-merger stages. In fact, it combines the pre-merger context variables of two main research streams on M&A that were described earlier, namely strategic fit and organizational fit, with the post-merger integration process. Thus, it is argued that the fit of integration approach mediates the relationships between synergy potential and cultural differences on one hand, and M&A performance on the other.

Part II: Research Agenda and Theoretical Development on Connection between M&A Stages and Context Variables

This part presents theoretical development about both context variables and linkage between variables in and from different M&A stages. Chapter 3, "A research agenda to increase mergers and acquisition success" by Marks and Mirvis, highlights that the processes used to put companies together is essential for M&A success. In these processes, the chapter focuses on the factors which matter most in eventual M&A success.

In Chapter 4, Reus, Ellis, Lamont and Ranft focus on context variables and connections between M&A stages. They present four models that place process factors along with contextual factors in M&A research. These models offer insight into ways in which the understanding of contextual and process factors can be enhanced in tandem.

In the last chapter of this part (Chapter 5) "The dynamics of knowledge transfer in mergers and acquisitions", Junni, Sarala and Vaara explore the relationships among context variables in both pre- and post-merger stages, such as collective and individual absorptive capacity and post-integration processes such as operational integration, cultural integration and political behavior. They present an integrative model that maps some of the complex interrelations between these factors, and provide suggestions for further theoretical and empirical work.

Part III: Methodological Issues in M&A Research

This part focuses on methodological limitations as well as suggestions for new directions with methodological considerations. In the first chapter of this part (Chapter 6), Risberg and Meglio challenge the methodological common wisdom that there is high failure rate of M&A based on common performance measures. They divide the research findings into different categories, and show how meaningless, if not misleading, it is to compare the results of various studies on M&A performance in an attempt to make any claims about merger and acquisition performance in general.

In "Researching mergers and acquisitions with the case study method: idiographic understanding of longitudinal integration processes" (Chapter 7) Bengtsson and Larsson review and summarize the comparative strengths and weaknesses of case studies as well as the most versus less influential M&A case studies. Their review argues that case study methodology has successfully contributed to the field. Following this they analyse the impact of different case study designs on findings and their impact through a survey of 55 M&A cases. They conclude with methodological recommendations about how to increase case study contributions to M&A research.

In last chapter of this part, "Individual values and organizational culture during a merger: immovable objects or shifting sands?" (Chapter 8) Kavanagh and Ashkanasy investigate four methods of acculturation. They present empirical findings of a longitudinal, multi-level quantitative study and focus in particular on the extent and direction of change to individual values and organizational culture during the acculturation process that occurs at post-merger integration stage. The results indicate that the method of acculturation depended on the approach taken to manage the merger.

Part IV: New and Under-explored Context and Process Variables in Various M&A Stages

This part includes chapters that investigate new variables such as grief in M&A, and other under-explored context variables such as communication. In Chapter 9, Søderberg focuses on how communication can serve strategic purposes after a complex merger where one of many challenges is to embrace national, organizational and professional cultures in a transnational organization. She also highlights some of the benefits of adding a communication perspective to studies of post-merger integration processes and draw attention to the impact for practice and research of the communicative issues touched upon.

In Chapter 10 Ahammad, Glaister, Weber and Tarba investigate the determinants of top management retention in cross-border acquisitions. Applying both the theory of relative standing and the financial incentive mechanism of retention, they find that post-acquisition autonomy of the acquired firm and the acquirer's commitment to the acquired organization significantly affect top management retention.

In "Grief and the management of mergers and acquisitions" Very, Metais and Hourquet investigate hostile mergers and mergers of equals. They examine the likely occurrence of employees' grieving for their former organization during the integration process and the consequences of this grief on performance.

An overarching theme of this book is that the failure of past research to find a consistent relationship between synergy and M&A success may stem from an over-emphasis on the pre-merger stage at the expense of the post-merger stage and the mechanisms inherent in processes of firm integration. This book contains chapters that highlight and clarify some of the complexities, interconnected processes, and synchronized activities of both pre- and post-merger stages.

REFERENCES

Chatterjee, S., Lubatkin, M.H., Schweiger, D.M. and Weber, Y. (1992), 'Cultural differences and shareholders value: Explaining the variability in the performance of related mergers', *Strategic Management Journal*, 13: 319–334.

Claus, L. (2006), 'Strategic global HR at Teva Pharmaceuticals', *Thunderbird International Business Review*, **48** (6): 891–905.

Ellis, K.M., Weber, Y., Raveh, A. and Tarba, S.Y. (2012). 'Integration in large, related M&As: Linkages between contextual factors, integration approaches, and process dimensions', *European Journal of International Management*.

Gomes, E., Weber, Y., Brown, C. and Tarba, S.Y. (2011), *Mergers, Acquisitions and Strategic Alliances: Understanding the Process*, New York and Basingstoke, UK: Palgrave Macmillan.

King, D.R., Dalton, D.R., Daily, C.M. and Covin, J.G. (2004), 'Meta-analyses of post-acquisition performance: Indications of unidentified moderators', *Strategic Management Journal*, 25: 187–200.

Lubatkin, M., Schweiger, D. and Weber, Y. (1999), 'Top management turnover in related M&As: An additional test of the theory of relative standing', *Journal of Management*, **25** (1): 55–74.

Palich, L.E., Cardinal, L.B. and Miller, C.C. (2000), 'Curvilinearity in the diversification-performance linkage: An examination of over three decades of research', *Strategic Management Journal*, 155–174.

Sarala, R.M. and Vaara, E. (2010), 'Cultural differences, convergence, and crossvergence as explanations of knowledge transfer in international acquisitions', *Journal of International Business Studies*, 41: 1365–1390.

Singh, H. and Montgomery, C.A. (1988), 'Corporate acquisitions and economic performance', *Strategic Management Journal*, **8** (4): 377–386.

Stahl, G.K. and Voigt, A. (2008), 'Do cultural differences matter in mergers and acquisitions? A tentative model for examination', *Organization Science*, **19** (1): 160–176.

Teerikangas, S. and Very, P. (2006), 'The culture-performance relationship in M&A: From yes/no to how', *British Journal of Management*, **17** (S1): S31–S48.

Weber, Y. (1996), 'Corporate culture fit and performance in mergers and acquisitions', *Human Relations*, **49** (9): 1181–1202.

Weber, Y. and Drori, I. (2011), 'Integrating organizational and human behavior perspectives on mergers and acquisitions: looking inside the black box', *International Studies of Management and Organizations*, **41** (3): 76–95.

Weber, Y. and Fried, Y. (2011a), 'The role of HR practices in managing culture clash during the post-merger integration process', *Human Resource Management*, **50** (5): 565–570.

Weber, Y. and Fried, Y. (2011b), 'The dynamics of employee reactions during post-merger integration process', *Human Resource Management*, **50** (6): 777–781.

Weber, Y. and Tarba, S.Y. (2010), 'Human resource practices and performance of mergers and acquisitions in Israel', *Human Resource Management Review*, 20: 203–211.

Weber, Y. and Tarba, S.Y. (2011), 'Exploring culture clash in related mergers: Post-merger integration in the high-tech industry', *International Journal of Organizational Analysis*, **19** (3): 202–221.

Weber, Y. and Tarba, S.Y. (2012), 'Mergers and acquisitions process: The use of corporate culture analysis', *Cross-Cultural Management: An International Journal*, **19** (3): 288–303.

Weber, Y., Shenkar, O. and Raveh, A. (1996), 'National and corporate culture fit in mergers/acquisitions: An exploratory study', *Management Science*, **42** (8): 1215–1227.

Weber, Y., Belkin, T. and Tarba, S.Y. (2011a), 'Negotiation, cultural differences, and planning in mergers and acquisitions', *Proceedings of the EuroMed Academy of Management 2010 Annual Conference*, 1249–1257. Nicosia, Cyprus, November 2010.

Weber, Y., Tarba, S.Y. and Reichel, A. (2011b), 'International mergers and acquisitions performance: Acquirer nationality and integration approaches', *International Studies of Management & Organization*, **41** (3): 9–24.

Weber, Y., Tarba, S. and Rozen-Bachar, Z. (2011c), 'Mergers and acquisitions paradox – the mediating role of integration approach', *European Journal of International Management*, **5** (4): 373–393.

Weber, Y., Rachman-Moore, D. and Tarba, S.Y. (2012), 'Human resource practices during post-merger conflict and merger performance', *International Journal of Cross-Cultural Management* (forthcoming).

Zollo, M. and Meier, D. (2008), 'What is M&A performance?' *Academy of Management Perspectives*, **22** (3): 55–77.

PART I

NEW MODELS AND EMPIRICAL FINDINGS ON CONNECTIONS BETWEEN M&A STAGES

1 The role of trust in mergers and acquisitions: a conceptual framework and empirical evidence
Günter K. Stahl

There is a massive and rapidly growing body of research on the sociocultural and human resources issues involved in the integration of acquired or merging firms. Variables such as cultural fit (Björkman et al., 2007; Stahl and Voigt, 2008; Weber et al., 1996), management style similarity (Datta and Grant, 1990; Larsson and Finkelstein, 1999), the combining firms' interaction history (Porrini, 2004), the pattern of dominance between merging firms (Cartwright and Cooper, 1996; Hitt et al., 2001), the acquirer's degree of cultural tolerance (Chatterjee et al., 1992; Pablo, 1994), issues of procedural and distributive justice (Ellis et al., 2009; Meyer and Altenborg, 2007), attention to cultural and HR issues in the due diligence process (Gebhardt, 2003; Pucik et al., 2010), the acquirer's leadership philosophy and style (Kavanagh and Ashkanasy, 2006; Sitkin and Pablo, 2005) and, more broadly, the social climate surrounding a merger (Birkinshaw et al., 2000; Vaara, 2003) have increasingly been recognized as being critical to the success of the post-merger integration.

Another potentially important, but underexplored, factor in the success of mergers and acquisitions (M&A) is trust. Indirect evidence about the critical role of trust in the M&A process can be drawn from a large body of research that suggests that the development of trust is critical to the successful formation and implementation of cooperative alliances between firms, such as joint ventures, research and development (R&D) collaborations, and marketing partnerships (Child, 2001; Inkpen and Currall, 2004; Krishnan et al., 2006; Zaheer et al., 1998). For example, trust built as firms engage in repeated alliances reduces the likelihood of opportunism and other transaction costs (Gulati, 1995). Krishnan et al. (2006) found that the benefits of trust on alliance performance are magnified when partner behavioral uncertainty is high. They argue that trust allows for the benefit of the doubt in interpreting partner actions which facilitates openness in sharing knowledge and reduces fear of opportunistic behavior by alliance partners. This research is also relevant to M&A, where behavioral uncertainty is generally high, especially among the acquired firm's managers and employees.

While few attempts have been made to systematically examine the role of trust in the context of M&A, qualitative case studies (for example, Chua et al., 2005; Olie, 1994) as well as interviews with managers and employees affected by M&A (for example, Krug and Nigh, 2001; Schweiger et al., 1987) suggest that trust is critical to the successful implementation of M&A because it helps management to overcome resistance and gain commitment from the employees. The following quote from Daniel Vasella, CEO of Novartis, concerning the merger that created the Swiss pharmaceutical giant highlights both the importance and fragility of trust in M&A:

> Only in a climate of trust are people willing to strive for the slightly impossible, to make decisions on their own, to take initiative, to feel accountable; trust is a prerequisite for working together effectively; trust is also an ally to fight bureaucracy. . . . We must fill this vacuum as fast as we can, we must restore confidence. We must earn it by "walking the talk", with candour, integrity, openness, fairness . . . We need to create a culture based on trust. (Chua et al., 2005: 391–392).

Despite the large body of anecdotal evidence supporting the critical role of trust in M&A, surprisingly little is known about the factors that facilitate or hinder the development of trust in acquired or merging organizations, and how that trust might influence the post-merger integration process. In the following sections, I attempt to provide some insight into when, why, and how trust matters in M&A. I present an integrative model that synthesizes our current understanding of the antecedents and consequences of trust in M&A, with target firm members' trustworthiness perceptions as a key mediating process, and provide empirical evidence supporting this model. This chapter is not intended as a critique of models that posit strategic and economic drivers of M&A activity and success; instead, it is intended to offer a supplement to that literature by synthesizing the growing body of research on the psychological and sociocultural factors that promote successful post-merger integration, with a particular focus on trust dynamics in M&A.

WHEN DOES TRUST MATTER IN MERGERS AND ACQUISITIONS?

M&A are driven by the quest for value. While some M&A may be motivated by purely financial reasons, the *raison d'être* of related-business acquisitions is to improve the competitive position of one or both of the firms by generating "synergies", whereby in combination the two firms create more value than each could achieve alone. Consistent with a value creation perspective on M&A (Haspeslagh and Jemison, 1991; Hitt et al., 2001; Stahl et al., 2005), the basic premise underlying this chapter is that following the M&A transaction, some degree of interorganizational integration is necessary to achieve the strategic intent of the deal. Except for the rare case when a target firm is acquired at a discount to its intrinsic value, the execution of a well-designed integration process that captures all forecasted synergies is therefore critical (Schweiger, 2002).

Processes related to the development of trust appear to be most important in related acquisitions that require substantial interdependence between the combining firms. While there are few cases when an acquired firm is either entirely absorbed or left completely autonomous, M&A researchers seem to agree that related acquisitions require higher levels of operational integration and lead to greater organizational changes in the target firm – and thus increase the potential for conflict (Buono and Bowditch, 1989; Datta, 1991; Larsson and Finkelstein, 1999; Schweiger, 2002; Weber et al., 1996). Trust does not appear as critical an issue in acquisitions that require lower levels of integration, because acquired units are usually granted a considerable degree of autonomy and there is less extensive interaction among the employees of the combining firms (David and Singh, 1994; Slangen, 2006).

WHY DOES TRUST MATTER IN MERGERS AND ACQUISITIONS?

Central to most definitions of trust are the notions of risk and vulnerability. In the absence of risk, trust is irrelevant because there is no vulnerability (Lewicki and Bunker, 1996; Mayer et al., 1995; Rousseau et al., 1998). In this study, we refer to trust as "a psychological state comprising the intention to accept vulnerability based upon positive expectations of the intentions or behavior of another" (Rousseau et al., 1998: 395). Conversely, distrust can be defined as negative expectations of another's intentions or behavior (Sitkin and Roth, 1993; Lewicki et al., 1998). This conceptualization of trust has also been applied to interorganizational relationships. For instance, in joint ventures, factors such as open communication and information exchange, task coordination, informal agreements, and levels of surveillance are all manifestations of trust based on a willingness to rely on, or be vulnerable to, another party under a condition of risk (Currall and Inkpen, 2002; Inkpen and Currall, 1997).

It has been observed that the turbulence following the announcement of a merger or an acquisition creates a breeding ground for distrust because the situation is unpredictable, easy to misinterpret, and people feel vulnerable (Hurley, 2006; Jemison and Sitkin, 1986; Schweiger and Walsh, 1990). Social networks and mutual understanding established through years of working together are sometimes destroyed in an instant. With a new organization, a new top management team and a new superior, there is little trust initially and employees are left wondering what the next wave of changes will bring and whether they will be negatively affected (Datta and Grant, 1990; Hambrick and Cannella, 1993; Lubatkin et al., 1999). The period following the announcement of a merger or takeover is thus one of intense risk assessment in which employees have to judge whether the acquiring firm's management (or their own management) can be trusted.

Theoretical work on trust has suggested that trust can take various forms, ranging from cognitive-based (or "calculative") trust, which is based on the predictability, dependability, and consistency of another party's behavior, to affect-based (or "identification-based") trust, which is rooted in emotional attachment and concern for the other party's welfare (Lewicki et al., 2006; Mayer et al., 1995). Consistent with prior research on interorganizational trust, the focus of this chapter is mainly on calculus-based trust, which involves a predominantly cognitive assessment of others' trustworthiness. This does not imply that employees affected by M&A have an unbiased and accurate view of the acquiring managers' (or their own managers') trustworthiness. Research suggests that following the announcement of a merger or takeover, employees tend to place disproportionate weight on rumors and other unreliable information sources while selectively searching for, discounting, or reinterpreting important information (Kramer, 1999; Marks and Mirvis, 2001; Sitkin and Stickel, 1996). Given the high degree of uncertainty and limited amount of information that is often available after the announcement of a merger, the effects of such perceptual and attributional biases on employees' trust judgments may be profound.

HOW DOES TRUST MATTER IN MERGERS AND ACQUISITIONS?

Research on trust within and between organizations has shown that trust exists at different levels. While most research on interorganizational trust has been carried out at the firm level of analysis (Ariño, de la Torre and Ring, 2001; Das and Teng, 1998; Ring and Van de Ven, 1992; Vlaar et al., 2007), trust has also been conceptualized at the individual, dyadic or group level or as a multilevel phenomenon (for example, Currall and Inkpen, 2002; Zaheer et al., 1998).

Figure 1.1 presents the theoretical model developed in the following

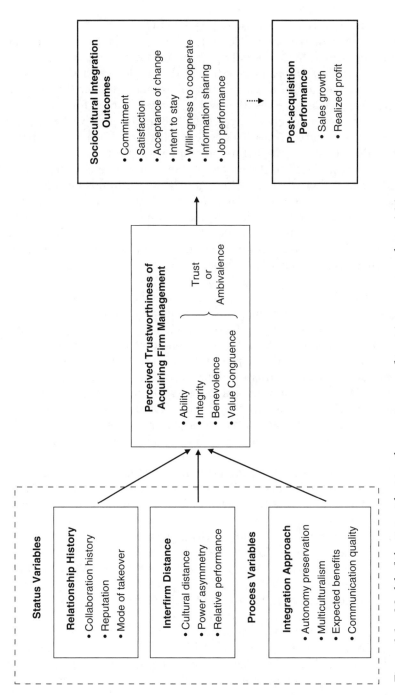

Figure 1.1   Model of the antecedents and consequences of trust in mergers and acquisitions

discussion. It focuses on trust relations between the two main parties involved in a merger or an acquisition: the top management of the acquiring firm or, in the case of a merger, the dominant partner (henceforth, *acquiring firm management*); and the employees of the acquired firm or, in the case of a merger, the subordinate partner (henceforth, *target firm members*). Thus, the level of analysis chosen for the trustor is the individual or, on an aggregated level, the group (that is, the members of the target firm). This conceptualization of trust is consistent with Zaheer et al.'s (1998) definition of interorganizational trust as "the extent of trust placed in the partner organization by the members of a focal organization" (p. 142). Although trust expectations do ultimately reside within the individual, this conceptualization of trust does not preclude the possibility that individuals within an organization have a collectively-held trust orientation toward another group (that is, the acquiring firm management) or the organization as a whole (that is, the acquiring firm) (Gulati, 1995; Nooteboom et al., 1997; Zaheer et al., 1998).

The model proposes that target firm members' perceptions of the acquiring firm management's trustworthiness are affected by a set of factors related to the firms' relationship history, interfirm distance, and integration approach. Although trust is composed of distinct elements or dimensions that can vary independently, it is proposed that the different dimensions of perceived trustworthiness form an overall trust impression that lead the target firm members to assess how much the acquiring firm management can be trusted (Mayer et al., 1995). More specifically, the model suggests that target firm members' perceptions of the acquiring firm managers' trustworthiness in terms of their ability, benevolence, integrity, and value congruence converge into a generalized trust judgment or result in a state of ambivalence, depending on whether the trustworthiness attributions are consistent or conflicting (see Stahl and Sitkin, 2010). These trust dynamics are posited to affect a variety of attitudinal and behavioral outcomes, as discussed below.

One approach to understanding why a given party will have a greater or lesser amount of trust for another party is to consider attributes of the trustee (Gabarro, 1978; Hurley, 2006; Mayer et al., 1995; Whitener et al., 1998). Mayer et al. (1995) proposed that individuals' trust in others is based on their propensity to trust and their perceptions of others' trustworthiness, rooted in their interpretation of the attributes and behavior of others. Their model of organizational trust suggests that three characteristics of a trustee are particularly critical for the development of trust: ability, integrity, and benevolence. In addition, trust research has shown that value congruence is another important element of trust (Gabarro,

1978; Sitkin and Roth, 1993). These characteristics are important if researchers are to understand the factors that influence the development of trust in the aftermath of a merger or takeover.

Ability. The perceived ability or competence of a party is an essential element of attributions about that party's trustworthiness (Butler, 1991; Mayer et al., 1995; Sitkin and Roth, 1993). Gabarro (1978), from interviewing executives, identified nine bases of trust, of which four – functional competence, interpersonal competence, business sense, and judgment – are related to the ability dimension. Competence perceptions also play an important role in interorganizational relationships. For example, Mishra (1996) observed that to the extent that a supplier's products meet a buyer's quality standards, the buyer will no longer inspect those products before accepting delivery, evidencing greater trust in the supplier's competence.

Benevolence. Trust in another party in terms of benevolence, goodwill or concern does not mean that the other party lacks any self-interest; rather, "trust in terms of concern means that such self-interest is balanced by interest in the welfare of others" (Mishra, 1996: 267). For instance, in manager–subordinate relationships, acting in a way that protects employees' interests, being sensitive to employees' needs, and refraining from exploiting employees for the benefit of one's own interests all affect the degree to which managers are judged to have benevolence (Whitener et al., 1998). In interorganizational relationships, a party can logically expect another party to act benevolently if both parties share the same goals and interests. Research on cooperative alliances between firms has shown that goal congruence and the perceived benefits derived from an alliance have a positive impact on the mutual trust and commitment of the parties involved (Ring and van de Ven, 1992; Sarkar, et al., 1997).

Integrity. Integrity perceptions can be explained in terms of expectations about the reliability, dependability, or consistency of a person's behavior (Butler, 1991; Hurley, 2006; Mayer et al., 1995). For example, in manager–subordinate relationships, if managers behave consistently over time and across situations, employees can better predict manager's future behavior and become willing to take risks in their relationship with their supervisor (Whitener et al., 1998). If, on the other hand, employees notice a discrepancy between what managers preach and what they practice, perceptions of managers' trustworthiness will deteriorate. The consistency of a party's past actions, credible communications about the trustee from other parties, and the extent that the party's actions are congruent with his or her words all affect the degree to which that party is judged to have integrity (Mayer et al., 1995).

Value Congruence. In addition to the ability, integrity and benevolence perceptions, research indicates that perceived value congruence helps to establish trust between individuals, groups, and organizations (Gabarro, 1978; Sitkin and Stickel, 1996; Young-Ybarra and Wiersema, 1999). Trustworthiness attributions often involve the perception that the trustee adheres to a set of principles that the trustor finds acceptable. Such perceptions are facilitated by value congruence between the parties involved in a relationship. In contrast, distrust may be engendered when an individual is perceived as not sharing key values, because "[w]hen a person challenges an organization's fundamental values, that person may be perceived as operating under values so different from the group's that the violator's underlying world view becomes suspect" (Sitkin and Roth, 1993: 371). In interorganizational relationships, it has been shown that shared norms and values facilitate the creation and maintenance of trust between firms (for example, Gulati, 1995; Sarkar et al., 1997).

Next, we will explore how, in the context of M&A, factors related to the relationship history, interfirm distance, and integration approach may influence target firm members' perceptions of the acquiring managers' trustworthiness along these four dimensions.

ANTECEDENTS OF TARGET FIRM MEMBERS' TRUST IN THE ACQUIRING FIRM MANAGEMENT

Figure 1.1 suggests that target firm members' trustworthiness perceptions are affected by a set of status variables, which comprise aspects of the acquirer–target relationship, as well as process variables related to the acquirer's integration approach. These two sets of variables are not independent of each other. For instance, factors such as collaboration history, cultural distance or mode of takeover will likely affect the degree of control imposed on the target, that is, whether the acquirer will adopt a more "hands-on" or "hand-off" integration strategy (Haspeslagh and Jemison, 1991; Hunt, 1990; Pablo, 1994). Also, variables within each of the two sets of antecedents cannot be assumed to be completely independent of each other. For example, the degree to which the acquirer removes autonomy from the target firm is likely to affect the quality of communication between the two firms (Jemison and Sitkin, 1986).

Next, we discuss each of the variables and their proposed relationships.

Relationship history is composed of the target firm's preexisting relationship with the acquiring firm, the acquiring firm's reputation, and the mode of takeover. We propose that the extent to which the members of a target firm perceive the acquiring firm's management to be trustworthy is a function of prior interfirm contact or, in the absence of a history of collaboration, the reputation of the acquirer. *Reputation* represents a cumulative record of past behaviors, serving as a reliable signal of the ability, dependability, benevolence, and value congruence of a counterpart. The behavior of firms in relationships with other partners allows potential partners to infer their future behavior and may thus facilitate or hinder the emergence of trust (Johnson et al., 1997; Parkhe, 1993).

Even more powerful than reputation is direct experience, or a *history of collaboration*. A large body of research on the role of trust in work groups, strategic alliances, and socially embedded partnerships suggests that trust evolves over time through repeated interactions between partners (Gulati, 1995; Ring and Van de Ven, 1992; Zaheer et al., 1998). Like romantic relationships, interfirm relationships mature with interaction frequency, duration, and the diversity of challenges that partners encounter and face together (Lewicki et al., 1998). As Rousseau et al. (1998: 399) have noted, "[r]epeated cycles of exchange, risk taking, and successful fulfillment of expectations strengthen the willingness of trusting parties to rely upon each other and expand the resources brought into the exchange". Furthermore, partners come to learn each other's idiosyncrasies and develop deeper mutual understanding over time, which improves the affective quality of the relationship (Inkpen and Currall, 2004; Parkhe, 1993). This indirect evidence from the alliance literature suggests that in acquisitions, familiarity through prior contact may facilitate the emergence of a shared identity and trust. However, Ring and Van de Ven (1992) have argued that trust can be expected to emerge between organizations only when they have *successfully* completed transactions in the past and they perceive one another as complying with norms of equity. If members of the target firm and the acquiring firm had a conflict-rich or inequitable exchange prior to the acquisition, this is likely to limit the potential for trust to emerge. Thus, both the length and the quality of the prior relationship with the acquiring firm will be critical in influencing target firm members' trust.

Finally, we propose that the *mode of takeover* or tone of the negotiations – whether it is friendly or hostile – is an important factor in determining target firm members' trust. It has been argued that hostile takeover tactics can result in sharp interorganizational conflict and difficulties integrating acquired firms (Buono and Bowditch, 1989; Hambrick and Cannella, 1993; Hitt et al., 2001). Hambrick and Cannella (1993) have observed that the atmosphere surrounding a hostile takeover is often characterized by bitterness and acrimony, making smooth social integration after the deal less likely; and that trust can erode quickly when executives from a hostile takeover target and those of the acquiring firm battle each other in a public forum, each being suspicious of the other's intentions and claiming the other party's lack of integrity. Social Identity Theory (Tajfel, 1982; Turner, 1982) suggests that under conditions of external threat, such as in a hostile takeover attempt, "us-versus-them" thinking is likely to set in, with individuals striving to maintain their positive social identity by idealizing their own group and denigrating the other. Support for this proposition can be found in research findings that show that hostile takeover attempts lead to resistance and increased cohesiveness among the target firm members (Elsass and Veiga, 1994; Krug and Nigh, 2001).

Collectively, these arguments suggest that the relationship history, which is made up of the direct experiences that the members of the target firm had with the acquiring firm in the past, as well as the reputation that the acquirer brings to the relationship, will be critical in influencing trust. If the acquirer's executives have repeatedly demonstrated their ability, integrity, benevolence and value congruence over an extended period of time, they are more likely to be perceived as trustworthy.

<u>Interfirm distance.</u> The second set of trust antecedents proposed in this chapter affect trustworthiness attributions through perceptions of interfirm distance. These variables include cultural distance, power asymmetry, and relative performance.

The *cultural distance* hypothesis (Hofstede, 1980) suggests that the difficulties, costs, and risks associated with cross-cultural contact increase with growing cultural differences between two individuals, groups, or organizations. Although studies that tested the cultural distance hypothesis in the context of M&A have yielded inconclusive results (see Cartwright and Schoenberg, 2006; Stahl and Voigt, 2008; Teerikangas and Very, 2006; Weber and Drori, 2008 for reviews), trust research has shown that shared norms and values facilitate the development of trust and the emergence of a shared identity (Lewicki et al., 1998; Sarkar et al., 1997). Conversely, trust can erode and the potential for conflict increase when a person or group is perceived as not sharing key values (Sitkin and Roth, 1993). Social Identity Theory suggests that in a merger situation, the mere existence of two different cultures is enough to lead to in-group out-group bias and conflict: Organizational members, while emphasizing their own positive distinctiveness, tend to exaggerate the differences between their own and the partner's culture (for example, Hogg and Terry, 2000; Kleppestø, 2005; Vaara, 2003). In-group bias and out-group derogation are likely to be greatest when the out-group is perceived to be very different from the in-group, such as in cross-border acquisitions (Elsass and Veiga, 1994). As a result of social categorization processes, out-group members may be perceived "as uniformly unethical or malevolent, incompetent, and ill-informed – and the in-group is viewed in the opposite terms" (Sitkin and Stickel, 1996: 212). In cross-border acquisitions, feelings of resentment, hostility, and mistrust may be further fueled by cultural stereotypes, prejudices and xenophobia (Teerikangas and Very, 2006; Vaara, 2003).

Cultural distance is thus likely to affect trust not only through perceptions of value congruence, but also because it increases the likelihood that the other party is ascribed various negative attributes, such as incompetence, malevolence, or lack of integrity.

Power asymmetry refers to the extent to which there can be a unidirectionality of influence from acquirer to target. The capability and tendency of the acquiring firm for exercising power to enforce its preferences upon the target is particularly strong when the acquirer is significantly larger than the target firm. In such cases, target firm members' needs tend to get overlooked or trivialized by the acquirer (Datta and Grant, 1990; Hambrick and Cannella, 1993; Jemison and Sitkin, 1986). As Pablo (1994) has noted, the effect of power differences "is not simply the overwhelming and domination of the smaller entity through sheer magnitude, but also the intensification of beliefs about superiority and inferiority" (p. 810). Acquiring executives tend to adopt an attitude of superiority and treat the members of the target firm as inferior, thus leading to status degradation and the voluntary departure of key employees (Hambrick and Cannella, 1993; Lubatkin et al., 1999). Research suggests that the mere existence of power asymmetries may generate suspicion and mistrust through anticipation of dominance by the acquiring executives. For instance, it has been observed that target firm members altered their behavior in response to the threat of a powerful buyer even prior to being acquired, for example, by seeking employment elsewhere (Hambrick and Cannella, 1993; Krug and Nigh, 2001). Also, research on alliances suggests that as power asymmetry increases, the weaker party tends to become distrustful because the more powerful party has no need to be trusting and can use its relative power to obtain cooperation (Das and Teng, 1998; Kumar, 1996).

Underperformance of the target relative to the acquirer may have a similar effect on trust. Poor target firm performance in the past is likely to increase an acquirer's tendencies toward arrogance and domination (Datta and Grant, 1990; Jemison and Sitkin, 1986). Hambrick and Cannella (1993) have observed that even if executives of a poorly performing firm are not fired outright after their acquisition, they may feel inferior or depart voluntarily because they are anticipating the dominating behaviors of their "conquerors". Lower-level employees are likely to experience anxiety from fears they might lose their jobs or be unable to meet the acquirer's performance standards. Paradoxically, though, it has been observed that when a smaller or underperforming firm is acquired by a significantly larger or financially healthy buyer, target firm members often welcome the takeover and are energized to become part of something larger or more successful than themselves (for example, Chaudhuri, 2005; Evans et al., 2002). This is especially true when they see the acquiring company as being a savior or having a more enlightened culture, or when they see other positive outcomes in being associated with the acquirer (better pay, more prestige, and so on). For example, Bastien (1987) observed that the overall mood of target employees was celebratory and optimistic after a "white knight" acquisition by a healthy buyer. Being liberated from weak and ineffective management may enhance target firm employees' trust, because they perceive the acquirer's executives as more effective and competent than their own. Thus, we propose that there is not a general effect of power asymmetry and relative performance on target firm members' trust. Rather, these attributes will lead to conflicting trustworthiness perceptions: while being acquired by a significantly larger, more powerful, and more successful company may be a frightening prospect to the members of a target firm, the greater power and superior performance of the acquirer relative to the target may at the same time elicit perceptions of managerial competence and, thus, trustworthiness.

Integration approach. In addition to the status variables discussed above, our analysis suggests that trust is influenced by a set of process variables relating to how the acquirer approaches the post-acquisition integration. Although, theoretically, integration can result in a balanced merging of two organizations, cultures and workforces, this balance rarely occurs in practice. Instead, the acquirer or dominant partner typically *removes autonomy* from the target firm and imposes a rigorous set of rules, systems, and performance expectations upon it in order to gain quick control (Datta and Grant, 1990; Hambrick and Cannella, 1993; Jemison and Sitkin, 1986; Pablo, 1994). Because tight controls tend to signal the absence of trust, their use typically hampers its emergence, thus resulting in a cycle of escalating distrust (Inkpen and Currall, 2004; Jemison and Sitkin, 1986). Autonomy removal can be devastating from the perspective of the members of the target firm and lead to feelings of helplessness and open hostility, as managers and employees vigorously defend their autonomy – a situation that Datta and Grant (1990) have termed the "conquering army syndrome". In such a situation, it seems likely that the acquirer's executives are perceived as uniformly malevolent and not to be trusted. They may also be seen as lacking integrity, especially if target firm members perceive a gap between the acquirer's stated goals and intentions, and the actual integration approach taken, as in the case of the DaimlerChrysler "merger" (Epstein, 2004; Vlasic and Stertz, 2000).

The degree to which an acquiring firm tends to impose its policies, norms and expectations on the target firm depends on the acquirer's *multiculturalism* (Chatterjee et al., 1992; Nahavandi and Malekzadeh, 1988; Pablo, 1994). The term multiculturalism refers to the degree to which an organization values cultural diversity and is willing to tolerate and encourage it (Nahavandi and Malekzadeh, 1988). A multicultural acquirer considers diversity an asset, and is therefore likely to allow an acquired firm to retain its own values and modus operandi. In contrast, a unicultural acquirer emphasizes conformity and adherence to a unique organizational ideology, and is therefore more likely to impose its culture on the target firm. Jemison and Sitkin (1986) have observed that cultural arrogance and insensitivity can trigger feelings of resentment, anger and hostility on the part of the target firm members. Cultural intolerance is also likely to increase the tendency to overemphasize cultural differences, thereby resulting in perceived value incongruence and an attitude polarization toward distrust (Sitkin and Roth, 1993).

There is evidence that the *expected benefits* of the organizational changes that result from the takeover, particularly the quality of the post-acquisition reward and job security changes, is a critical factor in determining employees' reactions to an acquisition (Hunt, 1990; Schweiger and Walsh, 1990; Van Dick et al., 2006). For instance, Graves (1981), in a case study of an acquisition of a firm of brokers in the reinsurance industry found that the employee reactions depended to a large extent on the personal benefits and losses attributed to the takeover. If the members of a target firm see the takeover as a chance for more job security and increased prospects for compensation and promotion, this is likely to affect their attitudes toward the acquirer in a positive way, and reduce the potential for conflict (Cartwright and Cooper, 1996; Schweiger, 2002). As an illustration, Bartels et al. (2006) found that the expected utility of the merger (anticipated benefits such as salary increases or more job security) was the strongest predictor of employees' identification with the post-merger organization.

Finally, we propose that the *quality of communication* is a key factor in determining the level of trust that target firm members have in the acquirer's management. Mergers and acquisitions are associated with high degrees of stress and uncertainty for the individuals affected by them, especially those of the target firm. Providing acquired employees with credible and relevant information has been shown to reduce the uncertainty associated with a takeover and to mitigate the negative effects on perceptions of managers' trustworthiness (Bastien, 1987; Schweiger and DeNisi, 1991). The quality of communication has also been shown to increase employees' identification with the post-merger organization (Bartels et al., 2006). A lack of credible and open communication, on the other hand, has been found to result in intense rumor activity, anxiety over job security, and feelings of suspicion and mistrust (Buono and Bowditch, 1989; Marks and Mirvis, 1998). While the credibility of the information provided by the acquirer can be considered a *sine qua non* for trust to

emerge, Hogan and Overmyer-Day (1994) found that too much information disseminated to employees in acquisitions characterized by high levels
of integration exacerbated undesirable attitudes and behaviors, because it
increased anxiety in a situation where employees already felt overwhelmed
and uncertain about their jobs. Thus, the quality and proper timing of
the communication may be more important in affecting trust than the
amount of information provided by the acquirer. For example, failure to
share relevant information in a timely manner may be judged to be typical
of the acquiring executives' incompetence; ambiguous, contradictory, or
incorrect information disseminated by the acquirer may be perceived as
a sign of managers' duplicity or dishonesty; the use of detached language
devoid of emotion when informing employees about necessary layoffs
may convey the impression that managers lack compassion and care;
and differences in communication style may be seen as an indicator of
fundamental value incongruence. Because ineffective communication can
promote a distorted picture of the acquiring executives' motives, intentions and actions, we propose that communication quality will affect
trustworthiness perceptions along all four dimensions.

HOW THE DIMENSIONS OF PERCEIVED TRUSTWORTHINESS COMBINE IN MERGERS AND ACQUISITIONS

The above evidence suggests that aspects of the firms' relationship history,
interfirm distance, and the acquirer's integration approach affect target
firm members' trust through perceptions of the acquiring managers'
ability, integrity, benevolence, and value congruence. However, from the
trust literature it is not clear how the bases of trust combine in influencing
overall trust. While some scholars have suggested that the dimensions of
perceived trustworthiness combine multiplicatively in determining overall
trust (for example, Mishra, 1996), others have argued that there may be
situations in which a meaningful amount of trust can develop with lesser
degrees of one or more of the factors, thus suggesting an additive effect
on trust (for example, Mayer et al., 1995). Yet others have proposed that
the different bases of trust do not combine, but, rather, that individuals
tend to "partition" their trust and work with interaction partners around
specific and compartmentalized interdependencies (Lewicki et al., 1998).
   The model presented in this chapter rests on the idea that the four
dimensions of perceived trustworthiness vary largely independently of
one another and represent different components of an overall trust construct. This implies that each of the dimensions contributes to a general-

ized assessment of how much the other party can be trusted (or must be mistrusted). The simplest cases of generalized trust or generalized distrust assume high or low levels of all four factors. In these cases, target firm members' perceptions of the acquiring firm management's ability, benevolence, integrity, and value congruence will converge into one overall trust judgment.

However, there are several reasons why "complex trust" – that is, some combined level of trust and distrust, resulting in a state of ambivalence – is more common in the aftermath of M&A (Stahl and Sitkin, 2010). One reason is conflicting trustworthiness perceptions on the part of the acquired employees. For example, high performance of the acquirer relative to the target may elicit perceptions of managerial competence, but at the same time raises concerns about the acquiring executives' benevolence. In other words, target firm employees may trust the acquiring managers to make competent decisions, but not necessarily trust them to act in accordance with their needs and interests. Such conflicting trustworthiness perceptions are likely to undermine the development of a singular overall trust expectation (Lewicki and Wiethoff, 2000). Moreover, the specific configuration of antecedent variables may facilitate the development of trust in terms of some dimensions but hamper the emergence of trust on others. For example, a powerful acquirer may be inclined to remove autonomy from the target firm and impose its culture, systems, and performance expectations upon it in order to gain quick control, yet at the same time provide strong incentives for the target firm members to conform (for example, Chaudhuri, 2005). In such a situation, target firm members have reason to trust the acquirer in some respects, but have reason to be wary and suspicious in other respects. This should alert us to the fact that trust relations between the members of the merging firms are multifaceted and inherently ambivalent.

CONSEQUENCES OF TARGET FIRM MEMBERS' TRUST IN THE ACQUIRING FIRM MANAGEMENT

Figure 1.1 proposes that the degree to which the target firm members trust the acquiring firm management is likely to affect a variety of behavioral and attitudinal outcomes, as well as the post-acquisition performance.

Sociocultural integration outcomes. Sociocultural integration represents an important dimension of acquisition success from an organizational and human resources perspective. It has been defined as the creation of positive attitudes towards the new organization, the development of a sense of shared identity and compatible values, and the gaining of commitment and motivation from acquired personnel (Birkinshaw et al., 2000; Björkman et al., 2007; Shrivastava, 1986). In M&A research, the level and success of sociocultural integration has been assessed using various behavioral and attitudinal measures, including employee commitment (for example, Weber et al., 1996), satisfaction (Stahl, Larsson, Kremershof and Sitkin, 2011), resistance (for example, Larsson and Finkelstein, 1999), turnover (for example, Schoenberg, 2004), acculturation (for example, Larsson and Lubatkin, 2001) and cooperation (for example, Weber et al., 1996). These variables capture different aspects of the sociocultural integration process, but have been shown to be highly interrelated (Stahl and Voigt, 2008; Weber et al., 1996).

Most of these attitudes and behaviors require a willingness to be vulnerable on the part of the target firm members and to engage in behaviors that put them at risk – and thus require some degree of trust (Lewicki et al., 2006; Mayer et al., 1995). In the aftermath of a takeover, the willingness to be vulnerable may be manifested in target firm employees who engage in open and candid communication with managers of the acquiring firm, who are willing to subjugate their personal goals for the goals of the new organization, and who remain with the organization even though they could get attractive jobs elsewhere. Conversely, the negative employee reactions and integration outcomes often observed in M&A, such as employee resistance, lack of commitment to the new organization, a focus on personal security rather than organizational goals, a tendency to not pass information up or down, and high rates of turnover (Buono and Bowditch, 1989; Marks and Mirvis, 1998; Olie, 1990; Schweiger, 2002) may reflect an unwillingness on the part of the target firm members to engage in behaviors that put them at risk. These dysfunctional attitudes and behaviors can thus be partly explained in terms of trust (or a lack thereof). This reasoning is supported by the results of two meta-analyses of research on the role of trust in organizational settings (Dirks and Ferrin, 2001, 2002), which suggest that trust affects a variety of attitudinal and behavioral outcomes, including communication and information sharing, organizational commitment, citizenship behavior, and intent to stay in the organization – the very variables that have been observed to be suffering during the post-merger integration phase.

Post-acquisition performance. The model presented in this chapter proposes that a lack of trust on the part of the target firm members will not only undermine the sociocultural integration process, but will also lead to poor performance in the post-acquisition period. A growing body of research (for example, Birkinshaw et al., 2000; Haspeslagh and Jemison, 1991; Larsson and Lubatkin, 2001; Schweiger, 2002) has shown that the execution of a well-designed integration process that minimizes interorganizational, interpersonal and intercultural friction is essential to capturing anticipated synergies. For example, Birkinshaw et al. (2000), in a study of foreign acquisitions made by Swedish multinationals, found that mutual respect and trust made the post-acquisition capability transfer and resource sharing easier; successful efforts to transfer knowledge and capabilities, in turn, facilitated the development of a shared identity and trust. These findings suggest that poor sociocultural integration and lack of trust may limit the effectiveness of the task integration efforts and hinder the exploitation of synergies. Failure to realize anticipated synergies may be reflected in accounting-based performance measures such as declining sales, profits, or return on assets (Harrison et al., 1991).

Collectively, these arguments suggest that lack of trust may affect the post-acquisition performance in two ways: first, through its adverse effect on the sociocultural integration process; and, second, by undermining the transfer of capabilities, resource sharing, and interorganizational learning.

DOES TRUST MATTER IN MERGERS AND ACQUISITIONS? EMPIRICAL EVIDENCE

Preliminary evidence for the model of trust presented in this chapter comes from qualitative case studies (Chua et al., 2005; Köster and Stahl, 2012), as well as several empirical studies that used a variety of methodologies (Stahl et al., 2006, 2012; Stahl et al., 2011). These studies focused on different aspects of trust dynamics in M&A (trust antecedents, consequences of trust, contextual factors affecting trust) and different stages of the M&A process (trust at announcement, trust during integration, trust several years after the deal), but they all support the critical role of trust in M&A. Table 1.1 provides a synopsis of the main findings and conclusions.

Two of the studies will be described in more detail below, as they offer some particularly interesting insights into the antecedents and consequences of trust in M&A.

Case Survey Research. Stahl et al. (2011) used a case survey design to test hypotheses derived from the model of trust dynamics in M&A presented in this chapter. Case surveys involve the quantification of a group of case studies for statistical analysis (Bullock and Tubbs, 1987; Jauch et al., 1980). A total of 50 cases that addressed trust issues during the post-acquisition integration period were identified and content-analyzed. The final sample comprised both domestic and cross-border acquisitions in a variety of industries.

The case survey results suggest that while aspects of the combining firms' relationship history and interfirm distance, such as pre-acquisition

Table 1.1 Empirical research on the role of trust in mergers and acquisitions: synopsis of study findings

Reference	Methodology	Key Findings and Conclusions
Stahl, Chua and Pablo, 2012	Policy Capturing	This policy capturing study revealed that target firm member trust in the acquirer is positively related to the firms' collaboration history, the friendliness of the takeover, and the attractiveness of the acquirer's HR policy and reward system, and negatively related to autonomy removal. The results suggest significant national dissimilarities between Germany and Singapore in the relationship of trust and four predictor variables (collaboration history, friendliness of takeover, domestic versus cross-border, autonomy removal). No significant differences between the Singaporean and German samples were found in the relationship between trust and the attractiveness of acquirer's HR policies and reward systems.
Stahl, Larsson, Kremershof and Sitkin, 2011	Case Survey	The model tested in this case survey proposes that the acquiring and target firms' relationship history, interfirm distance, and acquirer's integration approach will affect target firm member trust in the acquirer. Target firm trust, in turn, is proposed to influence several sociocultural integration outcomes as well as post-acquisition performance. The results suggest that certain aspects of the relationship history and interfirm distance, such as the firms' collaboration history and pre-acquisition performance differences, are poor predictors of trust, whereas integration process variables, such as speed of integration, communication quality, and acquirer multiculturalism are major factors influencing trust.

| Köster and Stahl, 2012 | Case Study | The Lenovo-IBM case study presents the attempts on the part of the former IBM and Lenovo sides to manage the integration process, particularly the cultural and people issues involved. Lenovo's approach aimed at increasing IBM members' trust by emphasizing that this was a "marriage of equals, based on trust, respect and compromise" (Lenovo CEO Yang stepped down to make way for IBM's Steve Ward; Lenovo's new global headquarters was set up in New York; the top management restructuring foresaw an even split between Chinese and Western executives), as well by promoting shared values and implementing communication enhancement programs ("Trash Bin Project"; "East Meets West Program") and achieving tighter integration through organizational restructuring (e.g., new management structure leading to closer integration of various functions). However, after only eight months Steve Ward resigned as CEO, which leaves room for speculation that the sociocultural integration was not as successful as previously assumed. |
| Chua, Engeli and Stahl, 2005 | Case Study | The case study about the merger of Ciba-Geigy and Sandoz is an example of the importance of trust in M&A. By the surprisingly sudden announcement of the planned merger and a lack of communication, trust on both sides was damaged. By openly addressing the issue of mistrust and dealing with the cultural and people issues involved in the integration of the two firms, Novartis' CEO Daniel Vasella aimed at restoring the trustworthiness of top management by demonstrating integrity, openness and competence, all key factors associated with trust. |

performance differences, power asymmetry, and cultural distance, are relatively poor predictors of trust, integration process variables such as the speed of integration, acquirer multiculturalism, quality of communication, and perceived employee benefits are major factors influencing target firm member trust at announcement and during integration. Given that trust requires a willingness to be vulnerable and to engage in behaviors that put one at risk (Mayer et al., 1995), it is understandable that target firm members' trust is closely associated with aspects of the integration approach taken by the acquirer. Integration-related factors such as the acquirer's tolerance for diversity, the adoption of a hands-off integration approach, and the quality of the post-acquisition reward and job security changes not only have a major impact on acquired employees' lives and careers; they also reveal much about the acquiring executives' competence, integrity, value congruence and concern – and, thus, their trustworthiness.

This study further suggests that not only does trust have a powerful effect on target firm members' attitudes and behaviors, it may also contribute to the realization of synergies, as reflected in accounting-based performance improvements. This is consistent with research on post-merger integration that indicates that aspects of the sociocultural integration process, such as the acquirer's ability to build an atmosphere of mutual respect and trust, facilitate the transfer of capabilities, resource sharing and learning; and that, conversely, sociocultural and human resources problems can undermine the realization of projected synergies (for example, Birkinshaw et al., 2000; Larsson and Finkelstein, 1999; Stahl and Voigt, 2008).

Policy Capturing Research. Another study (Stahl et al., 2006; 2012) tested the assumption that the way target firm employees respond to a takeover is contingent on their national origin, thus requiring a country-compatible post-acquisition integration strategy. The antecedents of target firm members' trust in the acquiring firm management were examined in a cross-national sample of German, Canadian and Singaporean employees using a policy-capturing design. Policy capturing involves presenting respondents with a set of scenarios in which multiple theoretically determined decision criteria are embedded, and asking respondents to make decisions (for example, the decision to trust another party) based on each scenario. The policy-capturing method provides for the degree of standardization and experimental control necessary to make cross-national comparisons.

Five factors hypothesized to affect target firm members' trust after a takeover were found to be significant influences on employees' trust judgments: the combining firms' collaboration history; the mode of takeover; whether it was a domestic or cross-border acquisition; the degree of autonomy removal; and the attractiveness of the acquiring firm's HR policies and reward system. While the perceived benefits to the target employees (in terms of the acquirer's HR policies and compensation and benefits system) was by far the most powerful predictor of employee trust in all three groups, this study found significant differences in the way the German, Canadian and Singaporean employees reacted to an acquirer's integration approach. For instance, German employees responded more negatively to hostile takeover tactics, removal of autonomy, and acquisition by a foreign acquirer (as opposed to an acquirer from the home country) than Singaporeans. For Singaporean employees, the history of collaboration between the two firms prior to the acquisition was a major factor in determining their reactions to the takeover, while for the German respondents the firms' interaction history was largely irrelevant in affecting the level of trust in the acquiring firm management.

Collectively, the results of this policy-capturing study support Goulet and Schweiger's (2006) observation that "acquirers may be culturally predisposed in the way they approach integration, and that targets may be culturally predisposed in the way they respond to integration" (p. 410). We conclude that companies engaged in cross-border acquisitions need to consider contingencies in the cultural and institutional contexts and adapt their approaches for integrating acquired firms.

WHEN, HOW AND WHY TRUST MATTERS IN MERGERS AND ACQUISITIONS: IMPLICATIONS FOR RESEARCH AND PRACTICE

Scholars have long criticized the lack of theory development and the fragmented nature of research in the area of M&A integration, arguing that M&A are multifaceted phenomena that require a research approach that integrates concepts and ideas from various disciplines (Larsson and Finkelstein, 1999; Schweiger and Goulet, 2000; Shimizu et al., 2004). In an effort toward a more theoretically grounded understanding of the process of sociocultural integration (Birkinshaw et al., 2000; Shrivastava, 1986), I applied trust theory to the domain of M&A integration. By linking organizational, cultural, and human resource perspectives on M&A to notions drawn from the trust literature, it is possible to gain a better understanding of the mechanisms by which aspects of the acquirer–target relationship, as well as process variables related to the acquirer's integration approach affect target firm members' reactions to a takeover.

Despite a large body of anecdotal evidence that supports the critical role that trust plays in M&A, surprisingly little is known about the factors that facilitate or hinder the development of trust in acquired organizations. Our analysis of the role that trust perceptions play in the post-merger integration period is very much in line with recent research on the process of sociocultural integration in M&A (for example, Birkinshaw et al., 2000; Calipha et al., 2010; Goulet and Schweiger, 2006). This research has shown that in the aftermath of M&A, trust is fragile – it is easily broken and hard to repair. For instance, M&A case studies (Chua et al., 2005; Olie, 1994; Sales and Mirvis, 1984) suggest that the uncertainty associated with M&A, impending layoffs, and the disruption of social networks create a breeding ground for distrust. In such situations, relatively minor trust violations may be sufficient to "tip the scales" (Dirks and Ferrin, 2001: 461) and result in a drift towards distrust, because individuals will tend to perceive the violation in ways consistent with their already low levels of trust – as yet another sign of the acquiring managers' incompetence, duplicity, or malevolence. The tendency to interpret trust violations in ways consistent with initial trust levels seems particularly strong in situations characterized by some degree of ambiguity. In these cases, trust (or distrust) provides a perceptual "lens" that affects the interpretation of the other party's past actions, the conclusions one draws about the factors motivating the other party's actions, and predictions of the other party's future behavior (Dirks and Ferrin, 2001; Kramer, 1999). These cognitive processes and perceptual biases can go a long way toward explaining the negative and self-reinforcing trust cycles often observed in M&A (for example, Jemison and Sitkin, 1986). They also explain why it may take a long time to build trust after a merger or takeover, but only an instant to destroy it.

Of particular interest to management practice are the findings pertaining to the antecedents of target firm members' trust in the acquiring firm management. Collectively, the results support a "process perspective" on acquisitions (Haspeslagh and Jemison, 1991), which holds that the extent to which synergies are realized depends to a large extent on the ability of the acquirer to manage the integration process effectively. More specifically, the case survey results suggest that trust problems are probably better dealt with through careful planning and management of the integration process than through incorporating trust considerations in the selection and due diligence investigation of targets. A number of actions can be taken by the acquiring firm's executives to build trust and secure commitment from acquired employees. In particular, resisting the temptation to impose one's culture on the target firm, improving the quality of communication, and offering proper incentives are likely to generate more positive trust dynamics and thereby contribute to better sociocultural integration outcomes. In terms of perceived benefits, HR policies and practices that are seen as transparent and fair, financial incentives to employees who ought to be retained, and adequate support of those who are negatively affected by the takeover can go a long way towards building trust and securing commitment from acquired employees.

While this may sound straightforward, there are often practical constraints, such as delays, physical distance, psychological "we versus them" defenses, and economic considerations that limit these recommendations when it comes to implementing them. In addition, the results of our policy-capturing research suggest that companies engaged in cross-border acquisitions need to consider contingencies in the national environment and adapt their approaches to integrating acquired firms. Despite these obstacles and complexities, the above suggestions largely coincide with the advice given in the HR-oriented literature on M&A (for example, Chaudhuri, 2005; Pucik et al., 2010; Schuler et al., 2004) and highlight the importance of trust building in overcoming implementation barriers and avoiding negative sociocultural outcomes.

The arguments and findings presented in this chapter provide some new insights into the trust dynamics in M&A. However, there are several possible limitations that need to be discussed, as well as avenues for future research. Our theoretical model, as well as studies designed to test the model, treat the main party affected by an acquisition – the members of the target firm – as a single, homogeneous entity, implicitly assuming that different groups within the target firm will respond the same to an acquisition. However, individuals may vary in their responses to a takeover, depending on their personalities, experiences, and roles in the organization (for example, Buono and Bowditch, 1989; Hambrick and Cannella, 1993; Stahl and Sitkin, 2010). For example, some of the proposed relationships may depend on the hierarchical level in the organization, that is, whether senior executives, middle managers, or rank-and-file employees are affected. Hostile takeover tactics and autonomy removal, for instance, are likely to affect acquired top managers more strongly than lower-level employees. While the potential moderating effects of individual difference variables are beyond the scope of this chapter, we believe that the role of individual-level moderators is critical to more fully understanding the trust dynamics in M&A.

The main focus of this chapter was on the motivational and behavioral reactions of acquired personnel. This bias toward the target firm's perspective notwithstanding, the proposed model points to the important role of the acquiring managers in building and restoring trust in acquisitions. One fruitful avenue for future research is to consider the role of trust repair strategies in restoring damaged relationships after M&A. Research on trust repair (for example, Bottom et al., 2002; Kim et al., 2006; Tomlinson et al., 2004) points to the potentially critical role of reconciliation tactics and conflict management strategies such as apology, repentance or reticence in interrupting, and possibly reversing, negative trust spirals.

Finally, the temporal dimension of trust in acquisitions warrants more attention. Prior research on organizational trust suggests that trust changes over time, developing, deteriorating, and sometimes resurfacing in long-standing relationships (Das and Teng, 1998; Lewicki et al., 2006; Rousseau et al., 1998). The quality of trust may change over the course of a relationship, from calculus- or deterrence-based trust to a more relational-based trust, as the parties gradually expand the resources brought into the exchange, form emotional bonds, and identify with each other's goals (Lewicki and Bunker, 1996; Tomlinson et al., 2004). Although this chapter does not explicitly address how trust is incrementally built and sustained over time, our emphasis on integration process variables implies that trust is a dynamic phenomenon. A more complete understanding of trust in acquisitions would come from consideration of its evolution over time, beginning at the time of the announcement of an acquisition and ending when the acquired firm is either successfully integrated or integration has failed.

CONCLUSION

This chapter extends existing research on the sociocultural dynamics of M&A by showing why trust matters in M&A, when it matters, how it matters, and what can be done to develop, repair and maintain trust. In particular, the findings point to the important role of the acquiring firm's integration approach in building trust and contributing to the success of the post-acquisition integration.

REFERENCES

Ariño, A., de la Torre, J. and Ring, P.S. (2001), 'Relational quality: Managing trust in corporate alliances', *California Management Review*, 44: 109–131.

Bartels, J., Douwes, R., De Jong, M. and Pruyn, A. (2006), 'Organizational identification during a merger: Determinants of employees expected identification with the new organization', *British Journal of Management*, 17: 49–67.

Bastien, D.T. (1987), 'Common patterns of behavior and communication in corporate mergers and acquisitions', *Human Resource Management*, 26: 17–34.

Birkinshaw, J., Bresman, H. and Hakanson, L. (2000), 'Managing the post-acquisition integration process: How the human integration and task integration processes interact to foster value creation', *Journal of Management Studies*, 37: 395–425.

Björkman, I., Stahl, G.K. and Vaara, E. (2007), 'Cultural differences and capability transfer in cross-border acquisitions: The mediating roles of capability complementarity, absorptive capacity, and social integration', *Journal of International Business Studies*, 38: 658–672.

Bottom, W.P., Gibson, K., Daniels, S.E. and Murnighan, J.K. (2002), 'When talk is not cheap: Substantive penance and expressions of intent in rebuilding cooperation', *Organization Science*, 13: 497–513.

Bullock, R.J. and Tubbs, M.E. (1987), *The Case Meta-Analysis for OD. Research in Organizational Change and Development*, Greenwich, CT: JAI Press, pp. 171–228.

Buono, A.F. and Bowditch, J.L. (1989), *The Human Side of Mergers and Acquisitions: Managing Collisions Between People, Cultures, and Organizations*, San Francisco, CA: Jossey-Bass.

Butler, J.K. 1991. 'Toward understanding and measuring conditions of trust: Evolution of a conditions of trust inventory', *Journal of Management*, 17: 643–663.

Calipha, R., Tarba, S. and Brock, D. (2010), 'Mergers and acquisitions: A review of phases, motives, and success factors', in S. Finkenstein and C.L. Cooper (eds), *Advances in Mergers and Acquisitions*, volume 9: 1–24, Bingley, UK: Emerald.

Cartwright, S. and Cooper, C.L. (1996), *Managing Mergers, Acquisitions, and Strategic Alliances: Integrating People and Cultures* (2nd edn), Oxford: Butterworth and Heinemann.

Cartwright, S. and Schoenberg, R. (2006), 'Thirty years of mergers and acquisitions research: Recent advances and future opportunities', *British Journal of Management*, **17** (1): 1–5.

Chatterjee, S., Lubatkin, M.H., Schweiger, D.M. and Weber, Y. (1992), 'Cultural differences and shareholder value in related mergers: Linking equity and human capital', *Strategic Management Journal*, 13: 319–334.

Chaudhuri, S. (2005), 'Managing human resources to capture capabilities: Case studies in high-technology acquisitions', in G.K. Stahl and M.E. Mendenhall (eds), *Mergers and Acquisitions: Managing Culture and Human Resources*, Stanford, CA: Stanford University Press, pp. 277–301.

Child, J. (2001), 'Trust – the fundamental bond in global collaboration', *Organizational Dynamics*, **29** (4): 274–288.

Chua, C.H., Engeli, H.P. and Stahl, G. (2005), 'Creating a new identity and high performance culture at Novartis: The role of leadership and human resource management', in G.K. Stahl and M. Mendenhall (eds), *Mergers and Acquisitions: Managing Culture and Human Resources*, Stanford, CA: Stanford University Press, pp. 379–400.

Currall, S.C. and Inkpen, A. (2002), 'A multilevel approach to trust in joint ventures', *Journal of International Business Studies*, 33: 479–495.

Das, T.K. and Teng, B-S. (1998), 'Between trust and control: Developing confidence in partner cooperation in alliances', *Academy of Management Review*, 23: 491–512.

Datta, D.K. (1991), 'Organizational fit and acquisition performance: Effects of post-acquisition integration', *Strategic Management Journal*, 12: 281–297.

Datta, D.K. and Grant, J.H. (1990), 'Relationships between type of acquisition, the autonomy given to the acquired firm, and acquisition success: An empirical analysis', *Journal of Management*, 16: 29–44.

David, K. and Singh, H. (1994), 'Sources of acquisition cultural risk', in G. Krogh, A. Sinatra and H. Singh (eds), *The Management of Corporate Acquisitions*, Basingstoke: Macmillan, pp. 251–292.

Dirks, K.T. and Ferrin, D.L. (2001), 'The role of trust in organizational settings', *Organization Science*, 12: 450–467.

Dirks, K.T. and Ferrin, D.L. (2002), 'Trust in leadership: Meta-analytic findings and implications for research and practice', *Journal of Applied Psychology*, 87: 611–628.

Ellis, K.M., Reus, T.H. and Lamont, B.T. (2009), 'The effects of procedural and informational justice in the integration or related acquisitions', *Strategic Management Journal*, 30: 137–161.

Elsass, P.M. and Veiga, J.F. (1994), 'Acculturation in acquired organizations: A force-field perspective', *Human Relations*, 47: 431–453.

Epstein, M.J. (2004), 'The drivers of success in post-merger integration', *Organizational Dynamics*, **33** (2): 174–189.

Evans, P., Pucik, V. and Barsoux, J-L. (2002), *The Global Challenge: Frameworks for International Human Resource Management*, Boston, MA: McGraw-Hill.

Gabarro, J.J. (1978), 'The development of trust, influence, and expectations', in A.G. Athos and J.J. Gabarro (eds), *Interpersonal Behavior: Communication and Understanding in Relationships*, Englewood Cliffs, NJ: Prentice-Hall, pp. 290–303.

Gebhardt, J. (2003), 'What "due diligence" really means: Intangible capital and organizational reality', in A.F. Buono (ed.), *Enhancing Inter-firm Networks and Interorganizational Strategies* (volume 3), Greenwich, CT: Information Age Publishing.

Goulet, P.K. and Schweiger, D.M. (2006), 'Managing culture and human resources in mergers and acquisitions', in G.K. Stahl and I. Björkman (eds), *Handbook of Research in International Human Resource Management*, Cheltenham, UK and Northampton, MA, USA: Edward Elgar Publishing, pp. 405–429.

Graves, D. (1981), 'Individual reactions to a merger of two small firms of brokers in the reinsurance industry: A total population survey', *Journal of Management Studies*, 18: 89–113.

Gulati, R. (1995), 'Does familiarity breed trust? The implications of repeated ties for contractual choice in alliances', *Academy of Management Journal*, 38: 85–112.

Hambrick, D.C. and Cannella, A.A. (1993), 'Relative standing: A framework for understanding departures of acquired executives', *Academy of Management Journal*, 36: 733–762.

Harrison, J.S., Hitt, M.A., Hoskisson, R.E. and Ireland, R.D. (1991), 'Synergies and post-acquisition performance: Differences versus similarities in resource allocations', *Journal of Management*, 17 (1): 173–190.

Haspeslagh, P. and Jemison, D.B. (1991), *Managing Acquisitions: Creating Value Through Corporate Renewal*, New York: The Free Press.

Hitt, M.A., Harrison, J.S. and Duane Ireland, R. (2001), *Mergers and Acquisitions: A Guide to Creating Value for Stakeholders*, New York: Oxford University Press.

Hofstede, G. (1980), *Culture's Consequences: International Differences in Work Related Values*, Beverly Hills, CA: Sage.

Hogan, E.A. and Overmyer-Day, L. (1994), 'The psychology of mergers and acquisitions', *International Review of Industrial and Organizational Psychology*, 9: 247–281.

Hogg, M.A. and Terry, D.J. (2000), 'Social identity and self-categorization processes in organizational contexts', *Academy of Management Review*, 25: 121–140.

Hunt, J.W. (1990), 'Changing pattern of acquisition behavior in takeovers and the consequences for acquisition processes', *Strategic Management Journal*, 11: S.69–77.

Hurley, R.F. (2006), 'The decision to trust', *Harvard Business Review*, September, 55–62.

Inkpen, A.C. and Currall, S.C. (1997), 'International joint venture trust: An empirical examination', in P.W. Beamish and J.P. Killing (eds), *Cooperative Strategies: North American Perspectives*, San Francisco, CA: New Lexington, pp. 308–334.

Inkpen, A.C. and Currall, S.C. (2004), 'The coevolution of trust, control, and learning in joint ventures', *Organization Science*, 15 (5): 586–599.

Jauch, L.R., Osborn, R.N. and Martin, T.N. (1980), 'Structured content analysis of cases: A complementary method for organizational research', *Academy of Management Review*, 5: 517–525.

Jemison, D.B. and Sitkin, S.B. (1986), 'Corporate acquisitions: A process perspective', *Academy of Management Review*, 11: 145–163.

Johnson, J.L., Cullen, J.B., Sakano, T. and Takenouchi, H. (1997), 'Setting the stage for trust and strategic integration in Japanese–U.S. cooperative alliances', in P.W. Beamish and J.P. Killing (eds), *Cooperative Strategies: North American Perspectives*, San Francisco, CA: New Lexington, pp. 227–254.

Kavanagh, M.H. and Ashkanasy, N.M. (2006), 'The impact of leadership and change management strategy on organizational culture and individual acceptance of change during a merger', *British Journal of Management*, 17: 81–103.

Kim, P.H., Dirks, K.T., Cooper, C.D. and Ferrin, D.L. (2006), 'When more blame is better than less: The implications of internal vs. external attributions for the repair of trust after a competence- vs. integrity-based trust violation', *Organizational Behavior and Human Decision Processes*, 99: 49–65.

Kleppestø, S. (2005), 'The construction of social identities in mergers and acquisitions', in G.K. Stahl and M. Mendenhall (eds), *Mergers and Acquisitions: Managing Culture and Human Resources*, Stanford, CA: Stanford University Press, pp. 130–151.

Köster, K. and Stahl, G.K. (2012), 'Lenovo-IBM: Bridging cultures, languages, and time zones', in G.K. Stahl, M. Mendenhall and G. Oddou (eds), *Readings and Cases in International Human Resource Management* (5th edn). London: Routledge, pp. 351–365.

Kramer, R.M. (1999), 'Trust and distrust in organizations: Emerging perspectives, enduring questions', *Annual Review of Psychology*, 50: 569–598.

Krishnan, R., Martin, X. and Noorderhaven, N.G. (2006), 'When does trust matter to alliance performance?' *Academy of Management Journal*, **49** (5): 894–917.

Krug, J.A. and Nigh, D. (2001), 'Executive perceptions in foreign and domestic acquisitions', *Journal of World Business*, 36: 85–105.

Kumar, N. (1996), 'The power of trust in manufacturer-retailer relationships', *Harvard Business Review*, 74: 92–106.

Larsson, R. and Finkelstein, S. (1999), 'Integrating strategic, organizational, and human resource perspectives on mergers and acquisitions: A case survey of synergy realization', *Organization Science*, 10: 1–26.

Larsson, R. and Lubatkin, M. (2001), 'Achieving acculturation in mergers and acquisitions: An international case survey', *Human Relations*, 54: 1573–1607.

Lewicki, R.J. and Bunker, B.B. (1996), 'Developing and maintaining trust in work relationships', in R.M. Kramer and T.R. Tyler (eds), *Trust in Organizations: Frontiers of Theory and Research*, Thousand Oaks, CA: Sage, pp. 114–139.

Lewicki, R.J. and Wiethoff, C. (2000), 'Trust, trust development, and trust repair', in M. Deutsch and P.T. Coleman, *The Handbook of Conflict Resolution*, San Francisco, CA: Jossey-Bass, pp. 86–107.

Lewicki, R.J., McAllister, D.J. and Bies, R.J. (1998), 'Trust and distrust: New relationships and realities', *Academy of Management Review*, 23: 438–458.

Lewicki, R.J., Tomlinson, E.C. and Gillespie, N. (2006), 'Models of interpersonal trust development: Theoretical approaches, empirical evidence, and future directions', *Journal of Management*, 32: 991–1022.

Lubatkin, M., Schweiger, D. and Weber Y. (1999), 'Top management turnover in related M&As: An additional test of the theory of relative standing', *Journal of Management*, 25: 55–74.

Marks, M.L. and Mirvis, P.H. (1998), *Joining Forces: Making One Plus One Equal Three in Mergers, Acquisitions, and Alliances*, San Francisco, CA: Jossey-Bass.

Marks, M.L. and Mirvis, P.H. (2001), 'Making mergers and acquisitions work: Strategic and psychological preparation', *Academy of Management Executive*, 15: 80–92.

Mayer, R.C., Davis, J.H. and Schoorman, F.D. (1995), 'An integrative model of organizational trust', *The Academy of Management Review*, 20: 709–734.

Meyer, C.B. and Altenborg, E. (2007), 'The disintegrating effects of equality: a study of a failed international merger', *British Journal of Management*, **18** (3): 257–271.

Mishra, A.K. (1996), 'Organizational responses to crisis: The centrality of trust', in R.M. Kramer and T.R. Tyler (eds), *Trust in Organizations, Frontiers of Theory and Research*, Thousand Oaks, CA: Sage, pp. 261–287.

Nahavandi, A. and Malekzadeh, A.R. (1988), 'Acculturation in mergers and acquisitions', *Academy of Management Review*, 13: 79–90.

Nooteboom, B., Berger, H. and Noorderhaven, N.G. (1997), 'Effects of trust and governance on relational risk', *Academy of Management Journal*, 40: 308–338.

Olie, R. (1990), 'Culture and integration problems in international mergers and acquisitions', *European Management Journal*, 8: 206–215.

Olie, R. (1994), 'Shades of culture and institutions in international mergers', *Organization Studies*, 15: 381–405.

Pablo, A.L. (1994), 'Determinants of acquisition integration level: A decision making perspective', *Academy of Management Journal*, 37: 803–836.

Parkhe, A. (1993), 'Strategic alliance structuring: A game theoretic and transaction cost examination of interfirm cooperation', *Academy of Management Journal*, 36: 794–829.

Porrini, P. (2004), 'Can a previous alliance between an acquirer and a target affect acquisition performance?', *Journal of Management*, 30: 545–562.

Pucik, V., Evans, P., Björkman, I. and Stahl, G.K. (2010), 'Human resource management in cross-border mergers and acquisitions', in A-W. Harzing and A. Pinnington (eds), *International Human Resource Management* (3rd edn), London: Sage, pp. 119–152.

Ring, P.S. and Van de Ven, A.H. (1992), 'Structuring cooperative relationships between organizations', *Strategic Management Journal*, 13: 483–498.

Rousseau, D.M., Sitkin, S.B., Burt, R.S. and Camerer, C. (1998), 'Not so different after all: A cross-discipline view of trust', *Academy of Management Review*, 23: 393–404.

Sales, A.L. and Mirvis, P.H. (1984), 'When cultures collide: Issues of acquisition', in J. Kimberly and R.E. Quinn (eds), *Managing Organizational Transitions*, Homewood, IL: Irwin, pp. 107–133.

Sarkar, M., Cavusgil, T. and Evirgen, C. (1997), 'A commitment-trust mediated framework of international collaborative venture performance', in P.W. Beamish and J.P. Killing (eds), *Cooperative Strategies: North American Perspectives*, San Francisco, CA: New Lexington Press, pp. 255–285.

Schoenberg, R. (2004), 'Dimensions of management style compatibility and cross-border acquisition outcome', *Advances in Mergers and Acquisitions*, 3: 149–175.

Schuler, R.S., Jackson, S.E. and Luo, Y. (2004), *Managing Human Resources in Cross-border Alliances*, London: Routledge.

Schweiger, D.M. (2002), *M&A Integration: A Framework for Executives and Managers*, New York: McGraw-Hill.

Schweiger, D.M. and DeNisi, A.S. (1991), 'Communication with employees following a merger: A longitudinal field experiment', *Academy of Management Journal*, 34: 110–135.

Schweiger, D.M. and Goulet, P.K. (2000), 'Integrating mergers and acquisitions: An international research review', *Advances in Mergers and Acquisitions*, 1: 61–91.

Schweiger, D.M. and Walsh, J.P. (1990), 'Mergers and acquisitions: An interdisciplinary view', *Research in Personnel und Human Resources Management*, 8: 41–107.

Schweiger, D.M., Ivancevich, J. and Power, F.R. (1987), 'Executive actions for managing human resources before and after acquisition', *Academy of Management Executive*, 1: 127–138.

Shimizu, K., Hitt, M.A., Vaidyanath, D. and Pisano, V. (2004), 'Theoretical foundations of cross-border mergers and acquisitions: A review of current research and recommendations for the future', *Journal of International Management*, 10: 307–353.

Shrivastava, P. (1986), 'Postmerger integration', *Journal of Business Strategy*, 7: 65–76.

Sitkin, S. and Pablo, A. (2005), 'The neglected importance of leadership in mergers and acquisitions', in G.K. Stahl and M.E. Mendenhall (eds), *Mergers and Acquisitions: Managing Culture and Human Resources*, Stanford, CA: Stanford University Press, pp. 208–223.

Sitkin, S.B. and Roth, N.L. (1993), 'Explaining the limited effectiveness of legalistic "remedies" for trust/distrust', *Organization Science*, 4: 367–392.

Sitkin, S.B. and Stickel, D. (1996), 'The road to hell: The dynamics of distrust in an era of "quality" management', in R. Kramer and T. Tyler (eds), *Trust in Organizations*, Thousand Oaks, CA: Sage, pp. 196–215.

Slangen, A.H.L. (2006), 'National cultural distance and initial foreign acquisition performance: The moderating effect of integration', *Journal of World Business*, 41: 161–170.

Stahl, G.K. and Sitkin, S. (2010), 'Trust dynamics in acquisitions: The role of relationship history, interfirm distance, and acquirer's integration approach', *Advances in Mergers and Acquisitions*, 9: 51–82.

Stahl, G.K. and Voigt, A. (2008), 'Do cultural differences matter in mergers and acquisitions? A tentative model and meta-analytic examination', *Organization Science*, 19: 160–176.

Stahl, G.K., Mendenhall, M., Pablo, A. and Javidan, M. (2005), 'Sociocultural integration in mergers and acquisitions', in G.K. Stahl and M.E. Mendenhall (eds), *Mergers and Acquisitions: Managing Culture and Human Resources*, Stanford, CA: Stanford University Press, pp. 3–16.

Stahl, G.K., Chua, C.H. and Pablo, A. (2006), 'Antecedents of target firm members' trust in the acquiring firm's management: A decision-making simulation', *Advances in Mergers and Acquisitions*, 5: 69–89.

Stahl, G.K., Larsson, R., Kremershof, I. and Sitkin, S. (2011), 'Trust dynamics in acquisitions: A case survey', *Human Resource Management*, 50: 575–603.

Stahl, G.K., Chua, C.H. and Pablo, A. (2012), 'Does national context affect target firm employees' trust in acquisitions? A policy-capturing study', *Management International Review*, 52: 395–423.

Tajfel, H. (1982), *Social Identity and Intergroup Relations*, New York: Cambridge University Press.

Teerikangas, S. and Very, P. (2006), 'The culture-performance relationship in M&A: From yes/no to how', *British Journal of Management*, 17 (1): 31–48.

Tomlinson, E.C., Dineen, B.R. and Lewicki, R.J. (2004), 'The road to reconciliation: Antecedents of victim willingness to reconcile following a broken promise', *Journal of Management*, 30: 165–187.

Turner, J.C. (1982), 'Towards a cognitive redefinition of the social group', in H. Tajfel (ed.) *Social Identity and Intergroup Relations*, New York: Cambridge University Press.

Vaara, E. (2003), 'Post-acquisition integration as sensemaking: Glimpses of ambiguity, confusion, hypocrisy, and politicization', *Journal of Management Studies*, 40: 859–894.

Van Dick, R., Ullrich, J. and Tissington, P.A. (2006), 'Working under a black cloud: how to sustain organizational identification after a merger', *British Journal of Management*, 17: 69–79.

Vlaar, P.W.L., Van den Bosch, F.A.J. and Volberda, H.W. (2007), 'On the evolution of trust, distrust, and formal coordination and control in interorganizational relationships', *Group and Organization Management*, 32: 407–429.

Vlasic, B. and Stertz, B. (2000), *How Daimler-Benz drove off with Chrysler*, New York: Morrow.

Weber, Y. and Drori, I. (2008), 'The linkages between cultural differences, psychological states, and performance in international mergers and acquisitions', *Advances in Mergers and Acquisitions*, 7: 119–142.

Weber, Y., Shenkar, O. and Raveh, A. (1996), 'National and corporate fit in mergers and acquisitions: An exploratory study', *Management Science*, 4 (8): 1215–1227.

Whitener, E.M., Brodt, S.E., Korsgaard, M.A. and Werner, J.M. (1998), 'Managers as initiators of trust: An exchange relationship framework for understanding managerial trustworthy behavior', *Academy of Management Review*, 23: 513–539.

Young-Ybarra, C. and Wiersema, M. (1999), 'Strategic flexibility in information technology alliances: The influence of transaction cost economics and social exchange theory', *Organization Science*, 10: 439–459.

Zaheer, A., McEvily, B. and Perrone, V. (1998), 'Does trust matter? Exploring the effects of interorganizational and interpersonal trust on performance', *Organization Science*, 9: 141–159.

2 Integration of international mergers and acquisitions: test of a new paradigm
Yaakov Weber, Shlomo Yedidia Tarba, Günter K. Stahl and Ziva Bachar-Rozen

An extensive body of literature has investigated financial and strategic variables as predictors of merger and acquisition (M&A) performance without finding clear relationships. This includes a meta-analytic study that recommends the use of other variables that may help predict M&A performance (King et al. 2004). Despite this vast body of research, the key factors of M&A success and the reasons why so many M&A fail remain poorly understood (Stahl et al. 2005). Studies of the financial and strategic aspects of M&A generally focus on the pre-merger stage, although all the value creation in an M&A takes place after the deal, and it hinges on the ability of the combined firms to effectively integrate their operations (Haspeslagh and Jemison 1991; Weber and Fried 2011a).

A central dilemma in managing post-merger integration is the decision about whether to integrate the newly acquired organization by traversing its structural boundaries and changing its culture, and what degree of autonomy should the acquired management be granted. Such intrusion may have a detrimental effect on M&A, including the departure of key talents and executives (Cannella and Hambrick 1993; Lubatkin et al. 1999), productivity losses in the technical core (Paruchuri et al. 2007), innovation disruption in technology acquisition (Puranam et al. 2006; Ranft and Lord 2002), executive behavior (Weber et al. 1996), shareholder values (Chatterjee et al. 1992), integration effectiveness, and return on assets (Weber 1996). These findings point to an integration paradox. On one hand, if the top management of the acquired firm retains full autonomy and the acquired firm is not integrated, synergy manifested in such processes as knowledge transfer, which is a main reason for many technology acquisitions, is not exploited. On the other hand, autonomy removal during the post-merger integration process may have a negative effect, especially when combined with a high level of national and organizational cultural differences.

Decisions about merger integration are important and difficult, especially in the high-tech industry where the loss of key talent specializing in specific R&D areas can have dramatic effects on integration effectiveness and M&A success. To address this dilemma and paradox, some scholars have suggested various integration solutions. Their studies focus on theoretical issues based on literature reviews (for example, Nahavandi and Malekzadeh 1988; Weber et al. 2009) or on case studies (Haspeslagh and Jemison 1991; Schweizer 2005) rather than on systematic empirical studies based on any sample size. Furthermore, some of the integration solutions (Haspeslagh and Jemison 1991; Nahavandi and Malekzadeh 1988) were suggested approximately 20 years ago and therefore do not incorporate findings from the last two decades about possible important factors in the post-merger integration process, such as national and organizational culture differences.

This chapter seeks to fill some of these gaps. The goal of this chapter is to explore systematically, based on a sample of international M&A, the vital but neglected role of the integration approach in the implementation of international M&A. To this end, we developed a theoretical framework for integration approaches that incorporates empirical findings from the last two decades to test whether the fit between the recommended and the actually implemented integration approaches explains integration effectiveness. The findings of the study can lead future research to consistent findings on international M&A success and help shape practices for achieving success.

BACKGROUND AND THEORY

Post-merger Integration and M&A Performance

Merging organizational units into a new structural form and administrative boundaries by structural integration requires highly imaginative problem-solving in the use of systems, authority, and processes in order to simplify coordination and facilitate mutual adaptation. Post-merger integration efforts are of utmost importance for exploiting the potential synergies between the acquired and acquiring firms (Ellis et al. 2009; Larsson and Finkelstein 1999). The level of integration is a pivotal factor in determining whether the objectives of M&A are achieved. The level of integration practiced by the buying company involves a degree of autonomy removal from the target firm. To achieve effective post-merger integration, the acquiring top management typically intervenes in the decision-making process of the acquired management team and imposes standards, rules, and expectations on it. In some cases this has a positive effect on M&A performance (for example, Larsson and Finkelstein 1999; Weber 1996). But as noted above, loss of autonomy may elicit tensions, negative attitudes toward the merger, a low level of top management cooperation and commitment to the success of the merger, and the leaving of key talents and top executives (Weber et al. 1996; Lubatkin et al. 1999).

It appears, therefore, that the efforts invested in exploiting the synergy potential can cause human problems, destroy the synergy, and compromise the success of the integration process (Weber and Fried 2011b). Furthermore, the integration of the two firms requires contact (not necessarily physical) in the decision-making process between the two top management teams (Nahavandi and Malekzadeh 1988). This contact may result in conflict because it exposes the cultures of the two teams to each other and makes the differences between them salient (Weber 1996). But some frameworks used for the integration of two organizations following M&A do not take into account cultural differences (Haspeslagh and Jemison 1991, Nahavandi and Malekzadeh 1988).

Cultural Differences and Merger Integration

Although national and corporate cultural differences have frequently been used to explain the poor performance of domestic and international M&A, findings are contradictory and confusing (for recent reviews, see among others, Reus and Lamont 2009; Stahl and Voigt 2008; Weber et al. 2009). On one hand, several studies have provided support for the idea that corporate (Chatterjee et al. 1992; Datta 1991, Weber 1996) or national (Datta and Puia 1995; Weber et al. 1996; Weber et al. 2012) cultural differences are detrimental to M&A performance. Studies also found this negative effect to be present under conditions of both low and high levels of integration, when autonomy was removed from the acquired managers (Lubatkin et al. 1999; Very et al. 1997; Weber 1996). On the other hand, some studies found that cultural differences have a positive effect on international M&A performance (Reus and Lamont 2009; Weber et al. 1996; Weber et al. 2012). Moreover, when considering cultural differences and level of integration together, Weber (1996) found a positive moderating effect of autonomy removal on financial performance. He suggested that this finding may be the result of better coordination between the two merged firms, which in turn enabled better synergy realization. But synergy potential was not a variable in this, as is the case in most studies.

Furthermore, the combination of national cultural distance and corporate cultural differences adds to the complexity of the above findings. It is unclear how national culture interacts with organizational culture and what might be the effect of this interaction on M&A performance.

For example, Lubatkin et al. (1998) compared French and British acquirers and found that a greater need for uncertainty avoidance and greater acceptance of power distance were associated with a higher level of integration (more centralized control). Similarly, Morosini et al. (1998) reported that national cultural distance was positively related to the degree of integration (post-acquisition strategy), but whereas cultural distance was positively related to performance, integration did not show any significant relationship with performance. By contrast, Morosini and Singh (1994) found that uncertainty avoidance and individualism were positively related to level of integration.

Furthermore, it seems that the national culture of the acquirer also has its effects (Weber et al. 2012. Based on interviews with directors of acquired UK companies, Child et al. (2000) and Pitkethly et al. (2003) found that national differences, rather than national cultural distance, are associated with the level of integration. For example, American acquirers tended to implement a high level of integration of subsidiaries, whereas Japanese and German companies preferred low levels of integration. French companies inclined toward an average level of integration. Calori et al. (1994) found that French acquirers exerted greater centralized formal control (that is, higher levels of integration) over the strategy and operations of their acquired businesses than did British acquirers (lower uncertainty avoidance), who leaned toward informal communication and cooperation that required lower levels of formal integration. The differential exercise of control mechanisms was found to correlate with acquisition performance. Similarly, Morosini and Singh (1994) found that in highly individualistic societies a lower level of post-acquisition integration appeared to result in higher productivity growth one year after the completion of the deal. The conclusions reached by Very et al. (1996) that "cross-national mergers are a complex phenomenon, sometimes influenced by national cultural differences, sometimes by organizational influences, sometimes by both and sometimes by neither" are apparently still valid. Nevertheless, studies of cross-border M&A have rarely included both national and organizational culture dimensions in the same analysis (for an exception, see Weber et al. 1996), possibly because of the complexity of these constructs. Schneider (1988) suggested: "a paradox that national culture may play a stronger role in the fact of a strong corporate culture. The pressures to conform may create the need to reassert autonomy and identity, creating a national mosaic rather than a melting pot."

In sum, although the factors of integration, national culture, and corporate culture are important for M&A success, as is evident from previous research, the interrelationships between them and their effects on M&A success are yet to be tested.

Theory and Hypotheses

Several possible explanations exist for the lack of consistency that permeates recent studies on the relationship between cultural differences and M&A performance. For example, Teerikangas and Very (2006) focused on the sources of complexity underlying these relationships. Others suggested that different measures of performance (Zollo and Meier 2008) that ignore the negotiation process (Weber et al. 2011), or national culture of the acquirer (Weber and Tarba 2010), focus on micro- or macro-levels of analysis only, or take into account either pre- or post-merger variables are not sufficient to find consistent relationships (Weber et al. 1996; Weber 1996; Weber and Fried 2011a). Despite these criticisms, the study of cultural differences should not be abandoned altogether. Rather, the implication of the studies is that greater elaboration is needed in the cultural analysis of the various processes and mechanisms involved.

The literature review directs attention to two essential issues for M&A performance. Most M&A studies do not simultaneously incorporate pre- and post-merger factors, and important factors are not considered simultaneously in the same study. This failure has major implications that lead to inconsistent and contradictory findings about M&A success. The limitations of current literature are many. First, national cultural distance, corporate cultural differences, synergy potential, and integration are important factors that can explain M&A success or failure. Second, empirical research especially aimed at the relationships between national cultural distance, corporate culture, and level of integration is rare. Third, studies usually do not include all these factors, and few studies include synergy potential as a factor in their investigation. Fourth, the national culture of the acquirer, and therefore the differences between acquirer cultures (rather than differences between the acquirer and target companies) may have an important effect on post-merger integration, but these were rarely considered in the study of M&A performance. Fifth, although more than 20 years ago integration solutions have been suggested to improve M&A performance (Haspeslagh and Jemison 1991; Nahavandi and Malekzadeh 1988), empirical testing of these approaches remains rare. Similarly, the choice of the actually implemented integration approach and the "recommended" one within the framework of integration approaches has been neglected. These limitations are discussed below.

Toward a New Paradigm

While the trade-off between level of integration and synergy potential has been recognized in the current literature, theoretical conceptualiza-

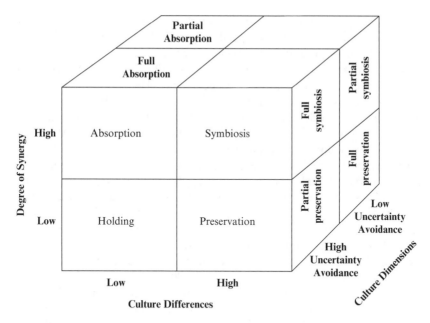

Figure 2.1   Integration approaches, cultural differences and cultural dimensions

tion and empirical testing remain limited because in the last two decades other variables, such as cultural differences, have appeared to be essential for M&A performance. For example, Haspeslagh and Jemison's (1991) framework for post-merger integration does not include cultural differences as an important variable, possibly because the first systematic study that tested their effects was published later (Chatterjee et al. 1992).

Individually taken, the level of integration, cultural differences, and synergy potential variables are not sufficient to explain M&A performance. Post-merger integration is a complex process that appears to need a better conceptualization than the simple linear relationship suggested by the studies mentioned above. We suggest using a combination of these factors together with the concept of *configurational fit* to explain integration effectiveness.

Given the limitations of the current literature and the importance of cultural differences to integration effectiveness, we propose a new paradigm for post-merger integration that requires high creativity in the choice of structural integration taking into account synergy and culture considerations. Figure 2.1 presents the recommended integration approaches as they are affected by synergy potential and cultural differences.

Corporate and national cultural factors are expressed on two dimensions: cultural differences and specific cultural dimensions. The straightforward synergy potential dimension of the matrix parallels dimensions in other frameworks such as relatedness (Nahavandi and Malekzadeh 1988) and the need for strategic interdependence (Haspeslagh and Jemison 1991). But the suggested framework uses the cultural differences variable as the determinant of the recommended integration approach instead of need for autonomy (Haspeslagh and Jemsion 1991) or cultural attractiveness and multiculturalism (Nahavandi and Malekzadeh 1988). There are several reasons, clarified in the literature review, for this approach. First, since Haspeslagh and Jemison (1991) suggested their framework, empirical findings have clearly indicated the critical importance of the effects of culture clash on integration effectiveness (for example, Cartwright and Cooper 1992, 1993; Datta 1991; Chatterjee et al. 1992; Weber 1996; Weber and Pliskin 1996; Stahl and Voigt 2008), on international M&A (for example, Datta and Puia 1995; Morosini et al. 1998; Lubatkin et al. 1998), and on both (for example, Weber et al. 1996.) Second, the need of the acquired managers for autonomy has not been measured directly in previous studies, but other measures were used that suggest its importance for M&A performance. The empirical findings are not clear, however (Weber et al. 2009; Schweiger and Goulet 2000). Third, the extent of cultural differences reflects to some degree the need for autonomy (Weber et al. 2009).

The integration terminology used here is similar to that used by Haspeslagh and Jemison (1991) and explained elsewhere (Weber et al. 2009). Here, *absorption* refers to a high level of integration and the lowest level of autonomy for the acquired management. It is recommended for achieving a high level of synergy when the level of cultural differences is low. *Preservation* refers to the lowest level of integration and the highest autonomy for the acquired management. It is recommended for low synergy potential and high cultural differences. *Symbiosis*, with high levels of both synergy and cultural differences, refers to a sophisticated level of integration to be considered in challenging situations (Haspeslagh and Jemison 1991).

The principal advantages of this new framework are that they close some of the gaps in the current literature, described above. First, it considers cultural differences. Second, it allows the simultaneous inclusion of the important variables that the purchasing firm managers must consider in their creative choice. Third, it allows inclusion of the acquirer's national cultural dimension (third dimension in the cube), which, according to the literature review, appears to affect integration and M&A performance (for example, Child et al. 2000; Weber and Tarba 2011, 2012). Fourth, it combines the pre- and post-merger stages. Cultural differences and synergy potential are part of the creative decision-making process to acquire or not, but they also determine the integration approach that should be implemented after the deal is consummated.

Finally, the matrices that proposed the integration solutions (Haspeslagh and Jemison 1991) and modes of acculturation (Nahavandi and Malekzadeh 1988) were implicit about the relationship between each selected approach and M&A performance. By contrast, the framework presented here, based on different factors and considerations, treats integration solutions as creative choices to be applied according to specific situations. Thus, the chosen integration approach, based on its specific configurational fit that is congruent with the three characteristics of each M&A (synergy potential, cultural differences, and cultural dimensions), can lead the acquiring company to superior performance.

HYPOTHESES

Appropriate Integration Approach

The framework presented here is based on a different set of factors and considerations than previous matrices, and it treats integration as creative choices to be applied given specific situations. Thus, a given integration approach, based on a fit between the recommended integration approach and the actual choice of integration approach being implemented, consistent with the characteristics of a specific M&A (synergy potential and cultural differences), can lead to superior integration effectiveness. Because cultural differences can be of critical importance to performance, the framework presented here takes them into consideration in the creative decision-making used to select the integration approach. This point of view combines the pre- and post-merger stages. It suggests that both cultural differences and synergy potential are parts of the creative choice of integration approach, and that a fit between the recommended and actual integration approach can lead to an effective integration process.

No integration approach fits all cases. Managers must creatively determine the best integration approach that fits their specific M&A and leads to effective post-merger integration. The choice of the appropriate integration approach based on synergy potential and cultural differences should lead to effective integration of functions, capability transfer, and so on. In other words, if the acquiring top management actually implements an appropriate integration approach, a fit emerges between the "right" integration approach (according to the framework presented here) and the approach being implemented. This leads to the following hypothesis:

H1: *A fit between the appropriate integration approach, based on synergy potential and national and corporate cultural differences, and the actual integration approach implemented is associated with higher integration effectiveness than is the absence of such a fit.*

Interaction Effect between the Fit of Integration Approach and Synergy Potential

Strategic theories, especially the concept of strategic fit, suggest that the relatedness between the acquiring and target firms determines the synergy potential, and is therefore the key determinant of value creation. But the empirical evidence derived from the studies of M&A characterized by relatedness is mixed at best. More important, synergy potential was rarely measured in these studies. In other words, the presence of synergy potential was assumed based on indications of relatedness versus unrelatedness; it was not measured directly. Furthermore, most of these studies followed the implicit assumption that the activities and actions of the acquiring firm during the pre-merger stage are the sole determinants of value. But the pre-merger stage can predict only the potential of integration effectiveness, based on the assumption that synergy is present and that management knows how to harness it. In practice, the failure to find a consistent relationship between indicators of synergy based on relatedness and M&A success may stem from measures that are not appropriate and an over-emphasis on the pre-merger stage at the expense of the post-merger stage (Weber and Fried 2011b), including the approach used during the processes of integration. With a few exceptions, the strategic and finance literature has not considered the possibility that the problematic interaction (because of cultural differences) between the acquiring and target firms in the management of the merger may play a key role in M&A success.

The reason for the conflicting results of previous studies may be the broad terms in which relatedness and synergy have been defined, often using similarity and complementarity synergies interchangeably, or ignoring complementarity altogether (Makri et al. 2010). Moreover, because the effects of synergy may depend on cultural differences, the effects of the synergy potential must be controlled by cultural differences.

Finally, if the appropriate integration approach is implemented, more of the synergy potential can be realized. Therefore, when both a high synergy potential and a fit of integration approach exist, it is easier to achieve the main objective of the M&A, namely to harness as much as possible of the synergy potential.

The following two hypotheses follow from the above discussion:

H2: *The higher the synergy potential, the higher the integration effectiveness is.*

H3: *The fit of integration approach moderates the relationship between the synergy potential and integration effectiveness. Specifically, the positive effects of the synergy potential are greatest if a fit of integration approach exists.*

METHODOLOGY

Industry Context and Integration Dilemma

Biotech companies are increasingly considering mergers and acquisitions as the best way to realize value from their holdings (Ernst & Young 2011). Companies in the biotech industry range from research-focused startups to large pharmaceutical firms. Important new technologies have emerged in this industry in the last three decades. Being dependent on emerging new knowledge, companies in the biotech industry cannot rely exclusively on internal knowledge development and need to absorb relevant knowledge from external sources. The acquisition of biotech companies takes place because other companies want to gain access to the knowledge and research capabilities of smaller biotech companies.

Furthermore, in the biotech industry small research firms are functionally limited because they lack strong production, marketing, and other capabilities. Therefore, small, functionally limited R&D firms in this industry turn to larger and functionally inclusive pharmaceutical firms for these capabilities because of the strength of the latter in all areas of activity.

At the same time, the integration dilemma in this industry may be more profound than in other industries and require a high level of organizational ingenuity. The knowledge of biotech companies is highly context-specific and cannot simply be transferred from the biotech company to the pharmaceutical company. Bower (2001) points out that the organic nature of biotech products and technologies makes their integration far more difficult than that of computer or chip components. Thus, pharmaceutical companies face a dilemma: on one hand they need to integrate biotech companies in order to gain access to desired research and innovative capabilities; on the other hand, they must preserve the autonomy of the biotech company not to endanger the future of the desired capabilities.

Considering the substantial differences in culture and organizational styles between pharmaceutical and biotech companies, the challenge of gaining access to the desired capabilities becomes even greater and asks for innovative solutions. Internally, biotech firms have forged their own entrepreneurial, creative, and risk-taking culture. They are usually organized into flexible, overlapping, interdisciplinary project teams with low levels of hierarchy, open communication, and informal organizational structures that produce a dynamic, lean, and effective organization for fostering innovation. Furthermore, employees often have a significant ownership stake in the firm, so that they have strong incentives to quickly develop new technologies at the lowest cost possible. These are key strong capabilities (Barney 1986, 1991) that lead to innovative results. By contrast, pharmaceutical companies have a relatively formal structure, more levels of hierarchy that result in long and slow decision-making processes, and a more risk-averse culture than that of biotech companies (Powell 1996).

The dilemma between the post-acquisition integration level and the motivation to realize the synergy potential is especially salient in the acquisition of biotech companies and depends on imaginative solutions. Because forms of knowledge that are tacit and socially complex (Ranft and Lord 2002; Ranft 2006) are difficult to transfer, a high degree of post-acquisition integration may be required in order to realize the anticipated benefits of these mergers (Puranam et al. 2003, 2006; Puranam and Srikanth 2007). But integration may lead to the ultimate destruction of the knowledge-based resources of the acquired firms through employee turnover and the disruption of organizational routines (Puranam et al. 2003; Ranft and Lord 2002).

In these M&A, managers find themselves torn between the competing needs of preserving and changing the culture of the acquired company, and at the same time encouraging knowledge transfer, integration, and cooperation between managers from both companies in order to harness the synergy. The high synergy potential requires intense efforts and sophisticated processes of interaction and coordination (Weber and Tarba 2010) to evade the human resources problems resulting from cultural differences and to achieve high commitment and cooperation from both management teams (Lubatkin et al. 1999; Weber et al. 1996; Weber 1996; Weber et al. 2012). Therefore, the need to select an appropriate approach that considers a specific combination with many complex factors to achieve high integration effectiveness is more important in this industry than in others.

Sample

The sample of firms was drawn from a list of mergers that took place during 2008–2009 obtained from the archive of the Israel Antitrust

Authority. A sample of M&A was selected based on the following criteria: the mergers were from the biotechnology industry, the acquiring company gained a controlling interest in the acquired firm, and the names and addresses of the top managers affiliated with the acquiring companies immediately before the merger were available. Data were collected during 2008–2009.

A questionnaire was sent directly to top managers of each of the buying or acquired company in Israel. Twenty-two companies out of 30 responded, a response rate of 73 percent. Previous M&A studies used small samples such as 23 M&A in some of their regression models (for example, Chatterjee et al. 1992: 329) and even smaller sample sizes. For example, Weber et al. (1996) used two samples, one of which was eight international M&A. Potential non-respondent biases were checked by comparing respondent and non-respondent firms with respect to relative size and the time that had elapsed since the date of the merger. These variables may affect the emotions and objectivity of the managers, and therefore their perceptions (Chatterjee et al. 1992; Lubatkin et al. 1999). The t-test of mean differences was not significant, showing no evidence of non-respondent bias

Questionnaire and Procedure

Ideally, cultural differences are investigated before the merger, and the results of the investigation are compared with data collected after the merger. It is extremely difficult, however, to gain access to such data in large samples during the negotiation period, and it is also inefficient because many negotiations do not result in M&A. This problem is compounded by another difficulty associated with the measure of corporate culture. Many elements of culture are unclear to its members because people take them for granted (Schein 1985). Dramatic events, such as M&A, and contacts with other cultures, however, make differences salient (Louis 1983), especially in conflict situations (Sales and Mirvis 1984). Greenwood et al. (1994) pointed out that it may take months or years for the acquired managers to form stable impressions about the compatibility of the cultures of the merging organizations. Therefore, retrospective data can be useful in studying the cultural differences and attitudes of top managers. It has been observed that attitudinal and behavioral data do not become less accurate over time, even after periods of 10 years (Finkelstein 1992; Gutek 1978; Pettigrew 1979). Studies of this type, however, should follow the recommendations of Huber and Power (1985) regarding access to top management and the use of retrospective data.

A second methodological difficulty has to do with how data about corporate cultural differences and their outcomes are collected. Recently, several studies have used questionnaires to measure perceived organizational culture (for example, Cartwright and Cooper 1993; Hofstede et al. 1990) and perceived cultural differences in M&A (Chatterjee et al. 1992; Lubatkin et al. 1999; Weber et al. 1996) and found them to have high reliability and validity. Self-report questionnaires of perceived cultural differences that can be used to reach large samples have the additional advantage that the reported behaviors and attitudes are determined by the people's perceptions rather than the "actual" or "objective" situation (Rentch 1990). Finally, perceptual outcomes, such as the effectiveness of the integration process, are useful because they provide a direct connection with cultural values (Earley and Singh 1995) and avoid problems inherent in the use of other performance measures (Zollo and Meier 2008).

All respondents were guaranteed anonymity (the only identification on the questionnaires was the name of the acquiring or buying company). Completed surveys were returned directly to the authors. Because the unit of analysis was not the individual manager but the merger management, responses were summed and averaged for each variable to arrive at merger management means (see Enz 1988). This procedure permitted control for team size variations across firms. Similarly, the aggregation of respondent perceptions to arrive at group scores resulted in findings that were less distorted by individual biases. Such distortion was further reduced by the fact that top managers were asked to evaluate not their own perception of cultural differences but those of the merger management. Moreover, multiple-respondent evaluations of each merger management made it possible to check reliability through a later calculation of consensus. Responses were aggregated only if a high level of consensus was demonstrated between the perceptions of top managers in each merger. Finally, to avoid problems of common method variance and the creation of pseudo-relationships between variables by methodological and process artifacts, provisions were made against consistency and priming effects following the recommendation of Podsakoff et al. (2003). As explained below, the most important variable, the fit of integration approach, was evaluated by a procedure that involves respondents only partially minimizing pseudo-relationships.

Measures

Corporate Cultural Differences. We used the instrument employed by Chatterjee et al. (1992), Lubatkin et al. (1999), Weber et al. (1996), and Weber (1996) to measure *corporate culture differentials*. Based on the assumption that relative phenomena are best suited for comparison, particularly in contrast situations (Louis 1983), respondents were asked to indicate the degree of pre-merger similarity between the acquired and acquiring top management on each item. Items were constructed to elicit responses about cultural differences on a 5-point scale, ranging from "very similar" to "very different". Following a test for inter-rater reliability, described below, a cultural difference index was computed across seven dimensions, each consisting of three to five items, with a total of 29 items. The seven dimensions (and the number of items used to measure each) were: innovation and action orientation (five items); risk-taking (five items); lateral integration (four items); top management contact (three items); autonomy and decision-making (five items); performance orientation (three items); and reward orientation (four items). Following the preliminary analysis described below, we collapsed the data into a single cultural difference index (Cronbach's alpha = 0.92) by summing the scores for all 29 items and taking their average.

National Cultural Distance. The GLOBE practices scores (House et al. 2004) were used. National cultural distance measures utilizing Hofstede's (1980) scores have been widely criticized (Harzing and Sorge 2003; McSweeney 2002; Shenkar 2001; Tayeb 1994). The extensive validity tests conducted for the GLOBE scores are reported in House et al. (2004).

Synergy Potential. We used an instrument based on the concept of "economy of sameness" (the synergy that can be achieved from accumulating similar operations), the concept of "economy of fitness" (synergies that can be achieved by combining different but complementary operations), and its measurement (Larsson and Finkelstein 1999). Synergy from similarities was measured using 11 items concerning the similarity of various operational functions such as marketing operations (geographic markets, customer groups, and industries) and production operations (types of input, process, and product). Synergy from complementarities was measured using 11 items concerning the complementarity of various operational functions such as marketing operations (possible transfer of marketing capabilities to new markets and products) and complementarity of production operations (possible transfer of production capabilities). The internal consistency is high (Cronbach's alpha = 0.90).

Fit of Integration Approach. To determine whether the fit between the appropriate integration approach and the one actually implemented by management was present in the merger, both recommended and actual integration approaches were evaluated separately and compared. To evaluate the recommended integration approach, the values of corporate culture differences and of synergy potential were classified into two categories, that is, two levels of dichotomy were determined for every variable: low and high. The cross-tabulation of the categories between the two variables created four groups, which made it possible to identify the integration approach that was recommended after completion of each individual M&A.

To identify the integration approach actually implemented by the M&A, managers were asked to choose the description of the integration process from a list of descriptions of integration approaches used by Ellis (2004). The characteristics of integration approaches consistently described by Haspeslagh and Jemison (1991), Nahavandi and Malekzadeh (1988), and Marks and Mirvis (1998) served as the basis for developing the coding scheme in the list of integration approaches. They included descriptions of the primary motives for the current acquisition; the extent to which the combined firm followed the operating procedures of the acquiring firm or sought to implement the best practices of both firms; whether any plans existed for restructuring and downsizing initiatives; and whether words such as assimilate, absorb, blend, or retain were used in describing the process of integrating the operations of the two firms. Statistical analysis comparing these integration approaches significantly confirmed the presence of differences between them (Ellis 2004). Note that these descriptions of the integration process do not use any evaluation of synergy potential or cultural differences in order to prevent creating any association between the two evaluations of the integration approach that may result from methodological and process artifacts.

Integration Effectiveness. The instrument used by Weber (1996) to measure integration effectiveness was employed. The effectiveness of the integration process measure was based on 12 questionnaire items that addressed effectiveness along such organizational dimensions as operations, production, marketing, research and development, and personnel. Use of key informants to assess effectiveness is common in organizational research, and self-report measures provide respondents with an opportunity to incorporate implicitly economic and non-economic considerations (for example, Dess 1987; Zollo and Meier 2008). A 5-point scale, ranging from "very ineffective" (1) to "very effective" (5) was used. The internal consistency is high (Cronbach's alpha = 0.86).

RESULTS

Table 2.1 presents the means, standard deviations, reliabilities, and inter-correlations of the seven dimensions of cultural difference measures.

Table 2.1 Mean, standard deviation, and Pearson correlations between dimensions of cultural differences and reliabilities

Dimension	Mean	S.D	IAO	RA	LI	TMC	ADM	PO	RO
IAO	3.4273	0.707	(0.767)						
RA	3.3364	0.713	0.797***	(0.854)					
LI	2.8864	0.862	0.291	0.224	(0.814)				
TMC	3.0305	1.053	0.574***	0.675***	0.507**	(0.743)			
ADM	3.1818	0.788	0.541***	0.527**	0.670***	0.739***	(0.740)		
PO	2.9095	0.868	0.444**	0.642***	0.282	0.431**	0.136	(0.711)	
RO	2.8750	0.739	0.544***	0.563***	0.528**	0.713***	0.564***	0.661***	(0.688)

Note: p< 0.10*, p< 0.05**, p< 0.01***.

Statistical analyses showed that most of the inter-correlations between the seven cultural difference dimensions are relatively high and significant, and internally consistent (Cronbach's alpha ranging from a low of 0.688 to a high of 0.854). In keeping with the theory underlying the construction of the culture measures, the dimensions demonstrated discriminant validity (Cronbach's alpha for each dimension was higher than the dimension's correlations with all or most of the other six dimensions).

The data also provide strong evidence of convergent validity, indicating, as expected, that the seven dimensions are part of the same general construct (Buchanan 1974; Rosenthal and Rosnow 1984). Although each dimension measures a unique aspect of the phenomenon, all the dimensions refer to the same content domain, making it possible to combine them all into a single index, a procedure for which prior research provides theoretical and statistical support (for example, Buchanan 1974; Chatterjee et al. 1992; Porter et al. 1974). The combined internal consistency of the single cultural difference index was high (Cronbach's alpha = 0.92).

Table 2.2 shows the means, standard deviations, and inter-correlations of the key constructs of the study. The results show some preliminary support for Hypothesis 1 that the fit is significantly and positively associated with integration effectiveness ($r = 0.364$, $p < 0.10$). The results also show that synergy potential is significantly and positively associated with integration effectiveness ($r = 0.436$, $p < 0.05$). The correlation results do not confirm any effect of national and corporate cultural differences.

A composite index of national cultural distance following the formula that was used for Hofstede's measures was not used for the GLOBE measures. The present study tests each dimension separately, similarly to previous studies of international M&A. Because the sample size does not allow handling of all 9 dimensions at the same time, we tested one dimension at a time; a practice that was used in many other studies. Some national dimensions did not show significant results. Table 2.3 presents three national dimensions that show significant results.

The results of Model 1 show that each variable is important for integration effectiveness. For example, cultural differences are significantly and negatively associated with integration effectiveness, except for the institutional collectivism dimension, which is significantly and positively associated with integration effectiveness. This dimension refers to the degree to which individuals are encouraged by societal institutions to be integrated into broader entities. Such differences may help integration process, and thus, contribute to integration effectiveness, a result that is consistent with some other studies (Stahl and Voigt 2008). The results also lend support to Hypothesis 2 stating that synergy potential is positively associated with integration effectiveness.

Most interesting is the result for the fit of integration approach, which is consistent with the theory and the paradigm developed in this study. The results lend support to Hypothesis 1 stating that such a fit is significantly and positively related to integration effectiveness. Furthermore, Model 2 that includes the interaction terms lends support for Hypothesis 3 stating that the interaction of synergy potential and fit of integration approaches will be positively and significantly ($p < 0.05$) associated with integration effectiveness.

DISCUSSION AND CONCLUSION

Mergers and acquisitions are complex phenomena that require a high level of organizational ingenuity; integrating people who are often strangers thrown together in a new organizational structure and system, at times against their will. In addition to maintaining the day-to-day business, managers and employees must build new relationships, often in different languages and in culture clash situations. These situations require innovative integration solutions that fit the specific conditions of the merger. The findings of the present study provide the first systematic evidence linking the fit of integration approach to integration effectiveness in international M&A. Specifically, when management selects an appropriate approach for the integration process, which fits the given M&A situation (level of synergy potential combined with levels of national and corporate or cultural differences), the integration is highly effective. If there is no fit between the selected and the appropriate integration approach, the integration process is not effective.

These findings suggest a direction in the quest for solving the long-overdue paradox of M&A success. Consistent positive association between synergy potential and international M&A success can be found when the management of the acquiring company selects the appropriate integration approach. These findings are of practical importance because they show that managers who choose the appropriate integration approach can realize the synergy potential and at the same time mitigate the negative effect of cultural differences. The implication is clear: the management of the acquiring firm must pay at least as much attention to issues of the integration approach to be implemented after the pre-merger search process, as they do to issues of strategic and organizational fit.

Measuring M&A success based on integration effectiveness is an attempt to bring the dependent variable of interest closer to the phenomenon under

Table 2.2   Descriptive statistics: mean, standard deviation, and correlations between the variables

Variable (N=22)	Min	Max	Mean	S.D	1	2	3	4
1. Effectiveness of Integration	2.58	4.42	3.43	0.586	(0.860)			
2. Fit Integration Approach					0.364*			
3. Synergy Potential	1.64	4.59	3.07	0.754	0.436**	0.063	(0.896)	
4. Organizational Culture Differences	2.00	4.24	3.124	0.619	−0.192	0.084	0.020	(0.917)
5. Assertiveness Practices	3.61	4.44	4.175	0.137	−0.122	−0.273	0.152	−0.051
6. Institutional Collectivism Practices	4.20	4.40	4.387	0.046	0.305	0.139	0.035	0.330
7. In Group Collectivism Practices	3.82	4.66	4.595	0.173	−0.007	−0.208	0.156	0.069
8. Future Orientation Practices	3.74	4.36	3.841	0.117	0.042	0.231	−0.157	−0.033
9. Gender Egalitarianism Practices	3.21	3.81	3.249	0.136	−0.0308	−0.147	−0.031	−0.331
10. Humane Orientation Practices	3.60	4.07	4.046	0.101	0.324	0.199	−0.002	0.331
11. Performance Orientation Practices	4.03	4.43	4.063	0.108	−0.261	−0.059	−0.076	−0.0305
12. Power Distance Practices	4.71	5.68	4.768	0.213	0.150	−0.0174	−0.014	−0.333
13. Uncertainty Avoidance Practices	3.97	5.05	4.05	0.267	−0.184	0.040	−0.116	−0.245

Note: p< 0.10* p< 0.05** p< 0.01***.

investigation. Traditional accounting and financial measures of M&A performance are problematic especially when examining the internal process of integration. Similarly, assessing the overall M&A potential based on similarities and complementarities is more direct than relying on Standard

5	6	7	8	9	10	11	12
−0.016							
0.935***	0.339						
−0.968***	−0.235	−0.994***					
0.045	−1.000***	−0.312	0.207				
−0.253	0.971***	0.106	0.003	−0.978***			
−0.259	−0.964***	−0.585***	0.493**	0.953***	−0.869***		
0.152	−0.991***	−0.208	0.100	0.994***	−0.995***	0.915***	
−0.556***	−0.822***	−0.814***	0.747***	0.747***	−0.663***	0.947***	0.737***

Industrial Classification (SIC) codes or other classification schemes that cannot differentiate between the various sources of value creation.

Selection of the integration solutions is often cited as an essential element in M&A success (for example, Haspeslagh and Jemison 1991;

Table 2.3   *Regression results of the fit of integration approach, synergy potential, and organizational culture on effectiveness of integration*

Variable (N=22)	Effectiveness of Integration					
	Model 1			Model 2 with Interaction		
	Beta (t)			Beta (t)		
Fit Integration Approach	0.318* (1.778)	0.314* (1.761)	0.302* (1.695)	−1.418** (−2.190)	−1.423** (−2.208)	−1.446** (−2.280)
Synergy Potential	0.411** (2.322)	0.412** (2.337)	0.419** (2.390)	0.010 (0.048)	0.011 (0.053)	0.014 (0.068)
Organizational Culture Differences	−0.346* (−1.849)	−0.347* (−1.860)	−0.351* (−1.892)	−0.297* (−1.860)	−0.299* (−1.879)	−0.305* (−1.943)
Institutional Collectivism Practices	0.360* (1.914)			0.295* (1.830)		
Gender Egalitarianism Practices		−0.364* (−1.936)			−0.301* (−1.871)	
Power Distance Practices			−0.376** (−2.003)			−0.320* (−2.010)
Fit Integration Approach* Synergy Potential				1.858** (2.757)	1.860** (2.773)	1.872** (2.836)
R^2	0.471	0.473	0.480	0.641	0.644	0.654
F	3.785**	3.818**	3.920***	5.724***	5.794***	6.043***
Adjusted R^2	0.347	0.349	0.357	0.529	0.533	0.546
R^2 change				0.170	0.171	0.174
F change				7.601**	7.688**	8.041**

Graebner 2004; Schweizer 2005; Nahavandi and Malekzadeh 1988), but no study has examined statistically its importance in a sample of international M&A and in conjunction with national and corporate cultural differences. The present study clearly shows that despite the negative effect of high cultural differences on M&A performance (Chatterjee et al. 1992; Weber 1996), it is possible to realize the synergy potential if the management creatively selects the integration approach that fits the characteristics of the merger. This finding is consistent with those of many previous studies (Larsson and Finkelstein 1999; Schweizer 2005; Weber et al. 1996; Weber and Tarba 2010; Weber and Drori 2011) and suggests that high synergy potential is not sufficient for M&A success: certain practices and structural changes must be undertaken to realize these synergies.

FUTURE RESEARCH

There are ample opportunities for further research following the findings and the theoretical framework presented here. For example, the present study warrants replication using an interdisciplinary approach, other forms of measurement (anthropological and other non-survey methods), expanded samples, and unrelated as well as related mergers. Replication studies should also attempt to measure M&A performance with other constructs (Zollo and Meier 2008) and management perceptions, over different time frames, to establish stronger causal links between the fit of integration approach and overall M&A performance. Although access to such data may be difficult, any attempt at triangulation would be useful in supporting both the internal and external validities of the present study.

Other research efforts could be directed toward understanding the fit of integration approach, degree of fit, its practices, and its effect on other factors in the post-merger integration process, for example, how the degree of fit affects such factors (observed in previous studies) as the turnover of top executives (Lubatkin et al.1999), intergroup conflict (Weber et al. 1996), drop in job commitment (Weber 1996), identification with the merger (Weber and Drori 2011), and human resource practices (Weber et al. 2012).

REFERENCES

Barney, J.B. (1986), 'Organizational culture: Can it be a source of sustained competitive advantage?', *Academy of Management Review*, 11: 656–665.
Barney, J.B. (1991), 'Firm resources and sustained competitive advantage', *Journal of Management*, **17** (1): 99–120.
Bower, J.L. (2001), 'Not all M&A are alike – and that matters', *Harvard Business Review* (Fall), 93–101.
Buchanan, B. (1974), 'Building organizational commitment: The socialization of managers in work organizations', *Administrative Science Quarterly*, **19** (4): 533–546.
Calori, R., Lubatkin, M. and Very, P. (1994), 'Control mechanisms in cross-border acquisitions: An international comparison', *Organization Studies*, 15: 361–379.
Cannella, A.A. Jr. and Hambrick, D.C. (1993), 'Effects of executive departures on the performance of acquired firm', *Strategic Management Journal*, 14: 137–152.
Cartwright, S. and Cooper, C.L. (1992), *Mergers and Acquisitions: The Human Factor*, Oxford: Butterworth–Heinemann.

Cartwright, S. and Cooper, C.L. (1993), 'The role of culture compatibility in successful organizational marriage', *Academy of Management Executive*, 7: 57–70.

Chatterjee, S., Lubatkin, M.H., Schweiger, D.M. and Weber, Y. (1992), 'Cultural differences and shareholders value: Explaining the variability in the performance of related mergers', *Strategic Management Journal*, 13: 319–334.

Child, J., Faulkner, D. and Pitkethly, R. (2000), 'Foreign direct investment in the UK 1985–1994: The impact on domestic management practice', *Journal of Management Studies*, **37** (1): 141–166.

Datta, D. (1991), 'Organizational fit and acquisition performance: effects of post-acquisition integration', *Strategic Management Journal*, 12: 281–297.

Datta, D.K. and Puia, G. (1995), 'Cross-border acquisitions: An examination of the influence of relatedness and cultural fit on shareholder value creation in U.S. acquiring firms. *Management International Review*, **35** (4): 337–359.

Dess, G.G. (1987), 'Consensus on strategy formulation and organizational performance: Competitors in a fragmented industry', *Strategic Management Journal*, 8: 259–277.

Earley, P.C. and Singh, H. (1995), 'International and intercultural management research: What's next?' *Academy of Management Journal*, **38** (2): 327–340.

Ellis, K.M. (2004), 'Managing the acquisition process: Do differences actually exist across integration approaches?', in A.L. Pablo and M. Javidan (eds), *Mergers and Acquisitions*: *Creating Integrative Knowledge*, Malden, MA, USA: Blackwell Publishing.

Ellis, K.M., Reus, T.H. and Lamont, B.T. (2009), 'The effects of procedural and informational justice in the integration of related acquisitions', *Strategic Management Journal*, 30: 137–161.

Enz, C.A. (1988), 'The role of value congruity in latent organizational power', *Administrative Science Quarterly*, 33: 284–304.

Ernst & Young (2011), 'Life sciences beyond borders – Global Biotechnology Report'.

Finkelstein, S. (1992), 'Power in top management teams: Dimensions, measurement, and validation', *Academy of Management Journal*, **35** (3): 505–538.

Graebner, M. (2004), 'Momentum and serendipity: How acquired leaders create value in the integration of technology firms', *Strategic Management Journal*, 25: 751–777.

Greenwood, R., Hinings, C.R. and Brown, J. (1994), 'Merging professional service firms', *Organization Science*, **5** (2): 239–257.

Gutek, B.A. (1978), 'On the accuracy of retrospective attitudinal data', *Public Opinion Quarterly*, 42: 390–401.

Harzing, A-W. and Sorge, A. (2003), 'The relative impact of country of origin and universal contingencies on internationalization strategies and corporate control in multinational enterprises: Worldwide and European perspectives', *Organization Studies*, **24** (2): 187–214.

Haspeslagh, P.C. and Jemison, D.B. (1991), *Managing Acquisitions: Creating Value through Corporate Renewal*, New York: Free Press.

Hofstede, G. (1980), *Culture's Consequences*, New York: Sage.

Hofstede, G., Neuijen, B., Ohavy, D.D. and Sanders, G. (1990), 'Measuring organizational culture: A qualitative and quantitative study across twenty cases', *Administrative Science Quarterly*, 35: 286–317.

House, R.J., Hanges, P.J., Javidan, M., Dorfman, P.W. and Gupta, V. (2004), *Leadership, Culture, and Organizations: The GLOBE Study of 62 Societies*, New York: Sage.

Huber, G.P. and Power, D.J. (1985), 'Retrospective reports of strategic-level managers: Guidelines for increasing their accuracy', *Strategic Management Journal*, **6** (2): 171–181.

King, D.R., Dalton, D.R., Daily, C.M. and Covin, J.G. (2004), 'Meta-analyses of post-acquisition performance: Indications of unidentified moderators', *Strategic Management Journal*, 25: 187–200.

Larsson, R. and Finkelstein, S. (1999), 'Integrating strategic, organizational, and human resource perspectives on mergers and acquisitions: A case survey of synergy realization', *Organization Science*, **10** (1): 1–26.

Louis, M.R. (1983), 'Organization as culture-bearing milieux', in L. Pondy, P. Frost, G. Morgan and T. Dandridge (eds), *Organizational Symbolism*, Greenwich, CT: JAI Press.

Lubatkin, M., Calori, R., Very, P. and Veiga, J.F. (1998), 'Managing mergers across borders: A two-nation exploration of a nationally bound administrative heritage', *Organization Science*, 9: 670–684.

Lubatkin, M., Schweiger, D. and Weber, Y. (1999), 'Top management turnover in related M&As: An additional test of the theory of relative standing', *Journal of Management*, **25** (1): 55–74.

Makri, M., Hitt, M.A. and Lane, P.J. (2010), 'Complementary technologies, knowledge relatedness, and invention outcomes in high technology mergers and acquisitions', *Strategic Management Journal*, 31: 602–628.

Marks, M.L. and Mirvis, P.H. (1998), *Joining Forces: Making One Plus One Equal Three In Mergers, Acquisitions, and Alliances*, San Francisco, CA: Jossey-Bass.

McSweeney, B. (2002), 'Hofstede's model of national cultural differences and their consequences: A triumph of faith; a failure of analysis', *Human Relations*, **55** (1): 89–118.

Morosini, P. and Singh, H. (1994), 'Post cross-border acquisitions: Implementing 'national culture-compatible' strategies to improve performance', *European Management Journal*, **12** (4): 390–400.

Morosini, P., Shane, S. and Singh, H. (1998), 'National cultural distance and cross-border acquisition performance', *Journal of International Business Studies*, **29** (1): 137–158.

Nahavandi, A. and Malekzadeh, A.R. (1988), 'Acculturation in mergers and acquisitions', *Academy of Management Review*, **13** (1): 79–90.

Paruchuri, S., Nerkar, A. and Hambrick, D.C. (2007), 'Acquisition integration and productivity losses in the technical core: Disruption of inventors in acquired companies', *Organization Science*, **17** (5): 545–562.

Pettigrew, A.M. (1979), 'On studying organizational cultures', *Administrative Science Quarterly*, 24: 570–581.

Pitkethly, R., Faulkner, D. and Child, J. (2003), 'Integrating acquisitions', in C. Cooper and A. Gregory (eds), *Advances in Mergers and Acquisitions*, Vol. 2, New York: JAI Press.

Podsakoff, P.M., MacKenzie, S.B., Jeong-Yeon, L. and Podsakoff, N.P. (2003), 'Common method biases in behavioral research: a critical review of the literature and recommended remedies', *Journal of Applied Psychology*, **88** (5): 879–903.

Porter, L.W., Steers, R.M., Mowday, R.T. and Boulian, P.V. (1974), 'Organizational commitment, job satisfaction, and turnover among psychiatric technicians', *Journal of Applied Psychology*, 59: 603–609.

Puranam, P., Singh, H. and Zollo, M. (2003), 'A bird in the hand or two in the bush? Integration trade-offs in technology-grafting acquisitions', *European Management Journal*, **21** (2):179–184.

Puranam, P., Singh, H. and Zollo, M. (2006), 'Organizing for innovation: Managing the coordination autonomy dilemma in technology acquisitions', *Academy of Management Journal*, **49** (2): 263–280.

Puranam, P. and Srikanth, K. (2007), 'What they know vs. what they do: How acquirers leverage technology acquisitions', *Strategic Management Journal*, 28: 805–825.

Ranft, A. and Lord, M.D. (2002), 'Acquiring new technologies and capabilities: A grounded model of acquisition implementation', *Organization Science*, **13** (4): 420–441.

Ranft, A. (2006), 'Knowledge preservation and transfer during post-acquisition integration', in C. Cooper and S. Finkelstein (eds), *Advances in Mergers and Acquisitions*, Vol. 5, New York: JAI Press.

Rentch, J.J. (1990), 'Climate and culture: interaction and qualitative differences in organizational meanings', *Journal of Applied Psychology*, 75: 668–681.

Reus, T.H. and Lamont, B.T. (2009), 'The double-edged sword of cultural distance in international acquisitions', *Journal of International Business Studies*, 40: 1298–1316.

Rosenthal, R. and Rosnow, R.L. (1984), *Essentials of Behavior Research: Methods and Data Analysis*, New York: McGraw-Hill.

Sales, M.S. and Mirvis, P.H. (1984), 'When cultures collide: Issues in acquisition', in J.R. Kimberly and R.E. Quinn (eds), *The Challenge of Managing Transitions*, Homewood, IL: Dow Jones–Irwin.

Schein, E.H. (1985), *Organizational Culture and Leadership: A Dynamic View*, San Francisco, CA: Jossey-Bass.

Schneider, S.C. (1988), 'National vs. corporate culture: Implications for human resource management', *Human Resource Management*, 27: 231–247.

Schweiger, M.D. and Goulet, P.K. (2000), 'Integrating mergers and acquisitions: An international research review', in C. Cooper and A. Gregory (eds), *Advances in Mergers and Acquisitions*, Vol. 1, New York: JAI Press.

Schweizer, L. (2005), 'Organizational integration of acquired biotech companies into pharmaceutical companies: The need for a hybrid approach', *Academy of Management Journal*, **48** (6): 1051–1074.

Shenkar, O. (2001), 'Cultural distance revisited: Towards a more rigorous conceptualization and measurement of cultural differences', *Journal of International Business Studies*, **32** (3): 519–535.

Stahl, G.K, Mendenhall, M.E. and Weber, Y. (2005), 'Research on sociocultural integration in mergers and acquisitions: Points of agreement, paradoxes, and avenues for future research', in G.K. Stahl and M.E. Mendenhall (eds), *Mergers and Acquisitions: Managing Culture and Human Resources*, Stanford, CA: Stanford Business Books.

Stahl, G.K. and Voigt, A. (2008), 'Do cultural differences matter in mergers and acquisitions? A tentative model and examination', *Organization Science*, 19: 160–176.

Tayeb, M.H. (1994), 'Japanese managers and British culture: A comparative case study', *International Journal of Human Resource Management*, **5** (1): 145–166.

Teerikangas, S. and Very, P. (2006), 'The culture-performance relationship in M&A: From yes/no to how', *British Journal of Management*, **17** (S1): S31–S48.

Very, P., Lubatkin, M. and Calori, R. (1996), 'A cross-national assessment of acculturative stress in recent European mergers', *International Studies of Management and Organization*, 26: 59–86.

Very, P., Lubatkin, M., Calori, R. and Veiga, J. (1997), 'Relative standing and the performance of recently acquired European firms', *Strategic Management Journal*, **18** (8): 593–614.

Weber, Y. (1996), 'Corporate culture fit and performance in mergers and acquisitions', *Human Relations*, 49: 1181–1202.

Weber, Y. and Pliskin, N. (1996), 'The effects of information systems integration and organizational culture on a firm's effectiveness', *Information & Management*, 30: 81–90.

Weber, Y., Shenkar, O. and Raveh, A. (1996), 'National vs. corporate cultural fit in mergers and acquisitions: An exploratory study', *Management Science*, 42: 1215–1227.

Weber, Y. and Tarba, S.Y. (2010), 'Human resource practices and performance of M&A in Israel', *Human Resource Management Review*, 20: 203–211.

Weber, Y., Belkin, T. and Tarba, S.Y. (2011), 'Negotiation, cultural differences, and planning in mergers and acquisitions', *Proceedings of the EuroMed Academy of Management 2010 Annual Conference*, 1249–1257. Nicosia, Cyprus, November 2010.

Weber, Y. and Drori, I. (2011), 'Integrating organizational and human behavior perspectives on mergers and acquisitions: Looking inside the black box', *International Studies of Management and Organization*, **41** (3): 76–95.

Weber, Y. and Fried, Y. (2011a), 'The role of HR practices in managing culture clash during the post-merger integration process', *Human Resource Management*, **50** (5): 565–570.

Weber, Y. and Fried, Y. (2011b), 'The dynamics of employee reactions during post-merger integration process', *Human Resource Management*, **50** (6): 777–781.

Weber, Y., Rachman-Moore, D. and Tarba, S.Y. (2012), 'Human resource practices during post-merger conflict and merger performance', *International Journal of Cross-Cultural Management*. Forthcoming.

Weber, Y. and Tarba, S.Y. (2011), 'Exploring culture clash in related merger: Post-merger integration in the hightech industry', *International Journal of Organizational Analysis*, **19** (3): 202–221.

Weber, Y. and Tarba, S.Y. (2012), 'Mergers and acquisitions process: The use of corporate culture analysis', *Cross-Cultural Management: An International Journal*. Forthcoming.

Weber, Y., Tarba, S.Y. and Reichel, A. (2009), 'International acquisitions and acquisitions performance revisited – the role of cultural distance and post-acquisition integration approach. in C. Cooper and S. Finkelstein (eds), *Advances in Mergers and Acquisitions*, Vol. 8, New York: JAI Press.

Zollo, M. and Meier, D. (2008), 'What Is M&A Performance?', *Academy of Management Perspectives*, **22** (3): 55–77.

PART II

RESEARCH AGENDA AND THEORETICAL DEVELOPMENT ON CONNECTION BETWEEN M&A STAGES AND CONTEXT VARIABLES

3 A research agenda to increase merger and acquisition success
Mitchell Lee Marks and Philip H. Mirvis

Scholars have been conducting serious research on the human, organizational and cultural aspects of mergers and acquisitions (M&A) for 30 years.[1] Yet, over this period, there have only been modest improvements in the M&A success rate (Schoenberg, 2006). In this chapter, we examine corporate combinations, describe how human factors contribute to their failure or success, and identify key research questions whose answers can help to improve the M&A success rate in both financial and human terms. We use our experience as both researchers and advisors in over 100 combinations – as well as our awareness of the scholarly literature and the work of other practitioners – to highlight the factors which matter most in eventual M&A success.

MERGERS AND ACQUISITIONS

Many motives prompt executives to acquire or merge with another organization. In some cases, a combination helps a firm move quickly into a new market or product space or pursue a strategy that would otherwise be too costly, risky, or technologically advanced to achieve on its own. Other times, deals are opportunistic, such as when a troubled competitor seeks a savior or when a bidding war ensues after a firm is "put into play". Still other times, acquisitions or mergers can be defensive moves to protect market share in a declining or consolidating industry. The overarching reason for combining with another organization is *the belief* that the union will enable a firm to attain strategic goals more quickly and inexpensively than acting on its own (Haspeslagh and Jamison, 1991).

Despite their popularity, most mergers and acquisitions are financial failures and produce undesirable consequences for the people and companies involved. While target-firm shareholders generally enjoy positive short-term returns, investors in bidding firms frequently experience share price underperformance in the months following acquisition, with negligible long-term gains (Agrawal and Jaffe, 2000). The most recent research shows that 83 percent of all deals fail to deliver shareholder value and 53 percent actually destroyed value (compare Cartwright and McCarthy, 2005; Harding and Rouse, 2007). In addition, M&A can exact a heavy toll on employees (DeMeuse and Marks, 2003; Mische, 2001). A longitudinal study of ten thousand US employees representing 4000 organizations found those from organizations that had been engaged in M&A reported significantly less favorable results than those who had not been involved. This held true for every industry group and every facet of working life measured (Wiley and Moechnig, 2005).

Many factors account for the dismal M&A track record, including paying the wrong price, buying the wrong company, or making the deal at the wrong time. Our own 30-year research program finds that the *processes* used to put companies together are integral to a deal's success versus failure (Marks and Mirvis, 2010). This encompasses the formation and operations of the buying team (Mirvis and Marks, 1992), how the firms are integrated (Marks and Mirvis, 2000), and learning from current deals to better manage future ones (Marks and Mirvis, 2001).

BUYING A COMPANY

Buying a company encompasses strategizing, scouting, assessing and selecting a partner, deal-making, and preparing for the eventual combination. The typical approach involves a "tunnel vision" on the financial aspects of the deal. Buyers concentrate on what a target is worth, what price premium, if any, to pay, and how to structure the transaction. The successful approach, by comparison, also emphasizes finance but adds careful attention to how a combination advances the business strategy of a firm, due diligence on behavioral and culture factors that might complicate the combination, and a clear picture of how the firms will be integrated.

Research Questions on Buying a Business

A review of relevant literature as well as practical experience suggests some key areas for future M&A research on the workings of buy teams:

M&A motives

To what extent are M&A "buy" decisions motivated by strategic intent (for example, market power, efficiency, asset redeployment, market discipline) versus manager's self-interest (for example, hubris, empire building, survival, personal financial gains)? This question applies to the overall make-versus-buy decision, the selection of a partner, and the price paid. Obviously, corporate pronouncements and executive talking points express the business case behind any deal. Yet a blue-ribbon panel of financial experts concluded that CEO ego was the primary force driving M&A in the United States (Boucher, 1980). Another study found that the bigger the ego of the acquiring company's CEO the higher the premium a company is likely to pay for a target (Sirower, 1997).

If the true motives behind a combination have more to do with "non-strategic" forces – say, the desire to run the largest company in an industry or fear of being swallowed up by competitors – then value creation is unlikely because there are few benefits to be leveraged by joining forces. To get at these factors, researchers might look into the pattern of purchases by regular acquirers and to what extent it builds out a clear and coherent business strategy. Those with a clinical mindset might, as Harry Levinson (1976) has done, explore the mindsets of buying CEOs and how their ambitions and fears factor into their M&A proclivities. They might also investigate instructions given to buy teams, pressures on them to do a particular deal, and considerations given to alternative courses of action.

Research question 1a: To what extent do strategic versus non-strategic motives drive M&A buy teams and what is the relationship between those motives and the price paid, partner selected, and synergies achieved by a deal?

Behavioral and cultural due diligence
When due diligence focuses exclusively on the financial makeup of potential M&A partners, analysts overestimate revenue gains and cost savings and underestimate the resource requirements and headaches involved in integrating businesses (Lodorfos and Boateng, 2006). Adding in behavioral due diligence – the process of investigating a potential partner's talent, organizational makeup and culture – enables a buyer to understand if the values of the potential partners are compatible, if the bench strength exists to replace managers who might depart, if all parties are on the same wavelength regarding synergies and what it takes to combine, and if there is enough trust and chemistry to propel the combined operation into becoming more than the sum of its parts (Gebhardt, 2003; Carlton and Lineberry, 2004).

Buyers are starting to use both qualitative and quantitative data for their behavioral and cultural due diligence efforts. Before moving ahead on any deal, one financial services firm begins a behavioral and cultural assessment of acquisition candidates using qualitative interviews and focus group discussions. This due diligence identifies a wide range of potential business and cultural barriers to integration success. All of these are then factored into buying decisions and, if the deal goes forward, into the integration manager's agenda. Other firms rely on validated organizational culture surveys to (1) examine cultural fit between two firms prior to a combination, (2) inform cross-cultural dialogue during their combination, and (3) establish a baseline measure to assess changes in culture later on.

The use of behavioral and cultural due diligence varies according to the type of deal. In a true merger, for example, the parties might use the data to generate discussion of the desired cultural end state for the combined entity. Dialogue about the end state should promptly raise up any disconnects between the partners' expectations as well as shared hopes for desired culture change (Marks and Mirvis, 2011). In acquisitions in which a target's culture might be assimilated into the buyer's, then the cultural assessment is more likely to be used to highlight potential sources of culture clash and provide integration managers with insights into potential cultural roadblocks down the road. Behavioral due diligence pays off: one study found that successful acquirers were 40 percent more likely to conduct thorough human and cultural due diligence than unsuccessful buyers (Anslinger and Copeland, 1996).

Research question 1b: How do buy teams consider behavioral versus financial due diligence in their analysis and to what extent does behavioral due diligence yield better M&A decisions?

Buy team make up
Most members of traditional due diligence teams come from financial positions or backgrounds. They bring a financial mindset to the study of a partner, and their judgments about synergies are informed by financial models and ratios. They do not necessarily bring an experienced eye to assessing a partner's "fit" in areas of engineering, manufacturing, or marketing. As a result, there is a tendency for "hard" criteria to drive out "soft" matters: if the numbers look good, any doubts about organizational or cultural differences tend to be scoffed at and dismissed.

We have argued that the traditional membership of due diligence teams (for example, financial analysts and strategists) be augmented by people from technical, operational, and HR functions. Beyond functional diversity, how important is it to have national and cultural diversity on a buy team? Our experience suggests that this is especially relevant to cross-border deals and to global combinations. But it is expensive and can be time-consuming. More research is needed to understand how this diversity in interests and expertise influences M&A analysis and team dynamics.

Research question 1c: To what extent does functional, operational, and national diversity in due diligence team membership contribute to better M&A decision making?

Buy team decision making

M&A underperformance is sometimes attributed to the "rush to close" the deal at the expense of attending to factors that could help or hurt its eventual success (Ashkenas and Francis, 2000). Why would companies buy something when their buy team has not thoroughly "looked under the hood?" Several scholars have documented how decision making traps – anchoring in initial perceptions, escalating commitments, and cognitive overload – can lead buyers to follow faulty assumptions and multiple misjudgments (Duhaime and Schwenk, 1985). Thus we have also proposed that buy teams be schooled in decision making biases and apply decision making tools and interventions to their deliberations. These include training in decision making effectiveness, the placement of "devil's advocates" on buy teams, and even the commissioning of a duplicate team to ensure that the deal's prospects passed muster with both teams. What are needed are studies of how these practices, studied in the lab, can operate in the field.

Research question 1d: What decision tools and interventions improve an M&A buy team's analyses and decisions?

PUTTING COMPANIES TOGETHER

After the deal receives legal clearance, the real work of integrating companies commences. Four aspects of M&A practice at this point beg research attention. First is the tendency for companies to fail to fully take account of the "human side" of M&A. Senior executives, once named to top posts, cannot relate to the uncertainty and insecurity experienced by employees down the line. Middle managers get caught up in their own anxiety and fail to communicate with their people. Meanwhile, HR departments are busy fire-fighting rather than moving the combination forward.

Second is the pace in which the integration occurs. There is a classic trade-off between moving quickly and moving carefully. Making quick decisions feels good in the short run by giving the impression of making progress and reducing stress and uncertainty. However, you have to live with the consequences of hasty decisions over the long run, which also can ultimately slow down progress and increase stress and uncertainty when early actions have to be undone.

Third is the increasingly common practice of forming integration planning teams with membership from both sides of a deal. Too often, however, these teams are ill-equipped to work together. They frequently are marred by conflict, engage in horse-trading, or simply settle for low-common-denominator decisions.

Fourth, the clash of cultures tends to be downplayed or ignored. A survey of European managers involved in acquisitions and alliances found that technical issues were less instrumental in producing conflicts in work relationships than differences between corporate and national cultures (Marks and Mirvis, 2010). A majority also reported that senior executives did not initially regard such differences as important.

Research Questions on Combining Businesses

Twenty-five years ago, we identified the symptoms of the "Merger Syndrome" as a prime cause of the individual, organizational, and culture problems in M&A (Marks and Mirvis, 1985). The Merger Syndrome is a fusion of uncertainty and the likelihood of change, both favorable and unfavorable, that produces stress and ultimately affects perceptions and judgments, interpersonal relationships, and the dynamics of the combination itself. At the organizational level, the Syndrome is manifested by increased centralization and lessened communication, leaving people in the dark about the combination and fueling rumors and insecurities. This often produces worst-case-scenario thinking that distracts employees from regular duties. All of this hampers integration, reduces productivity, and contributes to turnover of key people.

In response to these combination challenges, scholars have identified a range of interventions to counter adverse emotional reactions at the individual level (compare Seo and Hill, 2005), improve integration planning effectiveness at the group level (for example, Bradley, 2003), and ease the clash of cultures (Chatman and Cha, 2003).

Psychological preparation
One way to mollify the effects of the Merger Syndrome is a "realistic merger preview" that provides detailed information regarding the timeline of a combination, how it will affect employees, and other pertinent information. In a quasi-experimental study, researchers found that employees given a realistic preview of their merger rebounded more quickly from the negative effect in areas including job attitudes, trust toward the company, and job performance (Schweiger and DeNisi, 1991).

Other interventions include educating people through readings, presentations, or discussions of human factors in a combination. A more dynamic way is through merger sensitization workshops, role-plays, and other experiential activities that help people develop a true feeling of what it is like to acquire or be acquired (Marks, 2003). And then there is the role of communication. The employee desire for information in M&A has been described as "insatiable" and most prescriptions call for combining organizations to over-communicate, early and often. But little empirical work has sharpened insight regarding the content and processes of communications that work in the context of M&A.

Research question 2a: What kinds of interventions best prepare people to cope with the stresses of a combination? Does the efficacy of psychological preparation vary depending on whether people are acquired, acquiring, or merging?

Adapting to change

Concurrent with the development of insight into the range of human reactions to M&A has been the study of behavioral interventions to address their consequences (Jian, 2007). Many aim to help people to "let go" of past affiliations and practices and move toward the new behaviors and identifications (Bridges, 1991). But some address the socio-emotional aspects of adaptation. We have, for example, studied "grieving meetings" where people can mourn their losses and "bury" past associations. Others favor more cognitive approaches that have people, for instance, calculate the "plusses-and-minuses" of change. Still others emphasize acculturative interventions that bring people together quickly with counterparts from the other side. Finally, there are work-based interventions that stress the behavioral role of leaders and work groups in providing psychological support.

Research question 2b: What kinds of interventions – emotional, cognitive, acculturative, behavioral – help people to adapt to changes wrought by M&A? Is there a critical period in which interventions are more versus less effective in helping people prepare for and cope with the merger syndrome?

Pace of integration

Senior teams consistently underestimate the time and energy required to identify, assess, and address the many decisions that arise when two complex organizations combine. More than a few CEOs have done the glamour work of negotiating a deal and thereupon handed off the dirty work of meshing structures, systems, and procedures to operations managers. Other CEOs, by contrast, play an active role in the integration process and keep space available on their calendars for the many public and private activities required to steward a major organizational change.

How fast should the combination proceed? On the one hand, most involved want to move forward quickly – executives to capture synergies, managers to get refocused, and employees to get on with it or at least learn of their personal fate. Countering this is a more careful approach – one that is more time-intensive and stressful, but also likely to result in more well thought out decisions. The senior executive has the choice of insisting upon quick combination decisions – and living with the consequences – or of directing executives to take the time to make more careful choices. Realistic timetables take into account not only the many tasks involved in the combination phase, but also the need to run the two businesses effectively and efficiently! And, realistic timetables also consider what is going on in the partner organizations aside from the combination. Is a crucial new product launch or an important industry event scheduled during the integration period? Is a significant upgrade to IT or implementation of a major change like a reengineering project anticipated? If so, the time and resources allocated to these events detract from managing the combination and should be reflected in expected timing.

Research question 2c: What role does speed play in the integration process? Is there an ideal pace of integration, does it vary based on type of combination involved, and what are signals that the pace should be sped up or slowed down?

Transition teaming
Like any other start-up group, transition teams go through stages of development before they get down to performing effectively. What complicates this is that these teams are populated by representatives from each company that have their own accustomed ways of analyzing issues, sorting options, and arriving at decisions. Furthermore, they have their own and their organization's interests to protect. This is a setup for conflict (Mirvis, 1985). Undoubtedly, criteria used in team member selection, decisions about team leadership (for example, single or dual leaders? The person likely to head the function or an impartial figure?) and about team composition (for example, equal representation from both sides? Commensurate levels of skill and tenure?) influence team dynamics.

Research question 2d: What factors in transition team member selection, team composition and leadership, and team operations promote more or less effective team decisions?

Here, too, there have been interventions proposed to facilitate transition teaming that include team building exercises, third-party process facilitation, and training in conflict resolution.

Research question 2e: What kinds of interventions work best in building transition team effectiveness in M&A?

Combating culture clash
Just as an organization cannot effectively run with multiple incompatible information systems, it cannot succeed with multiple incompatible cultures. But successful combinations do not require the partners to be "cultural clones". In fact, a moderate degree of distinction between the partners' cultures results in the most successful integrations – the parties have sufficient similarities to take advantage of the differences, but they are not so disparate as to be like "oil and water".

A key question, then, is what drives a culture clash toward conflict versus synergy? Social identity theory suggests that people show a positive bias towards members of their own group and tend to hold a negative view about the members of an "out-group" in order to enhance the relative standing of their own kind (Tajfel, 1981; Turner, 1982). The in-group bias and "us-versus-them" comparisons are likely to be greatest when there is a perceived external threat, such as that posed by a combination.

A contrasting point of view is that cultural differences can be a source of value creation and learning. This perspective is largely based on the assumption that differences rather than similarities between combining organizations create opportunities for synergies and learning (Vermeulen and Barkema, 2001). Cultural differences, it is argued, can break rigidities in acquiring firms, help them to develop richer knowledge, and foster innovation and learning.

Research question 2f: When and in what circumstances do cultural differences contribute to, versus detract from, combination success?

A survey of CEOs who had attempted combinations found that "the major factor in failure was the underestimation of the difficulties of merging two cultures" and another study found that, while 80 percent of senior executives felt underprepared to deal with culture, those that did give early attention to it were more likely to realize synergies (Kelly, 2006). In a field study, Schweiger and Goulet (2005) examined three levels of cultural learning during an acquisition – none, shallow, and deep – and found an interesting relationship between them and the subsequent integration of plants in an acquired firm. In the case of no learning, they found, not surprisingly, no relationship to eventual integration success or failure. By contrast, deep culture learning interventions, involving cross-company dialogue, culture clarification workshops, and the like, had a strong, positive effect on integration success. Measured results included greater cross-cultural understanding, smoother resolution of cultural differences, more communication and cooperation between combining parties, and greater commitment to the combined organization. What fascinates in this study is that shallow learning – for example, show-and-tell presentations, official communiqués, informal Q&A, and such – did little to clarify and eliminate inaccurate cultural stereotypes or to reconcile differences between the partners. On the contrary, these had the undesirable effects of strengthening perceptions of cultural differences and reinforcing stereotypes that contributed to conflict between the organizations.

Research question 2g: Is it better to do nothing about culture clarification than something superficial and perfunctory? What are the best approaches to deepening cross-culture learning? In what conditions and under what circumstances are cultural interventions most effective in enabling a combination to achieve its desired financial and strategic objectives?

Part of a firm's cultural heritage is linked to its roots in the national culture of its home country. A review of academic studies has yielded competing points of view regarding the relationship between national culture differences and M&A performance. One set of studies finds that national cultural differences negatively impact functional integration and organizational effectiveness (Weber and Pliskin, 1996). The conclusion is that national differences can compound corporate cultural differences and thus slow the pace and hamper the physical integration of firms. Other studies, however, find that differences in national cultures between parent and target firms can have a positive effect on product synergies and sales growth (Morosini et al., 1998) as well as on reducing employee resistance (Larsson and Finkelstein, 1999). The rationale here is that differences rather than similarities between combining firms create more opportunities for synergies and learning. It may be that cross-border combinations are successful, despite their complexity, because the integration challenges are more obvious, prompting leaders to pay closer attention throughout the combination process (Stahl et al., 2005).

Research question 2h: Under what conditions are national cultural differences a bane or boon to desired M&A outcomes?

LEARNING TO BETTER MANAGE TRANSITIONS

To make a merger or acquisition work means learning how to translate theoretical synergies into real gains, how to recognize and deal with unintended consequences, and how to adapt to events as they unfold. Some of this learning comes from trial-and-error. But effective learning requires ongoing examination of progress and problems, all within a context that supports reflection and continuous improvement. This is aided by the use of valid data and studied attention.

Study after study confirms that execution is the real culprit in M&A failures (Lodorfos and Boateng, 2006; Schweiger and Goulet, 2000). Successful navigation through a complex organizational transition requires a constant flow of operational and behavioral information about how the business is performing and how people are acting and feeling (Marks and Baitch, 2006). This information helps managers monitor the impact of the combination and the effectiveness of the process. It also directs attention and resources to the issues that matter most in eventual success.

Proposed Research Agenda

Experience and learning matter: A study on the benefits of learning from M&A by Bain and Company shows that firms that do more than one acquisition per year generate higher average returns on them than those that do one a year (Hardy and Rovit, 2004). An A.T. Kearny study of large combinations found that nearly 60 percent reduced shareholder value; however, 74 percent of those that succeeded were run by managers with deep M&A expertise (Paulter, 2003). And, a McKinsey study found that committing internal financial and legal staff to M&A duties is not a differentiator of performance. Instead, the *tenure* of the team members did distinguish acquirers whose total returns to shareholders exceeded the returns of their peer group from those that did not (Palter and Srinivasan, 2006).

Learning from current combinations to better manage future ones
We would like to see these studies conducted by consulting firms repli-cated with scholarly rigor and independence. And, given that a flow of upward information is needed to understand when a combination is on track toward meeting its financial and strategic objectives or when it is veering off course – and that some firms now regularly conduct employee research to track the process and progress of their combinations – it is crit-ical to develop valid and reliable measures of M&A which can be applied consistently across combining organizations.

Research question 3a: What are the attitudinal and behavioral measures most directly linked to M&A success and how can they be measured through interviews, focus groups, surveys and other employee research methods?

One key way in which M&A is different today from when serious research on the phenomenon began 30 years ago is the effort taken by some organizations to develop a core competency in this area. We have identified three types of approaches organizations take to enhance their awareness of and readiness for what it takes to make a deal work (Marks and Mirvis, 2010): (1) periodic learning events in which managers accelerate the pace of disseminating lessons learned (Marks and Shaw, 1995); (2) a focus on refining combination methods and processes (Ashkenas et al., 1998); and (3) a "stepping stone" approach by first making small acquisitions and moving up to larger ones (Kumar, 2009).

Research question 3b: How does a firm effectively and efficiently transfer learning from one combination to build a core competency in M&A management to better manage future ones? To what extent are the lessons learned from one type of combination (say of a merger of equals) applicable to another (such as an outright acquisition)?

Overcoming transition burn-out

Finally, there is the matter of "transition burn-out". This is not about M&A per se but, more precisely, about the context within which many – if not most – mergers and acquisitions occur today. In many work organizations, discontinuous transitions have become a way of life: an acquisition, followed by a downsizing, a restructuring, a change in strategy, a subsequent restructuring, and then a second downsizing just in time for the organization to make another acquisition or itself be acquired. The effects of stressful events are cumulative and the costs of "ongoing change" mount (Kiefer, 2005). O'Toole (1995) notes that continual discontinuous change is not a natural condition of life, and that resistance is a to-be-expected response.

People become increasingly pessimistic when they experience one disruptive event after another and literally see no end in sight for all the instability (Kiefer, 2005). Pederit (2000) reports that, especially when numbed by constant and ongoing change and transition, employees may be more ambivalent to change rather than outright resistant to it.

Research question 3c: Is "continuous discontinuous change" sustainable for work organizations and their members? Can this continue at an even more accelerated pace?

CONCLUSION

As a final note, the methodology of conducting research in the area of M&A also deserves attention. First, more consistency is needed in how

M&A outcomes are measured. Current research spans a wide range of financial, operational, attitudinal, and behavioral measures. For example, some studies of financial outcomes examine fluctuations in share prices, others changes in cost savings or revenue generation, and still others the extent to which pre-deal financial targets were met. Second, more consistency is needed in the timing of measurements. When does the merger or acquisition "begin" – at its announcement or upon receiving regulatory and shareholder approval? And, when does it "end"? Typical academic studies use arbitrary time frames (for example, six months or one year) or rely on serendipitous measurement opportunities (for example, happening to have collected data before a deal or doing secondary analysis of data collected without M&A research in mind).

The methodological issues in generating reliable and useful M&A insights are substantial, but so, too, are the potential rewards for doing so. As industries consolidate and organizations increasingly become more global, more and more companies and their people will combine. The M&A success rate has not changed in the 30 years since serious research began. Perhaps the research agenda proposed here can make a difference.

NOTE

1. While the terms "merger" and "acquisition" tend to be used interchangeably by both practitioners and scholars, here merger is intended to mean the integration of two relatively equal entities into a new organization and acquisition is intended to mean the takeover of a target organization by a lead entity. The word "combination" is used here in reference to either a merger or an acquisition.

REFERENCES

Agrawal, A. and Jaffe, J. (2000). 'The post-merger performance puzzle'. In C. Cooper and A. Gregory (eds), *Advances in Mergers and Acquisitions Volume 1*, New York: Elsevier Science.

Anslinger, P.L. and Copeland, T.E. (1996). 'Growth through acquisitions: A fresh look'. *Harvard Business Review*, **74** (1), 126–135.

Ashkenas, R. and Francis, S.C. (2000). 'Integration managers: Special leaders for special times'. *Harvard Business Review*, **78** (6), 108–116.

Ashkenas, R.N., De Monaco, L.J. and Francis, S.C. (1998). 'Making the deal real: How GE Capital integrates acquisitions'. *Harvard Business Review*, **76** (1), 165–178.

Boucher, W.I. (1980). *The Process of Conglomerate Merger*. Washington, DC: Bureau of Competition, Federal Trade Commission.

Bradley, L. (2003). 'Mergers and acquisitions as collaborative challenges'. *Advances in Interdisciplinary Studies of Work Teams*, 9: 233–246.

Bridges, W. (1991). *Managing Transitions*. Reading, MA: Addison-Wesley.

Carlton, J.R. and Lineberry, C.S. (2004). *Achieving Post-Merger Success: A Stakeholder's Guide to Cultural Due Diligence, Assessment, and Integration.* San Francisco, CA: John Wiley and Sons.

Cartwright, S. and McCarthy, S. (2005). 'Developing a framework for cultural due diligence in mergers and acquisitions: Issues and ideas'. In G.K. Stahl and M.E. Mendenhall (eds), *Mergers and Acquisitions.* Stanford, CA: Stanford University Press, pp. 253–267.

Chatman, J.A. and Cha, S.E. (2003). 'Leading by leveraging culture'. *California Management Review,* **45** (4), 20–34.

DeMeuse, K. and Marks, M.L. (2003). *Resizing the Organization – Managing Layoffs, Divestitures, and Closings: Maximizing Gain While Minimizing Pain,* San Francisco, CA: Jossey-Bass Publishers.

Duhaime, I.M. and Schwenk, C.R. (1985). 'Conjectures on cognitive simplification in acquisition and divestment decision-making'. *Academy of Management Review,* 10: 287–295.

Gebhardt, J. (2003). 'What "due diligence" really means'. In A.F. Buono (ed.) *Enhancing Inter-firm Networks and Interorganizational Strategies.* Greenwich, CT: Information Age Publishing.

Harding, D. and Rouse, T. (2007). 'Human due diligence'. *Harvard Business Review,* **85,** 4, 124–131.

Hardy, D. and Rovit, S. (2004). *Mastering the Merger.* Boston, MA: Harvard Business School Press.

Haspeslagh, P. and Jamison, D.B. (1991). *Managing Acquisitions: Creating Value Through Corporate Renewal.* New York: Free Press.

Jian, G. (2007). 'Unpacking unintended consequences in planned organizational change: A process model'. *Management Communication Quarterly,* **21** (1), 5–28.

Kelly, J. (2006). *The Morning After.* London: KPMG.

Kiefer, T. (2005). 'Feeling bad: antecedents and consequences of negative emotions in ongoing change'. *Journal of Organizational Behavior,* 26: 875–897.

Kumar, N. (2009). *India's Global Powerhouses: How They Are Taking on the World.* Cambridge, MA: Harvard Business School Press.

Larsson, R. and Finkelstein, S. (1999). 'Integrating strategic, organizational, and human resource perspectives on mergers and acquisitions: A case survey of synergy realization'. *Organization Science,* **10** (1), 1–26.

Levinson, H. (1976). *Psychological Man.* Cambridge, MA: The Levinson Institute.

Lodorfos, G. and Boateng, A. (2006). 'The role of culture in the merger and acquisition process'. *Management Decision,* **44** (10), 1405–1421.

Marks, M.L. (2003). *Charging Back Up the Hill: Workplace Recovery after Mergers, Acquisitions, and Downsizings.* San Francisco, CA: Jossey-Bass Publishers.

Marks, M.L. and Baitch, D. (2006). 'Measuring employee opinions during mergers and acquisitions'. In A.I. Kraut (ed.) *Getting Action from Organizational Surveys: New Concepts, Methods, and Applications.* San Francisco, CA: Jossey-Bass Publishers.

Marks, M.L. and Mirvis, P.H. (1985). 'Merger syndrome: Stress and uncertainty', *Mergers and Acquisitions,* 20: 50–55.

Marks, M.L. and Mirvis, P.H. (2000). 'Creating an effective transition structure to manage mergers, acquisitions and alliances'. *Organizational Dynamics,* **28** (3), 35–47.

Marks, M.L. and Mirvis, P.H. (2001). 'Making mergers and acquisitions work: Strategic and psychological preparation'. *Academy of Management Executive,* **15** (2), 35–47.

Marks, M.L. and Mirvis, P.H. (2010). *Joining Forces: Making One Plus One Equal Three in Mergers, Acquisitions, and Alliances* (2nd edition), San Francisco, CA: Jossey-Bass Publishers.

Marks, M.L. and Mirvis, P.H. (2011). 'A framework for the Human Resources role in managing culture in mergers and acquisitions'. *Human Resource Management,* 50: 5.

Marks, M.L. and Shaw, R.B. (1995). 'Sustaining change: Creating the resilient organization'. In D.A. Nadler, R.B. Shaw, A.E. Walton, and Associates (eds), *Discontinuous Change,* San Francisco, CA: Jossey-Bass Publishers.

Mirvis, P.H. (1985). 'Negotiations after the sale: The roots and ramifications of conflict in an acquisition'. *Journal of Occupational Behavior*, 6: 65–84.

Mirvis, P.H. and Marks, M.L. (1992). 'The human side of merger planning: Assessing and analyzing "fit"'. *Human Resource Planning*, **15** (3), 64–92.

Mische, M.A. (2001). *Strategic Renewal*, Upper Saddle River, NJ: Prentice Hall.

Morosini, P., Shane, S. and Singh, H. (1998). 'National cultural distance and cross-border acquisition performance'. *Journal of International Business Studies*, **29** (1), 137–158.

O'Toole, J. (1995). *Leading Change*, San Francisco, CA: Jossey-Bass Publishers.

Palter, R.N. and Srinivasan, D. (2006). 'Habits of the busiest acquirers'. *McKinsey Quarterly*, 4: 18–27.

Paulter, P.A. (2003). *The Effects of Mergers and Post-Merger Integration: A Review of Business Consulting Literature*, Washington, DC: Federal Trade Commission.

Pederit, S.K. (2000). 'Rethinking resistance and recognizing ambivalence: A multidimensional view of attitudes toward an organizational change'. *Academy of Management Review*, 25: 783–795.

Schoenberg, R. (2006). 'Measuring the performance of corporate acquisitions: An empirical comparison of alternative metrics'. *British Journal of Management*, **17** (4), 361–370.

Schweiger, D.M. and DeNisi, A.S. (1991). 'Communication with employees following a merger: A longitudinal field experiment'. *Academy of Management Journal*, 34: 110–135.

Schweiger, D.M. and Goulet, P.K. (2000). 'Integrating mergers and acquisitions: An international research review'. In C. Cooper and A. Gregory (eds), *Advances in Mergers and Acquisitions, Volume 1*, New York: Elsevier Science.

Schweiger, D.M. and Goulet, P.K. (2005). 'Facilitating acquisition integration through deep-level cultural learning interventions'. *Organizational Studies*, **26** (10), 1477–1499.

Seo, M. and Hill, N.S. (2005). 'Understanding the human side of merger and acquisition: An integrative framework'. *Journal of Applied Behavioral Science*, **41** (4): 422–443.

Sirower, M.L. (1997). *The Synergy Trap*, New York: Free Press.

Stahl, G.K., Pucil, V., Evans, P. and Mendhall, M.E. (2005). 'Human resources management in cross-border mergers and acquisitions'. In G.K. Stahl and M.E. Mendenhall (eds), *Mergers and Acquisitions*, Stanford, CA: Stanford University Press.

Tajfel, H. (1981). *Human Groups and Social Categories*, Cambridge: Cambridge University Press.

Turner, J.C. (1982). 'Toward a cognitive redefinition of the social group'. In H. Taifel (ed.) *Social Identity and Intergroup Relations*, Cambridge: Cambridge University Press.

Vermeulen, F. and Barkema, H. (2001). 'Learning through acquisitions'. *Academy of Management Journal*, 44: 457–476.

Weber, Y. and Pliskin, N. (1996). 'The effects of information systems integration and organizational culture on a firm's effectiveness'. *Information and Management*, 30: 81–90.

Wiley, J.E. and Moechnig, S.A. (2005). 'The effects of mergers and acquisitions on organizational climate'. Paper presented at the annual meeting of the Society of Industrial/Organizational Psychology, Los Angeles.

4 Placing process factors along with contextual factors in merger and acquisition research

Taco H. Reus, Kimberly M. Ellis,
Bruce T. Lamont and Annette L. Ranft

Mergers and acquisitions (M&A), which commonly necessitate major organizational changes in at least one firm, show a clear case in point of the intricate, intertwined nature of contextual factors surrounding business combinations and process factors characterizing the way in which such combinations are implemented. M&A involve consequential strategic decision-making in which many contextual factors play a role. Strategic planners focus their initial attention on preexisting characteristics of the two firms and attributes of the acquisition itself in order to determine which deals provide the best opportunities to achieve improved performance, enhance strategic positioning, and attain other value-creating benefits. These contextual factors in turn influence the process through which the operations of previously separate firms are subsequently integrated so that strategic benefits are actually realized. From a practical perspective, this link between contextual and process factors necessitates a tight cooperation between strategy planners and integration teams. Ed Liddy, Chairman and Chief Executive Officer of Allstate, stressed this cooperation when he explained that at "Allstate, we have an integration team that works hand-in-hand with our strategic-planning area. They'll press the planners: 'What's the logic of this acquisition? . . . [W]hat processes do we have that we can transfer to the acquired company to bring it up to a level of performance that we're comfortable with? What can we borrow from them that would help us?'" (Carey, 2001: 15).

The complex nature of M&A is reflected in the large body of research conducted in the fields of strategic management, organization theory, organizational behavior, human resource management, and finance (Haleblian et al., 2009; Meglio and Risberg, 2010). Drawing on myriad theoretical perspectives, existing M&A research has identified an array of contextual factors and process factors that influence post-deal outcomes. Contextual factors such as relatedness, relative size, organizational fit, and cultural distance, represent characteristics of the M&A

at the time of announcement often denoting the similarity of or inter-dependency between the two firms involved in the deal. Process factors, such as mutual understanding, structural integration, and building of trust, characterize actions taken during M&A implementation that are designed to minimize disruptions and position the combined firm to realize deal benefits (see Table 4.1). While traditional discipline-based streams of research have examined many contextual and process factors as potential drivers of post-deal outcomes, specific effects are often mixed. For example, some studies reveal a positive relationship between relatedness and M&A performance, while others report negative or insignificant effects. One reason for this lack of consistent support may be the multiple, sometimes conflicting, effects of contextual factors like relatedness on different process dimensions required during M&A implementation.

As a result of equivocal findings, some M&A researchers are now calling for the development of a more holistic approach to examining post-M&A outcomes, which requires developing a deeper understanding of widely studied factors (Haleblian et al., 2009) and bridging traditional disciplinary boundaries to include multiple contextual and process factors (Cartwright and Schoenberg, 2006; Larsson and Finkelstein, 1999). However, conceptual and empirical examination aimed at enhancing our understanding of the interrelationships between context- and process-related factors remains largely unaddressed. One reason for the limited number of studies investigating both contextual and process factors and how they influence each other is that they call for more complex research designs (Meglio and Risberg, 2010). Some organization theorists have argued that theory building on variance in contextual data must be kept separate from theory building on process data because combining such theories creates confusion rather than clarity (Mohr, 1982). However, separation of contextual factors and process factors is artificial, and the insistence of isolation limits theory building because the phenomena under examination are essentially interwoven (Langley, 1999; Peterson, 1998). Particularly in the field of strategic management, where formulation and implementation of strategies are tightly connected, understanding requires cross-fertilization among multiple theoretical perspectives on strategy context and process (Ansoff, 1987; Mintzberg, 1990). So, there is a greater need for examining contextual and process factors together.

Though several seminal M&A studies stressed that the integration process and associated challenges vary by contextual factors (Buono and Bowditch, 1989; Jemison and Sitkin, 1986; Shrivastava, 1986), only recently has research begun to consider various ways in which contextual

Table 4.1 Theoretical perspectives in M&A research

	Perspective	Pre-acquisition Context	Pre-acquisition Process	Acquisition Implementation	Exemplars
CONTEXT	Diversification (Rumelt, 1974)	Relatedness			(Lubatkin, 1983)
	Resource-Based View (Penrose, 1959)	Resource complementary			(Harrison et al., 1991)
	Organizational learning (Huber, 1991)	Prior acquisition experience			(Pennings et al., 1994)
	Organization theory Hubris theory (Roll, 1986)	Organizational fit CEO's exaggerated self-confidence			(Datta, 1991) (Hayward and Hambrick, 1997)
	Theory of the MNC (Hymer, 1976)	Cultural distance, international experience			(Datta and Puia, 1995)
PROCESS	Process perspective (Kitching, 1967)		Ambiguity	Fit focus during integration; speed of integration	(Greenwood et al., 1994)
	Theory of escalation of commitment (Staw, 1981)		Managerial over-commitment to completing the deal		(Haunschild et al., 1994)

Theory		Concept	Citation
Theory of relative standing (Frank, 1986)		Status bestowal of executives; autonomy preservation	(Hambrick and Cannella, 1993)
Acculturation theory (Berry, 1980)		Resistance to change and culture clash among target employees	(Nahavandi and Malekzadeh, 1988)
Knowledge-Based View (Grant, 1996)		Acquiring, combining knowledge and capabilities	(Ranft and Lord, 2002)
Human resource management perspective (Buono and Bowditch, 1989)	Agreement	Rich communications; Trust; Mutual understanding Managerial retention	(Schweiger and DeNisi, 1991) (Walsh, 1988)
Organization theory (Haspeslagh and Jemison, 1991)	Preliminary planning Due diligence	Level of integration; Transition management	(Zollo and Singh, 2004)

and process factors interrelate (Greenwood et al., 1994; Homburg and Bucerius, 2006; Larsson and Finkelstein, 1999; Pablo, 1994; Reus and Lamont, 2009; Schweizer, 2005; Teerikangas and Very, 2006; Zaheer, Castañer, and Souder, forthcoming; Zollo and Singh, 2004). While these studies offer initial insight into the interrelationships between contextual factors and process factors, more research along these lines is warranted to help unravel when and how these factors interact to influence M&A outcomes. For example, rather than studying the simple, direct effect of a contextual factor such as relatedness on performance, there is a need to closely examine how relatedness impacts structural integration, mutual understanding and other process factors.

The overall aim of this chapter is to offer insight into ways in which our understanding of established contextual and process factors can be enhanced in tandem. In the first section of the chapter we provide a review of M&A research related to both contextual and process factors. The review highlights contextual factors that have received conflicting evidence and process research that has paid limited attention to contextual factors. In the second section of the chapter we highlight areas in which the two streams can be integrated to advance the M&A literature. We do this by raising four questions that place process factors and related arguments more solidly along with contextual factors in M&A research. It is important to note that while we focus mainly on relatedness in this section because it is the contextual factor having received the most empirical attention (that is, King et al., 2004), other contextual factors may also influence acquisition implementation decisions. Finally, in the last section we discuss further extensions and develop a research agenda for this relatively uncharted terrain within the M&A field. In doing so, we hope to encourage more research that incorporates both contextual and process factors to help enhance our understanding of the complexities associated with this common business phenomenon thereby advancing M&A theory.

MERGERS AND ACQUISITIONS RESEARCH

Since the first merger wave in the beginning of the twentieth century, researchers, particularly in the field of finance, have examined whether mergers and acquisitions (M&A) provide firms with performance benefits. The ominous conclusion drawn repeatedly is that on average M&A do not provide acquiring firms with any significant benefits for value creation. In fact, collective evidence from studies finds that shareholder value of acquiring firms tends to deteriorate after merger announcements (for example, Agrawal and Jaffe, 2000). In his seminal abridgment of this body of research, Lubatkin (1983) offered two suggestions for the counter-intuitive finding which have implications for management. M&A may not provide synergistic benefits because managers make mistakes or seek to maximize their own wealth at the expense of stockholders' wealth. Or, M&A may provide synergistic benefits that have not been detected in prior research. With the latter suggestion, Lubatkin (1983) conveyed a challenge for strategy researchers to identify factors that lead to the realization of synergistic benefits. In the decades that followed, management research on M&A has considered on a variety of contextual and process factors.

This review addresses the conceptual and empirical work related to contextual and process factors explaining acquisition performance. We follow Larsson and Finkelstein's conceptualization of acquisition performance in terms of synergy realization, defined as the "actual net benefits (reduced cost per unit, increased income, etc.) created by the interaction of two firms involved in a merger or acquisition" (Larsson and Finkelstein, 1999: 3).

Relatedness as a Key Contextual Factor

Since the early 1980s, M&A research in the field of strategy has emphasized the role of relatedness between combining firms. Building on Rumelt's (1974) diversification research, the relatedness hypothesis, sometimes referred to as strategic fit, argues that M&A involving firms operating in similar industries will outperform M&A where firms do not share this unifying feature. The underlying rationale for this hypothesis, based on the concept of synergy, posits that combining both firms' operations provides an opportunity to lower costs or make better use of scarce resources (Lubatkin, 1983). These opportunities for cost- and revenue-based synergies, which are not available to either firm as a standalone entity, stem from scale and scope economies as well as enhanced market power (Seth, 1990b). Also, from a learning perspective, managers are better able to understand activities of an acquired firm when they are familiar with its industry (Pennings et al., 1994). Greater relatedness facilitates acquiring firm managers' ability to discover hidden problems, understand the actions that should be taken to solve such problems, uncover potential sources of synergy, and transfer core skills (Salter and Weinhold, 1979).

In contrast, some studies have hypothesized factors that favor unrelated acquisitions. Unrelated acquisitions can yield economies of scope that are not specific to products or markets of the combining firms, such as administrative efficiencies or general managerial capability. Moreover, unrelated acquisitions often improve income stability by spreading financial risk across industries with different market conditions. This should reduce the probability of bankruptcy for the combined firm (Higgins and Shall, 1975). Nonetheless, since to some degree related acquisitions can provide such financial-based synergies as well, the common view is that related acquisitions should outperform unrelated acquisitions in the long term (Seth, 1990a; Singh and Montgomery, 1987).

Collectively, the abundant number of studies testing the relatedness hypothesis shows little clear support (Datta et al., 1992; King et al., 2004; Lubatkin, 1987). While some studies discovered that related acquisitions outperformed unrelated acquisitions (for example, Singh and Montgomery, 1987), many other studies did not find a significant positive effect of fit (for example, Lubatkin, 1987). Several reasons for the lack of support have been suggested in the literature. In particular, other contextual factors may need to be incorporated in research models tested (King et al., 2004; Lubatkin, 1987), or process dimensions may be key to post-acquisition performance (Larsson and Finkelstein, 1999). In the following sections, we will review how M&A research has dealt with these possible reasons for the lack of support of the relatedness hypothesis.

Other Contextual Factors

Resource complementarity
One reason for the lack of support of the relatedness hypothesis may be that emphasis on product-market similarities among acquisition partners is not a sufficient condition for above-average synergy realization. Barney (1988) argued that above-average post-acquisition performance also requires that synergistic cash and other resource flows resulting from the combination are unique and difficult to imitate by competitors. In a similar vein, Harrison et al., (1991) argue that *complementarity*, rather than similarity, of combining firms provides greater value through synergy and find that performance of acquisitions is higher when acquiring and acquired firms are in related industries but differ in R&D, capital, administrative and debt intensity. Making a similar argument, Larsson and Finkelstein (1999) highlight the important role of "economies of fitness" derived from leveraging complementary assets and resources, and Uhlenbruck et al., (2006) argue that acquisitions of online firms are successful because they provide complementary, synergistic resource exchange. More recently, Zaheer et al. (forthcoming) distinguish between the two forms of relatedness – similarity and complementarity and their independent as well as joint effects on two aspects of M&A implementation – structural integration and target autonomy. However, acquisition research still lacks closer examination of effects of resource complementarity on acquisition performance (Harrison et al., 2001). In particular the performance impli-

cations for effectively integrating these complementary resources have not been examined.

The lack of support for the relatedness hypothesis also led to the suggestion that other contextual factors may matter more (Lubatkin, 1987), thus facilitating an extensive broadening of the constructs examined in M&A research. A thorough review of all contextual factors investigated over the last two decades is beyond the scope of this chapter. Instead, we discuss the most prevalent contextual factors examined in existing M&A studies – relative size, prior acquisition experience, organizational fit, and cultural distance.

Relative size

Some authors contend that *relative size* (that is, the size of the acquired firm compared to the size of the acquiring firm) influences acquisition success. Early on, Kitching (1967) explained that a number of executives he interviewed ascribed acquisition failures to size mismatches. Executives argued that the acquired firm "was so small no one in corporate headquarters could get interested in it" and that "we couldn't get these little entrepreneurs to think like big businessmen" (Kitching, 1967: 92). This evidence, combined with Bergh's (1997) assertion that executives are often more dedicated to keeping large acquisitions from failure, suggest that larger acquisitions show better acquisition performance. On the other hand, some researchers argue that firms are better able to enter new markets by making small incremental steps (Lubatkin, 1983) as opposed to engaging in large-scale acquisitions which necessitate a far more complex integration of the two companies and require more managerial capacity (Schweiger et al., 1993). Empirical findings on the relative size-performance relationship are mixed. While some studies find a significant positive relationship between relative size and performance (for example, Hunt, 1990), several studies do not find a significant relationship (Bergh, 1997; Fowler and Schmidt, 1989; Very et al., 1997). In an effort to explain these contradictory findings, Bruton et al. (1994) argued that both very small and very large acquisitions create problems for acquiring firms and thus may harm shareholder value. However, Bruton et al. (1994) did not find support for such a curvilinear relationship.

Prior acquisition experience

Building on learning theories, researchers contend that experienced acquirers better know which targets to select and better understand complexities of the integration process (Lubatkin, 1983). In support of this argument, several studies find a positive relationship between *prior acquisition experience* and performance of subsequent acquisitions (Fowler and Schmidt,

1989). Most research, however, finds that prior experience effects only hold for certain types of acquisitions, such as acquisitions of related firms (Hayward, 2002), of distressed firms (Bruton et al., 1994), or foreign firms (Markides and Ittner, 1994). Providing further evidence that the prior acquisition experience–performance link may not be generalizable to M&A as a whole, a recent meta-analysis by King and his colleagues (2004) did not find support for any effect of prior acquisition experience on post M&A performance.

Organizational fit

Organizational theorists contributed to the acquisition literature by arguing that an exclusive focus on strategic issues will not explain the success of acquisitions (Greenwood et al., 1994). Rather, executives and scholars should examine organizational features when determining the potential success of an acquisition. The main contention is that greater levels of organizational fit, which refers to the "match between administrative practices, cultural practices, and personnel characteristics of the target and parent firms" (Jemison and Sitkin, 1986: 147) will ease the gradual combination of management styles, reward systems and organizational cultures thereby leading to higher performance of the acquisition. Most conceptual or anecdotal research in this stream identifies culture clash or the inability of combining firms to integrate different organizational cultures, which intensify stress and conflicts among organizational members as one of the major reasons for acquisition failure (Buono and Bowditch, 1989; Jemison and Sitkin, 1986; Nahavandi and Malekzadeh, 1988; Shrivastava, 1986). In contrast, higher levels of cultural similarities and tolerance for different subcultures are posited to ease acquisition implementation (Nahavandi and Malekzadeh, 1988; Pablo, 1994). The collective evidence from studies empirically testing the organizational fit hypothesis offers some support for cultural fit as denoted by shared values and beliefs for both firms' organizational members, and similarity in management styles of both firms' top management teams (Chatterjee et al., 1992; Datta, 1991; Datta et al., 1991; Weber et al., 1996). Conversely, no support has been found for a relationship between similarity of reward and evaluation systems and acquisition performance (Datta, 1991).

Cultural distance

With the increasing level of cross-border M&A activity, researchers have also examined the role of differences in national cultures of the countries in which the acquiring firm and the target are headquartered, often referred to as *cultural distance*. Attributes of national culture contribute to differences between countries in business practices, management styles, and organizational routines. Consequently, researchers have argued that when combining firms come from countries with diverging national cultures there is a higher likelihood of conflict, uncertainty, and culture clash during acquisition implementation (Cartwright and Cooper, 1992; Geringer et al., 1989). Following this conventional reasoning, Datta and Puia (1995) argued and found empirical evidence for a *negative* relationship between cultural distance and performance, but Markides and Ittner (1994) did not find support for such a relationship. Morosini et al. (1998), on the other hand, proposed a *positive* relationship between cultural distance and performance. These authors argued that by making acquisitions in culturally distant countries, firms are able to tap into diverse routines and repertoires embedded in national culture previously not available to them thereby facilitating their ability to enhance performance. Morosini et al. (1998) found empirical support for this revisionist perspective on the role of cultural distance on performance of international acquisitions. More recently, Reus and Lamont (2009) provided evidence that because cultural distance can impede and enrich M&A implementation efforts, its effect on performance is not as a simple as testing for a direct positive or negative relationship.

Collectively, contextual factors mostly have received mixed or weak support. Based on a recent meta-analysis of the most frequently researched contextual factors, such as relatedness and acquisition experience, King and his colleagues (2004) concluded that unidentified variables may explain significant variance in post-acquisition performance and that there is a clear need for further model development. This echoes earlier recommendations by Lubatkin (1987) and Datta et al. (1992). While we agree that further model development is needed, we, however, believe that instead of looking for new factors, similar to suggestions by Haleblian et al. (2009), an important route for M&A research is to consider in more depth the possible contingency conditions that may be responsible for the contradictory effects of the more widely studied contextual factors. Because contextual factors dictate implementation needs, such a fine-grained exploration of their effects on post-deal performance and other outcomes requires the concurrent consideration of process factors.

Process Factors that Characterize Acquisition Implementation

The emergence of a research stream examining the acquisition implementation process is at least in part a response to the mixed support for the effects of contextual factors (for a review see Risberg, 2003). The M&A process literature builds on the seminal work of Kitching (1967). After finding that related deals underperformed unrelated ones in the small sample of M&A he studied, Kitching argued that "managers of change" are the key source of acquisition success. He concluded that effective management of the acquisition implementation process is the most crucial determinant of synergy realization, not preexisting strategic fit as denoted by the relatedness of the two firms' primary operations. The M&A process research that ensued has further highlighted the importance of examining the implementation of acquisitions rather than just contextual factors that characterize the acquisition (for example, Jemison and Sitkin, 1986).

Proponents of process research regard acquisition implementation as a major organizational transition that involves several stages. A basic distinction has been made between two primary stages – the courtship and marriage stages of the acquisition process (Greenwood et al., 1994; Jemison and Sitkin, 1986). The courtship stage is the period prior to the official acquisition announcement that is characterized by the search for attractive acquisition candidates, negotiation of contract conditions, due diligence reviews, and preliminary assessments of potential synergies, cultural differences, and other critical operational issues (Buono and Bowditch, 1989). Research on the courtship stage remains largely anecdotal and lacks empirical testing because of the high level of secrecy that accompanies this period. The limited findings suggest that while effective management of the courtship stage facilitates signing the deal, it does not have a lasting effect on post-acquisition synergy realization (Greenwood et al., 1994).

Rather, success requires effective management of organizational changes that occur during the marriage stage of the acquisition. The marriage stage represents the actual implementation phase of the acquisition. This stage requires an integration of accounting and legal systems, the amalgamation of physical resources and assets, and, ultimately, the meshing of managements and cultures (Shrivastava, 1986). Research points to the critical need for leaders of the combined firm to foster partner interaction and manage the actual change as it is experienced by the integrating workforces as M&A partners aim to realize synergistic benefits. Consequently, acquisition implementation involves creating an integrated social community that blurs former firm boundaries. Of all the process factors that have been considered in M&A research, we can conceive of three underlying process qualities: developing mutual understanding, achieving structural integration, and fostering trust among workforces.

Developing mutual understanding
The development of an integrated social community first requires developing mutual understanding among workforces. Organizational members of

both firms need to be able to understand each other, and even more the expectations of change managers and top management. This component requires the development of a shared language because it facilitates the identification and interpretation of information (Galunic and Rodan, 1998; Nahapiet and Ghoshal, 1998). Network ties in the social community are of little use if members lack a "requisite manufacturability assessment expertise" (Adler and Kwon, 2002). Organizations, more so than market mechanisms, become vehicles for transferring resources and capabilities because organizational members develop shared language and mental models (Kogut and Zander, 1992). One way in which change managers can help develop such mutual understanding in the acquisition implementation process is through "realistic merger previews" (Schweiger and DeNisi, 1991). Schweiger and DeNisi (1991) highlight how these previews reduce uncertainty and ambiguity among workforces and streamline mutual understanding of M&A expectations (Schweiger and Weber, 1989).

Achieving structural integration
Integration is a delicate process where acquirers must exploit the acquired resources but at the same time avoid disruption of the acquired firm's capacity to explore and exploit resources (Puranam et al., 2006). In M&A, the integration of resources and capabilities can only occur when key organizational members do not disappear during acquisition implementation (Cannella and Hambrick, 1993; Coff, 1997). Moreover, the newly combined firm needs to develop ties across fading firm boundaries to create the opportunity for resource sharing. For example, transfer of organizational members from and to the acquired firm and frequent meetings of teams from the acquiring firm at the acquired firm's office provide rich communication links that make resource flows possible (Bresman et al., 1999; Gupta and Govindarajan, 2000; Inkpen and Dinur, 1998).

Kitching (1967) found that most successful acquisitions he examined appointed a top executive immediately after the acquisition to "ride the herd". Moreover, studies point to the importance of establishing a transition management structure (task forces, teams, and so on) comprised of individuals from both firms and various levels of the organization, responsible for identifying best practices, coordinating the integration of functional areas, and resolving differences (Haspeslagh and Jemison, 1991; Mirvis and Marks, 1994). In addition, managerial integration, personnel transfer, and new appointments on the board are considered critical to establishing "cross fertilization", meshing organizational cultures, and ensuring that acquired resources and capabilities are combined efficiently (Shrivastava, 1986).

Fostering trust

The mere presence of ties is not sufficient for the integration of resources and capabilities to realize synergies. Acquisitions often trigger an emotionally charged period for organizational members, particularly from the acquired firm (Vince, 2006). Buono and Bowditch (1989) refer to the period of "merger drift" in which much of management's time is consumed by the organizational change itself and organizational members' preoccupation with rumors about possible job changes and layoffs. As a result, daily work demands are disregarded and the trust to share resources and capabilities is minimal. Also, organizational hypocrisy, cultural confusion, and politicization of integration issues (Vaara, 2003) often make it difficult to achieve mutual trust among the newly combined workforces. Only those acquirers that overcome these issues by developing among their organizational members a sense of trust and identity with the newly combined firm will be able to cultivate a social community that encourages synergy realization (Citera and Rentsch, 1999).

Such development of trust also is important to develop commitment to the new company, particularly among acquired executives. Hambrick and Cannella (1993) build on Frank's (1986) theory of relative standing, to explain how acquired executives develop feelings of inferiority, hostility, and discomfort as status is taken away from them. As a result of a sudden plunge in their relative standing, acquired executives have a higher propensity to either exhibit less commitment to the ongoing success of the combined firm or leave the newly combined firm (Hambrick and Cannella, 1993). Similarly corporate scientists who lose most social status following acquisitions tend to be less productive (Paruchuri et al., 2006). Several studies have emphasized the importance of retaining key employees to secure post-acquisition stability and successful acquisition implementation (Jemison and Sitkin, 1986; Kitching, 1967), and empirical research examining retention indicates a negative effect of executive turnover on synergy realization (Bergh, 2001; Cannella and Hambrick, 1993; Krishnan et al., 1997; Very et al., 1997).

INTEGRATION OF CONTEXTUAL FACTORS AND PROCESS FACTORS

From a bird's eye view, the vast literature on M&A shows two rather distinct streams of research. One that emphasizes the role of context and another that emphasizes the process by which the acquisition is implemented. The research findings and recommendations to strategic managers are different from both streams. While research on contextual factors con-

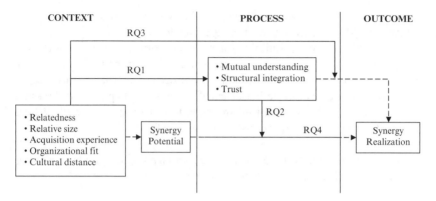

Note: ^a Dotted arrows indicate the current focus of M&A research, solid arrows show novel research questions.

Figure 4.1   A guiding framework to consolidate context and process research on M&A

siders the critical role of effective strategy formulation prior to the acquisition, the process research contends that careful attention to implementation is crucial. Needless to say, both research streams are necessary and provide important contributions to our thinking about M&A. However, the current isolation in which these two streams progress seriously hinders theory building, and may be the main cause for lack of support for critical contextual factors. For example, process research has not explained the effects of relatedness on the process of acquisition implementation.

We propose that integrating findings from the two streams of research provides a rich source for theory building and a conceptual basis for future empirical research. In this section we explore possible synergies between the two streams by explicitly addressing four critical questions. First, we ask how process qualities mediate the effects of contextual factors on realizing synergistic benefits. This question aims to stimulate researchers to unpack the black box that currently exists in context studies. Second, we ask how process qualities moderate the effects of contextual factors on synergy realization. By addressing this question researchers can better examine the role of change managers during acquisition integration. Third, we ask how contextual factors moderate the effects of process on synergy realization. And fourth, we ask at what stage in the acquisition implementation process contextual factors matter. Answers to this question will provide us with a better understanding of the role of contextual factors in the acquisition integration process. Figure 4.1 provides a guiding framework for posing these research questions.

Since the relatedness hypothesis has been widely studied with mixed support in M&A research, we take a closer look at what these questions mean for this argument. Building on evidence from research on contextual and process factors, we develop propositions specifically to clarify the relatedness construct. However, other contextual factors mentioned in the review section could be better clarified by more explicitly addressing their impact on the acquisition implementation process as well. Where plausible, we therefore also consider these constructs.

Research Question 1: How do process qualities mediate the effects of contextual factors on realizing synergistic benefits?

Many of the arguments made in research on contextual factors implicitly assume that contextual factors influence the process in which acquisitions are being implemented. For example, smaller relative size of the acquired firm is believed to reduce the attention acquiring managers pay to the implementation of that acquisition (Kitching, 1967). However, actual procedural effects of contextual factors are rarely examined. Instead, process qualities are treated as a black box, and contextual factors are posited to directly impact synergy realization.

While this facilitates empirical examination, it limits our ability to develop comprehensive theories about the performance of mergers and acquisitions, particularly because it forces a *friend or foe* approach to contextual factors. Researchers either argue for a positive or a negative effect of a particular contextual factor on synergy realization. Accordingly, conflicting arguments exist accompanied by inconsistent findings. Most noticeable is the contradictory arguments made about the role of cultural distance on acquisition performance. As mentioned earlier, Datta and Puia (1995) argued and found a negative effect of cultural distance because it complicates acquisition integration, while Morosini et al. (1998) argued and found support for a positive effect of cultural distance because the combination of culturally distinct capabilities leads to a more unique and difficult to imitate resource bundle. Moreover, the lack of attention to how the process is affected by contextual factors may be the root of the inability to find clear support for the relatedness hypothesis. In order to gain a better understanding about the complexities of acquisition performance, we need to unpack the black box – we need to investigate how contextual factors influence process qualities, and *indirectly* affect performance.

Figure 4.2 depicts the influence of relatedness on acquisition performance. As mentioned earlier, the relatedness hypothesis argues that related acquisitions outperform unrelated ones because the former are predicted to have more synergy potential (Lubatkin, 1983). Commonly, studies

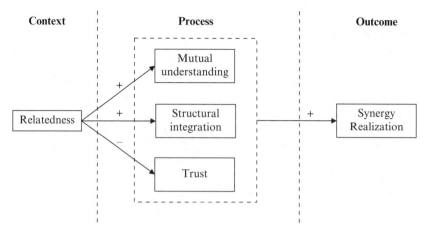

Figure 4.2   Process as mediator of the effect of relatedness on post-acquisition performance

examining the relatedness hypothesis emphasize that the acquirer has greater knowledge about firms operating in related industries, which should facilitate the integration process. The greater the relatedness of industries in which the acquirer and the acquired firm are active, the higher the likelihood that organizational members of both firms share a common language and can leverage their industry expertise. Accordingly, relatedness will increase the development of mutual understanding which enables the newly combined firm to better identify and realize synergistic benefits. Moreover, relatedness enhances the extent to which links can be made across former firm boundaries. Change managers are more likely to identify channels to achieve structural integration because firms' activities are more similar. Therefore the prediction is that relatedness *indirectly* has a positive effect on synergy realization through its *direct* effects on the development of mutual understanding and structural integration.

However, relatedness may also have negative effects on the acquisition integration process. Specifically, acquisitions made in related industries lead to greater redundancies because two firms in similar industries are likely have greater overlap than those from unrelated industries. Such overlap in related acquisitions will result in redundant staff and executives. On the other hand, human capital from firms in unrelated acquisitions will likely be more distinctive and less redundant. Consequently, the greater the relatedness of the two firms, the higher the likelihood of forced layoffs or termination of employees from the acquired firm during acquisition integration. As a result, related acquisitions are more likely to show symptoms of merger drift, which complicates the development of trust and commitment among workforces.

Even key employees from the acquired firm, such as top managers or those with critical expertise who are less affected by the redundancies, may depart the firm because they lose the power, autonomy, or status they held before the acquisition. Hambrick and Cannella (1993) predicted that this reduction of relative standing leads to a general sense of acrimony among acquired firm employees and a lack of commitment to the newly formed firm. Since related acquired firms are commonly more fully integrated into the acquirer, their key employees are likely to lose more decision-making power, which in turn lowers their relative standing. Indeed, Buchholtz et al. (2003) find that relatedness is positively associated with post-acquisition CEO departure. The disappearance of critical human capital reduces the ability for realizing synergies, particularly those rooted in economies of scope, since this requires that organizational members are motivated to share resources and capabilities. Moreover, since CEOs and other key employees are critical for managing the integration process, departure of such employees complicates the realization of other synergies. Accordingly, relatedness, through its effect on reducing trust, actually has a *negative indirect effect* on synergy realization. Thus, when we consider process-related mediators, we see that relatedness positively and negatively affects synergy realization.

Proposition 1a: Relatedness has a positive indirect effect on the realization of synergies through its positive direct effect on mutual understanding and structural integration, which positively affects synergy realization.

Proposition 1b: Relatedness has a negative indirect effect on the realization of synergies through its negative direct effect on trust and commitment to the newly formed firm, which negatively affects synergy realization.

Research Question 2: How do process qualities moderate the effects of contextual factors on realizing synergistic benefits?

M&A are complex strategic events that require the involvement of executives and key employees who can effectively manage a myriad of changes taking place in one or both firms during acquisition implementation. Changes that are necessary to realize synergistic benefits (Kitching, 1967). Unfortunately, there is little known about how change management, or process qualities in general, influence the performance of acquisitions. Such examination could shed light on the conflicting results associated with contextual factors discussed in earlier sections. Rather than arguing

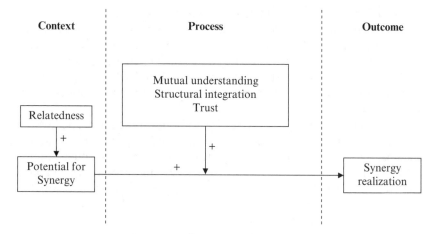

Figure 4.3 *Process as moderator of the effect of relatedness on post-acquisition performance*

that certain types of acquisitions perform better, we contend that acquisitions can create synergistic value in the combined firm, depending on key procedural qualities. By understanding which process qualities are critical for a specific context, we can develop more comprehensive theories about post-acquisition performance.

As shown in Figure 4.3, process qualities function as moderators of the effect of relatedness on acquisition performance. The relatedness hypothesis assumes that greater fit leads to greater *potential* for synergy realization. However, in order to become a source for above-average acquisition performance, potential synergies need to be transformed into *actual* realized synergy. Synergies can be exploited only if the acquiring firm can effectively combine the acquired firm's tangible and intangible assets that form the source of synergy potential into its existing bundle of resources and capabilities. Thus, while relatedness has a direct effect on the potential for synergies, its effect on synergy realization depends on a complex integration of the acquired firm's resources and capabilities into the operations of the acquiring firm. Kogut and Zander (1992) argue that this requires combinative capability rooted in the development of a general atmosphere which fosters voluntary knowledge sharing.

Integrating resources and capabilities in any organization is difficult primarily because they are embedded in the human capital of the firm (Grant, 1996). The significant organizational change that follows M&A can be expected to complicate matters. In this context two organizations that recently were sovereign entities have related and complementary resources, but can only exploit this synergistic potential if the two can truly become one organization (Barney, 1988; Capron and Pistre, 2002). Thus, integration of disparate systems, structures, and people needs to take place in order to cultivate the effect of relatedness on synergy realization. As argued earlier, we view mutual understanding, structural integration, trust, and commitment as the critical process factors in our organization framework.

At the outset, firms can only realize synergies rooted in relatedness, if mutual understanding between the acquiring and acquired organizational members exists during acquisition implementation. Mutual understanding of acquisition partners' operations, structures, and procedures enhances the combined firm's ability to transfer strategic knowledge and capabilities (Ellis et al., 2009; Jemison and Sitkin, 1986; Kitching, 1967). If partners do not understand each other they are not likely to be aware of each other's capabilities, let alone find ways to realize synergies among such capabilities. Even the realization of enhanced economies of scale requires that combining firms understand each other's manufacturing expertise (Sherman and Rupert, 2006).

In order to combine resources and capabilities in any organization, there needs to be a network of ties that make flows of resources and capabilities as well as knowledge sharing possible (Nahapiet and Ghoshal, 1998; Tsai and Ghoshal, 1998). In M&A, the potential synergies from related acquisition partners will only be realized if change managers can structurally integrate the newly combined companies. Such structural integration typically requires the use of task forces and teams comprised of individuals from both organizations and representing multiple organizational levels as well as functional areas (Haspeslagh and Jemison, 1991). Such acquisition process practices increase the ties among members of the acquiring and acquired firms that make synergy realization possible. Without structural integration the bundles of resources and capabilities remain separate entities with potential, but unrealized, synergies.

The presence of ties between organizational members of both firms alone is not sufficient for the actual transfer of resources and capabilities required to realize synergy. Organizational members also need to be motivated to share knowledge (Gupta and Govindarajan, 2000; Kogut and Zander, 1992). Specialists that hold the skills and expertise will only share these resources if they *voluntarily* decide to do so based on the trust and commitment that they have for the new organization (Kim and Mauborgne, 1998). Thus, knowledge transfer is a function of the relationships among organizational members (Szulanski, 1996).

While structural integration describes impersonal organizational characteristics, trust and commitment involve the personal relationships organizational members develop with each other (Adler and Kwon, 2002). Several social capital theorists have argued that trust limits negative behaviors such as employees seeking personal advantage with little regard for the firm while facilitating positive behaviors such as cooperation (for example, Kogut and Zander, 1992; Nahapiet and Ghoshal, 1998). As such, trust is a key factor in increasing the motivation of organizational members to share knowledge. Consequently, the resources and capabilities that relate so well to the acquirer's bundle of resources and capabilities can only become a source for synergy if the organizational members trust the new organization and are committed to its objectives.

Relatedness, in and of itself, may create the potential for various cost- and revenue-based synergies. In order to realize these synergies, the acquisition requires effective change management practices that create a general atmosphere which fosters the sharing of strategic resources and capabilities across former boundaries of the combining firms. Thus, realization of synergies depends on the development of mutual understanding, structural integration, and trust and commitment among acquiring and acquired employees.

Proposition 2: Mutual understanding, structural integration, and trust and commitment moderate the effect of relatedness on synergy realization, such that M&A that have or develop these process qualities show a stronger effect of relatedness on synergy realization.

Research Question 3: How do contextual factors moderate the process–synergy realization relationship?

Another approach is to examine how contextual factors influence the role of process qualities on synergy realization. A number of recent studies have specifically focused on particular types of acquisitions and their impact on the acquisition implementation process. For example, Homburg and Bucerius (2006) find that speed of the integration process is related to success only when acquisition partners operate in unrelated markets but have similar management styles. When acquisition partners are in highly related markets but have different management styles, rapid speed of integration is actually detrimental. Similarly, Puranam and colleagues (2006) emphasize that while structural integration facilitates exploitation through combination of resources, it hinders exploration activities of the acquired firm. As a result, structural integration causes disruption of exploratory activities and hurts innovativeness of acquired high-tech firms that have not yet launched products prior to the acquisition. When acquired firms have already launched products, the disruptive

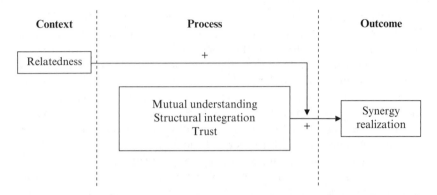

Figure 4.4   Relatedness as moderator of the effect of process factors on post-acquisition performance

effects are less harmful because these firms are more likely to be involved in refining earlier products. Thus, some research has begun to examine how process qualities differ for acquisitions in different contexts. However, our understanding of the role of context in the acquisition implementation process still is limited and provides a fruitful area for theorizing and empirical testing.

Related and unrelated M&A are such different strategic events that they require different acquisition implementation processes (Haspeslagh and Jemison, 1991; Jemison and Sitkin, 1986; Shrivastava, 1986). In the situation where an acquired firm operates in similar product markets as the acquirer, certain process qualities may be more important than when the firms have primary operations in unrelated industries (as depicted in Figure 4.4). Moreover, it is important to understand the different motives underlying related and unrelated acquisitions, and how these motives influence which process qualities are most critical in realizing synergies. For example, motives for engaging in related acquisitions are to achieve economies of scale and scope as well as enhance market power. Such motives necessitate the combination of both firms' previous capabilities and operations into a functioning whole to realize both cost and revenue based synergies. Accordingly, such acquisitions require additional invest-ments in the implementation process and integration of shared resources (Gary, 2005). This entails the establishment of a transition management structure to oversee critical integration efforts in order to realize syner-gistic benefits associated with related acquisitions. Moreover, a shared understanding of primary operations, industry conditions, and other factors facilitates the combined firm's ability to make decisions during the acquisition implementation that will enhance actual synergy realization. Finally, because related acquisitions often result in the elimination of redundancies, it is vital that the combined firm develops trust among and gains the commitment of organizational members who remain. This in turn minimizes negative behaviors which can derail implementation efforts and instead focuses attention on realizing synergies.

In contrast, unrelated acquisitions necessitate a rather different implementation process. Because these types of acquisitions are in unrelated industries, the specialized knowledge in acquired firms tends to be dissimilar from the acquirer's capabilities. As a result, there is less need to integrate the unrelated acquired firm, and in fact, the acquirer typically aims to keep such acquired firm's resources and capabilities intact (Haspeslagh and Jemison, 1991). Even when an unrelated acquired firm has expertise that is beneficial for the acquirer's value chain, a certain degree of autonomy of the acquired firm therefore is important to preserve the resources and capabilities. Thus, mutual understanding is not only unnecessary in unrelated acquisitions, but attempts to achieve it may have negative effects on synergy realization at the combined level. Finally, it is critical that employees of the acquired firm trust managers of the acquiring firm to allow them to continue operating autonomously and remain committed to creating value for the combined firm.

Proposition 3: Relatedness moderates the effect of process factors, such that relatedness elevates the positive effect of structural integration, mutual understanding and trust on synergy realization.

Research Question 4: At what stage in the acquisition implementation process do contextual factors matter?

A final reason why there may be a lack of support for many of the contextual factors is because research has not closely examined *when* contextual factors influence acquisition performance. The role of these factors can become clearer when we critically examine in what stage of the acquisition process they actually matter. Some contingencies may influence the performance of the acquisition during the entire process of acquisition implementation. Prior acquisition experience likely provides the acquirer with the expertise to manage various stages in the process effectively (Barkema and Schijven, 2008). Similarly, prior performance of the acquirer indicates that the acquirer has managerial and financial resources that can be used to achieve acquisition performance throughout acquisition implementation. For other contingencies it is less clear whether they can facilitate the acquisition implementation process in each stage. For example, CEO hubris may have a delayed detrimental effect on

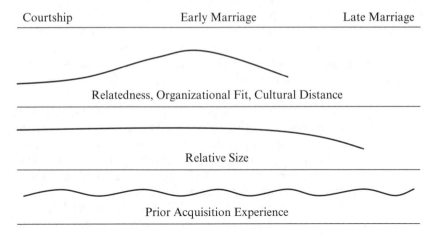

Figure 4.5   When do contextual factors matter?

acquisition performance. Such eager executives likely will enthusiastically manage the acquisition in the early acquisition stages. However, gradually the CEO focuses attention on the next acquisition of interest as immense costs of making the acquisition increasingly become a burden and the realized debt harder to manage. Figure 4.5 depicts the possible intensity of various contextual factors throughout acquisition implementation.

Relatedness may be particularly beneficial in the early stages of acquisition implementation because it facilitates mutual understanding of strategic objectives and operational issues. In addition, related acquisitions typically generate more opportunities to eliminate redundancies, close facilities, and initiate similar activities aimed at achieving economies of scale (Haspeslagh and Jemison, 1991). These actions, usually made shortly after completing the deal, allow the acquiring firm to realize substantial cost savings during early stages of the implementation process. Another reason may be that differences receive much attention in the early stages of acquisition implementation as combined firms seek to resolve problems based on dissimilarities quickly. As such, the effect of relatedness on synergy realization is only temporary.

However, over time these fit advantages disappear because even those M&A that are characterized by adequate fit are likely to encounter complexities of integration (Greenwood et al., 1994). In addition, firms involved in acquisitions that strategically fit tend to focus so much attention on achieving cost savings that they neglect daily operational issues as well as concerns of employees and customers, which have detrimental effects on longer-term synergy realization (Buono and Bowditch, 1989).

Proposition 4: Time influences the impact of relatedness, such that fit has a positive effect on synergy realization early in the M&A implementation process, but not later in the process.

IMPLICATIONS FOR M&A RESEARCH

Mergers and acquisitions have been a core topic of strategic management since its launch as an academic field (Schendel and Hofer, 1979). The numerous theoretical perspectives taken towards understanding the nature of this strategic phenomenon illustrate its complexity. However, researchers from the different streams of research work in relative isolation to proliferate ideas and arguments. Studies examining contextual factors often ignore factors that characterize the integration process, and studies examining process qualities tend to neglect key contextual factors. As a result, despite a body of research that spans over 30 years, we still lack a comprehensive theory of mergers and acquisitions.

We seek to address this gap in the existing literature by presenting research questions that have important implications for theory building on M&A. First, answers to Research Question 1 indicate that contextual factors could show contradictory effects on the acquisition implementation process. Research Question 2 points to the notion that some contextual factors only affect synergy realization provided the presence of certain process qualities. Research Question 3 implies that contextual factors influence the aptness of process characteristics. Finally, Research Question 4 addresses the importance of understanding when, in the acquisition integration process, contextual factors matter. In the remainder of this section, we provide some specific implications of the four research questions for M&A theory building. It is our hope that questions posed and implications provided will stimulate additional research that integrates both contextual factors and process qualities thereby improving our understanding of their interrelationships and enhancing the development of a more unified theoretical view of M&A.

M&A are such complex strategic phenomena that a contextual factor often has both positive and negative effects on various process qualities. For example, as discussed under Research Question 1, relatedness enhances the level of mutual understanding and structural integration between people from both companies which improves synergy realization, but it also increases the likelihood of drops in trust and commitment among key employees, which lead to employee departure (Buchholtz et al., 2003), and has been shown to hinder the realization of synergies (Cannella and Hambrick, 1993). Similarly, increasing relative size of an acquired firm enhances the process because top management of the acquirer feels it has more at stake in the acquisition (Bergh, 1995), but at the same time it increases the level of complexity of structural integration, which complicates synergy realization (Lubatkin, 1983). In the context of international acquisitions, Datta and Puia (1995) argue that cultural distance increases the likelihood of misunderstanding and miscommunication during acquisition implementation, and find support for a negative effect of cultural distance on post-acquisition performance, but Morosini and his colleagues (1998) argue that greater cultural distance enhances the ability to tap into a unique resource pool that is more difficult to imitate by competitors, which increases the potential for critical synergies. Clearly more comprehensive theories are needed to incorporate these disparate effects of contextual factors on elements of the acquisition integration process.

Research Question 2 indicates that the effect of contextual factors depends on the presence of certain process qualities. As such, it points to the effects of mutual understanding, structural integration, and trust and commitment on the combined firms' ability to integrate resources and capabilities. The opportunity exists to extend this notion to a fuller knowledge-based view of acquisition performance by highlighting the role of both firms' absorptive capacity and combinative capability. Absorptive capacity could be identified by contextual factors, such as prior related experience in the form of acquisition experience, and availability of related knowledge (Cohen and Levinthal, 1990; Lane and Lubatkin, 1998; Zahra and George, 2002). In contrast, combinative capability essentially is a process quality, which depends on the extent to which the separate units are combined into a single social community that fosters the transfer of knowledge and capabilities (Kogut and Zander, 1992). Indeed, Zollo and Singh (2004) find that structural integration facilitates the codification process of important knowledge during acquisition implementation. Absorptive capacity is expected to have a negligible effect on acquisition performance if the firms do not develop combinative capabilities. Similarly, combinative capability is of no value if combining firms do not possess absorptive capacity. In order to affect synergy realization, contextual factors thus require the presence of specific process qualities.

Research Question 3 indicates that effective management of the implementation process depends on contextual factors that characterize the acquisition. A relatively underrepresented M&A research topic is the role that motives have on the acquisition process. Trautwein (1990) discussed seven groups of widely dispersed motives underlying the decision to make acquisitions. Each motive is predicted to have distinct impacts on the type of acquisition process (Haspeslagh and Jemison, 1991). For example, when acquisitions are made to achieve market power, an acquirer chooses to buy a competitor and, subsequently, may combine purchasing functions, close down plants, and terminate most acquired personnel. Acquisition managers making acquisitions based on this motive are not so concerned about the trust and commitment of acquired organizational members. In contrast, when acquisitions are made to leverage complimentary product-market domains the implementation of the acquisition will require considerable commitment from all organizational members to combine resources and capabilities effectively. Consequently, it is important that M&A researchers are explicit about the underlying motives of acquisitions they examine. This enhances theory building about what constitutes effective process management.

Future research that builds on Research Question 3 can also facilitate understanding of conflicting evidence for process dimensions. For example, conflicting evidence of the role of executive retention can be explained by integrating seemingly contrasting theoretical arguments, and considering how context affects the role of retention. An important contextual factor may be the performance of the acquired firm before the acquisition. In cases where the acquired firm is performing poorly, the acquisition likely functions as a mechanism of the market for corporate control (Walsh, 1988). The acquiring top management is expected to do a better job managing the acquired company, and is not concerned about retaining acquired top management. In contrast, high performing targets can be seen as large and lucrative bundles of unique resources and capabilities, which can help the acquiring firm to grow and prosper. In the latter case, the acquiring firm greatly needs the acquired top management to facilitate the retention and dissemination of acquired expertise. Interestingly, researchers in the area of executive retention tend to focus on one argument only (for a resource perspective see for example Cannella and Hambrick, 1993; for a market for corporate control perspective see for example Jarrel et al., 1988; Walsh, 1988). Combining research on contextual and process qualities provides a more comprehensive model that incorporates both theoretical arguments.

Finally, Research Question 4 posits that many contextual factors may have performance effects, but only temporarily, during specific stages of acquisition implementation. Unfortunately, there is a dearth of M&A research that considers this timing issue (an important exception is Greenwood et al., 1994). The examination of this timing issue requires going beyond existing process models that tend to assume clear-cut phases of implementation because M&A integration commonly is more complex than that (Van de Ven, 1992). M&A researchers can build tremendously on recommendations provided by process theorists on the examination of sequences of events (Langley, 1999; Peterson, 1998). Research Question 4 also calls for a more explicit approach toward the time at which post-acquisition performance is measured. For example, event history measures of stock market reactions may be particularly suited for measuring short-term performance of the acquisition, whereas perceptual measures of post-acquisition performance two years following the M&A are better for assessing the longer term performance effects on the acquisition itself.

CONCLUSIONS

Mergers and acquisitions are complicated strategic events that require strategy formulation that is tightly connected to strategy implementation. Similarly, research on this phenomenon is complicated because it involves examination of relationships between contextual and process factors. The research questions offered in this chapter lead to more complex models to better understand the nature of these interrelationships and their interactive effects on M&A outcomes. As such, this makes it difficult to abide by the "less is more" rule that calls for simple models (Cohen, 1990). This is a complexity that is part of research on contingency theories in general, where a context of fit and the process of attaining fit inescapably require more complex models (Donaldson, 2001).

A way in which researchers can simplify the examination of M&A is by taking one contextual factor at a time, and studying how each impacts the process of acquisition implementation. For example, the propositions provided in this chapter begin to examine the manner in which relatedness influences the process of acquisition implementation. However, it is important that the field as a whole provides a more comprehensive model that is more closely akin to the reality of value creation through M&A. We hope that this chapter points the field to the many research opportunities that exist to discover how context impacts process, how context depends on process, how process differs per context, and how context effects change during process. Attention to these questions provides needed guidelines to develop a more unified theoretical view of M&A and unlock the keys to M&A value creation.

REFERENCES

Adler P.S. and Kwon S-W. (2002). 'Social capital: Prospects for a new concept', *Academy of Management Review*, 27 (1): 17–40.
Agrawal S. and Jaffe J.F. (2000). 'The post-merger performance puzzle', *Advances in Mergers and Acquisitions*, 1: 119–156.
Ansoff H.I. (1987). 'The emerging paradigm of strategic behavior', *Strategic Management Journal*, 8: 501–515.

Barkema H.G. and Schijven M. (2008). 'How do firms learn to make acquisitions? A review of past research and an agenda for the future', *Journal of Management*, 34: 594–634.

Barney J.B. (1988). 'Returns to bidding firms in mergers and acquisitions: Reconsidering the relatedness hypothesis', *Strategic Management Journal*, 9: 71–78.

Bergh D.D. (1995). 'Size and relatedness of units sold: An agency theory and resource-based perspective', *Strategic Management Journal*, 16: 221–239.

Bergh D.D. (1997). 'Predicting divestiture of unrelated acquisitions: An integrative model of *ex ante* conditions', *Strategic Management Journal*, 18 (9): 715–731.

Bergh D.D. (2001). 'Executive retention and acquisition outcomes: A test of opposing views on the influence of organizational tenure', *Journal of Management*, 27 (5): 603–622.

Berry J.W. (1980). 'Acculturation as varieties of adaptation'. In A. Padilla (ed.), *Acculturation: Theory, Models and Some New Findings*. Boulder, CO: Westview, pp. 9–25.

Bresman H., Birkinshaw J.M. and Nobel R. (1999). 'Knowledge transfer in international acquisitions', *Journal of International Business Studies*, 30 (3): 439–462.

Bruton G.D., Oviatt B.M. and White M.A. (1994). 'Performance of acquisitions of distressed firms', *Academy of Management Journal*, 37 (4): 972–989.

Buchholtz A.K., Ribbens B.A. and Houle I.T. (2003). 'The role of human capital in post-acquisition CEO departure', *Academy of Management Journal*, 46 (4): 506–514.

Buono A.F. and Bowditch J.L. (1989). *The Human Side of Mergers and Acquisitions: Managing Collisions Between People, Cultures, and Organizations*. San Francisco, CA: Jossey-Bass Publishers.

Cannella A.A., Jr. and Hambrick D.C. (1993). 'Effects of executive departures on the performance of acquired firms', *Strategic Management Journal*, 14: 137–152.

Capron L. and Pistre N. (2002). 'When do acquirers earn abnormal returns?', *Strategic Management Journal*, 23: 781–794.

Carey D. (2001). 'Lessons from master acquirers: A CEO roundtable on making mergers succeed', *Harvard Business Review on Mergers and Acquisitions*. Boston, MA: Harvard Business School Publishing, pp. 1–22.

Cartwright S. and Cooper C.L. (1992). *Mergers and Acquisitions: The Human Factor*. Oxford: Butterworth-Heinemann.

Cartwright S. and Schoenberg R. (2006). 'Thirty years of mergers and acquisitions research: Recent advances and future opportunities', *British Journal of Management*, 17: S1–S5.

Chatterjee S., Lubatkin M.H., Schweiger D.M. and Weber Y. (1992). 'Cultural differences and shareholder value in related mergers: Linking equity and human capital', *Strategic Management Journal*, 13: 319–334.

Citera M. and Rentsch J.R. (1999). 'Is there justice in organizational acquisitions? The role of distributive and procedural fairness in corporate acquisitions'. In R. Cropanzano (ed.), *Justice in the Workplace: Approaching Fairness in Human Resource Management*. Hillsdale, NJ: Erlbaum, pp. 211–230.

Coff R.W. (1997). 'Human assets and management dilemmas: Coping with hazards on the road to resource-based theory', *Academy of Management Review*, 22 (2): 374–402.

Cohen J. (1990). 'Things I have learned (so far)', *American Psychologist*, 45 (12): 1304–1312.

Cohen W.M. and Levinthal D.A. (1990). 'Absorptive capacity: A new perspective on learning and innovation', *Administrative Science Quarterly*, 35 (1): 128–153.

Datta D.K. (1991). 'Organizational fit and acquisition performance: Effects of post-acquisition integration', *Strategic Management Journal*, 12: 281–297.

Datta D.K., Grant J.H. and Rapagopolan N. (1991). 'Management incompatibility and postacquisition autonomy: Effects on acquisition performance'. In P. Shrivastava (ed.), *Advances in Strategic Management*, Vol. 7: 157–182.

Datta D.K., Pinches G.E. and Narayanan V.K. (1992). 'Factors influencing wealth creation from mergers and acquisitions: A meta-analysis', *Strategic Management Journal*, 13: 67–84.

Datta D.K. and Puia G. (1995). 'Cross-border acquisitions: An examination of the influence of relatedness and cultural fit on shareholder value creation in U.S. acquiring firms', *Management International Review*, 35 (4): 337–359.

Donaldson L. (2001). *The Contingency Theory of Organizations*. Thousand Oaks, CA: Sage Publications.

Ellis K.M., Reus T.H. and Lamont B.T. (2009) 'The effects of procedural and informational justice in the integration of related acquisitions', *Strategic Management Journal*, 30: 137–191.

Fowler K.L. and Schmidt D.R. (1989). 'Determinants of tender offer post-acquisition financial performance', *Strategic Management Journal*, 10: 339–350.

Frank R.H. (1986). *Choosing the Right Pond: Human Behavior and the Quest for Status*. New York: Oxford University Press.

Galunic D.C. and Rodan S. (1998). 'Resource recombinations in the firm: Knowledge structures and the potential for Schumpeterian innovation', *Strategic Management Journal*, 19: 1193–1201.

Gary M.S. (2005). 'Implementation strategy and performance outcomes in related diversification', *Strategic Management Journal*, 26: 643–664.

Geringer J.M., Beamish P.W. and daCosta R.C. (1989). 'Diversification strategy and internationalization: Implications for MNE performance', *Strategic Management Journal*, 10: 109–119.

Grant R.M. (1996). 'Toward a knowledge-based theory of the firm', *Strategic Management Journal*, 17 (Winter Special Issue): 109–122.

Greenwood R., Hinings C.R. and Brown J. (1994). 'Merging professional service firms', *Organization Science*, 5 (2): 239–257.

Gupta A.K. and Govindarajan V. (2000). 'Knowledge flows within multinational corporations', *Strategic Management Journal*, 21: 473–496.

Haleblian J., Devers C.E., McNamara G., Carpenter M.A. and Davison R.B. (2009). 'Taking stock of what we know about mergers and acquisitions: A review and research agenda', *Journal of Management*, 35: 469–502.

Hambrick D.C. and Cannella A.A., Jr. (1993). 'Relative standing: A framework for understanding departures of acquired executives', *Academy of Management Journal*, 36 (4): 733–762.

Harrison J.S., Hitt M.A., Hoskisson R.E. and Ireland R.D. (1991). 'Synergies and post-acquisition performance: differences versus similarities in resource allocations', *Journal of Management*, 17 (1): 173–190.

Harrison J.S., Hitt M.A., Hoskisson R.E. and Ireland R.D. (2001). 'Resource complementarity in business combinations: extending the logic to organizational alliances', *Journal of Management*, 27 (6): 679–690.

Haspeslagh P. and Jemison D.B. (1991). *Managing Acquisitions: Creating Value Through Corporate Renewal*. New York: Free Press.

Haunschild P.R., Davis-Blake A. and Fichman M. (1994). 'Managerial overcommitment in corporate acquisition processes', *Organization Science*, 5 (4): 528–540.

Hayward M.L.A. (2002). 'When do firms learn from their acquisition experience? Evidence from 1990–1995', *Strategic Management Journal*, 23: 21–39.

Hayward M.L.A. and Hambrick D.C. (1997). 'Explaining the premiums paid for large acquisitions: Evidence of CEO hubris', *Administrative Science Quarterly*, 42: 103–127.

Higgins R.C. and Shall L.D. (1975). 'Corporate bankruptcy and conglomerate merger', *Journal of Finance*, 30: 1003–1014.

Homburg C. and Bucerius M. (2006). 'Is speed of integration really a success factor of mergers and acquisitions? An analysis of the role of internal and external relatedness', *Strategic Management Journal*, 27: 347–367.

Huber G.P. (1991). 'Organizational learning: The contributing processes and the literatures', *Organization Science*, 2 (1): 88–115.

Hunt J.W. (1990). 'Changing patterns of acquisition behaviour in takeovers and the consequences for acquisition processes', *Strategic Management Journal*, 11 (1): 69–77.

Hymer S. (1976). *International Operations of National Firms: A Study of Direct Investment*. Cambridge, MA: The MIT Press.

Inkpen A.C. and Dinur A. (1998). 'Knowledge management processes and international joint ventures', *Organization Science*, 9 (4): 454–468.

Jarrel G.A., Brickley J.A. and Netter J.M. (1988). 'The market for corporate control: The evidence since 1980', *Journal of Economic Perspectives*, 2: 49–68.

Jemison D.B. and Sitkin S.B. (1986). 'Corporate acquisitions: A process perspective', *Academy of Management Review*, 11: 145–163.

Kim W.C. and Mauborgne R. (1998). 'Procedural justice, strategic decision making, and the knowledge economy', *Strategic Management Journal*, 19: 323–338.

King D.R., Dalton D.R., Daily C.M. and Covin J.G. (2004). 'Meta-analyses of post-acquisition performance: Indications of unidentified moderators', *Strategic Management Journal*, 25: 187–200.

Kitching J. (1967). 'Why do mergers miscarry?' *Harvard Business Review*: 84–101.

Kogut B. and Zander U. (1992). 'Knowledge of the firm, combinative capabilities, and the replication of technology', *Organization Science*, 3 (3): 383–397.

Krishnan H.A., Miller A. and Judge W.Q. (1997). 'Diversification and top management team complementarity: Is performance improved by merging similar or dissimilar teams?', *Strategic Management Journal*, 18 (5): 361–374.

Lane P.J. and Lubatkin M. (1998). 'Relative absorptive capacity and interorganizational learning', *Strategic Management Journal*, 19 (5): 461–477.

Langley A. (1999). 'Strategies for theorizing from process data', *Academy of Management Review*, 24 (4): 691–710.

Larsson R. and Finkelstein S. (1999). 'Integrating strategic, organizational, and human resource perspectives on mergers and acquisitions: A case survey of synergy realization', *Organization Science*, 10 (1): 1–26.

Lubatkin M. (1983). 'Mergers and the performance of the acquiring firm', *Academy of Management Review*, 8: 497–512.

Lubatkin M. (1987). 'Merger strategies and stockholder value', *Strategic Management Journal*, 8: 39–53.

Markides C.C. and Ittner C.D. (1994). 'Shareholder benefits from corporate international diversification: Evidence from U.S. international acquisitions', *Journal of International Business Studies*, 25 (2): 343–366.

Meglio O. and Risberg A. (2010). 'Mergers and acquisitions – time for a methodological rejuvenation in the field', *Scandinavian Journal of Management*, 26: 87–95.

Mintzberg H. (1990). 'The design school: Reconsidering the basic premises of strategic management', *Strategic Management Journal*, 11: 171–195.

Mirvis P.H. and Marks M.L. (1994). *Managing the Merger: Making it Work*. Upper Saddle River, NJ: Prentice-Hall.

Mohr L.B. (1982). *Explaining Organizational Behavior*. San Francisco, CA: Jossey-Bass Publishers.

Morosini P., Shane S. and Singh H. (1998). 'National cultural distance and cross-border-acquisition performance', *Journal of International Business Studies*, 29 (1): 137–158.

Nahapiet J. and Ghoshal S. (1998). 'Social capital, intellectual capital, and the organizational advantage', *Academy of Management Review*, 23: 242–266.

Nahavandi A. and Malekzadeh A.R. (1988). 'Acculturation in mergers and acquisitions', *Academy of Management Review*, 13 (1): 79–90.

Pablo A.L. (1994). 'Determinants of acquisition integration level: A decision-making perspective', *Academy of Management Journal*, 37 (4): 803–836.

Paruchuri S., Nerkar A. and Hambrick D.C. (2006). 'Acquisition integration and productivity losses in the technical core: Disruption of inventors in acquired companies', *Organization Science*, 17 (5): 545–562.

Pennings J.M., Barkema H. and Douma S. (1994). 'Organizational learning and diversification', *Academy of Management Journal*, 37 (3): 608–640.

Penrose E. (1959). *Theory of Growth of the Firm*. New York: Wiley.

Peterson M.F. (1998). 'Embedded organizational events: The units of process in organization science', *Organization Science*, 9 (1): 16–33.

Puranam P., Singh H. and Zollo M. (2006). 'Organizing for innovation: Managing the coordination-autonomy dilemma in technology acquisitions', *Academy of Management Journal*, 49 (2): 263–280.

Ranft A.L. and Lord M.D. (2002). 'Acquiring new technologies and capabilities: A grounded model of acquisition implementation', *Organization Science*, 13: 420–441.

Reus T.H. and Lamont B.T. (2009). 'The double-edged sword of cultural distance in international acquisitions', *Journal of International Business Studies*, 40: 1298–1316.

Risberg A. (2003). 'The merger and acquisition process', literature review at *Journal of International Business Studies*, accessed online at http://www.jibs.net.

Roll R. (1986). 'The hubris hypothesis of corporate takeovers', *Journal of Business*, 59: 197–216.

Rumelt R.P. (1974). *Strategy, Structure, and Economic Performance*. Boston, MA: Harvard Business School Press.

Salter M.S. and Weinhold W.A. (1979). *Diversification through Acquisitions: Strategies for Creating Economic Value*. New York: Free Press.

Schendel D.E. and Hofer C.W. (1979). 'Research needs and issues in strategic management'. In D.E. Schendel and C.W. Hofer (eds), *Strategic Management: A New View of Business Policy and Planning*. Boston, MA: Little, Brown and Company, pp. 515–530.

Schweiger D.M. and DeNisi A.S. (1991). 'Communication with employees following a merger: A longitudinal field experiment', *Academy of Management Journal*, 34 (1): 110–135.

Schweiger D.M. and Weber Y. (1989). 'Strategies for managing human resources during mergers and acquisitions', *Human Resource Planning*, 12: 69–87.

Schweiger D.M., Csiszar E.N. and Napier N.K. (1993). 'Implementing international acquisitions', *Human Resource Planning*, 16: 53–70.

Schweizer L. (2005). 'Organizational integration of acquired biotechnology companies into pharmaceutical companies: The need for a hybrid approach', *Academy of Management Journal*, 48 (6): 1051–1074.

Seth A. (1990a). 'Sources of value creation in acquisitions: An empirical investigation', *Strategic Management Journal*, 11 (6): 431–446.

Seth A. (1990b). 'Value creation in acquisitions: A re-examination of performance issues', *Strategic Management Journal*, 11: 99–115.

Sherman H.D. and Rupert T.J. (2006). 'Do bank mergers have hidden or foregone [sic] value? Realized and unrealized operating synergies in one bank merger', *European Journal of Operational Research*, 168 (1): 253–268.

Shrivastava P. (1986). 'Postmerger integration', *Journal of Business Strategy*, 7: 65–76.

Singh H. and Montgomery C. (1987). 'Corporate acquisition strategies and economic performance', *Strategic Management Journal*, 8: 377–386.

Staw B.M. (1981). 'The escalating commitment to a course of action', *Academy of Management Review*, 6: 577–587.

Szulanski G. (1996). 'Exploring internal stickiness: Impediments to the transfer of best practice within the firm', *Strategic Management Journal*, 17: 27–43.

Teerikangas S. and Very P. (2006). 'The culture-performance relationship in M&A: From yes/no to how', *British Journal of Management*, 17: S31–S48.

Trautwein F. (1990). 'Merger motives and merger prescriptions', *Strategic Management Journal*, 11: 283–295.

Tsai W. and Ghoshal S. (1998). 'Social capital and value creation: The role of intrafirm networks', *Academy of Management Journal*, 41 (4): 464–476.

Uhlenbruck K., Hitt M.A. and Semadeni M. (2006). 'Market value effects of acquisitions involving internet firms: A resource-based analysis', *Strategic Management Journal*, 27: 899–913.

Vaara E. (2003). 'Post-acquisitions integration as sensemaking: Glimpses of ambiguity, confusion, hypocrisy, and politicization', *Journal of Management Studies*, 40 (4): 859–894.

Van de Ven A.H. (1992). 'Suggestions for studying strategy process: A research note', *Strategic Management Journal*, 13: 169–188.

Very P., Lubatkin M., Calori R. and Veiga J. (1997). 'Relative standing and the performance of recently acquired European firms', *Strategic Management Journal*, 18 (8): 593–614.

Vince R. (2006). 'Being taken over: Managers' emotions and rationalizations during company takeover', *Journal of Management Studies*, 43 (2): 343–365.

Walsh J.P. (1988). 'Top management turnover following mergers and acquisitions', *Strategic Management Journal*, 9: 173–183.

Weber Y., Shenkar O. and Raveh A. (1996). 'National and corporate cultural fit in mergers/acquisitions: An exploratory study', *Management Science*, 42: 1215–1228.

Zaheer A., Castañer X. and Souder S. (Forthcoming). 'Synergy sources, target autonomy, and integration in acquisitions', *Journal of Management*, published online at http://jom.sagepub.com/content/early/2011/04/29/0149206311403152.full.pdf+html.

Zahra S.A. and George G. (2002). 'Absorptive capacity: A review, reconceptualization, and extension', *Academy of Management Review*, 27 (2): 185–203.

Zollo M. and Singh H. (2004). 'Deliberate learning in corporate acquisitions: post-acquisition strategies and integration capability in U.S. bank mergers', *Strategic Management Journal*, 25 (13): 1233–1257.

5 The dynamics of knowledge transfer in mergers and acquisitions
Paulina Junni, Riikka M. Sarala and Eero Vaara

INTRODUCTION

Mergers and acquisitions (M&A) are a popular means to enter new markets, access new resources and transfer knowledge (Ahuja and Katila, 2001; Haspeslagh and Jemison, 1991; Vermeulen and Barkema, 2001) despite the fact that acquisition outcomes are often disappointing (King et al., 2004). While acquisition performance is affected by a large number of variables, one of the key determinants is *knowledge transfer* (Birkinshaw et al., 2000; Haspeslagh and Jemison, 1991) – defined as the level of utilization of the source's knowledge by the recipient (Minbaeva et al., 2003). Through knowledge transfer, the merging firms create value by accessing new knowledge that resides in the acquisition partner or from combining the resources of the two firms in new ways (Capron and Pistre, 2002; Eschen and Bresser, 2005).

Regardless of the importance of knowledge transfer in M&A, relatively few studies have examined the complex mechanisms that impact knowledge transfer in this context (for exceptions see for example Björkman et al., 2007; Ranft and Lord, 2002; Sarala and Vaara, 2010; Westphal and Shaw, 2005). In particular, there is a lack of integrative models that spell out how key mechanisms facilitate or impede knowledge transfer in general (Kane, 2010), and in acquisitions in particular (Haleblian et al., 2009). This is what we aim to provide in this chapter. We portray post-acquisition knowledge transfer as a dynamic process, which ultimately relies on organizational absorptive and disseminative capacities that depend on knowledge complementarity, operational and cultural integration, and political behavior.

The chapter is structured as follows. We will first discuss the knowledge transfer process in general and in the particular context of M&A. Then, we will present our theoretical model of the dynamic aspects of post-acquisition knowledge transfer: knowledge complementarity, organizational absorptive and disseminative capacities, operational and cultural integration, as well as political behavior. We conclude the chapter by discussing the implications of our model and avenues for future research in this area.

THEORETICAL BACKGROUND

Knowledge Transfer Process

Although researchers differ in their definitions of knowledge transfer, most agree that it is a complex process that involves much more than simple sharing of information (for example Hedlund 1994; Kogut and Zander, 1993; Nonaka and Takeuchi, 1995). Knowledge consists of individuals' conceptual understanding ("know-what"), practical skills and expertise ("know how"). Knowledge results from personal experiences (Blackler, 1995) and increases individuals' capacity to do something more efficiently and effectively (Zander and Kogut, 1995). Knowledge is socially constructed by individuals, based on their interpretations and explanations of reality, which in turn are shaped by previous learning experiences, values and the social context (Boisot and Canals, 2004; Schulz, 2001; Zander and Kogut; 1995). Thus, we view knowledge as subjective and dynamic – changing as new information is received and interpreted, and expectations are changed – rather than something objective or passive.

In a similar vein, knowledge transfer is influenced by individuals' values and accumulated learning experiences. We understand knowledge transfer as a dual process that includes both the dissemination of knowledge from the source and the consequent absorption and use by the recipient (Minbaeva et al., 2003). Thus, knowledge transfer requires effective framing and articulation of knowledge by the source and the subsequent recontextualization and reapplication of knowledge in a new context by the recipient (Foss and Pedersen, 2002; Minbaeva et al., 2003).

The type of knowledge that is transferred can vary extensively, depending on what the source has available and what is useful for the recipient. For instance, external knowledge is related to the business environment and includes detailed knowledge about the local institutional environment and business practices and networks (Hamel, 1991; Kostova and Roth, 2002; Simonin, 1999) whereas internal knowledge is connected to the firm's different functions, such as management, manufacturing or R&D (Kogut and Zander, 1993; Zander and Kogut, 1995). Also, knowledge can be explicit or tacit, which relates to how easily it can be articulated, codified, and transferred (Kogut and Zander, 1993; Simonin, 1999). Furthermore, knowledge can reside at different organizational levels. While individual knowledge refers to the skills and competencies possessed by single organizational members, an organization's knowledge base is not simply the sum of individuals' knowledge (Zhao and Anand, 2009). Rather, it also includes collective knowledge, which relates to interpersonal routines and requires coordination and information sharing between individual members. More specifically, Zhao and Anand (2009: 962) define collective knowledge as "the knowledge embedded among organizational members regarding how to coordinate, share, distribute, and recombine individual knowledge". Thus, an organization's knowledge base consists of both individuals' knowledge as well as collective knowledge, which coexist and complement each other (Zhao and Anand, 2009).

A number of issues have been identified that can influence knowledge transfer. In general these factors can be divided into four categories: characteristics of knowledge, characteristics of the source and recipient including their similarities and differences, the relationship between the source and recipient, and knowledge integration mechanisms. Regarding the characteristics of knowledge, one of the most commonly cited barriers to knowledge transfer relates to the level of tacitness of knowledge because such knowledge is difficult to identify and "package" in a way that is useful for the recipient. This contributes to what Szulanski (1996) calls "stickiness" of knowledge. Another barrier to knowledge transfer is complexity, defined as the number of interdependent individuals, routines, and/or technologies that knowledge is related to (Simonin, 1999). In contrast, knowledge that is reliable (Szulanski, 1996) and/or complementary (Lane and Lubatkin, 1998) can facilitate knowledge transfer.

As to the characteristics of the source and recipient, the level of absorptive capacity has been described as a central determinant of knowledge transfer (Gupta and Govindarajan, 2000; Lane and Lubatkin 1998, Szulanski, 1996). Cohen and Levinthal (1990: 128, emphasis added) define absorptive capacity as "the *ability* to recognize the value of new external information, assimilate it, and apply it to commercial ends". Minbaeva et al. (2003), however, argue that individuals' *motivation* to take up and make use of new knowledge is an equally important component of absorptive capacity. Similar to absorptive capacity, disseminative capacity refers to the source's *ability* and *motivation* to share their knowledge with the recipient (Minbaeva, 2007). The ability to absorb (Cohen and Levinthal, 1990) and to disseminate (Minbaeva, 2007) knowledge is enhanced when the source and recipient have relevant prior knowledge, are familiar with each other's knowledge and practices, and share the same language. Thus, differences in key organizational aspects such as knowledge bases, organizational structures, compensation policies (Lane and Lubatkin, 1998), as well as strategy, practices and culture (Lam, 1997; Westphal and Shaw, 2005) can undermine knowledge transfer efforts. However, some differences in the source's and recipient's knowledge bases – stemming for instance from cultural differences – may be necessary to generate knowledge transfer because completely overlapping knowledge stocks may offer few benefits for the recipient (Lane and Lubatkin, 1998).

Further, the relationship between the source and the recipient organizations is likely to influence knowledge transfer. Organizational members are more likely to be motivated to absorb knowledge if they trust the source and expect to benefit from knowledge transfer (Cabrera and Cabrera, 2005). Similarly, organizational members are more likely to be motivated to disseminate their knowledge in a reciprocal trusting relationship in which they expect to receive something valuable in return (Husted and Michailova, 2002). Simonin's (1999) study highlights the importance of the source's motivation to share its knowledge by identifying organizational members' protectiveness of their knowledge as one of the main barriers to knowledge transfer.

Finally, operational and sociocultural integration can facilitate knowledge transfer by increasing coordination and control through the alignment of structures, practices and values (Birkinshaw et al., 2000). Operational integration combines the operational aspects of different firm units and includes factors such as the level of decision-making autonomy (Nohria and Ghoshal, 1994) and ongoing task related inter-unit communication (Gupta and Govindarajan, 2000). Sociocultural integration, in turn, increases interpersonal linkages and creates a shared culture and identity between different organizational units in order to create trust and increase the organizational members' understanding of each other (Gupta and Govindarajan, 2000; Björkman et al., 2004). Cross-functional meetings and projects (Zhao and Anand, 2009), joint training programs and the use of expatriates (Björkman et al., 2004) are examples of factors that contribute to socio-cultural integration.

Knowledge Transfer in Mergers and Acquisitions

It has been argued that knowledge transfer is particularly important in the context of M&A because it is essential for value creation (Haspeslagh and Jemison, 1991; Larsson and Finkelstein, 1999). Furthermore, the knowledge transfer process can be more complex in M&A than in other settings, because it deals with knowledge transfer between two previously separate organizations that are in the process of being integrated. In addition, M&A often involve high levels of ambiguity and uncertainty about the future (Bresman et al., 1999; Vaara et al., 2003), which may reduce the ability and motivation of the organizational members to transfer knowledge (Empson, 2001).

Since the late 1990s, when research on knowledge transfer in M&A commenced, empirical studies have shown that a number of variables can impact knowledge transfer. Large-scale surveys have tended to focus on only a few explanatory variables. For example, one of the more comprehensive studies by Bresman, Birkinshaw and Nobel (1999) only includes four variables. Case studies have typically provided more comprehensive views on the interaction of specific variables. For example, Westphal and Shaw's (2005) extensive study includes 20 variables. Table 5.1 provides an overview of key empirical studies from scholarly journals in this area. It includes the variables studied and their impact on knowledge transfer.

Regarding knowledge characteristics, M&A researchers have mostly emphasized the role of tacitness (Bresman et al., 1999; Castro and Neira, 2005; Ranft and Lord, 2002; Westphal and Shaw, 2005), social embeddedness (Ranft and Lord, 2002; Tsang, 2008), ambiguity (Junni and Sarala, 2011) and context specificity of knowledge (Schweizer, 2005; Westphal and Shaw, 2005). Whereas tacit and/or embedded knowledge may offer knowledge transfer potential, such knowledge may be more difficult to identify and "package" to a transferable form (Lam, 1997). In addition, very specific knowledge may be less useful for the recipient because it is more difficult to adapt to a new context (Schweizer, 2005).

As to the source and recipient and their similarities/differences, M&A studies have included factors such as the size of the target company's knowledge base (Ahuja and Katila, 2001), personnel retention (Ranft and Lord, 2000; 2002), the age of the recipient company, and the recipient's tendency to revert back to old practices (Tsang, 2008). Out of these factors, the size of the target firm and its knowledge base, and personnel retention have been identified as facilitators of knowledge transfer while the tendency to revert to old practices is a major barrier for knowledge transfer. Researchers have also focused on the interrelatedness of the knowledge bases in terms of their relative size and relatedness (Ahuja and Katila, 2001), complementarity (Westphal and Shaw, 2005; Zou and Ghauri, 2008), asymmetry (Capron et al., 1998; Westphal and Shaw, 2005), strategic similarity (Capron et al., 2001; Westphal and Shaw, 2005), and overall differences (Lam, 1997). In addition, differences between the firms due to national and organizational cultural differences have been examined (Castro and Neira, 2005; Sarala and Vaara, 2010; Vaara et al., 2010). These studies have found that strategic similarity, knowledge complementarity and asymmetry tend to facilitate knowledge transfer whereas dissimilarities in relative sizes, knowledge bases, and cultures often hinder knowledge transfer, but the empirical evidence is not clear-cut. For instance, whereas Castro and Neira (2005) suggest an overall negative effect of cultural differences, other studies have found a positive relationship (Sarala and Vaara, 2010; Vaara et al., 2010). Ahuja and Katila (2001), in turn, established an inverted U-curve

Table 5.1 An overview of empirical knowledge transfer studies in M&A

Authors	Method	Category	Variables studied	Impact on knowledge transfer
Lam (1997)	Case study (one)	Source/recipient Knowledge	Differences in knowledge bases Different functional areas of knowledge	+ + in R&D, manufacturing and marketing – in managerial capabilities in general
		Source/recipient Relationship	Knowledge asymmetry Direction of knowledge transfer	+ + in R&D, manufacturing, marketing in both directions + in managerial capabilities from acquirer to target
Bresman et al. (1999)	Survey and interviews	Knowledge Relationship	Tacitness Direction of knowledge transfer	– – in the beginning more from acquirer to target, later bilateral knowledge flows
		Management Relationship	Elapsed time Communication Direction of knowledge transfer	+ +
Capron (1999)	Survey	Relationship	Direction of knowledge transfer	Multilateral flows: + Unilateral flow from target to acquirer: –
Ranft and Lord (2000)	Survey	Source/recipient	Employee retention	+

Table 5.1 (continued)

Authors	Method	Category	Variables studied	Impact on knowledge transfer
Ahuja and Katila (2001)	Survey	Source/recipient	Nontechnological acquisitions Absolute size of the target's knowledge base Relative size of knowledge bases Relatedness of knowledge bases	Not significant + – Inverted U-curve
Capron et al. (2001)	Survey	Source/recipient Relationship	Strategic similarity Direction of knowledge transfer	+ + for multilateral flows in strategically similar acquisitions Also used as explanatory variable to predict asset divestiture: +
Empson (2001)	Case studies (three)	Relationship	Fear of exploitation and contamination	–
Schoenberg (2001)	Survey	Knowledge	Different functional areas of knowledge	+ in marketing, distribution, finance – in R&D, supply, investment appraisal
Capron and Pistre (2002)	Survey	Relationship	Direction of knowledge transfer	Used as explanatory variable to predict abnormal returns: + for unilateral flows from acquirer to target but not vice versa, and + for multilateral flows

Author (year)	Method	Category	Factor	Effect
Ranft and Lord (2002)	Case studies (seven)	Knowledge	Tacitness	–
			Social embeddedness	–
		Management	Communication	+
			Integration speed	– Inverted U-curve
Bröchner et al. (2004)	Small survey (32 cases)	Source/recipient	Knowledge asymmetry	+ influences direction of knowledge transfer
		Management	Type of communication (email, face-to-face etc.)	Different effect on KT depending on language skills and preferences
Castro and Neira (2005)	Case studies (three)	Knowledge	Tacitness	–
		Source/recipient	Employee retention	+ (especially tacit knowledge)
			Cultural differences	–
		Relationship	Acquisition motive (to achieve market presence or access complementary knowledge)	+
Schweizer (2005)	Case studies (four)	Knowledge	Specificity	–
		Relationship	Target autonomy	–
Westphal and Shaw (2005)	Case studies (seven)	Knowledge	Tacitness	–
			Specificity	–
			Usefulness	+
		Source/recipient	Knowledge complementarity	+
			Knowledge asymmetry	+
			Organizational and strategic differences	–
			Performance differences	+

Table 5.1 (continued)

Authors	Method	Category	Variables studied	Impact on knowledge transfer
		Relationship	Affinity for partner	+
			Professional respect	+
			Positive attitude toward deal	+
			Relative identification with the new firm	+
			Relationship quality	+
		Management	High structural flux	+
			Information-sharing norms	+
			Acquirer commitment	+
			Procedural fairness	+
			Level of normative integration	–
			Informal vs. formal interaction	+
			User- vs. source-initiated knowledge transfer	+
			Group vs. individual work	+
			Group vs. individual incentives	+
Tsang (2008)	Case studies (eight)	Knowledge	Social embeddedness	–
		Source/recipient	Age of company	–
			Tendency to revert to old routines	–
		Relationship	Elapsed time	+
			Perceived expertise of source by recipient	+
		Management	Deployment of experts/expatriates	+

Zou and Ghauri (2008)	Case studies (four)	Source/recipient	Knowledge complementarity	+
		Management	Target autonomy	+
			Communication	+
Sarala and Vaara (2010)	Survey	Source/recipient	National cultural differences	+
			Organizational cultural differences	Not significant
		Management	Cultural integration	+ for cultural convergence and crossvergence
Vaara et al. (2010)	Survey	Source/recipient	National cultural differences	+
			Organizational cultural differences	+
		Relationship	Social conflict	–
		Management	Operational integration	+
Junni and Sarala (2011)	Survey	Knowledge	Causal ambiguity	–
		Relationship	Partner attractiveness	+
		Management	Cultural integration	+ for cultural crossvergence on KT in both directions
				+ for cultural convergence on KT from acquirer to target
Junni (2011)	Survey	Relationship	Fears of exploitation and contamination	–

relationship between differences in knowledge bases and knowledge transfer.

In terms of the relationship between the acquirer and target firms, knowledge transfer in the M&A context has been suggested to be particularly problematic due to uncertainty and ambiguity inherent in acquisitions, as well as the lack of a social community between the merging firms in early stages of the integration process (Bresman et al., 1999). More specifically, studies have concentrated on elapsed time (Bresman et al., 1999), fear of exploitation in part of the source and fear of contamination in part of the recipient (Empson, 2001; Junni, 2011), the perceived expertise of the source (Tsang, 2008), social conflict (Vaara et al., 2010), procedural fairness (Westphal and Shaw, 2005), as well as the perceived quality of the relationship with the partner (Junni and Sarala, 2011; Westphal and Shaw, 2005).

Another popular topic has been the direction of knowledge transfer in acquisitions (Bresman et al., 1999; Bröchner et al., 2004; Capron, 1999). In general, the findings of the above mentioned studies indicate that a "negative" relationship characterized by fears of exploitation and contamination as well as social conflict impede M&A knowledge transfer. In contrast, a "positive" relationship – in which the acquisition process is perceived as fair and just, and the acquisition partners have a high affinity for each other – supports M&A knowledge transfer. Further, concerning the direction of knowledge transfer, the study of Bresman et al. (1999) showed that whereas acquirers mostly "imposed" knowledge on targets in early post-acquisition integration stages, knowledge flows tended to become more mutual in later stages. The direction of knowledge transfer is also affected by acquisition strategy. More specifically, in "absorption" acquisitions the acquirer is more likely to impose its knowledge on the target, in order to achieve synergies (Haspeslagh and Jemison, 1991). In contrast, "symbiosis" and "preservation" acquisitions – where the acquirer is interested in preserving and accessing knowledge from the target (Haspeslagh and Jemison, 1991) – are likely to involve more knowledge transfer from the target or even mutual two-directional transfer.

Finally, management of the post-acquisition integration is vital for successful knowledge transfer. One of the topics has been the optimal speed of integration (Westphal and Shaw, 2005). In addition, operational integration, mostly in terms of the level of autonomy granted for the target (Castro and Neira, 2005; Ranft and Lord, 2002; Schweizer, 2005; Zou and Ghauri, 2008; Vaara et al., 2010) has been studied. Furthermore, researchers have explored the effect of sociocultural integration (Bresman et. al., 1999; Castro and Neira, 2005; Junni and Sarala, 2010; Sarala and Vaara, 2010). Finally, regarding specific integration mechanisms that support operational and sociocultural integration, previous research has focused on the positive role of inter-firm communication and interaction (Bresman et al., 1999; Bröchner et al., 2004; Castro and Neira, 2005; Ranft and Lord, 2002; Zou and Ghauri, 2008), deployment of experts and expatriates (Tsang, 2008), and creation of information-sharing norms (Westphal and Shaw, 2005).

The results indicate that a fast paced integration process contributes to knowledge transfer by keeping recipients used to receiving new knowledge (Westphal and Shaw, 2005). Ranft and Lord (2002) argue, however, that the effect of integration pace is a more complex inverted U-curve: a "too" fast integration process is disruptive for the target firm's knowledge base, but a "too" slow integration process reduces opportunities to collaborate and share knowledge. Also, in general a high level of sociocultural integration facilitates knowledge transfer (Bresman et al., 1999; Castro and Neira, 2005; Junni and Sarala, 2011; Sarala and Vaara, 2010). However, the findings are more mixed related to the effects of operational integration. While it has been argued that too much integration can destroy the target firm's knowledge base (Castro and Neira, 2005) and thus undermine knowledge transfer potential (Westphal and Shaw, 2005; Zou and Ghauri, 2008), other studies have shown a positive relationship between operational integration and M&A knowledge transfer (Vaara et al., 2010). Similar to this, studies have found that high levels of target autonomy reduce knowledge transfer (Ranft and Lord, 2002). However, autonomy may be beneficial if the target is converted into a center of excellence (Schweizer, 2005).

As discussed above, a number of factors have been found to influence knowledge transfer in M&A. However, there is a need to develop more complex and integrative models in general (Kane, 2010; Minbaeva, 2007; Van Wijk et al., 2008) and in M&A in particular (Haleblian et al., 2009). In particular, the socio-political aspects require further specification. First, few studies have explicitly addressed the more complex associations between knowledge complementarity, acquisition integration strategy, and political behavior in order to examine the processes through which knowledge transfer is realized (for notable exceptions see Björkman et al., 2007; Haspeslagh and Jemison, 1991, see also Table 5.1). In this chapter, we build on previous research and explicitly address how knowledge complementarity influences the post-acquisition integration strategy in terms of operational and cultural integration. Second, concerning source/recipient characteristics, while individual absorptive capacity has been linked to M&A knowledge transfer (Björkman et al., 2007), disseminative capacity as well as collective aspects of absorptive and disseminative capacity have received little attention. Third, regarding relationship

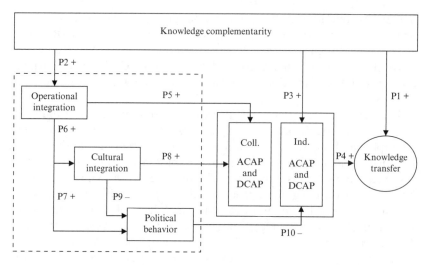

Figure 5.1   A theoretical framework of knowledge transfer in mergers and acquisitions

characteristics, scant research has been devoted to explaining the role of political behavior (for exceptions see Empson, 2001; Tsang, 2008; Vaara et al., 2003). Fourth, the influence of post-acquisition integration impacts on knowledge transfer needs further specification (Haleblian et al., 2009). As discussed earlier, the results concerning operational integration are mixed and relatively few studies have addressed the complexities of cultural integration. In the following, we will propose an integrative theoretical model that focuses on these strategic and socio-political aspects of knowledge transfer and maps out their relationships in M&A. Figure 5.1 provides a summary of this model.

KNOWLEDGE TRANSFER IN M&A: A DYNAMIC THEORETICAL FRAMEWORK

Knowledge Complementarity

It is a common theme in M&A research that synergies contribute to value creation (Haspeslagh and Jemison, 1991), and several studies indicate that knowledge transfer is actively sought by acquiring companies to achieve this aim. In order to create synergies, acquirers tend to either seek targets with complementary knowledge that can strengthen their existing knowledge base, or targets with weaknesses that they can overcome with the acquirer's knowledge (Capron et al., 1998; Capron et al., 2001; Castro and Neira, 2005; Schoenberg, 2001). *Knowledge complementarity* refers to the extent of gaps in the knowledge bases of the acquiring and acquired companies that can be filled by using the partner's knowledge to create synergies, which the acquisition partners could not have created on their own (Eschen and Bresser, 2005). Thus, knowledge complementarity increases the potential to create synergies through knowledge transfer (Björkman et al., 2007; Eschen and Bresser, 2005; Larsson and Finkelstein, 1999). Although some acquisitions can involve the transfer of substitutable or duplicative knowledge, in order to standardize processes and create economies of scale or scope, the transfer of complementary knowledge has been argued to be a more common acquisition motive because it offers greater potential for value creation than the transfer of duplicative knowledge (Castro and Neira, 2005; Eschen and Bresser, 2005; Haspeslagh and Jemison, 1991; Westphal and Shaw, 2005). Consequently, the presence of complementary knowledge is likely to increase M&A knowledge transfer (Björkman et al., 2007; Eschen and Bresser, 2005; Westphal and Shaw, 2005; Zou and Ghauri, 2008).

The existence of knowledge complementarities, in turn, increases the need for operational integration due to greater interdependencies between the merging firms (Haspeslagh and Jemison, 1991). Because knowledge is embedded in organizational structures, collective procedures and practices of the merging firms, knowledge can only be transferred through operational integration that increases coordination and task related inter-unit interaction between the merging firms so that complementarities can be realized (Haspeslagh and Jemison, 1991; Zhao and Anand, 2009).

Further, knowledge complementarity is likely to increase individuals' motivation to share their knowledge, because of the potential to create synergies (Björkman et al., 2007), as well as reduced fears on part of the sender that their knowledge will be "exploited" by the recipient without receiving equally valuable knowledge in return (Empson, 2001). Further, knowledge complementarities tend to be associated with greater value of knowledge to the recipient and thereby increase the recipient's motivation to absorb knowledge from the source, whilst detaching itself from its old knowledge, by reducing fears of knowledge contamination and "not-invented-here syndrome" (Empson, 2001; Gupta and Govindarajan, 2000). In addition, acquisitions characterized by complementary rather than supplementary knowledge are less likely to involve large-scale personnel reductions (Capron et al., 2001; Larsson and Finkelstein, 1999), which can make knowledge transfer less threatening (Westphal and Shaw, 2005).

Organizational Absorptive and Disseminative Capacities

Organizational absorptive capacity

Absorptive capacity is a central concept in the literature on knowledge transfer and learning. In their seminal paper Cohen and Levinthal (1990: 128) describe a firm's *organizational absorptive capacity* as "the firm's ability to recognize the value of new information, assimilate it, and apply it to commercial ends". Organizational absorptive capacity is influenced by a wide variety of factors, such as individual members' knowledge bases, cognitive processes, and experience, training and communication, compensation structure, organization's culture and structure, as well as R&D expenditure (Cohen and Levinthal, 1990). This suggests that we can distinguish between individual and collective components of organizational absorptive capacity, which together make up an organization's absorptive capacity (Zhao and Anand, 2009). In addition, we argue that organizational absorptive capacity involves the recipient firm members discarding old knowledge, also referred to as organizational "unlearning" (Hedberg, 1981; Yildiz and Fey, 2010). When the recipient organization is attached to its old knowledge, knowledge transfer becomes less effective because the new knowledge is not fully used (Tsang, 2008; Vaara et al., 2003). Discarding old knowledge can be both intentional and unintentional (Tsang and Zahra, 2008). For example, in M&A acquisition partners can intentionally set out to eliminate old knowledge and practices, in favor of new knowledge (Vaara et al., 2003) whereas unintentional discarding of old knowledge may result from unexpected personnel turnover (Tsang and Zahra, 2008).

Concerning *individual absorptive capacity*, the outcomes of any human endeavor can be described as depending on both individuals' ability and motivation to behave in a certain way (Baldwin et al., 1991). An individual's *ability* has been defined as "a group of skills, competencies, and characteristics that enable a party to have influence within some specific domain" (Mayer et al., 1995: 717). In relation to individuals' absorptive capacity in M&A, ability thus refers to individuals' skills, competencies and characteristics that enable them to make use of the acquisition partner's knowledge, and to discard their old knowledge. The '*ability*' dimension of individual absorptive capacity consists of developing new frames of reference that increase understanding about past and future actions, and how effective these are likely to be (Fiol and Lyles, 1985). The more familiar the recipient is with the source's knowledge base or domain, the easier it will be to understand and learn the source's knowledge (Simonin, 1999). In line with this, Lam (1997) found that a lack of experience with the source's knowledge base impeded post-merger knowledge transfer.

The 'ability' dimension of individual absorptive capacity is also related to discarding of old cognitive frames of reference, in order to be able to take up new ones (Yildiz and Fey, 2010). If recipients are not familiar with the partner's knowledge, and thus less able to recognize the value and usefulness of new knowledge, they will be less likely to actively give up their old knowledge and practices in order to take up new ones (Tsang, 2008), which reduces their individual absorptive capacity.

Concerning the 'motivational' side, an individual's work *motivation* can be understood as "a set of energetic forces that originate both within as well as beyond an individual's being, to initiate work-related behavior and to determine its form, direction, intensity, and duration" (Pinder, 1998: 11). The motivational dimension of individual absorptive capacity relates to the recipient's intention to learn from the partner (Hamel, 1991; Simonin, 2004). The recipient's motivation to absorb new knowledge also relates to normative aspects. More specifically, if the source's knowledge is not perceived as legitimate by the recipient, (s)he will be less motivated to take up the source's knowledge, even if it is more useful than the recipient's old knowledge (Kostova and Roth, 2002). This is more likely to happen if the recipient is not familiar with the sender's knowledge base (Empson, 2001). In the context of M&A, decision makers commonly try to legitimize their motives and actions to others. Such legitimization activities can enhance the motivation on part of individuals to be receptive to new knowledge and related actions considered necessary for knowledge transfer (Vaara and Monin, 2010). The 'motivation' dimension of individual absorptive capacity is also linked to discarding old knowledge. In order for knowledge transfer to take place individuals need to be motivated to give up old practices (Yildiz and Fey, 2010). De-legitimizing and de-institutionalizing old practices can be time consuming and difficult, requiring significant effort from the source (Yildiz and Fey, 2010). In addition, organizational members are often emotionally attached to their existing practices and routines, which can reduce the motivation to discard them, and thus hamper knowledge transfer (Vaara et al., 2003). Individuals' attachment to their old knowledge depends on the length of time that they have worked in the recipient firm: the longer they have worked there, the more attached they are likely to be to their existing ways of thinking and working, and will thus be less motivated to detach themselves from their old knowledge and change their practices (Fiol and Lyles, 1985; Tsang, 2008). In addition, if the partners are afraid that they will lose their existing power structures from adopting new knowledge and practices, they will be less willing to "give up" their old knowledge structures (for example, Empson, 2001; Vaara et al., 2003). Although ability and motivation are separate dimensions of individual absorptive capacity, they have been shown to support knowledge transfer best in combination (Minbaeva et al., 2003). Low ability can negatively affect motivation whereas low or absent motivation may hinder realizing employee's potential ability (Vroom, 1964).

Concerning *collective absorptive capacity*, while Minbaeva et al. (2003) and Minbaeva (2007) view organizational absorptive capacity as being the sum of individuals' motivation and ability to absorb knowledge, Zhao and Anand (2009) expand the concept by including a 'collective dimension' of organizational absorptive capacity. They argue that knowledge is not limited to individual abilities and skills but is also embedded within the organizational structure and organizational culture (Nonaka and Takeuchi, 1995; Zhao and Anand, 2009). Collective absorptive capacity is thus defined as the "structural and cultural attributes of the receiving organization as a whole that are conducive to acquiring and assimilating new knowledge" (Zhao and Anand, 2009: 962). To extend this definition, we maintain that collective absorptive capacity also involves supporting the discarding of old knowledge.

We suggest that structural and cultural attributes conducive for knowledge transfer include an organizational structure that is characterized by extensive task-related inter-unit interaction and routines (Gupta and Govindarajan, 2000; Jansen et al., 2005), as well as a cohesive organizational culture that encourages informal communication, mutual understanding and respect (Bock et al., 2005; Kayworth and Leidner, 2004; Khoja and Maranville, 2010). A functionally and socially interconnected organizational structure enhances individuals' *ability* to interpret issues and build new frames of reference that allow them to better understand new knowledge (Daft and Lengel, 1986). Also, a culture that is cohesive and encourages informal communication will generate a high level of shared meaning, affiliation and trust between individuals, which is likely to *motivate* them to seek out knowledge from their colleagues (Bock et al., 2005). Furthermore, a cohesive organizational structure and culture create cognitive systems, and memories that are shared by organizational members (Fiol and Lyles, 1985), which increases the likelihood that new knowledge which has been absorbed by individuals will impact the organization as a whole (Crossan et al., 1999; Zhao and Anand, 2009).

Collective absorptive capacity also involves discarding old knowledge. An organizational structure that is characterized by extensive cross-functional activities and routines is likely to make recipient firm members more used to interacting with individuals from different functions with diverse backgrounds, which increases their *ability* to reconsider and reevaluate their existing knowledge base (Jansen et al., 2005). Furthermore, a cohesive organizational culture that encourages informal communication is likely to create trust in the partner's knowledge (Bock et al., 2005; Kayworth and Leidner, 2004), and thus *motivate* the recipient to discard old knowledge. This kind of structural and cultural environment is thus likely to encourage individuals to question their existing assumptions and cognitive maps and to discard them in favor of new and potentially more useful knowledge (Yildiz and Fey, 2010).

To conclude, the recipient's organizational absorptive capacity – which consists of individual and collective aspects – is expected to influence knowledge transfer by increasing individuals' ability and motivation to absorb new knowledge from the partner, whilst discarding their old knowledge. Further, we contend that while individual and collective absorptive capacities are distinctive factors, they also influence and support each other. On the one hand, organizational structure and culture lay out the internal context that individuals need to operate within, and adapt their behavior to (Zhao and Anand, 2009). On the other hand, individuals' abilities, attitudes and personalities also shape the organization and can, over time, change aspects of the organization's structure and culture. Together, individual and collective absorptive capacities make up the recipient's organizational absorptive capacity.

Organizational disseminative capacity
Few studies have addressed knowledge transfer from the source's viewpoint by including disseminative capacity (for notable exceptions, see Gupta and Govindarajan, 2000; Minbaeva, 2007; Zhao and Anand, 2009). Similar to organizational absorptive capacity, we understand *organizational disseminative capacity* as consisting of individual and collective aspects that are distinctive but support each other.

Concerning *individual disseminative capacity*, we distinguish between the individuals' *ability* and *motivation* to convey or teach knowledge to the recipient (Minbaeva, 2007). The '*ability*' dimension of the source's individual disseminative capacity relates to how well the members of the source organization are able to make their knowledge understandable to the recipient firm members. If members of the source firm are familiar with the recipient firm's knowledge domain and its organizational practices, it is better able to teach its knowledge to individuals in the recipient firm (Lane and Lubatkin, 1998). In addition, it is necessary to legitimize the knowledge that is intended for knowledge transfer, in order to increase the recipient's motivation to learn while giving up its old practices (Kostova and Roth, 2002). Thus, it is important that individuals in the source firm can communicate and convey their knowledge to members of the recipient firm in such a way that it is viewed as legitimate, for example, by showing how the new knowledge can contribute to the recipient firm's existing knowledge and practices. As to the '*motivation*' dimension of disseminative capacity, if the members of the source firm are afraid that individuals in the recipient firm may exploit their knowledge, without offering anything valuable in return, they will be less motivated to depart from valuable knowledge (Empson, 2001; Husted et al., 2005). This will reduce opportunities for learning about the source's knowledge, and consequently reduce knowledge transfer. Although studies on alliances and M&A have focused on the motivation dimension (Empson, 2001; Simonin, 1999), we maintain that both individuals' ability and motivation play important roles in facilitating knowledge sharing (Minbaeva et al., 2003). More specifically, we suggest that the ability and motivation dimensions are interconnected through perceived self-efficacy: when individuals believe that they are able to disseminate knowledge, they are also more motivated to do so (Cabrera et al., 2006).

Similar to collective absorptive capacity that encompasses both structural and cultural aspects of the recipient organization (Kayworth and Leidner, 2004; Van den Bosch et al., 1999), we define *collective disseminative capacity* as the structural and cultural attributes of the source organization as a whole that are conducive to teaching and disseminating knowledge to the recipient. Concerning the '*ability*' dimension of collective disseminative capacity, if the source organization's structure supports inter-unit task related communication and collaboration among its members, the members are likely to have a better understanding of the kind of knowledge possessed by different organizational members and teams/units (Zhao and Anand, 2009), which will increase their ability to identify and to recombine their knowledge in such a way that it is more useful for the recipient. This is also likely to improve the source's ability to communicate and "teach" its knowledge to the recipient (Zhao and Anand, 2009) because otherwise knowledge is easily misinterpreted or distorted by the recipient (Zellmer-Bruhn, 2003). This is especially important when the knowledge that is to be transferred is highly tacit and requires more teaching (Winter, 1987). Concerning '*motivational*' aspects of collective disseminative capacity, if the organizational culture is cohesive, individuals are more likely to feel that their culturally embedded knowledge is valuable, and thus be motivated to transfer this knowledge to others (Nahavandi and Malekzadeh, 1988). Furthermore, in a cohesive organizational culture that encourages informal and open social interaction among individual members, individuals are more likely to trust that knowledge transfer will be reciprocal, and will thus be more motivated to share their knowledge (Bock et al., 2005).

In sum, we conceptualize individual and collective disseminative capacity as distinctive yet interrelated factors, which together constitute the source's organizational disseminative capacity. Thus, if the source's structure supports horizontal cross-functional interaction as opposed to having clear boundaries between departments (Van den Bosch et al., 1999) and the source's culture is collaborative and open (Bock et al., 2005), we expect individuals to be better able and motivated to disseminate their knowledge to the recipient. We contend that while individual and collective absorptive capacities are distinctive factors, they also influence and support each other.

Post-acquisition Integration Process

Operational integration

We understand *operational integration* as coordination and control between the merging firms through organizational structures and systems (Pablo, 1994), the aim of which is to create value by being able to reach organizational goals more effectively (Birkinshaw et al., 2000). Previous research suggests that post-acquisition operational integration takes place primarily through assimilation of the target firm to the acquirer or through symbiotic combination of the structures and systems of both firms (Haspeslagh and Jemison, 1991). In absorption acquisitions, coordination and control are achieved by imposing the acquirer's structures and systems on the target so that the acquirer and the target are fully consolidated (Haspeslagh and Jemison, 1991). In contrast, in symbiosis acquisitions the merging firms combine their existing structures and systems in order to "get the best out of both worlds" (Evans et al., 2011; Haspeslagh and Jemison, 1991).

Operational integration is likely to improve *collective absorptive and disseminative capacities*. By aligning structures and systems of the two organizations, creating shared goals, structures and activities (Pablo, 1994), enhancing inter-firm coordination, and creating functional ties between the acquisition partners (Birkinshaw et al., 2000), operational integration creates a 'collective structural platform' that increases the individuals' ability to convey their knowledge to the members of the partner organization, as well as take up new knowledge from the partner (Jansen et al., 2005; Van den Bosch et al., 1999; Westphal and Shaw, 2005).

However, operational integration can involve extensive organizational restructuring in the merging firms, including personnel reduction to achieve economies of scales and scope. Thus, operational integration can have "unintended" negative consequences in terms of increased political behavior as individuals try to "protect their turfs" from an "invading enemy" (Haspeslagh and Jemison, 1991; Jemison and Sitkin, 1986). The extent to which operational integration is likely to increase political behavior, however, depends on whether an absorption or symbiosis integration approach is used. Absorption acquisitions may require coercion and direct pressure on part of the acquirer, which reduces the individuals' motivation to collaborate (Jemison and Sitkin, 1986; Steensma and Van Milligen, 2003). Symbiosis acquisitions are likely to involve less coercive operational changes in a sense that they have to be "negotiated" and "reasoned" between the merger partners in order to decide how different organizational aspects are to be integrated, which is likely to create perceptions of procedural fairness amongst organizational members in the target firm (Steensma and Van Milligen, 2003) and, as a result, reduce the risk of disruptive political behavior.

Because of the possible negative effects on individuals, operational integration increases the need for cultural integration that is aimed to enhance the merging firm's motivation to collaborate by creating positive interactions and a shared identity and understanding of why operational integration is needed to achieve the common organizational goals. Birkinshaw et al. (2000) warn that if operational integration is achieved without paying attention to cultural integration, it can create a hostile environment between the acquisition partners and reduce their willingness to cooperate. Thus, in order to achieve the strategic objectives of operational integration, cultural integration is required to support morale and gain the commitment of people to the merger objectives (Shrivastava, 1986). Therefore we will next focus on cultural integration and discuss in more detail how cultural integration can further support collective absorptive capacity, while also reducing political behavior that results from operational integration.

Organizational cultural integration

Cultural integration represents the ideological and human side of the integration process. Following Shrivastava (1986), we understand *organizational cultural integration* as the development of a common organizational culture with shared espoused values and belief systems (Shrivastava, 1986). Previous research suggests that cultural integration takes place primarily through the mechanisms of organizational cultural convergence and organizational cultural crossvergence (Sarala and Vaara, 2010). Organizational cultural convergence describes the process of the acquiring and target firms becoming increasingly similar along existing cultural dimensions (Sarala and Vaara, 2010). Usually, this is driven by changes in the target firm that are mandated by the dominant acquiring firm (Haspeslagh and Jemison, 1991) – that is, the acquirer's culture is imposed on the target. In contrast, organizational cultural crossvergence describes cultural integration through the creation of a new shared culture that is distinct from the previous cultures of both the acquiring and the target firms (Sarala and Vaara, 2010). Crossvergence is thus inherently a more mutual, collaborative process in which specific cultural characteristics of both partners are combined or entirely new cultural dimensions are created by introducing values and beliefs distinct from those of the acquirer and the target and specific for the new merged organization.

We suggest that organizational cultural integration has a significant effect on *collective* absorptive and disseminative capacities. A common organizational culture created by cultural integration creates a shared frame of reference and vision for the members of both organizations (Schweiger et al., 1987; Schweiger and Goulet, 2005), which increases their ability to receive and disseminate knowledge by allowing for the reception and dissemination of tacit, complex, and culturally embedded knowledge (Haspeslagh and Jemison, 1991). A common organizational culture thus creates a shared 'cultural platform' that allows the merged organization, as a collective, to more efficiently store and process culturally embedded knowledge without having to separate it from the organizational context. Also, when cultural integration is supported by specific social integration mechanisms, such as cultural seminars, the process of cultural integration by itself creates a network of informal social ties between the merged organizations (Jansen et al., 2005; Van den Bosch et al., 1999) that supports the absorption and dissemination of knowledge between them.

Without cultural integration, social identification with the pre-merger organizations can become problematic because it leads to stronger ingroup-outgroup categorizations between the acquirer and the target (Lipponen et al., 2004). The outgroup is perceived as threatening the status and legitimacy of the ingroup (Terry and O'Brien, 2001). Organizational members respond to this 'threat' by attempting to enhance and protect their power bases by increased political behavior (Steensma and Van Milligen, 2003). Thus, cultural integration reduces disruptive political behavior through the creation of a shared culture and identity.

We would expect that both convergence and crossvergence can effectively contribute to the creation of a shared frame of reference and shared 'cultural platform' that enhance the acquisition partners' collective absorptive and disseminative capacities. However, we suggest that the positive effect may be stronger for crossvergence (Junni and Sarala, 2011), which – as a more mutual and collaborative process – is more conducive for the creation of an inter-organizational social network that increases individuals' motivation to absorb and disseminate knowledge. While convergence has been shown to enhance M&A knowledge transfer (Sarala and Vaara, 2010), it is likely to better support the acquirer's ability to disseminate its knowledge to the target than vice versa (Junni and Sarala, 2011). Although convergence reduces potential ingroup-outgroup categorizations (Birkinshaw et al., 2000), it usually involves assimilation of the target's culture to the acquirer (Harding and Rouse, 2007) and is thus more likely to encourage knowledge dissemination from the culturally more dominant acquirer to the target. In conclusion, we contend that cultural integration – be it through cultural convergence or crossvergence – is likely to have a positive effect on the acquisition partners' collective absorptive and disseminative capacities by creating a shared identity and trust between them. This is also likely to reduce the risk of potentially disrupting political behavior that can result from social ingroup-outgroup categorizations (Steensma and Van Milligen, 2003; Terry and O'Brien, 2001).

Political behavior
Political behavior can be viewed as an integral part of organizational life (Mintzberg, 1985), especially in acquisitions (Cartwright and Cooper, 1990). In line with Hickson et al. (1971) and Salanick and Pfeffer (1974) we view power as the influence that one party has on the decisions or actions of another. *Politics*, in turn, refers to behavior intended to influence others (Mayes and Allen, 1977; Farrell and Petersen, 1982) in order to preserve or increase one's power. In general however, individuals are more likely to resort to politicking, when they feel that their position is threatened, that is, when they fear that they run the risk of losing outcomes (Steensma and Van Milligen, 2003). Power and politics are often overlooked aspects of M&A because most M&A research has tended to focus on "legitimate" aspects, such as value creation through synergies (Haspeslagh and Jemison, 1991, Larsson and Finkelstein, 1999). However, political behavior can have negative consequences on acquisition outcomes (Empson, 2001; Vaara, 2003). For example, Trautwein (1990) points to "managerialism"– which can be described as an attempt to increase managerial power at the expense of shareholders – as a motivation for conducting M&A. In addition, the post-acquisition integration process can also be riddled with power games, which can impede value creation (Vaara, 2003).

Previous research suggests that both the acquiring and target companies can resort to political behavior, in order to defend or enhance their position against each other (Vaara, 2003), as they deal with uncertainties concerning future outcomes (Steensma and Van Milligen, 2003). This can impede individuals' absorptive and disseminative capacities because motivation to make use of the partner's knowledge or to depart from knowledge is diminished (Empson, 2001; Vaara et al., 2003). Regarding absorption of knowledge, the acquirer has "position power", that is, the ability to use rewards, coercion and their authority in order to influence the target (Steensma and Van Milligen, 2003). By drawing on this power base acquirers often use "hard" political tactics that are coercive and controlling, such as direct pressure, that does not give the target a choice of whether to comply with the acquirer (Steensma and Van Milligen, 2003). In line with this, it is common that the acquiring company views itself as "the conqueror" of the target, perceiving itself – along with its practices and knowledge – to be superior to the target (Jemison and Sitkin, 1986). This often leads to the acquirer trying to impose its "superior" knowledge and practices to the target – even when they are not directly applicable – which creates defensiveness and change resistance in the target (Haspeslagh and Jemison, 1991; Jemison and Sitkin, 1986; Steensma and Van Milligen, 2003), and reduces its motivation to absorb the acquirer's knowledge. For example, Vaara et al. (2003) found that members in the four merging firms in their study used rational persuasion – a "softer" political tactic (Steensma and Van Milligen, 2003) – to try to convince members of the other firms of why their practices were superior and should not be changed. Imposed changes can reduce the target's collective absorptive capacity if these changes break down existing social ties – for example, through increased employee turnover (Haspeslagh and Jemison, 1991). The acquirer's individual absorptive capacity can also be reduced if organizational members are unwilling to adopt the target's "inferior" knowledge and practices, corresponding to Empson's (2001) fear of contamination'– defined as the fear on the part of individuals that their image will suffer as a result of absorbing new knowledge from the acquisition partner. This fear of contamination can be present on both sides of the merging firms. The decision to reject knowledge absorption may also be rooted in the desire to maintain the status quo, in order to shield the organization from disruptive changes (Haspeslagh and Jemison, 1991; Husted et al., 2005), as well as protecting individual positions and organizational identities (Buono and Bowditch, 1989).

Regarding knowledge dissemination, Husted et al. (2005) argue that individuals are more likely to use political tactics – such as hoarding knowledge – in the context of acquisitions, because of low levels of perceived psychological safety, and a fear of losing personal bargaining power, which reduces the source's individual disseminative capacity. In line with this, empirical studies have shown that fears of knowledge "exploitation" by members of the source firm can severely impede M&A knowledge transfer (Empson, 2001; Junni, 2011). This type of fear can be especially prevalent among individuals in the target firm, who often perceive that their status and relative standing are lowered after an acquisition (Hambrick and Cannella, 1993).

Taken together, power games and political behavior are likely to disrupt M&A knowledge transfer by reducing individual absorptive and

Table 5.2   Propositions

P1:	Knowledge complementarity will be *positively* associated with knowledge transfer.
P2:	Knowledge complementarity will be *positively* associated with operational integration.
P3:	Knowledge complementarity will be *positively* associated with individual absorptive and disseminative capacities (ACAP and DCAP).
P4:	Organizational ACAP and DCAP, consisting of collective and individual ACAP and DCAP, will be *positively* associated with knowledge transfer.
P5:	Operational integration will be *positively* associated with collective ACAP and DCAP.
P6:	Operational integration will be *positively* associated with cultural integration.
P7:	Operational integration will be *positively* associated with political behavior.
P8:	Cultural integration will be *positively* associated with collective ACAP and DCAP.
P9:	Cultural integration will be *negatively* associated with political behavior.
P10:	Political behavior will be *negatively* associated with individual ACAP and DCAP.

disseminative capacities; especially when the acquirer uses "hard" political tactics that create resentment and resistance in the target. Further, the individuals in the target firm may be especially reluctant to share their knowledge because of fears of losing their bargaining power vis-à-vis the acquirer.

We summarize our propositions in Table 5.2.

DYNAMICS BETWEEN THE VARIABLES

We have discussed how knowledge transfer is influenced by knowledge complementarity as well as organizational absorptive and disseminative capacities. More specifically, we argue that knowledge complementarity provides the basis within which acquisition partners aim to achieve synergies by transferring knowledge: the greater knowledge complementarities the greater potential there is for knowledge transfer. Further, we view organizational absorptive and disseminative capacities as consisting of individual and collective dimensions that together influence the effectiveness of knowledge transfer. While several studies have examined absorptive capacity, the recipient's ability and motivation to discard old knowledge ('unlearning') as an important component of absorptive capacity has received less attention. Also, the source's role in knowledge transfer – conceptualized as disseminative capacity – has not been applied to the M&A context.

Organizational absorptive capacity – individual and collective – relates to the recipient's ability and motivation to receive knowledge from the partner firm and let go of 'old' non-compatible knowledge. At the individual level of analysis we distinguish between ability and motivation to absorb knowledge. The recipient's ability to understand the source's knowledge and perceive it as valuable will influence the extent of receiving new knowledge (Simonin, 1999) and letting go of old knowledge (Tsang, 2008). The motivational dimension of the recipient's individual absorptive capacity in turn is related to whether the recipient views the source's knowledge as valuable and legitimate in its own context; if the source's knowledge is viewed as legitimate the recipient is more likely to be motivated to adopt it (Kostova and Roth, 2002). Similarly, discarding old knowledge requires that the recipient de-legitimizes its old practices, which can be difficult and time consuming (Yildiz and Fey, 2010). Collective absorptive capacity includes structural and cultural aspects of the organization that influences knowledge transfer by shaping the organizational framework to either encourage or constrain knowledge transfer (Bock et al., 2005; Zhao and Anand, 2009).

Disseminative capacity – individual and collective – refers to the source's ability and motivation to support the recipient in understanding and taking up its knowledge. The source's ability to teach and disseminate its knowledge influences the recipient's ability to absorb the source's knowledge (Zellmer-Bruhn, 2003). The source's ability to package and convey its knowledge, so that it fits with the recipient's existing context and is viewed as legitimate, also influences the recipient's motivation to absorb the source's knowledge (Kostova and Roth, 2002). Similarly, the source's ability to de-legitimize the recipient's knowledge will facilitate the discarding of old knowledge, which otherwise may hinder the recipient from effectively making use of the source's knowledge (Yildiz and Fey, 2010). Furthermore, collective disseminative capacity is likely to support knowledge transfer in two ways. First, an organizational structure that supports inter-unit task related communication increases organizational members' understanding of how to combine their individual knowledge, which supports their ability to teach it to recipient firm members (Zhao and Anand, 2009). Second, a cohesive organizational culture creates stronger informal social ties between organizational members and increases organizational members' motivation to share knowledge because of increased interpersonal trust and expectations of reciprocity (Empson, 2001; Husted et al., 2005).

Absorptive and disseminative capacities are in turn influenced by operational and cultural integration, as well as political behavior. First, we propose that operational integration will enhance the acquisition partners' collective absorptive and disseminative capacity by creating a 'collective structural platform' that enhances inter-firm coordination and creates operational ties between the acquisition partners (Birkinshaw et al., 2000). However, because restructuring can threaten the status quo of the merging firms, operational integration can give rise to political behavior (Jemison and Sitkin, 1986). More specifically, planned structural changes are likely to create a greater concern for the acquisition partners' own interests, which is likely to make them engage more readily in political behavior in order to protect or enhance their power base (Steensma and Van Milligen, 2003). Thus, we contend that operational integration increases the need for cultural integration, which aligns the acquisition partners' cultures and identities in order to create mutual understanding and respect (Birkinshaw et al., 2000) that overcome at least some of the negative effects of operational integration. Second, we propose that organizational cultural integration has a positive effect on collective absorptive and disseminative capacities by creating a "collective cultural platform" of shared values and norms (Schweiger et al., 1987), which increases the organization's ability to convey and absorb complex and culturally embedded knowledge. In addition, when the acquisition partners share an organizational culture, they are likely to be more motivated to share and absorb knowledge due to reduced fears of "contamination" and "exploitation" (Empson, 2001). Furthermore, the alignment of the acquisition partners' cultures through cultural integration mechanisms, such as cultural awareness seminars or informal gatherings, enhances informal communication between the acquisition partners and strengthens their inter-unit social ties, and is thus likely to increase their motivation to collaborate (Jansen et al., 2005; Schweiger and Goulet, 2005) and engage in knowledge transfer. Third, we suggest that political behavior on part of the organizational members, which aims to increase or defend their existing power bases (Mayes and Allen, 1977; Farrell and Petersen, 1982), undermines individual aspects of absorptive and disseminative capacities by reducing motivation to depart from own knowledge as well as make use of the partner's knowledge (Husted et al., 2005; Vaara et al., 2003). Regarding individual absorptive capacity, the recipient will be less reluctant to take up the source's knowledge, if it fears that it will be "contaminated" by the source (Empson, 2001) or (s)he fears that knowledge absorption will cause disruptive changes to existing social ties and power structures (Husted et al., 2005). Concerning disseminative capacity, individuals may fear losing personal bargaining power from "giving away" their knowledge, without receiving anything valuable in return (Empson, 2001; Husted et al., 2005).

CONCLUSION

In this chapter we set out to explore key mechanisms of knowledge transfer in M&A. We concentrated on the dynamic relationships between variables that influence knowledge transfer, highlighting aspects that have not received adequate attention in previous research. We argued that knowledge complementarity, as well as organizational absorptive and disseminative capacities are central in explaining M&A knowledge transfer. While previous studies have mainly focused on the effects of absorptive capacity at the individual level (Gupta and Govindarajan, 2000; Minbaeva et al., 2003; Simonin, 1999; Szulanski, 1996) we suggest that it is necessary to consider the effects of both individual and collective absorptive capacities (Zhao and Anand, 2009), as well as individual (Minbaeva, 2007) and collective disseminative capacities.

Several M&A studies have examined the influence of operational and cultural integration on performance in general (for a review of operational integration see for example Zollo and Meier, 2008, and for cultural integration see Stahl and Voigt, 2008) and on knowledge transfer in particular (for example Björkman et al., 2007; Ranft and Lord, 2002; Vaara et al., 2010). However, the relationship between these integration processes and absorptive and disseminative capacities remains less explored. We suggested that operational and cultural integration increase collective absorptive and disseminative capacities by creating a collective "structural platform" and "cultural platform" that increase the acquisition partners' ability and motivation to disseminate and absorb knowledge respectively.

Finally, we proposed that operational integration can indirectly reduce individual absorptive and disseminative capacities by increasing political behavior (Steensma and Van Milligen, 2003), which decreases organizational members' motivation to share and absorb knowledge. More specifically, operational integration is likely to lead to the politicization of integration issues and create organizational resistance (Jemison and Sitkin, 1986), which reduces individual absorptive and disseminative capacities by increasing fears of "contamination" and "exploitation" reported in the previous literature (Empson, 2001; Simonin, 1999; Szulanski, 1996).

Our contribution is two-fold. First, we integrate novelties from knowledge transfer research in other contexts to the specific context of M&A. A key aspect here is the specification of not only absorptive capacity but also disseminative capacity as main mechanisms of knowledge transfer in M&A. Also, distinguishing between different levels of absorptive and disseminative capacities in terms of the individual/collective and ability/motivation dimensions provides further depth for these concepts. Integrating these essential mechanisms enriches discussions and understanding on knowledge transfer in M&A. Instead of linking factors directly to knowledge transfer, our model recognizes knowledge transfer in M&A as a process that depends on the individual and collective capabilities, which has been called for in previous research (Haleblian et al., 2009).

Second, we highlight special complexities of the knowledge transfer process in the context of M&A integration. This is done by including socio-political factors that are likely to play a particularly important role in M&A. Operational post-acquisition changes are likely to pose a threat to the acquisition partners' existing structures (Steensma and Van Milligen, 2003), which increases the likelihood of politicization of integration decisions. Also, because M&A involve a high level of uncertainty about future outcomes (Steensma and Van Milligen, 2003), it can be expected that power games and political behavior have an especially disruptive effect on M&A knowledge transfer. Thus operational integration increases the need for cultural integration that creates a more positive atmosphere between the acquisition partners (Birkinshaw et al., 2000), in order to reduce the likelihood of disruptive political behavior that can result from ingroup-outgroup categorizations of culturally separate groups (Lipponen et al., 2004; Terry and O'Brien, 2001). Thus M&A represent a unique situation of strategic and social integration processes mixed in with political behavior, the effects of which have not yet been explored on knowledge transfer processes in the more general literature on knowledge transfer.

While we aimed to provide an integrative model on knowledge transfer in M&A, there are several aspects that could be developed in the future. It is crucial to keep integrating developments of the more general knowledge transfer literature (such as disseminative capacity) to our models of knowledge transfer in M&A. This assures that the most current knowledge is integrated in the M&A studies, ensures consistent terminology and methodology across knowledge transfer studies, and enables comparisons of knowledge transfer in different contexts. At the same time, researchers need to be aware of the specifics of the M&A integration process related to, in particular, the strategic and socio-political dynamics of post-acquisition integration. This means acknowledging the vital role of knowledge complementarity – which increases the need for operational integration, but also requires cultural integration in order to increase acquisition partners' motivation to engage in knowledge transfer, whilst undertaking efforts to structurally integrate the two previously separate firms. Here the key is to integrate advancements in the strategic and socio-cultural aspects of M&A to the context of knowledge transfer. The message we want to send is that knowledge transfer is ultimately about knowledge transfer potential and people, which makes it crucial to focus on understanding the complex interactions between the members of the acquiring and target firms in M&A.

Future studies should also address the limitations of our model. We have focused in this chapter on how operational and cultural integration, as well as political behavior build or undermine organizational absorptive and disseminative capacities, which in turn influence M&A knowledge transfer. We want to point out, however, that these variables are not static, but dynamic, and thus can influence each other in the "opposite direction" as well. For example, while organizational absorptive and disseminative capacities facilitate knowledge transfer (for example, Minbaeva et al., 2003; Minbaeva, 2007; Zhao and Anand, 2009), knowledge transfer also influences subsequent organizational absorptive and disseminative capacities. Once the recipient accepts the source's knowledge as "legitimate" and begins using it as part of its routines and processes, the knowledge becomes institutionalized (Kostova and Roth, 2002) and embedded within the recipient's organization structure, processes and culture. This in turn influences the conditions for future knowledge transfer endeavors by giving rise to different types of organizational behavior (Bock et al., 2005; Fiol and Lyles, 1985). Thus, an important topic for future research would concern the possibly reverse relationships between the constructs identified in our model, as well as the long term consequences of processes such as operational and cultural integration.

Similarly, our model primarily included mediating effects in order to illustrate the interrelatedness of the variables. Further examination is required, however, to establish the complex nature of the relationships. One should look further into whether some of the variables could actually be moderators (Kane, 2010) and whether we could find not only linear relationships, but also curvilinear ones (Ahuja and Katila, 2001).

In addition, whilst we focused on the negative aspects of power and politics "neutral" or "softer" political tactics such as consultation, inspirational appeals, rational persuasion and negotiation (Steensma and Van Milligen, 2003) could contribute to creating a better relationship between the acquisition partners and increase their motivation to share knowledge. Thus we consider another fruitful area for future research the examination of the use of political tactics on the micro-level, in order to increase our understanding of how "hard"/"neutral"/"soft" political tactics influence M&A knowledge transfer.

Furthermore, the role of managerial interventions requires further specification. While we focused on the role of operational and cultural integration in value creation, it is important to distinguish the exact managerial actions that contribute to these processes. For instance, future human resource oriented studies could outline the HR practices most conducive for achieving operational and/or cultural integration, and how these practices should be adjusted to reflect different strategic and cultural contexts (Hunt and Downing, 1990; Schuler and Jackson, 2001).

As a final point, although we have outlined a "process model" of M&A knowledge transfer, future research could go further in processual analysis. Our model is a variance model as it tries to explain why certain variables influence others (Van de Ven, 1992). Future analyses could build on the emerging process studies approach (Hernes and Maitlis, 2010; Langley, 2004; Van de Ven and Poole, 1995) and for example focus on the dialectical or dialogical processes in knowledge transfer. Some studies have already examined the *dynamics* of post-merger integration (Clark et al., 2010; Graebner, 2004; Vaara and Monin, 2010; Vaara and Tienari, 2011), but not in the case of knowledge transfer. Among other things, such analyses could elucidate the way in which previous actions and phases impact future ones – including emerging problems and opportunities and unintended consequences.

REFERENCES

Ahuja, G. and Katila, R. (2001). 'Technological acquisitions and the innovation performance of acquiring firms: a longitudinal study'. *Strategic Management Journal*, 22: 197–220.
Baldwin, T., Magjuka, R.J. and Loher, B.T. (1991). 'The perils of participation: effects of choice of training on trainee motivation and learning'. *Personnel Psychology*, 44: 51–65.
Birkinshaw, J., Bresman, H. and Håkanson, L. (2000). 'Managing the post-acquisition integration process: how the human integration and task integration processes interact to foster value creation'. *Journal of Management Studies*, 37: 395–425.
Björkman, I., Barner-Rasmussen, W. and Li, L. (2004). 'Managing knowledge transfer in MNCs: the impact of headquarters control mechanisms'. *Journal of International Business Studies*, 35: 443–456.
Björkman, I., Stahl, G.K. and Vaara, E. (2007). 'Cultural differences and capability transfer in cross-border acquisitions: the mediating roles of capability complementarity, absorptive capacity, and social integration'. *Journal of International Business Studies*, 38: 658–672.
Blackler, F. (1995). 'Knowledge, knowledge work and organisations: an overview and interpretation'. *Organisation Studies*, 16: 1021–1046.
Bock, G.W., Zmud, R.W., Kim, Y.G. and Lee, J.N. (2005). 'Behavioral intention formation in knowledge sharing: examining the roles of extrinsic motivators, social-psychological factors, and organizational climate'. *MIS Quarterly*, 29: 87–111.
Boisot, M. and Canals, A. (2004). 'Data, information and knowledge: have we got it right?' *Journal of Evolutionary Economics*, 14: 43–67.
Bresman, H., Birkinshaw, J. and Nobel, R. (1999). 'Knowledge transfer in international acquisitions'. *Journal of International Business Studies*, 30: 439–463.
Bröchner, J., Rosander, S. and Waara, F. (2004). 'Cross-border post-acquisition knowledge transfer among construction consultants'. *Construction Management and Economics*, 22: 421–427.

Buono, A.F. and Bowditch, J.L. (1989). *The Human Side of Mergers and Acquisitions: Managing Collisions between People, Cultures, and Organizations*. San Francisco, CA: Jossey-Bass.

Cabrera, E. and Cabrera, A. (2005). 'Fostering knowledge sharing through people management practices'. *International Journal of Human Resource Management*, 16: 720–735.

Cabrera, Á., Collins, W.C. and Salgado, J.F. (2006). 'Determinants of individual engagement in knowledge sharing'. *International Journal of Human Resource Management*, 17: 245–264.

Capron, L., Dussauge, P. and Mitchell, W. (1998). 'Resource redeployment following horizontal acquisitions in Europe and North America, 1988–1992'. *Strategic Management Journal*, 19: 631–661.

Capron, L. (1999). 'The long-term performance of horizontal acquisitions'. *Strategic Management Journal*, 20: 987–1018.

Capron, L., Mitchell, W. and Swaminathan, A. (2001). 'Asset divestiture following horizontal acquisitions: a dynamic view'. *Strategic Management Journal*, 22: 817–844.

Capron, L. and Pistre, N. (2002). 'When do acquirers earn abnormal returns?' *Strategic Management Journal*, 23: 781–794.

Cartwright, S. and Cooper, C.L. (1990). 'The impact of mergers and acquisitions on people at work: existing research and issues'. *British Journal of Management*, 1: 65–76.

Castro, C. and Neira, E. (2005). 'Knowledge transfer: analysis of three internet acquisitions'. *International Journal of Human Resource Management*, 16: 120–135.

Clark, S.M., Gioia, D.A., Ketchen, D.J. and Thomas, J.B. (2010). 'Transitional identity as a facilitator of organizational identity change during a merger'. *Administrative Science Quarterly*, **55** (3): 397–438.

Cohen, W.M. and Levinthal, D.A. (1990). 'Absorptive capacity: a new perspective on learning and innovation'. *Administrative Science Quarterly*, 35: 128–152.

Crossan, M.M., Lane H.W. and White, R.E. (1999). 'An organizational learning framework: from intuition to institution'. *Academy of Management Review*, 2: 522–537.

Daft, R.L. and Lengel, R.H. (1986). 'Organizational information requirements, media richness and structural design'. *Management Science*, 32: 554–571.

Empson, L. (2001). 'Fear of exploitation and fear of contamination: impediments to knowledge transfer in mergers between professional service firms'. *Human Relations*, 54: 839–863.

Eschen, E. and Bresser, R. (2005). 'Closing resource gaps: toward a resource-based theory of advantageous mergers and acquisitions'. *European Management Review*, 2: 167–178.

Evans, V., Pucik, V. and Björkman, I. (2011). *The Global Challenge: International Human Resource Management* (2nd edition). New York: McGraw-Hill.

Farrell, D. and Petersen, J.C. (1982). 'Patterns of political behavior in organization'. *Academy of Management Review*, 7: 403–412.

Fiol, M.C. and Lyles, M. (1985). 'Organizational learning'. *Academy of Management Review*, 10: 803–813.

Foss, N.J. and Pedersen, T. (2002). 'Transferring knowledge in MNCs: the role of sources of subsidiary knowledge and organizational context'. *Journal of International Management*, 8: 49–67.

Graebner, M.E. (2004). 'Momentum and serendipity: how acquired leaders create value in the integration of technology firms'. *Strategic Management Journal*, 25: 751–777.

Gupta A.K. and Govindarajan, V. (2000). 'Knowledge flows within multinational corporations'. *Strategic Management Journal*, 21: 473–496.

Haleblian, J., Devers, C.E., McNamara, G., Carpenter, M.A. and Davidson, R.B. (2009). 'Taking stock of what we know about mergers and acquisitions: a review and research agenda'. *Journal of Management*, 35: 469–502.

Hambrick, D.C. and Cannella A.A. (1993). 'Relative standing: a framework for understanding departures of acquired executives'. *Academy of Management Journal*, 36: 733–762.

Hamel, G. (1991). 'Competition for competence and interpartner learning within international strategic alliances'. *Strategic Management Journal*, 12: 83–103.
Harding, D. and Rouse, T. (2007). 'Human due diligence'. *Harvard Business Review*, 85: 124–131.
Haspeslagh, P. and Jemison, D.B. (1991). *Managing Acquisitions: Creating Value through Corporate Renewal*. New York: The Free Press.
Hedberg, B. (1981). *How Organizations Learn and Unlearn*. New York: Oxford University Press.
Hedlund, G. (1994). 'A model of knowledge management and the N-form corporation'. *Strategic Management Journal*, 15: 73–90.
Hernes, T. and Maitlis, S. 2010. *Process, Sensemaking and Organizing*. Oxford: Oxford University Press.
Hickson, D.J., Hinings, C.R., Lee, C.A., Schneck, R.E. and Pennings, J.M. (1971). 'A strategic contingencies' theory of intraorganizational power'. *Administrative Science Quarterly*, 16: 216–229.
Hunt, W. and Downing, S. (1990). 'Mergers, acquisitions and human resource management'. *International Journal of Human Resource Management*, 8: 213–225.
Husted, K. and Michailova, S. (2002). 'Diagnosing and fighting knowledge-sharing hostility'. *Organizational Dynamics*, 31: 60–73.
Husted, K., Gammelgaard, J. and Michailova, S. (2005). 'Knowledge-sharing behaviour and post-acquisition integration failure'. In A.F. Buono and F. Poulfelt (eds), *Challenges and Issues in Knowledge Management*. Charlotte, NC: Information Age Publishing, pp. 209–226.
Jansen, J.J.P., Van den Bosch, F.A.J and Volberda, H.W. (2005). 'Managing potential and realized absorptive capacity: how do organizational antecedents matter?' *Academy of Management Journal*, 48: 999–1015.
Jemison, D.B. and Sitkin, S.B. (1986). 'Corporate acquisitions: a process perspective'. *Academy of Management Review*, 11: 145–163.
Junni, P. (2011). 'Knowledge transfer in acquisitions: fear of exploitation and contamination'. *Scandinavian Journal of Management*, 27: 307–321.
Junni, P. and Sarala, R.M. (2011). 'Causal ambiguity, cultural integration and partner attractiveness as determinants of knowledge transfer: evidence from Finnish acquisitions'. *European Journal of International Management*, 5: 346–372.
Kane, A.A. (2010). 'Unlocking knowledge transfer potential: knowledge demonstrability and superordinate social identity'. *Organization Science*, 21: 643–660.
Kayworth, T. and Leidner, D. (2004). 'Organizational culture as a knowledge resource'. In C.W. Holsapper (ed.), *Handbook on Knowledge Management. Volume 1: Knowledge Matters*. Berlin: Springer Verlag, pp. 235–252.
Khoja, F. and Maranville, S. (2010). 'How do firms nurture absorptive capacity?' *Journal of Managerial Issues*, 22: 262–278.
King, D.R., Dalton, D.R., Daily, C.M. and Covin, J.G. (2004). 'Meta-analyses of post-acquisition performance: indications of unidentified moderators'. *Strategic Management Journal*, 25: 187–200.
Kogut, B. and Zander, U. (1993). 'Knowledge of the firm and the evolutionary theory of the multinational corporation'. *Journal of International Business Studies*, 24: 625–645.
Kostova, T. and Roth, K. (2002). 'Adoption of organizational practice by subsidiaries of multinational corporations: institutional and relational effects'. *Academy of Management Journal*, 45: 215–233.
Lam, A. (1997). 'Embedded firms, embedded knowledge: problems of collaboration and knowledge transfer global cooperative ventures'. *Organization Studies*, 18: 973–996.
Lane, P. and Lubatkin, M. (1998). 'Relative absorptive capacity and interorganizational learning'. *Strategic Management Journal*, 19: 461–477.
Langley, A. (2004). 'Qualitative researching'. *Organizational Research Methods*, **7** (3): 354–356.

Larsson, R. and Finkelstein, S. (1999). 'Integrating strategic, organizational, and human resource perspectives on mergers and acquisitions: a case survey of synergy realization'. *Organization Science*, 10: 1–27.

Lipponen, J., Olkkonen, M-E. and Moilanen, M. (2004). 'Perceived procedural justice and employee responses to an organizational merger'. *European Journal of Work and Organizational Psychology*, 13: 391–413.

Mayer, R.C., Davis, J.H. and Schoorman, F.D. (1995). 'An integrative model of organizational trust'. *Academy of Management Review*, 20: 709–734.

Mayes, B.T. and Allen, R.W. (1977). 'Toward a definition of organizational politics'. *Academy of Management Review*, 2: 672–678.

Minbaeva, D. (2007). 'Knowledge transfer in multinational corporations'. *Management International Review*, 47: 567–593.

Minbaeva, D., Pedersen, T., Björkman, I., Fey, C.F. and Park, H.J. (2003). 'MNC knowledge transfer, subsidiary absorptive capacity, and HRM'. *Journal of International Business Studies*, 34: 586–599.

Mintzberg, H. (1985). 'The organization as a political arena'. *Journal of Management Studies*, 22: 133–154.

Morosini, P., Shane, S. and Singh, H. (1998). 'National cultural distance and cross-border acquisition performance'. *Journal of International Business Studies*, 29: 137–158.

Nahavandi, A. and Malekzadeh, A.R. (1988). 'Acculturation in mergers and acquisitions'. *Academy of Management Review*, 13: 79–90.

Nohria, N. and Ghoshal, S. (1994). 'Differentiated fit and shared values: alternatives for managing headquarters-subsidiary relations'. *Strategic Management Journal*, 15: 491–502.

Nonaka, I. and Takeuchi, H. (1995). *The Knowledge Creating Company: How Japanese Companies Create the Dynamics of Innovation*. New York, Oxford University Press.

Pablo, A. (1994). 'Determinants of acquisition integration level: a decision-making perspective'. *Academy of Management Journal*, 37: 803–836.

Pinder, C.C. (1998). *Work Motivation in Organizational Behavior*. Upper Saddle River, NJ: Prentice-Hall.

Ranft, A.L. and Lord, M.D. (2000). 'Acquiring new knowledge: the role of retaining human capital in acquisitions of high-tech firms'. *Journal of High Technology Management Research*, 11: 295–319.

Ranft, A.L. and Lord, M.D. (2002). 'Acquiring new technologies and capabilities: a grounded model of acquisition implementation'. *Organization Science*, 13: 420–441.

Salancik, G.R. and Pfeffer, J. (1974). 'The bases and use of power in organizational decision making: the case of a university'. *Administrative Science Quarterly*, 19: 453–473.

Sarala, R.M. and Vaara, E. (2010). 'Cultural differences, convergence, and crossvergence as explanations of knowledge transfer in international acquisitions'. *Journal of International Business Studies*, 41: 1365–1390.

Schoenberg, R. (2001). 'Knowledge transfer and resource sharing as value creation mechanisms in inbound continental European acquisitions'. *Journal of Euromarketing*, 10: 99–114.

Schuler, R.S. and Jackson, S.E. (2001). 'HR issues and activities in mergers and acquisitions'. *European Management Journal*, 19: 59–75.

Schulz, M. (2001). 'The uncertain relevance of newness: organizational learning and knowledge flows'. *Academy of Management Journal*, 44: 661–681.

Schweiger, D.M. and Goulet, P.K. (2005). 'Facilitating acquisition integration through deep-level cultural learning interventions: a longitudinal field experiment'. *Organization Studies*, 26: 1477–1499.

Schweiger, D.M., Ivancevich, J.M. and Power, F.R. (1987). 'Executive actions for managing human resources before and after acquisition'. *Academy of Management Executive*, 1: 127–138.

Schweizer, L. (2005). 'Knowledge transfer and R&D in pharmaceutical companies: a case study'. *Journal of Engineering and Technology Management*, 22: 315–331.

Shrivastava, P. (1986). 'Postmerger integration'. *Journal of Business Strategy*, 7: 65–76.

Simonin, B. (1999). 'Ambiguity and the process of knowledge transfer in strategic alliances'. *Strategic Management Journal*, 20: 595–623.

Simonin, B. (2004). 'An empirical investigation of the process of knowledge transfer in international strategic alliances'. *Journal of International Business Studies*, 35: 407–427.

Stahl, G.K. and Voigt, A. (2008). 'Do cultural differences matter in mergers and acquisitions? A tentative model for examination'. *Organization Science*, 19: 160–176.

Steensma, H. and Van Milligen, F. (2003). 'Bases of power, procedural justice outcomes of mergers: the push and pull factors of influence tactics'. *Journal of Collective Negotiations*, 30: 113–134.

Szulanski, G. (1996). 'Exploring internal stickiness: impediments to the transfer of best practice within the firm'. *Strategic Management Journal*, 17: 27–43.

Terry, D.J. and O'Brien, A.T. (2001). 'Status, legitimacy, and ingroup bias in the context of an organizational merger'. *Group Processes Intergroup Relations*, 4: 271–289.

Trautwein, F. (1990). 'Merger motives and merger prescriptions'. *Strategic Management Journal*, 11: 283–295.

Tsang, E.W.K. (2008). 'Transferring knowledge to acquisition joint ventures: an organizational unlearning perspective'. *Management Learning*, **39** (1): 5–20.

Tsang, E.W.K. and Zahra, S. (2008). 'Organizational unlearning'. *Human Relations*, 61: 1435–1462.

Vaara, E. (2003). 'Post-acquisition integration as sensemaking: glimpses of ambiguity, confusion, hypocrisy, and politicization'. *Journal of Management Studies*, 40: 859–894.

Vaara, E. and Monin, P. (2010). 'A recursive perspective on discursive legitimation and organizational action in mergers and acquisitions'. *Organization Science*, 21: 3–22.

Vaara, E. and Tienari, J. (2011). 'On the narrative construction of MNCs: an antenarrative analysis of legitimation and resistance in a cross-border merger'. *Organization Science*, 22: 370–390.

Vaara, E., Tienari, J. and Björkman, I. (2003). 'Best practice is West practice? A sensemaking perspective on knowledge transfer'. In A-M. Søderberg and E. Vaara (eds) *Merging Across Borders*. Denmark: Copenhagen Business School Press, pp. 111–138.

Van de Ven, A.H. (1992). 'Suggestions for studying strategy process: a research note'. *Strategic Management Journal*, 13: 169–191.

Van de Ven, A.H. and Poole, M.S. (1995). 'Explaining development and change in organizations'. *Academy of Management Review*, **20** (3): 510–540.

Van den Bosch, F.A.J., Volberda, H.W. and de Boer, M. (1999). 'Coevolution of firm absorptive capacity and knowledge environment: organizational forms and combinative capabilities'. *Organization Science*, 10: 551–568.

Van Wijk, R., Jansen, J.J.P. and Lyles, M.A. (2008). 'Inter- and intra-organizational knowledge transfer: a meta-analytic review and assessment of its antecedents and consequences'. *Journal of Management Studies*, 45: 830–853.

Vermeulen, F. and Barkema, H. (2001). 'Learning through acquisitions'. *Academy of Management Journal*, 44: 457–476.

Vroom, V. (1964). *Work and Motivation*. New York, London and Sydney: John Wiley and Sons.

Westphal, T. and Shaw, V. (2005). 'Knowledge transfers in acquisitions – an exploratory study and model'. *Management International Review*, 45: 75–100.

Winter, S.G. (1987). 'Knowledge and competence as strategic assets'. In D. Teece (ed.) *The Competitive Challenge: Strategies for Industrial Innovation and Renewal.* Cambridge, MA: Ballinger, pp. 159–184.

Yildiz, H.E. and Fey, C.F. (2010). 'Compatibility and unlearning in knowledge transfer in mergers and acquisitions'. *Scandinavian Journal of Management*, 26: 448–456.

Zander, U. and Kogut, B. (1995). 'Knowledge and the speed of the transfer and imitation of organizational capabilities: an empirical test'. *Organization Science*, 6: 76–92.

Zellmer-Bruhn, M.E. (2003). 'Interruptive events and team knowledge acquisition'. *Management Science*, 49: 514–528.

Zhao, Z.J. and Anand, J. (2009). 'A multilevel perspective on knowledge transfer: evidence from the Chinese automotive industry'. *Strategic Management Journal*, 30: 959–983.

Zollo, M. and Meier, D. (2008). 'What is M&A performance?' *Academy of Management Perspectives*, 22: 55–77.

Zou, H. and Ghauri, P.N. (2008). 'Learning through international acquisitions: the process of knowledge acquisition in China'. *Management International Review*, 48: 207–226.

PART III

METHODOLOGICAL ISSUES IN M&A RESEARCH

6 Merger and acquisition outcomes – is it meaningful to talk about high failure rates?

Annette Risberg and Olimpia Meglio

INTRODUCTION

> Most mergers fail. Though this reality is uncomfortable, it is an indisputable fact. By whatever measure you choose – stock price, revenues, earnings, return on equity – most deals fall short of expectations. (Booz-Allen and Hamilton, 2001: 1)

The above statement well synthesizes the conventional discourse about mergers and acquisitions: they experience high failure rates. This view represents an enduring issue for merger and acquisition scholars ever since Kitching, as early as 1967, aimed at answering the question of why mergers and acquisitions miscarry. One finds claims of up to 50 percent merger and acquisition failure rates in academic studies (for example, Buckley and Ghauri, 2002; Cartwright, 1998, Hubbard, 1999; Hunt, 1990; Shrivastava, 1986); the same finding appears in more practitioner-oriented literature (Habeck et al., 2000).

Where do these numbers come from? Is this claim a fact or simply a taken-for-granted statement regarding mergers and acquisitions? The impressive number of studies offering numerical data on poor-performing mergers and acquisitions would imply that the statement is a fact. However, a deeper analysis of this literature shows that frequently the academic scholars making these claims are not actually conducting empirical studies on merger and acquisition performance. Rather their statements about failure seem to be a means of justifying the study at hand – studies which are generally not about performance or outcome but about other issues connected to merger and acquisition processes (for example, Appelbaum et al., 2000b; Appelbaum et al., 2000a; Bourantas and Nicandrou, 1998; Cartwright and Cooper, 1995; Child et al., 2001; DiGeorgio, 2002; Marks and Mirvis, 2001; Panchal and Cartwright, 2001; Very and Schweiger, 2001) (see Risberg, 2012, for further discussion).

However, that so many scholars justify their studies by arguing that many mergers and acquisitions fail signals a great interest in understanding how mergers and acquisitions perform, and what the variables are that may affect merger and acquisition performance. This interest is, to some extent, imported from the field of financial studies, which has long been concerned with the analysis of merger and acquisition performance. Large sample studies, generally employing an event study methodology, show that the target's shareholders earn abnormal returns, but no significant gain accrues to the acquirer's shareholders (Agrawal et al., 1992; Jarrell et al., 1988; Jensen and Ruback, 1983; Franks et al., 1991; Loderer and Martin, 1992; Mulherin and Boone, 2000). Therefore, merger and acquisition scholars have long been interested in the analysis of merger and acquisition performance from the acquiring firm's perspective, aiming to explain how mergers and acquisitions perform.

The frequent claims about failure in merger and acquisition literature led us to further investigate what the actual outcomes of mergers and acquisitions are. The aim of the chapter is to scrutinize studies about merger and acquisition success or failure. It also aims to bring to light that it is impossible in the research agenda to compare research that measures different variables. We do so through a selected review of literature on merger and acquisition performance. Our method differs from previous studies as our review is not another meta-analysis that attempts to cumulate existing research findings (Datta et al., 1992; King et al., 2004). It is instead a literature review with findings presented in narrative form (compare Huff, 2008). We decided to look into what conclusions the authors of a performance study made regarding merger and acquisition success or failure. This meant that we did not have to interpret the numbers from the study because the meaning of success or failure in this context is ambiguous. We chose this method as we believe it allows us to offer a more nuanced and informative account of merger and acquisition performance research. Based on our review, we describe in this chapter the average merger and acquisition outcomes found in the literature (positive or negative), what type of merger and acquisition the literature depicts to perform best, and what variables merger and acquisition scholars have employed so far to explain merger and acquisition performance. By doing so, by breaking the research findings down into different categories, we show how few studies are made using the same type of measures, and how meaningless, if not misleading, it is to then compare the results in an attempt to make any claims about merger and acquisition performance in general.

The remainder of the chapter is structured as follows. In the next section we describe the study method, and then we present and discuss our findings. In the concluding section we suggest how merger and acquisition scholars may move forward.

METHOD

The Sample

As specified above, our study is a literature review. In order to identify the sample of articles, we employed a multi-stage approach. The sample is the result of literature searches at two different points in time. The first one was carried out by the first author of this chapter in 2003 and was aimed at selecting articles dealing with failure or success in mergers and acquisitions. The second search was carried out by both authors in 2008 with the aim of identifying articles dealing with measuring merger and acquisition performance.

First stage: range of journals to include in the sample

We decided to limit our search to mainly management and organization journals. The decision of this disciplinary focus is driven by the awareness that management and organizational studies and financial studies regard mergers and acquisitions in rather different manners. For finance scholars, mergers and acquisitions are homogeneous and instantaneous events, while management scholars acknowledge that they are not alike and conceive of them as processes.

Among management and organization journals, we decided to search those journals that are defined as top-tier according to the Thomson ISI Journal Citation Report as they report the cutting edge research and set the standards in this field. We therefore searched in the following journals: *Academy of Management Journal* (AMJ), *Administrative Science Quarterly* (ASQ), *British Journal of Management* (BJM), *Human Relations* (HR), *Journal of Management* (JM), *Journal of Management Studies* (JMS), *Strategic Management Journal* (SMJ), *Organization Science* (OSc) and *Organization Studies* (OSt).

Second stage: search criteria and time frame

We made a Boolean search, using the keywords merger *or* acquisition and failure *or* success or merger *or* acquisitions *and* performance in each journal database. The time span for our article search covers almost two decades, from 1980 to 2008.

Third stage: criteria for inclusion in the sample

We decided to include empirical articles measuring post-acquisition performance in terms of market-based, accounting-based, or mixed performance. This includes actual market and accounting measures as well managers' and other experts' assessments or perceptions of them. In this way, we consider accounting- and market-based measures being regarded as either objective or as perceptual measures. We are well aware that merger and acquisition performance can be defined as a broader construct and that a multitude of measuring methods can be found in the literature. In a systematic narrative literature review, the authors of this chapter (compare Meglio and Risberg, 2011b) elicited the multitude of meanings attached to the label "merger and acquisition performance". From this review it emerges that merger and acquisition scholars measure different things in different settings, using broad or narrow definitions, relying on a wide array of indicators, each reflecting different time scales and units of analysis. In some instances, merger and acquisition performance is conceptualized as financial performance, generally measured through a market-based indicator, such as CAR, generally a few days after the deal is announced (for example, Hopkins, 1987). In other instances, scholars give the merger and acquisition performance a broader meaning, including, for example, survival measures (for example, Schweizer, 2005). While we acknowledge that an analysis of merger and acquisition performance should do justice to the array of outcomes a merger or an acquisition could pursue, we have, however, decided to narrow the focus of our analysis to the most used ways of measuring merger and acquisition performance. The reason for focusing on market- and accounting-based measures, objective or perceptual, is based on the notion of high failure rates mentioned in the start of this chapter. If one talks about failure or success rates for mergers and acquisitions in general, one probably does think about shareholder returns or market or sales growth and such types of measures. That is why we have excluded studies mainly defining performance in terms of, for example, top management turnover, innovation, R&D outcome, patents, knowledge transfer, or risk avoidance. Variables that are not purely market- or accounting-based are, however, still represented to some extent in our analysis as some studies mainly using accounting and market-based metrics also include other types of metrics.

Articles discussing merger and acquisition performance or success without measuring them were not included in the sample, and neither were research notes, as they rarely present empirical findings. Based on the above criteria, we first read, checked the adherence to the selection criteria, and discussed which articles to include and take out until we reached complete agreement. This produced a final sample of 55 articles. Compared to earlier meta-analyses made, the number of articles seems to be representative. King et al. (2004) analyzed 93 articles, and Datta et al. (1992) analyzed 41 articles.

The Categorization of Empirical Studies

All articles were read and registered in an Excel spreadsheet and coded according to the following categories: types of mergers and acquisitions under investigation, the research focus, the research method, the definition of performance used in the article, metrics used to measure performance, the perspective accounted for when measuring performance, and the research findings. We have reported the findings that the authors point out in a result or discussion section as we wanted to avoid making interpretations that the authors of the articles had not made themselves.

The outcome of our analysis is the categorization of articles according to type of measure of performance and what has been measured. As indicated above, we have chosen to focus our analysis on market-, accounting-, perception-based, or mixed measures of merger and acquisition performance. By market-based measures we refer to measures of performance that reflect the market value of the company, and they are, accordingly, available for public companies only. Accounting-based measures are those that rely upon the financial information reported in income statements, balance sheets, and statements of cash-flows. While the former measures look forward as they estimate how the company will perform from the financial market's standpoint, the latter measures are backward-looking as they are based on historical as well as internal figures from the company accounting system (see Carton and Hofer, 2006; Corvellec, 1997). In our review we have also included mixed measures. By mixed measures we mean those that rely on multiple measures, which may be accounting-, market-based measures, or operational measures.

Within each category we further categorize measures as objective or as perceptual. An objective measure remains constant no matter what measurement instrument is used or who is doing the measurement. A perceptual measure, on the other hand, is one that may change according to who is asked, what instrument is used, and when one is asked.

Finally we would like to note that for each type of measure, we found a huge number of different metrics used to operationalize the merger and acquisition performance. Among market-based measures, CAR is probably the most frequently used, while ROA dominates among the accounting-based measures, but we could easily claim that the variables and the metrics are as many as the studies under review (compare Meglio and Risberg, 2011b).

In the following section we will provide the result of the review, discussing what research has to say about failure and success in mergers and acquisitions. In presenting our findings, we will also account for the different ways merger and acquisition scholars measure performance and what factors they have found to affect the merger and acquisition performance.

FINDINGS

Before presenting the figures from our review, we would like to draw our readers' attention to two issues that will help us interpret and make sense of the figures we have found in merger and acquisition empirical research. These issues regard how the labels "mergers and acquisitions" as well as "merger and acquisition performance" are used within the merger and acquisition literature.

What Do Merger and Acquisition Scholars Actually Investigate?

The first issue concerns the great variety of mergers and acquisitions under investigation that are nonetheless referred to as mergers and acquisitions as a unitary phenomenon, as the two terms are generally used interchangeably. The idea that there is no major difference between mergers and acquisitions was put forward by Haspeslagh and Jemison (1991) when they contended that a distinction between the two categories is not relevant when discussing the implications of mergers and acquisitions on the organizations involved. Mergers and acquisitions both produce, at different paces and levels, turmoil and integration problems once the deal is completed.

Although this idea is commonplace, not everybody agrees with it. Epstein (2004), for example, claims that it is important to make a distinction between mergers and acquisitions. He defines mergers of equals as deals involving two entities of relatively equal stature coming together and taking the best of each company. An acquisition involves a much easier process of fitting one smaller company into the existing acquiring firm. While this distinction may appear sound, we would like to point out that it could be difficult to assess when two entities are of equal stature. Other suggestions in line with Epstein's have been put forward focusing on how to define a merger. For example, Søderberg and Vaara (2003) define the merger as the deal in which neither party prevails. In line with this, Piekkari et al. (2005) argue that the term "merger of equals" is used for political reasons to mean that there is no party prevailing over the other. Vaara and Tienari (2003) note that it is difficult to achieve a balance of power between parties, and we would add that it is also difficult to maintain such a balance throughout the integration process. Teerikangas and

Very (2006) propose to distinguish mergers from acquisitions by focusing attention on the percentage of controlling interest – which is more than 50 percent in an acquisition – regardless of the sizes of companies. From this array of proposals, one can argue that among merger and acquisition scholars there is, at the same time, the belief that mergers and acquisitions are different phenomena, but there is no agreement about how and in what regard they differ.

Not only is an acquisition different from a merger, but also mergers and acquisitions may differ in many regards, such as the typology (related versus unrelated), and the nature (friendly or hostile) of the transaction, the form of payment used, as well as the percentage of acquisition. Many more categorizations have been found in the existing literature. These categorizations are not simply a theoretical exercise by merger and acquisition scholars. On the contrary, since they provide the conditions shaping how the merger and acquisition process unfolds over time, they influence how the merger and acquisition will perform. In our review we have found studies of tender offers (for example Schmidt and Fowler, 1990), friendly and hostile acquisitions (for example, Sudarsanam and Mahate, 2006), acquisitions (for example, Loderer and Martin, 1992), mergers (for example, Arnold and Parker, 2007), or mergers and acquisitions (for example, Lubatkin, 1987).[1] Sometimes it is not clear if it is mergers or acquisitions that are studied as the terminology is mixed or unclear (for example, Blackburn et al., 1990). The label "mergers and acquisitions" is like a word pointing at different referents, and there is a lack of reflection on whether the word is pointing at different phenomena taking place at different times and time periods, in different places and in different kinds of organizations. Just to give an example, as different studies as Flanagan (1996) – aiming to introduce a new way to categorize related and unrelated mergers in order to get purely related and unrelated ditto and to be able to test the effect on shareholder returns for both firms with an event study method, and Risberg (2003) – aiming to show that acquisition processes can by understood as multiple realities among the managers and employees in the acquired company using a social constructionist methodology are both labeled merger and acquisition research. But as the studies are so different, their results can hardly be compared despite the same label. One can conclude that the term "mergers and acquisitions" is referring to many different things, while being used as a unifying label. Different types of mergers and acquisitions, involving different industries and taking place in different geographical areas are studied and simply labelled as "mergers and acquisitions" (for a more extensive discussion on this see Meglio and Risberg, 2011a).

What is Merger and Acquisition Performance?

The second issue, which in a way mirrors the first one, concerns how the label "merger and acquisition performance" is used by merger and acquisition scholars in empirical studies. This construct has been defined by the scholars in different ways. Some scholars measure the effect on R&D (for example, Hitt et al., 1991), change in market value (for example, Chatterjee, 1991), accounting profitability (for example, Ramaswamy, 1997), perceived effectiveness of the integration (for example, Weber, 1996), gain or loss from the divesture (for example, Kaplan and Weisbach, 1992), the endurance of an expansion (for example, Pennings et al., 1994), attitude toward the merger (for example, Greenwood et al., 1994), synergy as value creation (for example, Seth, 1990), subsidiary performance (for example, Slangen and Hennart, 2008) and earnings (for example, Very et al., 1997), just to mention a few. Others use more or less the same definition of performance, but measure it differently. For example, Krishnan and Park (2002) define post-acquisition performance as accounting performance and use ROE as a metric. Capron (1999), on the other hand, relies on a perceptual measure, assessing the acquisition performance along a number of metrics such as change in market share, sales, intrinsic profitability, relative profitability compared to industry average, cost based synergies, revenue based synergies, asset divestiture, and resource deployment.

What is evident from our findings is that merger and acquisition performance as a unitary construct does not exist (Meglio and Risberg, 2011b). As we will detail below in presenting and discussing our results, almost each study contains its own definition of merger and acquisition performance. This makes it as impossible to cumulate findings from existing research as it would be to compare oranges and apples. The notion of failure rates is probably built on such accumulation of findings (in systematic research or not). We believe this is a possible explanation for why so many scholars claim high failure rates.

After these remarks we move on to the presentation and discussion of our results (see Tables 6.1 and 6.2). We have divided the sample articles into three categories: those that discuss the outcome in general; those that discuss the outcome in relation to type of merger and acquisition; and those that discuss what variables affect the outcome. Some articles include more than one of these categories. We will start out by discussing results according to what the researchers have measured, and we will further detail the differences between types of measures according to the article's category.

Outcomes of Merger and Acquisition Activity on Average

In this section we focus on the research findings regarding the outcome of the mergers or acquisitions. Table 6.1 illustrates what scholars have to say about merger and acquisition outcomes on average. In summarizing research results, we faced some difficulties. The first difficulty is that it is not always clear what unit of analysis is under investigation. In other words, does merger and acquisition performance refer to the acquiring company, the target one, or the combination of the two? Another difficulty is that some studies' results can be interpreted in more than one way. For example, Arnold and Parker (2007) conclude that there are greater gains from a deal to the target company's shareholders than to the bidder company's. We have interpreted this to say that there are gains to both shareholders only differing in degree, but it may also be interpreted as claiming a loss to bidder shareholders. On the other hand, King et al. (2008) report on specific variables that positively affected outcome. Their study found that on average, acquisitions do not lead to higher performance, but that "complementary resource profiles in target and acquiring firms are associated with abnormal returns" (2008: 327). With these limitations at hand, Table 6.1 depicts how the researchers interpret their findings in terms of the average success or failure.

Some scholars report positive market-based performance for the target companies (for example, Chatterjee, 1991; Lubatkin, 1987). It is interesting to note that when the unit of analysis is the target company, scholars rely upon market-based measures of performance. Examples of studies reporting positive performance for the acquiring companies are Uhlenbruck et al. (2006) employing market-based measures, and Ingham et al. (1992) employing mixed measures of performance. Examples of positive performance for the combined entity are reported in Seth (1990), which employs market-based measures, in Lamont and Anderson (1985), which employs accounting-based measures, or in Graves (1981), which employs a perceptual measure of performance.

Among studies reporting negative performance, we did not find any with the target company as the unit of analysis. When the unit of analysis is the acquiring company, we found studies employing market-based measures of performance, such as Schmidt and Fowler (1990), and studies employing mixed measures of performance, such as Fowler and Schmidt (1988).

We have also found studies where it is not possible to conclude who gains from a merger or acquisition. In these studies the merger and acquisition performance is measured as market-based performance (for example, Beckman and Haunschild, 2002; King et al., 2008), or as a per-

Table 6.1 Summary of merger and acquisition outcome in general in the reviewed articles

Result/Type of study	Positive outcome on average			Negative outcome on average			No effect or about as many successful as unsuccessful	Number of articles (the parenthesis depicts the number of articles within the category)
	Target firm	Acquirer firm	Combined firm	Target firm	Acquirer firm	Combined firm (or not specified)		
Market-based	3	2	3	0	2	1	2	11 (25)
Accounting-based	0	0	1	0	0	0	0	1 (10)
Perception-based	0	0	2	0	0	0	2	4 (11)
Mixed methods	0	1	0	0	1	1	2	5 (9)
Sum	3	3	6	0	3	2	6	21 (55)

ceptual measure (for example, Very et al., 1997) as well as a mixed measure (for example, Graebner, 2004).

From the research findings presented in the table, one could conclude that mergers and acquisitions on average are seen as rather successful with more studies reporting on positive outcomes than negative outcomes. But we find such comparisons not very meaningful because we would have to compare completely different measures of performance. The types of performance measured vary almost as much as the studies. In most market-based studies, the metric is CAR, but the time frames vary a lot. The time scale of measurement may vary between a few days around the announcement date to several months after the deal. In the accounting-based studies the metrics used are average annual growth in sales, ROA, ROI, ROE, and the time scale of measurement is often three years after the deal. In the perception-based studies we also found a huge variety of measures, from assessments of retention or divestiture, synergy effects to assessment of accounting as well as market performance to the assessment of overall performance, and many, many more metrics. In other words, so many different metrics are used that it becomes meaningless, if not misleading, to compare the results of the different studies. One could say, though, that the average impression from the results is that in the end, mergers and acquisitions do not perform as badly as the general notion seems to be among merger and acquisition scholars and practitioners.

What Type of Merger and Acquisition Performs Better?

Instead of measuring merger and acquisition outcomes on average, it is more common in the research to compare different types of mergers and acquisitions to see which type performs better. A typical study of this kind is to compare related acquisitions to unrelated acquisitions (for example, Blackburn et al., 1990; Flanagan, 1996; Finkelstein and Haleblian, 2002), in order to see if related acquisitions perform better than unrelated acquisitions (for example, Shelton, 1988; Harrison et al., 1991). In fact, theories on strategic and organizational fit (Napier, 1989; Datta, 1991) are based on the notion that the more alike the combining firms are the better will the outcome be. In our review, 11 studies did some kind of comparison of the performance of different types of mergers and acquisitions, and among those the comparison between related and unrelated acquisitions was the most common. In our sample there were seven studies (for example, Finkelstein and Hableblian, 2002; Shelton, 1988; Ramaswamy, 1997; Park, 2002) reporting that related outperformed unrelated mergers and acquisitions. Datta and Grant (1990) and Harrison et al. (1991) found that unrelated mergers and acquisitions perform better than related ones.

Table 6.2   The performance of related and unrelated acquisitions

	Related performs better than unrelated	Unrelated performs better than related	Related do not outperform unrelated	Both create value
Market-based studies	5		1	1
Accounting-based studies	2	1		
Perception-based studies		1		
Mixed method				
Sum	7	2	1	1

The findings are compiled in Table 6.2. One possible conclusion from the results could be that related acquisitions perform better than unrelated.

From Table 6.2 it is possible to see that when the scholars compare different typologies of mergers and acquisitions they tend to use market-based and accounting-based measures of performance, with perceptual or mixed measures playing a minor role. Also in this type of study, the various results depend on what variables are measured. For example, Park (2002) found that related acquisitions in the sample were more profitable because they were more profitable than unrelated prior to the diversification. Datta and Grant (1990), however, found that unrelated acquisitions perform better than related because autonomy is positively associated with superior performance in unrelated acquisitions. As said above, based on the findings in the studies we reviewed, we cannot provide any definitive statement about which type of merger and acquisition performs better as the variables employed differ greatly from study to study.

What Variables Affect Merger and Acquisition Performance?

While the issue of what type of merger and acquisition performs better was a popular research question during the 1980s and early 1990s, we have more recently witnessed a shift towards the understanding of what variables explain the merger and acquisition performance. Some studies in our sample, especially from the 2000s, aim at unraveling what variables affect and therefore explain the merger and acquisition performance. Findings from empirical research are difficult to categorize, as so many variables have been tested to see if any significant and meaningful correlation would emerge. In this chapter we have tried to categorize them in a way that resembles the whole acquisition process. The results of our categorization are arranged in Table 6.3. In this table, we have presented only some of

Table 6.3   Variables explaining performance: a categorization

Pre-deal variables	Negotiation phase variables	Integration process variables
Complementary resources (for example, King et al., 2008) Early movers as opposed to late comers (for example, McNamara et al., 2008; Carow et al., 2004) Profitability of the companies before the merger (for example, Park, 2002)	Payment method (for example , Carow et al., 2004; Krishnan et al., 2007) The amount of premium (for example, Krishnan et al., 2007)	Transfer of acquirer's resources to target (for example, Capron and Pistre, 2002) Top managers turnover (for example, Krishnan et al., 1997; Zollo and Singh, 2004; Cannella and Hambrick, 1993; Saxton and Dollinger, 2004) Workforce reduction (for example, Krishnan et al., 2007; Krishnan and Park, 2002)

the variables employed in articles from our sample according to the phase of merger and acquisition process to which they belong. We have distinguished the variables as pre-deal, as belonging to the negotiation phase, and as belonging to the integration process. Under the label "Pre-deal variables" we indicate all variables that describe the merging companies' conditions before the deal is closed. Within this category we find variables that characterize the merging companies, such as the profitability or the resource endowments, but also those related to the type of control. Under the label "Negotiation phase variables" we arrange those variables pertaining to the legal transaction, such as the amount of premium paid or the form in which such premium is actually paid. In the third category, which we label as "Integration phase variables", we assemble variables affecting the post-acquisition integration process. Variables span from the transfer of resources to workforce reduction to top management turnover. The variables included in our table and the examples of empirical articles do not exhaust our sample but are illustrative of them.

The first impression from Table 6.3 is that merger and acquisition scholars have looked into the various phases of the acquisition process to select variables explaining performance. This reinforces the notion that mergers and acquisitions are processes (Jemison and Sitkin, 1986) within which it is difficult to put boundaries. The notion of mergers and acquisitions as processes also conveys the idea that performance is the outcome of several concurrent and partly conflicting sub-processes, each of which is intended to attain acquisition goals. Looking into the single variables employed in empirical studies, it emerges that the resource-based view has been frequently employed. Resources seem to play a key role in empirical research. Here we find that complementary resources (King et al., 2008) as well as transfer of acquirer's resources to target (Capron and Pistre, 2002) are associated with abnormal returns and that differences in the resource allocation create value in the post-merger period (Harrison et al., 1991) or that resource deployment can contribute to acquisition performance (Capron, 1999). Also, among resources, the human factor may negatively affect the merger and acquisition performance if not handled carefully. Empirical results point to that workforce reduction (Krishnan et al., 2007; Krishnan and Park, 2002) or top managers leaving the company have a negative impact on the performance (Krishnan et al., 1997; Zollo and Singh, 2004; Cannella and Hambrick, 1993; Saxton and Dollinger, 2004). Among the variables pertaining to the pre-deal phase, studies have, for example, found that acquisition early in a merger and acquisition wave perform better than latecomers (McNamara et al., 2008; Carow et al., 2004), or that companies that are profitable before the merger are also more profitable after (Park, 2002), or that success breeds success, meaning that firms with track records of durable ventures are more likely to replicate their good expansion performance in the future (Pennings et al., 1994). Among the variables belonging to the negotiation phase, we found that payment method (Carow et al., 2004; Krishnan et al., 2007) and amount of premium paid affect the outcome (Krishnan et al., 2007). Premiums paid in cash were found to realize superior stock returns than other types of payment methods (Carow et al., 2004) and higher premiums had a negative impact on merger and acquisition performance (Krishnan et al., 2007). The type of corporate control also affects the performance, and ownership (as opposed to management) control results in positive shareholder returns (Kroll et al., 1997; Blackburn et al., 1990). These are just a few of the many variables that scholars have tested and correlated for their effect on performance. However, our review shows that merger and acquisition researchers point to many different possible variables explaining acquisition performance. After reading all these articles, we are not sure we could tell what leads to positive merger and acquisition outcomes. One reason could be that, as some scholars claim, each merger and acquisition is unique (Bower, 2001; Lubatkin, 1987), and they each have different explanatory variables. This suggests that we should be very cautious when we review such a vast number of articles with the aim to cumulate existing findings. A serious reflection on what we can learn from such an exercise of reviewing a vast number of articles is therefore needed.

In the following section we will discuss what this variety of methods, perspectives, and metrics used in merger and acquisition studies might imply.

DISCUSSION

A general impression from research on merger and acquisition performance is the variety of type of studies, measures, metrics, and variables tested (compare Meglio and Risberg, 2011b). Despite this great variety, scholars use "merger and acquisition" as a unifying label without any critical reflection over the use of this label. In addition, what is defined as outcome or performance, or, to put it differently, what the different metrics are measured to have an effect on, differ greatly.

There are different types of studies based on different types of measures. In this review four categories are used: market-based studies, accounting-based studies, perception-based studies, and studies mixing these measures. Each type of measures is aimed at different types of stakeholders. There are mainly three categories of stakeholders that can be identified in these studies (even though they are not always made explicit). Accounting-based studies are using measures that are aimed to communicate with owners and managers, and they are historical, as accounting measures depict what has happened. When studies rely on perceptual measures they report how managers (mostly) and (sometimes other) employees perceive either accounting measures or other types of variables that are not accounted for in the formal accounting, such as attitudes, behaviors, and values.

Market-based studies are based on measures and information aimed towards stakeholders active on the so called market for corporate control. This could be owners in terms of shareholders, or different types of financial institutions, such as a venture capitalist. All market-based studies included in the sample were measuring the market performance and abnormal returns using the event study method. Whereas accounting-based studies are historical, event studies look forward as they say nothing about the actual performance of the acquisition, but how the market expects the acquisition to perform. Neither do these measures say anything about if the shareholders lose or gain on the announcement as they are just measuring the markets' predictions about what might happen, and the shareholders will not gain or lose anything unless they actually sell their stocks at that time. In market-based studies there is an underlying assumption that the market has an ability to know what will happen in the future. Moreover, some studies comparing accounting, efficiency, divestiture, and market measures claim that abnormal returns are good predictors of a long term acquisition outcome (Haleblian and Finkelstein, 1999; Harris and Shimizu, 2004). More recently, Oler et al. (2008) have provided empirical evidence that shows that financial markets correct themselves as soon as they get more accurate information about merging companies. Others claim that event studies are not able to capture the long term effects of merger and acquisition performance (Capron, 1999) or the historical context (Côté et al., 1999).

To group market-based studies together with other types of studies when one wants to find out if mergers and acquisitions are successful or not would be like comparing apples and oranges. Whereas market-based studies are focused on what the market believes the future performance will be, other types of studies are more focused on the companies' earlier performance. The studies are not measuring the same thing, and therefore one cannot lump the results together in order to say anything about merger and acquisition success or failure rates in general, as success and failure mean different things in different studies. In a market-based study, success might mean that the market believes the merger will be successful in the future, and therefore the market starts to trade the stock more and the stock price goes up. In an accounting-based study, success could mean that the measured metric has improved compared to before the merger. In a perception-based study, success means that the managers and employees perceive the merger to be successful, and this perception could be based on many different things (not just the metrics used in the study).

The time frames studied are also quite different depending on the type of measure used. In event studies, very short time frames are used, from a 3-day window around the announcement date (-1 to $+1$) (Carow et al., 2004), up to not so short, such as 200 trading days before and 50 trading days after the announcement (Chatterjee et al., 1992). There are also studies taking a longer term perspective with time frames of three years or more after the acquisition (Finkelstein and Haleblian, 2002; Krishnan et al., 1997) up to six years after the acquisition (Schweizer, 2005), just to give a few examples. In other articles, the time frame is not mentioned at all (for example, Datta, 1991).

It is quite natural that the time periods studied differ, but it may also affect the results of the research. Several studies that have compared different time periods have found that there were negative abnormal returns in the 1980s (Morck et al., 1990; Agrawal et al., 1992). If anyone making a literature review is not aware of this, and includes many market-based studies in the review from that time period, the result would of course indicate that the failure rates seem to be high. This could be one explanation why many scholars claim high failure rates in mergers and acquisitions.

Another reason was brought forward by Brouthers et al. (1998), who explain earlier studies' negative or various results on merger and acquisition performance. In their study of realization of management motives they claim that researchers have been looking at one type of measure (market- or accounting-based) while managers were pursuing and achieving other types of measures (motive realization). Shareholder values say nothing about managers' motives with mergers and acquisitions. This could explain the inconsistency between managers' assessments of the success of a deal and what objective indicators, such as ROA or the share price, indicate. We are not pointing to one measure as being more able than another to measure performance; we are pointing to their telling a different story (compare Corvellec, 1997). When managers claim that a deal was successful, it may be done in order to reinforce their reputation as managers able to carry out successful deals, or it could be that they are measuring something different from what most scholars do, like motive realization.

Before moving on to the concluding remarks, we would like to focus our attention on what all findings, taken together, may point to. As specified above, this is a selected review with findings presented in narrative form. Therefore we cannot, and do not want to, derive any statistically significant result from our analysis. However, our findings are illustrative of much of existing research on mergers and acquisitions, and they allow us to claim that to date, scholars have been mainly concerned with finding the right variables to explain and predict performance. That so many studies report statistically significant correlations between so many different variables and performance could mean that it is not possible to identify a single variable or a few variables that explain performance. The reason is simply that there are so many different variables affecting it. Changes in stock prices do not really say anything about how the acquisition affects the performance of the combined firm. It cannot even be of interest to shareholders unless they want to sell at that precise moment. Event studies made around the announcement of the takeover can thus be considered as quite irrelevant if one wants to find out how acquisitions affect company performance in the long term. They are only of interest if one wants to measure the effect of the stock price in the short or long term.

This is a reason why so many scholars doing longitudinal studies have discarded the event study methodology. One could conclude that event studies will not help us understand if acquisitions have a negative or positive effect on firms' performances (unless you define the performance as stock price). Claiming that one can only make short window event studies in order to control for other types of impacts is like looking for your lost keys under the street light even though you lost them five meters away in the darkness. In other words, it seems quite pointless to measure something because it is measurable if it does not say anything about what one really wants to find out. That in turn means that we should approach mergers and acquisitions through methods more suitable to study such a complex phenomenon. Looking for correlation between single variables and performance may probably produce a statistically significant result, but only a minor advancement in our understanding of what make mergers and acquisitions successful (Meglio and Risberg, 2010).

CONCLUSIONS

Even though we cannot provide statistically significant results of how mergers and acquisitions perform, we can still conclude that our review did not confirm the notion that mergers and acquisitions perform poorly. Instead our results indicate that the research on mergers and acquisitions outcomes is rather inconclusive. This is not very different from what Lubatkin found in his 1983 review. If no definitive findings support the idea that most mergers and acquisitions fail, and we thus believe that such a claim is more a taken-for-granted statement than a fact supported by conclusive empirical evidence.

Our findings also show how difficult, if not meaningless, it is to compare results from different studies. By breaking down the research findings from our review, we can point to researchers' extensive use of different types of measures and variables. The many different types make it meaningless to cumulate findings. If one believes mergers and acquisitions to be unique, such a variety of variables and measures is quite natural. But, it makes it less interesting to compare results across studies.

Having stated this position, we want to take the opportunity to reflect on what our findings may say to the merger and acquisition community. We also would like to reflect on how the studies of merger and acquisition scholars may move forward.

We believe that our findings demonstrate that high failure rate has become a taken-for-granted assumption regarding mergers and acquisitions (see, for example, Risberg, 2012). This is, in our view, the outcome of several different, yet intertwined, issues we would like to discuss in this concluding section.

The first issue is that the notions of success and failure as well as of merger and acquisition performance are often left unspecified in empirical research. Not only do merger and acquisition scholars leave undefined the constructs of performance or failure; they also use different types of performance and a huge variety of measurement methods and indicators in their research, as shown in our review. As a result, it is not possible to talk about merger and acquisition performance or failure as unitary constructs, and therefore it is not useful to compare, for example, how the financial markets react to a merger and acquisition announcement with how executives assess the attainment of a merger and acquisition's intended goals. We therefore posit that it is not possible to provide on average or general results about how mergers and acquisitions perform or if they experience high failure rates.

The community of merger and acquisition scholars has so far labeled this state of affairs as "fragmentation" and has suggested several distinct "recipes" to overcome such fragmentation. Some posit that the merger and acquisition community has not yet identified the right variables able to explain or predict merger and acquisition performance (King et al., 2004); others claim that the problem lies instead in performance measurement, which is currently too poor. Some scholars have attempted to devise a better way to measure performance (Cording et al., 2010; Zollo and Meier, 2008). The conventional discourse, therefore, assumes that merger and acquisition performance is something objective and unitary and that merger and acquisition scholars are called upon to find the best way to capture this construct. We do not share this view. Let us explicate why. The first reason lies in the inconsistency between how mergers and acquisitions are generally described and how they are investigated. Mergers and acquisitions are commonly depicted as heterogeneous events that may differ at various stages of their development. High technology deals are particular no one would doubt – compared to those taking place in manufacturing and mining industries. Moreover, friendly and hostile takeovers are not alike. Mergers and acquisitions may differ in terms of goals they intend to attain or in the way they are managed. These differences all have a role in producing merger and acquisition performance. Yet most empirical research does not do justice to such heterogeneity in its quest to find universal laws. We believe that the idea that the merger and acquisition literature is fragmented reflects a positivistic research paradigm, where knowledge accumulates through a linear process. If we assume a constructivist perspective, "this fragmentation entails a different meaning, becoming merely an outcome of the fact that researchers with different ontological, epistemological, and methodological stances investigate mergers and acquisitions in different ways. For example, the question of finding a coherent answer to the question of merger and acquisition failure and success becomes irrelevant as each merger and acquisition is different, with different motives and objectives" (Meglio and Risberg, 2010: 88). The aim of inquiry should instead be to reach understandings and reconstructions of the constructions people formulate about a phenomenon (Guba and Lincoln, 1994). If such a perspective is taken, multiple constructions can coexist as knowledge accumulates only in a relative sense through the formation of more informed and sophisticated constructions.

The existence of such a multitude of merger and acquisition performance measures does not, however, signal a method problem. As Corvellec (1997) contends, such a multiplicity of indicators can be conceived of both as a sign of disagreement as to what constitutes the notion of performance and a sign of agreement that the performance is not reducible to a single dimension, being that it is a multidimensional construct. It could also reflect that the multiple indicators found in the literature 'signals' the disagreement among scholars about what constitutes the correct performance measure, referring to the ongoing debate (compare Corvellec 1997) in the literature as to whether market-based or accounting-based measures best capture merger and acquisition performance. This, however, does not underline that we should give up investigating merger and acquisition performance. Rather it underlines that we should clearly define what it is that we are measuring under the label "merger and acquisition performance". Merger and acquisition performance, like organizational performance, is a construct that lacks universality; this implies that scholars should clearly specify what it is and define the boundary conditions where it does or does not apply (Suddaby, 2010). So, let us continue studying merger and acquisition performance from many different perspectives using many different metrics, but acknowledging that performance measures cannot be compared. Instead, they only represent many different views and perspectives of what mergers and acquisitions are and how merger and acquisition performance should be measured. A clear definition of the merger and acquisition performance construct can be easily reached if only scholars answer the following questions when they measure this construct.

1. What does merger and acquisition performance mean? Is it an accounting performance, a market-based performance, a combination of the two, or what else? Is it measured by an objective or a perceptual indicator?
2. What is the time scale of measurement? Is the performance measure a short-, medium-, or long-term performance? Is it measured after days, months, or years after the event?
3. What is the unit of analysis of merger and acquisition performance? The empirical research has mainly assumed the acquiring company as the unit of analysis. This is consistent with the idea that management is a discipline devoted to the improvement of organizational effectiveness. Other units of analysis could be possible, of course, apart from the target company or the combination of the merging companies.

For instance, to date, nobody has investigated if the end consumers gain from the acquisition game.

4. What is the level of analysis of merger and acquisition performance? Is the performance measured at the individual, the task, or the organizational level?

Answering such questions while measuring merger and acquisition performance could help the merger and acquisition community to better interpret findings and derive more effective managerial implications.

NOTE

1. A tender offer is an offer to purchase some or all of shareholders' shares in a company. A tender offer may be friendly or hostile. A hostile takeover is when the purchaser has not come to an agreement with the management of the company but goes direct to the shareholders with an offer, or the purchaser may fight to replace the management to get an agreement. An acquisition is when a company purchases a target company's ownership stakes in order to take control of the company. An acquisition may be friendly or hostile. A merger is when the management of two companies decides to become one. The decision tends to be mutual between the companies.

REFERENCES

Agrawal, A., Jaffe, J.F. and Mandelker, G.N. (1992). 'The post-merger performance of acquiring firms: a re-examination of an anomaly'. *The Journal of Finance*, **47**(4), 1605–1621.

Appelbaum, S.H., Gandell, J., Yortis, H., Proper, S. and Jobin, F. (2000a). 'Anatomy of a merger: behavior of organizational factors and processes throughout the pre- during- post-stages (part 1)'. *Management Decision*, **38**(9), 649–662.

Appelbaum, S.H., Gandell, J., Shapiro, B.T., Belisle, P. and Hoeven, E. (2000b). 'Anatomy of a merger: behavior of organizational factors and processes throughout the pre- during-post- stages (part 2)'. *Management Decision*, **38**(10), 674–684.

Arnold, M. and Parker, D. (2007). 'UK competition policy and shareholder value: the impact of merger inquiries'. *British Journal of Management*, **18**(1), 27–43.

Beckman, C.M. and Haunschild, P.R. (2002). 'Network learning: the effects of partners' heterogeneity of experience on corporate acquisitions'. *Administrative Science Quarterly*, 47: 92–124.

Blackburn, V.L., Lang, J.R. and Johnson, K.H. (1990). 'Mergers and shareholder returns: the roles of acquiring firm's ownership and diversification strategy'. *Journal of Management*, **16**(4), 769–782.

Booz-Allen and Hamilton (2001). 'Merger integration: delivering on the promise. A series of viewpoints on mergers, acquisitions and integration'. Available at www.bah.com, accessed on 14 March 2004.

Bourantas, D. and Nicandrou, I.I. (1998). 'Modelling post-acquisition employee behavior: typology and determining factors'. *Employee Relations*, **20**(1), 73–91.

Bower, J.L. (2001). 'Not all M&As are alike – and that matters'. *Harvard Business Review*, **79**(3), 92–101.

Brouthers, K.D., van Hastenburg, P. and van den Ven, J. (1998). 'If most mergers fail why are they so popular?' *Long Range Planning*, **31**(3), 347–353.

Buckley, P.J. and Ghauri, P.N. (2002). *International Mergers and Acquisitions. A Reader*. Singapore: Thomson.

Cannella Jr, A.A. and Hambrick, D.C. (1993). 'Effects of executive departures on the performance of acquired firms'. *Strategic Management Journal*, **14**(S1), 137–152.

Capron, L. (1999). 'The long-term performance of horizontal acquisitions'. *Strategic Management Journal*, **20**(11), 987–1018.

Capron, L. and Pistre, N. (2002). 'When do acquirers earn abnormal returns?' *Strategic Management Journal*, **23**(9), 781–794.

Carow, K., Heron, R. and Saxton, T. (2004). 'Do early birds get the returns? An empirical investigation of early-mover advantages in acquisitions'. *Strategic Management Journal*, **25**(6), 563–585.

Carton, R.B. and Hofer, C.W. (2006). *Measuring Organizational Performance. Metrics for Entrepreneurship in Strategic Management Research*. Cheltenham, UK and Northampton, MA, USA: Edward Elgar.

Cartwright, S. (1998). 'International mergers and acquisitions: the issues and challenges'. In Gersten, M.C., Søderberg, A-M. and Torp, J.E. (eds), *Cultural Dimensions of International Mergers and Acquisitions*. New York: Walter de Gruyter.

Cartwright, S. and Cooper, C.L. (1995). 'Organizational marriage: "hard" versus "soft" issues?' *Personnel Review*, **24**(3), 32–42.

Chatterjee, S. (1991). 'Gains in vertical acquisitions and market power: theory and evidence'. *Academy of Management Journal*, **34**(2), 436–448.

Chatterjee, S., Lubatkin, M.H., Schweiger, D.M. and Weber, Y. (1992). 'Cultural differences and shareholder value in related mergers: Linking equity and human capital'. *Strategic Management Journal*, **13**(5), 319–334.

Child, J., Faulkner, D. and Pitkethly, R. (2001). *The Management of International Acquisitions*. Oxford: Oxford University Press.

Cording, M., Christmann, P. and Weigelt, C. (2010). 'Measuring theoretically complex constructs: The case of acquisition performance'. *Strategic Organization*, **8**(1), 11–41.

Corvellec, H. 1997. *Stories of Achievement-narrative Features of Organizational Performance*. New Brunswick, NJ: Transaction Publisher.

Côté, L., Langley, A. and Pasquero, J. (1999). 'Acquisition strategy and dominant logic in an engineering firm'. *Journal of Management Studies*, **36**(7), 919–952.

Datta, D.K. (1991). 'Organizational fit and acquisition performance: effects of post-acquisition integration'. *Strategic Management Journal*, **12**(4), 281–297.

Datta, D.K. and Grant, J.H. (1990). 'Relationships between type of acquisition, the autonomy given to the acquired firm, and acquisition success: An empirical analysis'. *Journal of Management*, **16**(1), 29–44.

Datta, D.K., Pinches, G.E. and Narayanan, V.K. (1992). 'Factors influencing wealth creation from mergers and acquisitions: A meta-analysis'. *Strategic Management Journal*, **13**(1), 67–84.

DiGeorgio, R.M. (2002). 'Making mergers and acquisitions work: What we know and don't know – Part I'. *Journal of Change Management*, **3**(2), 134–148.

Epstein, M.J. (2004). 'The drivers of success in post-merger integration'. *Organizational Dynamics*, **33**(2): 174–189.

Finkelstein, S. and Haleblian, J. (2002). 'Understanding acquisition performance: The role of transfer effects'. *Organization Science*, **13**(1), 36–47.

Flanagan, D.J. (1996) 'Announcements of purely related and purely unrelated mergers and shareholder returns: Reconciling the relatedness paradox'. *Journal of Management*, 22: 823–850.

Fowler, K.L. and Schmidt, D.R. (1988). 'Tender offers, acquisition, and subsequent performance in manufacturing firms'. *Academy of Management Journal*, **31**(4), 962–974.

Franks, J., Harris, R. and Titman S. (1991). 'The post-merger share price performance of acquiring firms'. *Journal of Financial Economics*, 29: 81–96.

Graebner, M.E. (2004). 'Momentum and serendipity: How acquired leaders create value in the integration of technology firms'. *Strategic Management Journal*, **25**(8/9), 751–777.

Graves, D. (1981). 'Individual reactions to a merger of two small firms of brokers in the re-insurance industry: A total population survey'. *Journal of Management Studies*, **18**(1), 89–113.

Greenwood, R., Hinings, C.R. and Brown, J. (1994). 'Merging professional service firms'. *Organization Science*, 5: 239–257.

Guba, E.G. and Lincoln, Y.S. (1994). 'Competing paradigms in qualitative research'. In Denzin, N.K. and Lincoln, Y.S. (eds), *Handbook of Qualitative Research*. Thousand Oaks, CA: Sage, pp. 105–117.

Habeck, M.M., Kroger, F. and Tram, M.R. (2000). *After the Merger*. London and New York: *Financial Times*/Prentice Hall.

Haleblian, J. and Finkelstein, S. (1999). 'The influence of organizational acquisition experience on acquisition performance: A behavioral learning perspective'. *Administrative Science Quarterly*, **44**(1), 29–56.

Harris, I.C. and Shimizu, K. (2004). 'Too busy to serve? An examination of the influence of overboarded directors'. *Journal of Management Studies*, **41**(5), 775–798.

Harrison, J.S., Hitt, M.A., Hoskisson, R.E. and Ireland, R.D. (1991). 'Synergies and post-acquisition performance: differences versus similarities in resource allocation'. *Journal of Management*, **17**(1), 173–190.

Harrison, J.S., Hitt, M.A., Hoskisson, R.E. and Ireland, R.D. (2001). 'Resource complementarity in business combinations: Extending the logic to organizational alliances'. *Journal of Management*, **27**(6), 679–690.

Haspeslagh, P.C. and Jemison, D.B. (1991). *Managing Acquisitions*. New York: Free Press.

Hitt, M.A., Ireland, R.D., Harrison, J.S. and Hoskisson, R.E. (1991). 'The effects of acquisitions on R&D inputs and outputs'. *Academy of Management Journal*, **34**(3), 693–706.

Hopkins, D.H. (1987). 'Acquisition strategy and the market position of acquiring firms'. *Strategic Management Journal*, 8: 535–547.

Hubbard, N. (1999). *Acquisitions Strategy and Implementation*. Basingstoke, UK: Macmillan Business.

Huff, A.S. (2008). *Designing Research for Publication*. Thousand Oaks, CA: Sage.

Hunt, J.W. (1990). 'Changing pattern of acquisition behaviour in takeovers and the consequences for acquisition processes'. *Strategic Management Journal*, **11**(1), 69–77.

Ingham, H., Kran, I. and Lovestam, A. (1992). 'Mergers and profitability: A managerial success story?' *Journal of Management Studies*, **29**(2), 195–208.

Jarrell, G.A., Brickley, J.A. and Netter, J.M. (1988). 'The market for corporate control: The empirical evidence since 1980'. *Journal of Economic Perspectives*, 2: 49–68.

Jemison, D.B. and Sitkin, S.B. (1986). 'Corporate acquisitions: A process perspective'. *Academy of Management Review*, **11**(1), 145–163.

Jensen, M.C. and Ruback, R.S. (1983). 'The market for corporate control'. *Journal of Financial Economics*, **11**(1), 5–50.

Kaplan, S.N. and Weisbach, M.S. (1992). 'The success of acquisitions: evidence from divestiture'. *Journal of Finance*, **47**(1), 107–138.

King, D.R., Dalton, D.R., Daily, C.M. and Covin, J.G. (2004). 'Meta-analyses of post-acquisition performance: Indications of unidentified moderators'. *Strategic Management Journal*, **25**(2), 187–200.

King, D.R., Slotegraaf, R.J. and Kesner, I. (2008). 'Performance implications of firm resource interactions in the acquisition of R&D-intensive firms'. *Organization Science*, **19**(2), 327–340.

Kitching, J. (1967). 'Why do mergers miscarry?' *Harvard Business Review*, **45**(6), 84–101.

Krishnan, H.A. and Park, D. (2002). 'The impact of work force reduction on subsequent performance in major mergers and acquisitions. An exploratory study'. *Journal of Business Research*, **55**(4), 285–292.

Krishnan, H.A., Miller, A. and Judge, W.Q. (1997). 'Diversification and top management team complementarity: Is performance improved by merging similar or dissimilar teams?' *Strategic Management Journal*, **18**(5), 361–374.

Krishnan, H.A., Hitt, M.A. and Park, D. (2007). 'Acquisition premiums, subsequent workforce reductions and post-acquisition performance'. *Journal of Management Studies*, **44**(5), 709–732.

Kroll, M., Wright, P., Toombs, L. and Leavell, H. (1997). 'Form of control: A critical determinant of acquisition performance and CEO rewards'. *Strategic Management Journal*, **18**(2), 85–96.

Lamont, B.T. and Anderson, C.R. (1985). 'Mode of corporate diversification and economic performance'. *Academy of Management Journal*, **28**(4), 926–934.

Loderer, C. and Martin, K. (1992), 'Post-acquisition performance of acquiring firms'. *Financial Management*, autumn, pp. 69–79.

Lubatkin, M. 1987. 'Merger strategies and stockholder value'. *Strategic Management Journal*, 8: 39–53.

Marks, M.L. and Mirvis, P.H. (2001). 'Making mergers and acquisitions work: Strategic and psychological preparation'. *Academy of Management Executive*, **15**(2), 80–92.

McNamara, G.M., Haleblian, J. and Dykes, B.J. (2008), 'The performance implication of participating in an acquisition wave: early mover advantages, bandwagon effects, and the moderating influence of industry characteristics and acquirer tactics'. *Academy of Management Journal*, **51**(1), 113–130.

Meglio, O. and Risberg, A. (2010). 'Mergers and acquisitions – time for a methodological rejuvenation of the field?' *Scandinavian Journal of Management*, **26**(1), 87–95.

Meglio, O. and Risberg, A. (2011a). 'Are all mergers and acquisitions treated as if they were alike? A review of empirical evidence'. In Cooper C. and Finkelstein S. (eds), *Advances in Mergers and Acquisitions*, Vol. 10.

Meglio, O. and Risberg, A. (2011b). 'The (mis)measurement of M&A performance – a systematic narrative literature review'. *Scandinavian Journal of Management*, **27**(4) December issue.

Morck, R., Shleifer, A. and Vishny, R.W. (1990). 'Do managerial objectives drive bad acquisitions?' *The Journal of Finance*, **45**(1), 31–48.

Mulherin, J.H. and Boone, A.L. (2000), 'Comparing acquisitions and divestitures', *Journal of Corporate Finance*, **6**(6), 117–139.

Napier, N.K. (1989). 'Mergers and acquisitions, human resource issues and outcomes: a review and a suggested typology'. *Journal of Management Studies*, **26**(3), 271–289.

Oler, D.K., Harrison, J.S. and Allen, M.R. (2008). 'The danger of misinterpreting short event-window study findings in strategic management research: an empirical illustration using horizontal acquisitions'. *Strategic Organization*, **6**(1), 151–184.

Panchal, S. and Cartwright, S. (2001). 'Group differences in post-merger stress'. *Journal of Managerial Psychology*, **16**(6), 424–433.

Park C. (2002). 'The effects of prior performance on the choice between related and unrelated acquisitions: Implications for the performance consequences of diversification strategy'. *Journal of Management Studies*, **39**(7), 1003–1019.

Pennings, J.M., Barkema, H.G. and Douma, S. (1994). 'Organizational learning and diversification'. *Academy of Management Journal*, **37**(3), 608–640.

Piekkari, R., Vaara, E., Tienari, J. and Säntti, R. (2005). 'Integration or disintegration? Human resource implication of a common corporate language decision in a cross-border merger'. *International Journal of Human Resource Management*, **16**(3): 330–344.

Ramaswamy, K. (1997). 'The performance impact of strategic similarity in horizontal mergers: Evidence from the U.S. banking industry'. *The Academy of Management Journal*, **40**(3), 697–715.

Risberg, A. (2003). 'Notions of shared and multiple realities in acquisitions. Unfolding and critiquing dominating notions of acquisitions'. *Nordiska Organisasjonsstudier*, **5**(1), 58–82.

Risberg, A. (2012), 'The stake of high failure rates in mergers and acquisitions'. In Anderson, H., Havila, V. and Nilsson, F. (eds), *Mergers and Acquisitions – The Critical Role of Stakeholders*. New York: Routledge.

Saxton, T. and Dollinger, M. (2004). 'Target reputation and appropriability: picking and deploying resources in acquisitions'. *Journal of Management*, **30**(1), 123–147.

Schmidt, D.R. and Fowler, K.L. (1990). 'Post-acquisition financial performance and executive compensation'. *Strategic Management Journal*, **11**(7), 559–569.

Schweizer, L. (2005). 'Organizational integration of acquired biotechnology companies into pharmaceutical companies: the need for a hybrid approach'. *Academy of Management Journal*, **48**(6), 1051–1074.

Seth, A. (1990). 'Sources of value creation in acquisitions: An empirical investigation'. *Strategic Management Journal*, **11**(6), 431–446.

Seth, A., Song, K.P. and Pettit, A.R. (2002). 'Value creation and destruction in cross-border acquisitions: An empirical analysis of foreign acquisitions of U.S. firms'. *Strategic Management Journal*, **23**(10), 921–940.

Shelton, L.M. (1988). 'Strategic business fits and corporate acquisition: empirical evidence'. *Strategic Management Journal*, 9: 279–287.

Shrivastava, P. (1986). 'Postmerger integration'. *Journal of Business Strategy*, **7**(1), 65–76.

Singh, H. and Montgomery, C.A. (1987). 'Corporate acquisition strategies and economic performance'. *Strategic Management Journal*, **8**(4), 377–386.

Slangen, A.H.L. and Hennart, J.F. (2008). 'Do foreign greenfields outperform foreign acquisitions or vice versa? An institutional perspective'. *Journal of Management Studies*, **45**(7), 1301–1328.

Søderberg, A.M. and Vaara, E. (2003). *Merging Across Borders*. Copenhagen: Copenhagen Business School Press.

Sudarsanam, S. and Mahate, A. (2006). 'Are friendly acquisitions too bad for shareholders and managers? Long-term value creation and top management turnover in hostile and friendly acquirers'. *British Journal of Management*, Supplement, 17: S7–S30.

Suddaby, R. (2010). Editor's comments: 'Construct clarity in theories of management and organization'. *Academy of Management Review*, **35**(3), 346–357.

Teerikangas, S. and Very, P. (2006). 'The culture–performance relationship in M&A. From yes/no to how', *British Journal of Management*, **17**(S1), 31–48.

Uhlenbruck, K., Hitt, M.A. and Semadeni, M. (2006). 'Market value effects of acquisitions involving internet firms: A resource-based analysis'. *Strategic Management Journal*, **27**(10), 899–913.

Vaara, E. and Tienari, J. (2003). 'The "balance of power principle": Nationality, politics and the distribution of organizational positions'. In Søderberg, A-M. and Vaara, E. (eds) *Merging Across Borders: People, Cultures and Politics*. Copenhagen: Copenhagen Business School Press.

Very, P. and Schweiger, D.M. (2001). 'The acquisition process as a learning process: Evidence from a study of critical problems and solutions in domestic and cross-border deals'. *Journal of World Business*, **36**(1), 11–31.

Very, P., Lubatkin, M., Calori, R. and Veiga, J. (1997). 'Relative standing and the performance of recently acquired European firms'. *Strategic Management Journal*, **18**(8), 593–614.

Weber, Y. (1996). 'Corporate cultural fit and performance in mergers and acquisitions'. *Human Relations*, **49**(9), 1181–1203.

Zollo, M. and Meier, D. (2008). 'What is M&A performance?' *Academy of Management Perspectives*, **22**(3), 55–77.

Zollo, M. and Singh, H. (2004). 'Deliberate learning in corporate acquisitions: post-acquisition strategies and integration capability in U.S. bank mergers'. *Strategic Management Journal*, **25**(13), 1233–1256.

7 Researching mergers and acquisitions with the case study method: idiographic understanding of longitudinal integration processes

Lars Bengtsson and Rikard Larsson

There are two major ways of empirically studying various phenomena; broader nomothetic surveys of many observations and idiographic case studies of one or few in-depth cases (Larsson, 1993). In the area of mergers and acquisitions, as with many other management research areas, the scientific literature is dominated by nomothetic surveys (for example, Andrade et al., 2001; Chatterjee et al., 1992; Haleblian and Finkelstein, 1999; Hitt et al., 1991; Jensen and Ruback, 1983; King et al., 2004) and conceptual publications (for example, Haspeslagh and Jemison, 1991; Jemison and Sitkin, 1986; Schweiger and Walsh, 1990). These two categories tend together to outnumber the published M&A case studies (for example, Buono et al., 1985; Greenwood et al., 1994; Larsson, 1990; Sales and Mirvis, 1984) by more than 10 to 1 among the most referenced M&A articles and books (compare Haleblian et al., 2009).

One can speculate why case studies are much less prevalent in the M&A literature, such as dominating positivistic, quantitative research norms in the mainly American academic community that devalues more interpretive, qualitative case studies more often used by European researchers (Bengtsson et al., 1997, Collin et al., 1996). The classic example of this being the claim of case studies lacking scientific value, that fortunately Campbell himself retracted this quite exaggerated statement (Campbell, 1975). Comparing submission and acceptance rates of different kinds of studies rather show that it is not that case studies have a higher rejection rate, but rather a lower submission rate (Larsson and Löwendahl, 2005). Thus, case studies seem to be more discarded in advance by fears of them not being accepted rather than there being a much larger pool of rejected case studies.

Instead of perpetuating this self-fulfilling prophesy of case study doom, our purpose with this chapter is to highlight the comparative advantages of using case study research to contribute to the M&A field and provide some recommendations how this can be done well. The mere likelihood of diminishing marginal utility of continued nomothetic survey dominance suggests that case study contributions can be relatively greater by exploiting underutilized idiographic research benefits. We are certainly not arguing that the many decades of survey dominance should be replaced by equally long case study hegemony. On the contrary, surveys and case studies are quite complementary and therefore create more synergistic contribution through more balance over time.

The chapter is organized as follows. First, we briefly review the methodological literature to summarize the comparative strengths and weaknesses of case studies in general. Second, we review some of the most versus less influential M&A case studies to find out what this method has successfully contributed to the field. Third, we analyse the impact of different case study designs on findings and their impact through a case survey of 55 M&A case studies used by Larsson (1989, 1993). Finally, we conclude with some methodological recommendations about how to increase case study contributions to M&A research.

COMPARATIVE STRENGTHS OF CASE STUDY RESEARCH

Allport (1937, 1962), borrowing the terms from the neo-Kantian philosopher Windelband, introduced the terms nomothetic (general laws and procedures of exact science) and idiographic (understanding of particular cases) to represent two research methodologies in psychology. Management and organizational researchers (Burrell and Morgan, 1979; Larsson, 1993; Larsson and Bengtsson, 1993; Luthans and Davis, 1982; Tsoukas, 1989) have also used the terminology of nomothetic and idiographic research approaches when discussing different methodological approaches in this research field. These two methodological schools can also be observed in M&A research, the traditionally and dominant *nomothetic* approach which emphasizes quantitative analysis of a few aspects across large samples and the *idiographic* approach which focuses on the qualitative, multi-aspect in-depth study of one or a few cases (Burrell and Morgan, 1979; Luthans and Davis, 1982). Most empirical studies as well as most M&A researchers clearly fall into one of these methodological approaches.

The aim of idiographic researchers is to provide rich descriptions and/ or to make theoretical generalizations. This is in contrast with the nomothetic approach that emphasizes quantitative analysis of a few aspects across large samples in order to test hypotheses and make statistical generalizations. The idiographic perspective contributes especially by providing new and unexpected insights and by building new theories and concepts.

These kinds of contributions are often based on an in-depth understanding generated by rather time consuming studies of complex processes over a longer time period. Major disadvantages are that they tend to be so rich and specific that no statistical generalization is possible, and that the reliance on many empirical sources with sometimes vague research questions can make the validity and reliability questionable.

The case study method is the dominating idiographic research method within management and organizational research including M&A research. The strengths and weaknesses of the case study method in management and organizational research have in general interested a few select scholars. A study of well-published case study-based articles in major management research journals (Larsson and Löwendahl, 2005) found that these articles mostly referenced three sources; Glaser and Strauss (1967), Yin (1984) and Eisenhardt (1989). Since the Larsson and Löwendahl study at least three more recent articles have contributed to the case study method; Eisenhardt and Graebner (2007), Flyvbjerg (2006) and Siggelkow (2007). These leading scholars, articles and books concerning the case study method in management research will in the following form the base for a discussion of the strengths and weaknesses of case study research.

Glaser and Strauss wrote a classic book on qualitative research; *The Discovery of Grounded Theory* (1967). It argues for inductive development of theory from empirical data. It recommends constructing substantive theory, that is, theory pertaining to specific empirical phenomenon such as M&A, eventually moving also to formal theory, that is, more general theories that could be used on many empirical phenomena such as transaction-cost theory. Even though Glaser and Strauss (1967) focus "on defending building cases from theory rather than on actually how to do it" (Eisenhardt, 1989: 546) they were among the first to stress the strength of the case study method as a generator of new theory.

The case study method's generative purpose has strongly been advocated by Eisenhardt (1989) and Eisenhardt and Graebner (2007) in the management research field. Eisenhardt (1989: 546) states that case studies are particularly relevant "in the early stages of research on a topic or to provide freshness in perspective to an already researched topic". They largely recommend following the same process as outlined by Glaser and Strauss (1967) performing multi-case studies, usually some 2–10 cases, and then proceed with comparative analysis resulting in "the development of testable hypothesizes and theory which is generalizable across settings" (Eisenhardt, 1989: 548). Eisenhardt and Graebner (2007) maintain that the case study method probably is the best bridge between rich qualitative evidence to standard deductive research, making case study research complementary to the nomothetic research methodology. They (ibid.) also note that access to rich empirical data often creates theory which is interesting, accurate and testable as evidenced by articles based on case study research receiving a disproportionate portion of awards and references.

Eisenhardt and Graebner (2007) also discuss the weaknesses of case study research which mostly concerns the problems of getting published as case study research-based papers often are viewed upon with skepticism by reviewers and editors belonging to the mainstream nomothetic tradition. Eisenhardt and Graebner (2007) recommend researchers to justify their theory building purpose, to explain their theoretical sampling of cases, limit informant bias, and use rich presentation of evidence much in line with advice given by Bengtsson et al. (1997).

If Glaser and Strauss (1967) wrote the classic book on arguing for grounded theory building using case studies, Yin's original book (1984) on case study research is the classic book on case study design, that is, how to do case study research. Yin sees case study research as a research strategy which has its strengths when the research project has a purpose to explain or understand a contemporary phenomenon, especially when more complex and detailed explanations are required. Yin equates the case study method with the experiment as both are strong on causal explanations. However, if you do not control the research object and its environment, as in the experiment situation, case study research will be the only possible strategy. Thus case studies are the best research strategy for answering how and why questions when studying a contemporary phenomenon such as M&A.

Glaser and Strauss (1967) and Eisenhardt (1989) have largely the same view of case studies; it is a good research strategy when building new theory in an inductive fashion. Later on normal science, the nomothetic science approach, can take over and test hypothesizes, generated by case studies, on larger samples. Thus, the cases as such are not very valuable; it is their contribution to theory building which is valuable. Yin (1984) largely agrees with this notion, however, he also notes the existence of critical and unique cases. Sometimes cases are interesting in themselves because they are so unique and offer unique opportunities to study actions and reactions normally not visible to the researcher. A contemporary example of such a unique case would be the global financial crisis starting in 2008.

Siggelkow (2007) also argues for the interest in unique and critical cases as a source for motivation and inspiration to do case study research. Flyvbjerg (2006) takes this discussion further and argues for case studies as critical cases or "black swans", that is, they could be used in a Popperian way to falsify theories. Flyvbjerg (2006) also maintains that by selecting extreme cases or cases with extreme variations, they could also be used to test hypothesizes and/or the robustness of theories. Flyvbjerg also argues for case studies in their own right; good narratives add to the general and academic understanding of the social phenomenon.

In summary, the case study method, according to the well-referenced articles and books above, has the following strengths and uses in management research:

- Case studies are particularly good to use when building new theory for a new contemporary phenomenon.
- Case studies are also good to provide fresh and new perspectives to a well-known and previously studied phenomenon.
- Case studies are particularly good at studying complex causal and contextual explanations and understanding for a contemporary phenomenon, that is, how and why questions regarding, for example, multi-aspect and level interaction between joining organizations.
- The longitudinal strength of case studies can be utilized to better capture organizational processes over time, such as the combination and integration phases of M&A.
- Case studies can also be used to test theory using critical, extreme and maximum variation cases.
- Case studies can also be used in their own right to provide illustrations and general understanding of a complex contemporary phenomenon.

REVIEWING MORE INFLUENTIAL M&A CASE STUDIES

The disciplines of management and finance completely dominate research on M&A (Cartwright and Schoenberg, 2006; Haleblian et al., 2009), predominantly focusing on M&A activities in the USA and UK (Cartwright, 2005). Financially oriented research mostly focus on the issue whether M&A create value or not for the shareholders (Cartwright and Schoenberg, 2006; Larsson, 1990). Strategic management research has largely focused on the issue of strategic fit, that is, the link between performance and the fit between acquiring and acquired firm (Cartwright and Schoenberg, 2006). To an overwhelming degree these questions have been researched through various forms of nomothetic research methods using mainly quantitative archival data (Haleblian et al., 2009).

In a recent review of empirically based M&A research, between 1992 and 2007 published in leading US academic journals in management, finance, accounting, sociology and economics, Haleblian et al. (2009)

identified 167 articles. They found only five studies which had either "focused in great depth on one particular event ... or a small set of acquisitions" (Haleblian et al., 2009: 492) which gives a publication rate of 3 percent for case-based research in M&A. Thus, we may conclude that overall M&A research is of nomothetic orientation and only a small fraction is idiographic. Moreover, as Larsson and Finkelstein (1999) highlight, the different disciplines involved in M&A research; strategic management, finance, economics, organization theory and HRM tend to disregard research findings in the other disciplines. Thus, very few attempts have been made using integrative approaches using M&A research findings from different disciplines and research approaches.

Given this, which are the most influential case-based M&A studies and what are their findings? We used the Social Science Citation Index (SSCI) to identify the most referenced M&A studies published in the most prestigious scientific journals. We compared our list of articles with the recent reviews on M&A research mentioned above (Cartwright and Schoenberg, 2006; Haleblian et al., 2009) in order to make sure that we had not missed any important publication.

In order to limit our search we looked at the 200 most referenced publications in the M&A field in SSCI. Thus we used the logic that if the publication is one of the 200 most referenced publications in the field it is an influential publication. From those lists we identified the publications based on research using an idiographic approach. Altogether we identified 11 articles. This indicates that the idiographic research is a little more (6 percent) than the level indicated above by Haleblian et al.'s (2009) review of M&A research. Haleblian et al. (2009) used only articles published in US journals for their review. The SSCI index contains a selection of top-rated US, European and journals from other continents. Moreover, we used impact as a measure, meaning that we have only used articles that are heavily cited in the field. The 11 influential M&A case studies are summarized in Table 7.1.

The influential idiographic M&A studies show a different pattern in terms of origin of researchers, journals, discipline and research contexts than the pattern exhibited in the traditional nomothetic M&A studies of US dominance in origin of researchers, journals and research data and dominance of finance and strategic management disciplines. The idiographic M&A research exhibits a more varied and pluralistic pattern. Articles written by North American and European researchers are almost evenly distributed (six North American and five European articles) as are the research data (six studies based on North American data and five on European data) and journal location (six in European journals and five in North American journals). Strategic management dominates (five

Table 7.1 The summary of 11 influential case studies

Article (number of citations in SSCI)	Research aim/ question	Main research discipline	Research design + main method method references	Empirical context and length of study period	Main findings
Bresman, Birkinshaw and Nobel, 1999 (125)	To identify the factors that facilitate knowledge transfer in international acquisition and identifying patterns of international knowledge transfer from the acquiring company to acquired company and vice versa in the post-acquisition integration process	Strategic management	Questionnaires and case studies, three longitudinal cases of acquisitions based on 219 questionnaires and 40 interviews (no method references)	Post-acquisition integration process, specifically knowledge transfer, three Swedish MNCs' acquisitions of foreign companies, studied period 1988–1996 (8 years)	The knowledge transfer process in acquisitions is distinctly different from other modes of governance, due to the rapidly evolving relationship between the two parties. In the early stages, knowledge transfer is relatively hierarchical but then gives way to a reciprocal process. Over time knowledge being transferred shifts from relatively articulate (for example patents) to more tacit

Author, year	Purpose	Field	Method	Case description	Findings
Buono, Bowditch and Lewis, 1985 (112)	Clarify our understanding of organizational culture and its consequences for the merger process	HRM	Multi-method approach, before, during and after merger, based on questionnaires, interviews, observations and archival data.	One case study, two banks merging studied from pre-merger 1979–1980, during merger 1981 and post-merger 1982 (4 years)	Hard organizational factors such as compensation, amount of working hours and training policies showed no significant differences on organizational climate before and after the merger. Instead it was the subjective culture, such as organizational commitment and attitudes towards top management, producing the differences. More management attention should be directed to the culture aspect of the merger
Ranft and Lord, 2002 (64)	Explore the process of acquiring new technologies and capabilities from other firms with particular focus on the dynamics of knowledge transfer during acquisition implementation	Strategic management	Multiple case study research design for grounded-theory building and development of a conceptual model and propositions. Based on 17 interviews of high-level managers.	Post-acquisition integration process, seven retrospective cases of high-tech acquisitions with the intention of gaining new technologies and capabilities. Studied period	The transfer of technologies and capabilities to the acquirer is neither simple nor quick because of distinct acquisition implementation issues. Knowledge transfer is difficult within an existing firm and likely to be even more difficult in an acquisition context because, unlike in an existing firm, the acquirer and the

Table 7.1 (continued)

Article (number of citations in SSCI)	Research aim/ question	Main research discipline	Research design + main method references	Empirical context and length of study period	Main findings
Ranft and Lord, 2002 (64)			Glaser and Strauss (1967), Eisenhardt (1989), Yin (1994)	3 years of post-acquisition integration process	acquired firm do not share a common strategy, structure, history, and culture
Birkinshaw, Bresman and Håkanson, 2000 (56)	What is the process through which an acquisition delivers on the value creation sought by the acquiring firm?	Strategic management	Case studies based on interviews and questionnaires, to study a small number of recent acquisitions in great detail	Post-acquisition integration process, 3 longitudinal cases of cross-border acquisitions by three Swedish MNCs. Studied period 1991–1996 (5 years)	The task integration process and acquisition success is mediated by the current performance level and the human integration already in place in the individual operating units. A low level of performance and a low level of human integration will limit the effectiveness of task integration as a driver of acquisition success
Rhoades, 1998 (52)	Do bank mergers, especially horizontal (in-market) mergers, yield efficiency gains?	Finance	Case study approach to provide insights into firm (industry) behavior and	Post-merger integration efficiency effects. Nine retrospective large horizontal	In all cases significant cost cutting objectives were achieved or surpassed fairly quickly; four of the nine mergers showed clear efficiency gains relative to

Author (year)	Focus	Discipline	Method / Sample	Findings
			performance through the use of a wide range of data and institutional detail from unique firm or industry sources. Analyses of financial ratios and interviews with bank officials. No method references given	bank mergers. Studied period three years after the merger
				peers; and seven of the nine mergers exhibited an improvement in return on assets relative to peers
Bastien, 1987 (47)	Linking acquiring company communication and behavior with acquired company employee motivation, retention, and communications	HRM	Case studies based on 21 interviews of acquired lower level and mid-level managers. Yin, 1984	Post-acquisition integration process, three retrospective cases of acquisitions around or some months after formal take-over
				In stressful situations such as merger or acquisition, communication is key to managing uncertainty in the acquired organization. If communication is inadequate in quantity, quality (formal or collegial), or congruence for the acquired organization, rumor mills, a decrease in productivity, and an increase in employee turnover can result

Table 7.1 (continued)

Article (number of citations in SSCI)	Research aim/ question	Main research discipline	Research design + main method references	Empirical context and length of study period	Main findings
Vaara, 2002 (46)	To study narratives of success and failure in the case of mergers and acquisitions	Organization theory	Narrative approach, case studies based on 126 interviews with high level and mid-level managers.	Post-acquisition integration process, eight retrospective cases of Finnish-Swedish mergers and acquisitions. Studied period, circa one year after the formal merger	The study identifies four specific discourse types – 'rationalistic', 'cultural', 'role-bound' and 'individualistic' – that the narrators employed when (re)constructing success/ failure in the context of post-merger integration
Greenwood, Hinings and Brown, 1994 (45)	Empirically test the hypotheses: H1. The courtship stages of the merger process are characterized by a concern for strategic fit to the neglect of organization fit.	Strategic management	A longitudinal case study of two similar organizations whose members widely agreed to merge. Therefore appropriate to test the hypotheses in a situation where behavioral	Post-merger integration process involving a merger between two large accounting firms in Canada. Process studied from announcement	Contrary to Hypothesis 1, attention was given throughout the merger process to the importance of organizational as well as strategic fit. In the present case the unfolding of the merger did reveal significant variations of professional practice that were unanticipated in the

	Research aim	Theory	Method	Description	Findings
	H2. Ambiguous agreements made during the early stages of a merger lead to a cycle of escalating conflict as ambiguities are clarified during the consummation stage		difficulties might be least expected. Based on some 220 interviews with partners and managers during the studied period. Eisenhardt, 1989	of merger and four years after in real time, i.e., as the process unfolded	negotiation stages, which confirms Hypothesis 2
Olie, 1994 (43)	To study merger integration in an international context and how a new viable entity can be created	Organization theory	Case study approach to allow for greater understanding of the dynamics present within a single setting. Based on some 60 interviews from both parties. Yin, 1984	Post-merger integration process. Retrospective cases of three German-Dutch industrial mergers. Studied period 10 years	A high degree of cohesion is fundamental in creating a joint effort to fulfill the goals of the new organization. Obstacles were identified which may hinder effective consolidation. These include firm-specific, industry-specific and country-specific differences such as different legal requirements, co-determination practices, political environment, management styles and sales traditions

Table 7.1 (continued)

Article (number of citations in SSCI)	Research aim/ question	Main research discipline	Research design + main method references	Empirical context and length of study period	Main findings
Empson, 2001 (40)	Why do individuals resist knowledge transfer in the context of mergers between professional service firms?	HRM	Longitudinal and retrospective case studies (based on 177 interviews) in order to gain in-depth understanding of the complexities of the merger process, gather longitudinal data, triangulate data and combine multiple levels of analysis. No method references	Post-acquisition integration process, two longitudinal cases and one retrospective case study of mergers and acquisitions in accounting and management consulting, professional service firms. In all three cases the period studied was three years	In the context of PSF mergers, individuals will resist knowledge transfer when they perceive fundamental differences in the form of the knowledge base and the organizational image of the combining firms. These perceived differences give rise to the twin fears of exploitation and contamination

184

| Graebner, 2004 (40) | How do the leaders of the acquired firm influence value creation during the implementation process? | Strategic management | Grounded theory-building, multiple case designs with replication logic. Three data sources: interviews, follow-up emails and phone calls, archival data. Eisenhardt, 1989 | Post-acquisition integration process, 8 retrospective cases of acquisition in the ICT-industries. Based on 60 semi-structured interviews. Retrospective case studies six months after formal acquisition | Acquired leaders are instrumental in creating two types of value, expected and serendipitous. They create value in part by mitigating the potential conflicts between autonomy and integration. The most effective acquired leaders are able to foster multiple points of change within their organizations, including the completion of the acquired technology, the realization of planned synergies, and the discovery of unexpected sources of synergy |

articles), with HRM and organization theory having three and two articles respectively. The dominating discipline in nomothetic M&A research, finance, has only one article in the idiographic research tradition.

Analyzing the content of the 11 articles we arrive at some interesting patterns in relation to the strengths of the case study method discussed above.

1. Almost all idiographic M&A studies (10 of 11) focus on the post-acquisition or post-merger integration process. Thus, the relatively more complex and especially longitudinal part of the M&A process, that is, the messy post-acquisition integration process that is more extended over time than the more "snapshot" pre-acquisition process and stock-market reactions, seem to be fertile ground for case studies. In the eleventh article, Buono et al. (1985) study the whole merger process, before, during and after.
2. All studies were process studies in the sense that they studied the integration (or whole merger process) either retrospectively, sometime after the formal merger or acquisition, or longitudinally following the process as it unfolded. The time differed from some weeks after the formal merger or acquisition up to ten years after.
3. The majority of the studies (eight) argued for the case study approach as a good way to get a more detailed or fine-grained view of the study object and the dynamics. Two studies explicitly follow a grounded-theory, theory-building approach, making references to Glaser and Strauss (1967), Yin (1984 or 1994) and/or Eisenhardt (1989). One study (Greenwood et al., 1994) claimed to test theory using their two case studies of accounting firm mergers.
4. All studies have explicit or implicit research questions of "how and why" character. They all have the general purpose to provide further explanations and understanding of the integration process. While some studies also had questions like "when, who and what", their main contributions concerned the how and why questions.
5. Two studies had the aim to resolve current theoretical debates (Rhoades, 1998; Greenwood et al., 1994) using critical cases. Rhoades tried to resolve the debate regarding financial view of wealth-destruction caused by M&A contrary to the more positive view on M&A by strategic management researchers and practitioners. Rhoades selected cases that were most likely to show positive outcomes, horizontal M&A, as critical cases. Greenwood et al. (1994) used a case study of merging accounting firms that were not met with the usual resistance and instead were welcomed by all parties involved, to test two hypotheses derived from previous

M&A research, implicitly assuming resistance from several parties involved.

6. While no studies seem to fit the description of a "narrative in its own right" the contexts in which M&A studies are performed varies giving industry- and firm-specific understanding to M&A. Most studies were from industrial companies (five); there are also some from contexts such as bank and accounting industries (three), high-tech industries (two), and professional service firms (one). Moreover, as much nomothetic M&A research is based on US data, the idiographic M&A research also provided rich descriptions from different European countries such as Finland, Germany, the Netherlands, Sweden and the UK.

7. The studies based on one or two cases tend to focus on one industry, or one type of firm, professional service firms, or one aspect of the merger/acquisition such as communication. The longer the studied time period or the more the cases studied are not confined to one industry or type of firm, the more integration dimensions are discovered. For instance, in the longitudinal study by Olie (1994), studying three international mergers over ten years, he finds not only firm-specific differences affecting the integration process, but also industry-specific and country-specific differences affecting the integration process.

In summary, the influential M&A case studies focus on the post-acquisition or post-merger integration process and study this over time retrospectively and/or as it unfolds over time. They do it mainly to acquire a fine-grained perspective of the process and to understand the idiosyncrasies of the particular interaction between the joining organizations and their unfolding (inter)national-, industry-, and company-specific contexts. Some studies explicitly relate this to theory building and theory testing. Studies based on long time periods and/or many cases tend to discover and analyse more integration dimensions than studies based on fewer cases. Moreover the more limited data richness of most surveys of archival data typically lacks the number and flexible collection of data aspects to capture contextual and multi-level complexities as case studies are more able to do.

A METHODOLOGICAL CASE SURVEY OF 55 M&A CASES

Unfortunately, almost all development of the case study method seems to be largely conceptual and qualitatively experiential, that is, by researchers who have read and thought about case study methodology and done their own case studies. Systematic comparisons between various case studies, such as Larsson and Löwendahl's (2005) quantitative and qualitative meta-analysis of 12 well-published case studies, are rare indeed. Even rarer is the utilization of the *case survey* method for quantitatively, empirically analyzing and developing different case study designs, even though it is very suitable to do so (Larsson, 1993).

The case survey method is "an expensive and potentially powerful method of identifying and statistically testing patterns across studies . . . particularly suitable . . . when the unit of analysis is the organization [and] a broad range of conditions is of interest (Jauch et al., 1980) . . . The basic procedure of the case survey is (1) select a group of existing case studies relevant to the chosen research questions, (2) design a coding scheme for systematic conversion of the qualitative case descriptions into quantified variables, (3) use multiple raters to code the cases and measure their inter-rater reliability, and (4) statistically analyze the coded data" (Larsson, 1993: 1516–1517). It taps the vast prior research efforts of the many existing rich and longitudinal case studies and overcomes the individual limitations of case studies not being able to examine cross-sectional patterns and statistically generalize to larger populations. Case surveys are also replicable, systematically extendable, can measure the reliability of the case coding, and bridge traditional research gaps between idiographic and nomothetic as well as qualitative and quantitative methods (Larsson, 1993).

There are some good examples of case surveys that have contributed greatly to services (Yin and Yates, 1974); decision-making (Mintzberg et al., 1976), strategy and organizational transitions (Miller and Friesen, 1977, 1980), CEO succession (Osborn et al., 1981), gain sharing (Bullock and Lawler, 1984), and M&A (Larsson, 1989; Larsson and Finkelstein, 1999; Larsson and Lubatkin, 2001; Stahl et al., forthcoming). Even though there have been several well-published methodological articles on the case survey itself (Jauch et al., 1980; Larsson, 1993; Yin and Heald, 1975), we have yet to find any study that has focused on using the power of the case survey method to develop case study methodology. Given that systematic comparisons of how different case study designs ought to be a central part of the complete case survey method (Larsson, 1993), this method offers a great opportunity for empirically studying the effects of different case study designs. Unfortunately, very few (such as two of seven reviewed case surveys in Larsson, 1993) actually do this case study design analysis, which can be one explanation why there seem to be so few case surveys being used to develop the case study method.

We will here make use of the 55 M&A case survey that was used as an illustration in Larsson's methodological article from 1993 to highlight how different case study designs are related to M&A findings and newly collected reference impact data. Table 7.2 shows the means, standard deviations, and correlations between the different case study design variables of "Number of Cases" studied, how extensive ("Case Data Collection") and systematic ("Case Systematic Method") the data collection of the case study was, the "Case Calendar Year" (average integration year, ranging from 1 = throughout 1964 and 5 = from 1980 onwards), "Case Period Length", and "Acquired Case Perspective" (that is, mainly acquirer = 1, balanced mix = 2, and mainly acquired = 3) of the case studies. We also include the "Real Case Names" (that is, non-anonymous), "Case Pages", "Case Publication Status", and "Case Reference Impact" of the case study reports to analyse the possible impact of these case study reporting issues (no. 7–10). With the exception of the newly created variables Number of Cases (single = 1, double = 2, triple = 3, or quadruple or more = 4) and Case Reference Impact (rank from 1–55 based on number of references found to the case sources in Google Scholar searches in February 2011, where 55 = most references and 1 = least, since SSCI was not possible to use due to its exclusion of all books, dissertations, teaching cases, and conference papers that also were included in the case survey), all the other case study design variables are described in detail in Larsson (1989).

The strongest positive correlation between the case study design variables (no. 1–6) is the extent and systematic data collection (0.61 corr.coef.). This is a natural finding of good case study designs that combine both high quantity and quality of the data collection. One expected nuance here is the two multi-case studies with the most cases were Lindgren's (1982) doctoral dissertation with 11 cases and Ravenscraft and Scherer's (1987) research book with 15 cases, where the large number of cases reduced the extent of data collected *per case* relative to the the higher degree of systematic data collection.

More unexpected case design correlations include the extent of data collection and the Real Case Names which are both positively correlated to case studies with mainly the acquired firm's perspective (0.41 and 0.39 corr.coef.). These correlations are to some extent most likely artefacts of the characteristics of the specific case sample, where Lindgren's 11 anonymous foreign acquisitions were done with relatively less data collection per case and primarily the acquiring firm's perspective.

Larsson (1989; 1993) has already tested the impact on the different case study designs on this M&A sample and found that it was mainly the Case Period Length and Case Calendar Year that had significant impacts on the dependent variable Synergy Realization, when including the main independent variables and Case Data Collection in the same regression

Table 7.2   Means, standard deviation, and Pearson correlation coefficients

Variables:	Means	s.d.	N^a	1	2	3	4
Case design variables							
1. Number of Cases	2.82	1.31	55				
2. Case Data Collection	3.44	1.15	50	−0.64**			
3. Case Systematic Method	3.65	1.05	49	−0.04	0.61**		
4. Case Calendar Year	3.86	1.03	55	0.02	0.16	0.25*	
5. Case Period Length	3.92	1.30	47	0.45**	−0.19	−0.26	−0.21
6. Acquired Case Perspective	1.94	0.65	55	−0.47**	0.41**	−0.05	−0.10
Case publication variables							
7. Real Case Names	1.63	0.49	55	0.02	−0.04	−0.09	−0.27
8. Case Pages	44.6	17.0	55	−0.29*	0.56	0.50	0.14
9. Case Publi-cation Status	3.20	1.01	55	0.18	−0.24	−0.09	−0.15
10. Case Reference Impact	31.9	17.2	55	0.72**	−0.65**	−0.26	0.12
Substantive M&A variables							
11. Synergy Realization	2.03	1.82	55	−0.05	0.35**	0.32*	0.32**
12. Strategic Combin-ation Potential	12.2	3.90	51	−0.35*	−0.35*	0.56**	0.42**
13. Organ-izational Integration	2.92	1.08	54	−0.02	0.38**	0.34*	0.34*
14. Employee Resistance	2.58	1.16	48	−0.36*	0.36*	−0.02	0.03

Notes:
[a] Differences are due to insufficient information coding for some variables
* $p < 0.05$
** $p < 0.01$.

5	6	7	8	9	10	11	12	13
−0.08								
0.21	0.39**							
−0.26	0.18	0.18						
0.08	0.02	0.33*	−0.13					
0.44**	−0.18	0.17	−0.41**	0.50**				
0.05	−0.07	−0.11	0.05	−0.22	−0.13			
0.24	−0.26	−0.16	−0.27	0.41**	−0.52**	0.55**		
0.19	0.15	−0.21	0.14	0.22	−0.19	0.66**	0.62**	
−0.07	0.20	−0.11	0.31*	0.27	−0.32*	−0.24	0.25	0.06

equations. This suggested that when controlling for differences during the more than three decades over which the 55 M&A cases occurred (such as business cycles and population learning), the longer the case period studied, the more synergy realization was found. The implication of this is that M&A researchers should design case studies that preferably cover several years of the integration to capture as much as possible of the M&A performance. The longitudinal strength of case studies enables both practitioners sufficient time to actually realize even unexpected synergy potentials and researchers to identify this gradual value creation.

However, these past analyses of case study design impact of M&A findings did not include how many cases the design included. We have now added Number of Cases to the M&A database. It ranges from 15 single case studies, four double case studies, two triple case studies, one with eleven cases, and one with fifteen cases. To avoid the two extreme values of 11- and 15- cases, we simply used a scale from 1 to 4 as stated above. The strongest correlation with other case design variables is with Case Data Collection (−0.64). This is natural given the practical limitations of research resources hardly allows to spend as much time on each of so many cases as those who only do 1–3 cases in their studies. There is also a negative correlation between Acquired Case Perspective and Number of Cases (−0.47 corr.coef.). It can be expected that those researchers focusing on the acquired firm use the more unique single case study design, while those focusing on the acquiring firm are more likely to do multi-case studies of firms that do multiple acquisitions.

While Table 7.2 shows many significant correlations between case design and findings variables, the regression results in Table 7.3 show that only few of these relationships remain significant when tested simultaneously. The four main case findings variables of the Larsson (1989; 1993) case survey are the dependent variable Synergy Realization (measured by 11 different synergy sources, including cost savings from consolidating purchasing, production, administration, and vertical supply as well as added income from new market access and cross-selling) and the three main independent variables, Strategic Combination Potential (improved after the original 1989 study by measuring the production and market similarities and complementarities), Organizational Integration (measured from degree of interaction and coordination efforts between the joining firms), and Employee Resistance (measured in the first and second halves of the studied integration period).

The only main case findings variables that were substantially affected by the case design variables are Strategic Combination Potential where the adjusted R^2 is 0.41 but no single case design variable is significant and Organizational Integration where the adjusted R^2 is 0.27 and Acquired

Table 7.3 Results of regression analysis of M&A findings and case design variables

Variables	Synergy Realization		Strategic Combination Potential		Organizational Integration		Employee Resistance	
	β	s.e.	β	s.e.	β	s.e.	β	s.e.
Number of Cases	−0.06	0.23	−0.27	0.20	0.18	0.23	−0.22	0.29
Case Data Collection	0.48	0.30	0.36	0.26	0.78**	0.28	0.31	0.34
Case Systematic Method	−0.06	0.24	0.14	0.21	−0.26	0.22	−0.13	0.28
Case Calendar Year	0.38*	0.17	−0.05	0.15	0.19	0.16	−0.20	0.20
Case Period Length	0.25	0.19	−0.19	0.17	−0.18	0.18	−0.08	0.22
Acquired Case Perspective	−0.15	0.17	−0.17	0.15	−0.37*	0.17	−0.20	0.22
Adjusted R^2	0.17		0.41		0.27		0.01	
F	2.4		5.3**		3.4*		1.1	
N	39		37		38		33	

Notes:
* $p < 0.05$
** $p < 0.01$.

193

Case Perspective (negative) and especially Case Data Collection (positive) are significantly related. This can in part be explained by the more eventful and content-rich the studied integration period of the case was, the more data was collected as can be expected in contrast to unrelated M&A with little integration.

The only case design variable that was found to be significantly related to the dependent Synergy Realization variable case is Case Calendar Year. This positive relationship indicates the possibility of M&A learning at the population level and/or effects of changes in the US antitrust regulations (Larsson, 1993). In contrast, the 1989 regression analysis with Synergy Realization as dependent variable with five of the independent case design variables (that is, without Number of Cases) showed instead Case Data Collection as the only significant case design variable. The present addition of Number of Cases can be seen as controlling for the multi-case design effect on the Case Data Collection and thereby more clearly revealing the positive Case Calendar Year relationship (that also was found to be more significant than Case Data Collection in regressions with all the four main case findings variables).

TESTING THE PUBLICATION IMPACT OF CASE DESIGN

Turning to case publication issues, the correlations involving them in Table 7.2 include that the higher the extent of systematic data collection, the more pages are used to report the case studies (0.56 and 0.50 corr. coef.). This can suggest the difficulty of economically reporting well-designed case studies that can hinder article publications to some extent. While some of the design and publication findings have been observed in earlier works based on this M&A case sample (Larsson, 1989, 1993), the newly collected reference counts offer the opportunity to predict and test hypotheses on the effects of M&A case design and publication on how much subsequent research refers to the respective M&A case study. Based on the simple logic of the better case study design and publication are likely to result in greater impact on subsequent research, we propose the following hypotheses:

1. The more extensive the Case Data Collection, the (a) greater the achieved Case Publication Status and (b) more the Case Reference Impact.

2. The more the Case Systematic Method, the (a) greater the achieved Case Publication Status and (b) more the Case Reference Impact.

3. The greater the Number of Cases included in the case study, the (a) greater the achieved Case Publication Status and (b) more the Case Reference Impact.

4. The longer the Case Period Length, the (a) greater the achieved Case Publication Status and (b) more the Case Reference Impact.

5. Real Case Names are associated with (a) greater achieved Case Publication Status and (b) more Case Reference Impact.

6. The greater the achieved Case Publication Status, the more the Case Reference Impact.

We do not predict any clear impact of the acquired versus acquiring perspective of the case studies on publication status and reference impact. While a high number of case pages can be expected to limit high status publication in research journals and a more recent calendar year can limit the total number of references by subsequent research, we do not consider these two possible relationships as potentially relevant for developing the case study method in M&A research.

Case Publication Status was measured with a 5-point ordinal scale from unpublished = 1 (4 out of the 55 cases), teaching cases and conference papers = 2 (7 cases), and doctoral dissertations = 3 (22 cases) to published chapter or book (18 cases) = 4 and research journal = 5 (4 cases). We intended to measure the research impact through dual reference counts in the more selective SSCI and the broader Google Scholar. However, it turned out that only four out of the 55 case studies had any SSCI references at all, so we had to settle for using only the Google Scholar references. They ranged from one reference (including two Harvard Business School cases) to 340 references to Buono et al. (1985) and an outstanding 833 references, to the Ravenscraft and Scherer (1987) book with 15 M&A case studies. To avoid using this extreme value, we rank ordered the 55 cases from 1 having the least references to 55 having the most references.

The correlations in Table 7.2 indicate that Case Publication Status is only significantly correlated to Case Reference Impact (0.50 corr.coef.) and Real Case Names (0.33 corr.coef.). The former indicates the obvious relationship that subsequent research tends to use the previous works that are better published, while the latter suggests that the authenticity of real names may contribute somewhat to the publishability of M&A cases. That is, both these correlations support Hypotheses 5a and 6.

Case Reference Impact is significantly correlated to a couple more variables, namely Number of Cases (0.72 corr.coef.) and Case Time

*Table 7.4   Results of regression analysis of publication issues and case
            design variables*

Variables	Case Publication Status		Case Reference Impact	
	β	s.e.	β	s.e.
Number of Cases	−0.04	0.26	0.40*	0.16
Case Data Collection	−0.21	0.32	−0.35**	0.19
Case Systematic Method	0.04	0.26	0.06	0.15
Case Period Length	0.04	0.19	0.18	0.11
Real Case Names	0.22	0.18	−0.08	0.11
Case Publication Status			0.34**	0.10
Adjusted R^2	−0.005		0.3	
F	0.6		11.9**	
N	38		38	

Notes:
* $p < 0.05$
** $p < 0.01$.

Period (0.44 corr.coef.) in support of Hypotheses 3b and 4b, while it is
also negatively correlated with Case Data Collection (−0.65 corr.coef.) in
contradiction to Hypothesis 1b.

Table 7.4 shows the regression results for simultaneously testing these
publication hypotheses. Case Publication Status turns out to not be
explained at all by the set of Hypotheses 1a, 2a, 3a, 4a and 5a that have
an adjusted R^2 of 0.0. Thus, when controlling for the other case design
variables, the correlation support for Real Case Names (Hypothesis 5a)
disappears.

In sharp contrast, the whole set of independent variables explained
as much as 63 percent of the variance in Case Reference Impact, with
Number of Cases and Case Publication Status being the significant
variables in support for Hypotheses 3b and 6. The surprising negative
correlation with Case Data Collection is reduced to insignificance when
controlling for the other independent variables.

In summary, there seems to be no clear pattern of case study design that
explains the initial publication status of these 55 cases, at least not among
the design variables we have studied here. On the other hand, the publication status explains, in turn, a lot of the subsequent research impact in
terms of Google Scholar references together with the perhaps most con-
troversial of our proposed case design hypotheses above. We expect that
many case researchers would disagree that the more cases included in one
case study, the better. Among these 55 M&A cases, the number of cases

seems to contribute to the subsequent impact, albeit probably amplified by the fact that Ravenscraft and Scherer (1987) also contained a gigantic economic survey of M&A performance that has also contributed to its very many references.

CONCLUDING RECOMMENDATIONS FOR GREATER CASE STUDY CONTRIBUTIONS TO THE M&A FIELD

Based on the three reviews of the case study methodological literature, influential M&A case studies, and the methodological case survey of 55 M&A cases, we can conclude that the case study method is a powerful, yet much underutilized method in M&A research. Even though there seem to be perhaps more than 20 times as many M&A surveys as case studies (Haleblian et al., 2009), we find that especially influential M&A case studies contribute unique value to M&A research in terms of the rich idiographic understanding of the complex combination and especially integration processes where the longitudinal, multi-aspect, and multi-level strengths of the case study method excel.

It is also encouraging to find that several of the leading, mainly conceptual M&A books of, for example, Buono and Bowditch (1989), Haspeslagh and Jemison (1991), Cartwright and Cooper (1996), and Marks and Mirvis (1998) are substantially influenced by their authors' own M&A multi-case study experiences. These authors have used the size-wise less restrictive book format to not only give the readers powerful case illustrations, but also provide more conceptual integration of the otherwise quite fragmented M&A field (Larsson and Finkelstein, 1999) as illustrated by Haleblian et al.'s (2009) recent M&A research review. King et al.'s (2004: 188) extensive meta-analysis of 93 M&A performance studies found that existing research has failed to specify many variables that moderate M&A performance and concluded that an "implication is that changes to both M&A theory and research methods may be needed". Case studies represent a well-established research method that can discover missing pieces of the M&A performance puzzle as well as many other M&A issues and certainly deserves more than being 3–6 percent of the total empirical M&A research. We offer the following recommendations for more and better M&A case studies.

First and foremost, do *more M&A case studies*. So far, their absence seems to be more a result of pessimistic avoidance than actually higher publication rejection rates. The almost complete dominance of nomothetic surveys in empirical M&A research is most likely subject to diminishing marginal utility. We need to be focusing more on how the methodological strengths of idiographic case studies can be utilized to complement the nomothetic hegemony and the blind spots that it has created. Greater awareness, more utilization, further development, better reporting, and greater appreciation of the idiographic strengths of the case study method as well as stronger arguments for its use should lead to more break-throughs, greater methodological balance and complementarities, higher publication status, and more subsequent impact on research.

Second, do a *series of cases* to generate more case comparisons, re-utilization of case data, and multiple publication opportunities. Those who have not done any case studies before can try to do a first pilot case to explore both the case study method itself and the first interesting find-ings that it can generate. Then one can complement this first case with other cases sequentially as can those who already have done previous case studies. The key point here is that doing related cases (such as being in the same theoretical domain of certain research questions, Bullock and Tubbs, 1987) creates great research synergies between them in contrast to unrelated single case studies of disparate phenomena. Glaser and Strauss (1967) have recommended initially selecting as similar cases as possible to facilitate discoveries of new categories and possible relationships between them and then gradually maximizing the differences between the cases to identify the limits and variations of the initial discoveries. This sequencing of similarities and differences has proven to be quite useful in M&A case study research (Larsson, 1990).

Many researchers that have tried once or twice to do case studies are concerned about how much data is collected versus how little of it is then reported, especially when using the article format. The use of serial case studies can utilize another idiographic strength of the case study method, namely the flexible use of collected data. Due to their multi-aspect rich-ness, case studies are very amenable to being reused for different purposes (Larsson, 1993). For example, the 55 M&A cases reanalyzed here were made from an array of purposes including theory building, theory testing, description, and teaching. Serial case designs can enable first a single case publication, followed by a dual case study that can be economically made by reusing the first case with a different focus and adding the second case and the cross-case comparison it contributes as a second publication opportunity. A third case can then be used as part of a new dual or triple case study with yet again different focus and so forth. At some point, it can be economical to also reuse case studies made by others through the case survey method to further strengthen the cross-case comparative power.

Third, make use of the *longitudinal power* of case studies to capture the complex unfolding processes of combining and integrating two or more organizations that last for many years. Nomothetic surveys of archival data typically offer at best a superficial time series of snapshots in contrast to the rich idiographic capture of interacting people, groups, organizations, and contexts over time that make up the complex processes of the pre- and post-combination phases of M&A. The length of the 55 cases here varied from covering at least six months to more than 10 years, with a median of 4+ years of studied integration period and significantly impacting how much synergy realization was found. While real time observations have advantages such as reducing post-rationalizations, almost all cases are mainly reconstructive where one can economically collect data from the past.

Fourth, use mainly *balanced case perspectives* rather than choosing to only look at M&A from either the acquiring or acquired perspective. Getting both sides of the story should be essential in the perhaps most two-sided management phenomena of corporate marriages. It can guard against the post-rationalizations that often occur when acquirers, for example, emphasize positive developments, while acquired people mainly remember the "good old company spirit" in cultural defence of their collective identity (Larsson, 1990). Comparing what both sides say makes it also easier to identify what one side does *not* say, such as collective repressions of less "pure" parts of the acquired companies' histories.

As an example, management style similarity was one of the many other variables that were coded for the 55 cases but not discussed here due to the limited scope of this chapter. It was strongly negatively correlated with Acquired Case Perspective. Thus, case studies focusing on the acquired firm's perspective tended to find less management style similarity and thereby more cultural clash than those focusing on the acquiring firms. This indicates that the culturally more threatened acquired side tends to find and even rally against management style differences, while acquirers acknowledge less of such cultural clashes. Collecting both sides of M&A stories enables informed choices of which of the acquirer, balanced, and acquired perspectives to use when interpreting the data instead of being stuck with only one side of the story.

Finally, make use of both the *multi-level and contextual strengths* of case studies to better grasp the complexities of M&A processes than the often single-level archival data of nomothetic surveys. Interviews are the main data collection vehicle of case studies and they can easily involve questions about individual interpretations and actions as well as group reactions, whole organizational processes, and contextual issues such as competitors, customers, national societies, industries, and so forth. Buono et al. (1985)

and Birkinshaw and Bresman's two case studies (1999, 2000) are examples of how also quantitative questionnaires were used for complementary case data collection and analysis to find patterns among individuals within the M&A cases.

M&A are unique and complex events that highlight both value-creating and value-destroying organizational processes. As such they deserve not only the strongly dominating nomothetic study of quantitative surveys, but also the idiographic case studies that can provide very complementary understanding of M&A. We hope that this chapter has provided some further insights and even enthusiasm regarding how increased and better use of the case study method can substantially contribute to greater M&A knowledge overall.

REFERENCES

Allport, G.W. (1937) *Personality: A Psychological Interpretation*, New York: Holt.

Allport, G.W. (1962) 'The general and unique in psychological science', *Journal of Personality*, 30: 405–422.

Andrade, G., Mitchell, M. and E. Stafford (2001) 'New evidence and perspectives on mergers', *The Journal of Economic Perspectives*, 15 (2): 103–120.

Bastien, D.T. (1987) 'Common patterns of behavior and communication in corporate mergers and acquisitions', *Human Resource Management*, 26: 17–33.

Bengtsson, L., Elg, U. and J-I. Lindh (1997) 'Bridging the transatlantic publishing gap: how North American reviewers evaluate European idiographic research', *Scandinavian Journal of Management*, 13 (4): 473–492.

Birkinshaw, J., Bresman, H. and L. Håkanson (2000) 'Managing the post-acquisition integration process: how the human integration and task integration processes interact to foster value creation', *Journal of Management Studies*, 37 (3): 395–424.

Bresman, H., Birkinshaw, J.M. and R. Nobel (1999) 'Knowledge transfer in international acquisitions', *Journal of International Business Studies*, 30 (3): 439–462.

Bullock, R.J. and Lawler, E.E. (1984) 'Gain sharing: a few questions, and fewer answers', *Human Resource Management*, 23: 23–40.

Bullock, R.J. and Tubbs, M.E. (1987) 'The case meta-analysis for OD', *Research in Organizational Change and Development*, 1: 171–228.

Buono, A.F. and Bowditch, J.L. (1989) *The Human Side of Mergers and Acquisitions*, San Francisco, CA: Jossey-Bass.

Buono, A.F., Bowditch, J.L. and J.W. Lewis (1985) 'When cultures collide: the anatomy of a merger', *Human Relations*, 38 (5): 477–500.

Burrell, G. and Morgan, G. (1979) *Sociological Paradigms and Organizational Analysis*, London: Heinemann.

Campbell, D.T. (1975) 'Degrees of freedom and the case study', *Comparative Political Studies*, 8 (2): 178–193.

Cartwright, S. (2005) 'Mergers and acquisitions: an update and appraisal', in G.P. Hodgkinson and J.K. Ford (eds), *International Review of Industrial and Organizational Psychology*, Chichester: John Wiley, 20, pp. 1–38.

Cartwright, S. and Cooper, C.L. (1996) *Managing Mergers, Acquisitions and Strategic Alliances: Integrating People and Cultures*, Oxford: Butterworth-Heinemann.

Cartwright, S. and Schoenberg, R. (2006), 'Thirty years of mergers and acquisitions research: recent advances and future opportunities', *British Journal of Management*, 17: S1–S5.

Chatterjee, S., Lubatkin, M.H., Schweiger, D.M. and Y. Weber (1992), 'Cultural differences and shareholder value in related mergers: linking equity and human capital', *Strategic Management Journal*, 13: 319–334.

Collin, S.-O., Johansson, U., Svensson, K. and P.-O. Ulvenblad (1996), 'Market segmentation in scientific publications: research patterns in American vs European management journals', *British Journal of Management*, 7: 141–154.

Eisenhardt, K. (1989) 'Building theories for case study research', *Academy of Management Review*, 14: 532–550.

Eisenhardt, K.M. and Graebner, M.E. (2007) 'Theory building from cases: opportunities and challenges', *Academy of Management Journal*, 50: 1.

Empson, L. (2001) 'Fear of exploitation and fear of contamination: impediments to knowledge transfer in mergers between professional service firms', *Human Relations*, **54** (7): 839–862.

Flyvbjerg, B. (2006) 'Five misunderstandings about case study research', *Qualitative Inquiry*, **12** (2): 219–245.

Glaser, B.G. and Strauss, A.L. (1967) *The Discovery of Grounded Theory: Strategies for Qualitative Research*, Chicago IL: Aldine.

Graebner, M.E. (2004) 'Momentum and serendipity: how acquired leaders create value in the integration of technology firms, *Strategic Management Journal*, 25: 751–777.

Graebner, M.E. and Eisenhardt, K.M. (2004) 'The seller's side of the story: acquisition as courtship and governance as syndicate in entrepreneurial firms', *Administrative Science Quarterly*, **49** (3): 366–403.

Greenwood, R., Hinings, C.R. and J. Brown (1994) 'Merging professional service firms', *Organization Science*, **5** (2): 239–257.

Haleblian, J. and Finkelstein, S. (1999) 'The influence of organizational acquisition experience on acquisition performance: a behavioral learning perspective', *Administrative Science Quarterly*, 44: 29–56.

Haleblian, J., Devers, C.E., McNamara, G., Carpenter, M.A. and R.B. Davison (2009) 'Taking stock of what we know about mergers and acquisitions: a review and research agenda', *Journal of Management*, **35** (3): 469–502.

Haspeslagh, P. and Jemison, D. (1991) *Managing Acquisitions*, New York: Free Press.

Hitt, M., Hoskisson, R.E., Ireland, R.D. and J.S. Harrison (1991) 'Effects of acquisitions on R&D inputs and outputs', *Academy of Management Journal*, **34** (3): 693–706.

Jauch, L.R., Osborn, R.N. and T.N. Martin (1980) 'Structured content analysis of cases: a complementary method for organizational research', *Academy of Management Review*, 5: 517–525.

Jemison, D.B. and Sitkin, S.B. (1986) 'Corporate acquisitions: a process perspective', *Academy of Management Review*, 11: 145–163.

Jensen, M.C. and Ruback, R.S. (1983) 'The market for corporate control: the scientific evidence', *Journal of Financial Economics*, 11: 5–50.

King, D.R., Dalton, D.R., Daily, C.M. and J.G. Covin (2004) 'Meta-analysis of post-acquisition performance: indications of unidentified moderators', *Strategic Management Journal*, 25: 187–200.

Larsson, R. (1989) *Organizational Integration of Mergers and Acquisitions: A case survey of realization of synergy potentials*, Lund, Sweden: Lund Studies in Economics and Management.

Larsson, R. (1990) *Coordination of Action in Mergers and Acquisitions: Interpretive and systems approaches towards synergy*, Doctoral dissertation. Lund, Sweden: Lund University Press.

Larsson, R. (1993) 'Case survey methodology: quantitative analysis of patterns across case studies', *Academy of Management Journal*, 36: 1515–1546.

Larsson, R. and Bengtsson, L. (1993) 'Integrating method and substance in strategic research. A case survey of individual versus collective organizational learning', Paper presented at the Strategic Management Society's Annual International Conference in Chicago.

Larsson, R. and Finkelstein, S. (1999) 'Integrating strategic, organizational, and human resource perspectives on mergers and acquisitions: a case survey of synergy realization', *Organization Science*, pp. 1–26.

Larsson, R. and Löwendahl, B.R. (2005) 'The qualitative side of management research: a meta-analysis of espoused and used case study methodologies', in Lines, R., Stensaker, I. and A. Langley (eds) *Handbook of Organizational Change and Learning*, Norway: Fagbokforlaget, pp. 390–412.

Larsson, R. and Lubatkin, M. (2001) 'Achieving acculturation in mergers and acquisitions: an international case survey', *Human Relations*, **54** (12): 1573–1607.

Lindgren, U. (1982) *Foreign Acquisitions: Management of the integration process*, Doctoral dissertation, Stockholm School of Economics, Sweden: IIB/EFI.

Luthans, F. and Davis, T.R.V. (1982) 'An idiographic approach to organizational behavior research: the use of single case experimental designs and direct measures', *Academy of Management Review*, 8: 218–225.

Marks, M.L. and Mirvis, P.H. (1998) *Joining Forces: Making One Plus One Equal Three In Mergers, Acquisitions, and Alliances*, San Francisco, CA: Jossey-Bass.

Miller, D. and Friesen, P.H. (1977) 'Strategy-making in context: ten empirical archetypes', *Journal of Management Studies*, pp. 253–280.

Miller, D. and Friesen, P. (1980) 'Archetypes of organizational transition', *Administrative Science Quarterly*, pp. 268–292.

Mintzberg, H., Raisinghani, D. and A. Theoret (1976) 'The structure of 'unstructured' decision processes', *Administrative Science Quarterly*, pp. 246–275.

Olie, R. (1994) 'Shades of culture and institutions in international mergers', *Organization Studies*, **15** (3): 381–405.

Osborn, R.N., Jauch, L.R., Martin, T.N. and W.F. Glueck (1981) 'The event of CEO succession, performance, and environmental conditions', *Academy of Management Journal*, pp. 183–191.

Ranft, A.L. and Lord, M.D. (2002) 'Acquiring new technologies and capabilities: a grounded model of acquisition implementation', *Organization Science*, **13** (4): 420–441.

Ravenscraft, D.J. and Scherer, F.M. (1987) *Mergers, Sell-offs, and Economic Efficiency.* Washington, DC: Brookings Institution.

Rhoades, S.A. (1998) 'The efficiency effects of bank mergers: an overview of case studies of nine mergers', *Journal of Banking and Finance*, 22: 273–291.

Sales, A.L. and Mirvis, P.H. (1984) 'When cultures collide: issues in acquisition', in J. Kimberly and R. Quinn (eds), *The Challenge of Managing Corporate Transition*, Homewood, IL: Dow Jones and Irwin.

Schweiger, D.M. and Walsh, J.P. (1990) 'Mergers and acquisitions: an interdisciplinary view', *Research in Personnel and Human Resource Management*, 8: 41–107.

Siggelkow, N. (2007) 'Persuasion with case studies', *Academy of Management Journal*, **50** (1): 20–24.

Stahl, G., Larsson, R., Kremershof, I. and S. Sitkin (forthcoming) 'Trust dynamics in acquisitions: a case survey', *Human Resource Management.*

Tsoukas, H. (1989) 'The validity of idiographic research explanations', *Academy of Management Review*, 14: 551–561.

Vaara, E. (2002) 'On the discursive construction of success/failure in narratives of post-merger integration', *Organization Studies*, **23** (2): 211–248.

Yin, R.K. (1984/1994) *Case Study Research*, Beverly Hills, CA: Sage.

Yin, R.K. and Heald, K.A. (1975) 'Using the case survey method to analyze policy studies', *Administrative Science Quarterly*, pp. 371–381.

Yin, R.K. and Yates, D. (1974) *Street-level Governments: Assessing decentralization and urban services*, Lanham, MD: Lexington Books.

8   Individual values and organizational culture during a merger: immovable objects or shifting sands?
Marie H. Kavanagh and Neal M. Ashkanasy

Mergers and acquisitions continue to be a popular model for organizational growth but, as Cartwright and Schoenberg (2006) note, often with mixed success. In this respect, scholars (for example, Korman et al. 1978; Cartwright and Cooper 1992; Sagiv and Schwartz 1995; Weber 1996, 2000) have acknowledged the role human factors play in determining the success or otherwise of mergers. In line with Cartwright and Cooper (1996), we argue that whether or not individuals view the merger as presenting a threat, providing an opportunity or having little (or no) impact on future working life will depend on the proposed direction and clarity of future change, acceptability of the change, and the values held by the individuals affected.

Moreover, as Major (2000) suggested, organizational culture is the active critical ingredient of mergers (Cartwright and Cooper 1992, 1996; Ashkanasy and Holmes 1995; Weber 2000). As such, the individual becomes merely a 'thing' to be brought into the organization. This view had led to ambivalence about the role of individuals (Ashkanasy et al. 2000b, 2011) and the importance of individual values when leading change (Kavanagh and Ashkanasy 1996). Weber and Drori (2008) suggest further that most research about human factors in mergers has been prescriptive and atheoretical; and note the role of the individual, especially in cases affected by cultural difference, has rarely been investigated empirically. The approach we adopted in our study, therefore, was to incorporate the human side by studying mergers from an insider point of view (Louis 1985; Martin 2002). As such, we considered individual values in relation to organizational culture and processes and how these contribute to effective or ineffective mergers (Whiteley 1995).

According to Cartwright and Cooper (1996), key to understanding individual values and cultural shift or change is the issue of management of change and acculturation following a merger. In this respect, Nahavandi and Malekzadeh (1988) and Schnapper (1992) posit that acculturation in mergers and acquisitions will involve changes that occur as a result of contact between individuals of differing cultural origin. Nahavandi and

Malekzadeh propose in particular that there are four methods of acculturation: assimilation, integration, separation and deculturation.

To address these issues we conducted a longitudinal study to investigate how individual values of people, cultural shifts in organizations, and acculturation approaches affect post-merger process and interaction. Our study illustrates how individuals react, and how organizational culture shifts occur during the merger acculturation process in three large public sector tertiary education organizations.

INDIVIDUAL VALUES AND ORGANIZATIONAL CULTURE

In much of the organizational literature dealing with values, the framework and definition advanced by Rokeach (1969) has been particularly popular. According to Rokeach, values represent "an enduring belief that a specific mode of conduct or end-state of existence is personally and socially preferable to alternative modes of conduct or end-states" (p. 160). Schwartz and Bilsky (1987, 1990) and Schwartz (1992; see also Schwartz and Boehnke 2004) suggest further that values may be grouped into motivational domains. For example, a motivational domain of *achievement* would incorporate values such as successful, capable, ambitious, and influential. As such, values are cognitive/social representations of important human goals. In this respect, Amis et al. (2002) note that if external pressures for change are largely viewed as consistent with the values held then change is likely to be embraced.

Consistent with this idea, we propose that an understanding of the values of individuals in each of the merging partners is critical to merger management. It follows therefore that, where a level of congruence exists between the individual values of persons involved in a merger, a smoother process will result, or:

Hypothesis 1: At the commencement of the merger, there will be congruence between the collective values of individuals in each of the merger partners within each institution.

Cartwright and Cooper (1996) note further that, while individual values determine how people act and feel and conduct themselves within an organization, the essence of organizational culture is usually a set of basic assumptions and beliefs which operates in an often unconscious 'taken for granted' fashion (see also Ashkanasy et al. 2000a, 2011). Culture helps us to understand what Schein (1992) refers to as "the hidden and complex aspects or organizational life" (p. 9) that are important to the success or otherwise of the merger (Angwin and Vaara 2005; Cartwright 2005; Teerikangas and Very 2006).

We define culture according to Harrison's (1975) typology in terms of four types: power, role, task/accomplishment and person/support. When two cultures merge, the degree of cultural congruence or homogeneity that exists will affect how individuals draw on similarities to form relationships and collaborate (Earley and Mosalkowski 2000). Cartwright and Cooper (1996) suggest that success in a merger depends on identifying partners who represent both a good strategic and cultural match. This implies that choice of a merger partner includes assessment of the level of congruence or similarity that exists between cultures of merging parties. Thus:

Hypothesis 2: At the commencement of the merger there will be differences in the existing culture types across merger partner status within each institution.

CHANGING INDIVIDUAL VALUES AND ORGANIZATIONAL CULTURE

Hinrichs (1972) and Van Maanen and Schein (1979) examined the role organizations play in modifying personal values, and have demonstrated that organizations do influence the values of their members over time. According to Rokeach (1973), confronting an individual with information or an event (such as a merger) that is discordant with her or his values may influence those values or lead the person to alter them. Lord and Brown (2001) noted further that leaders might also influence the values of others through action or the process of making 'my values' known (see also Frontiera 2010). Thus:

Hypothesis 3: Individual values within each institution will change significantly following the merger.

We note, however, that others (for example, Bareil et al. 2007) argue that individuals usually do not want to move out of their perceived comfort zone. Thus, in making this hypothesis, we are not confident it will be supported. Nonetheless, we opted to hypothesize that values would change based on the notion that individuals in a merger context may need somehow to adapt to the change. Thus, the extent and direction of individual value change which might occur in a merger remains uncertain.

In a similar vein, although organizational cultures tend to be relatively

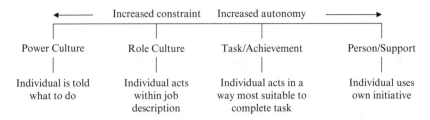

Source: Cartwright and Cooper (1996) p. 80.

*Figure 8.1   Relationship between culture types and individual constraint/
autonomy*

stable, they are neither uniform nor static. They evolve over time and it seems reasonable to posit that all cultural systems will exhibit continuous, incremental changes punctuated on occasion by more episodic, radical change (Watzlawick et al. 1974; Weick and Quinn 1999). Goffee and Jones (2001) suggest that cultural change may often occur as subtle shifts within, rather than between, elements that characterize a particular culture. Meyerson and Martin (1987) suggest further that any change process must be viewed in terms of different organizational cultures. Martin (1992, 2002) advocates a three-perspective view of organizational culture (integrated, differentiated and fragmented), suggesting that all three views might exist in an organization at the same time. In particular, cultures can become fragmented when under stress, with consequent implications for the management of the change process, so that:

Hypothesis 4a: Merger activity will cause organizational culture to change over time.

Cartwright and Cooper (1996) point out also that mergers are rarely marriages between equals. Consequently, as the process unfolds and the organization is reframed, the distribution of power is likely to evolve over time. These authors suggest further that, during times of rapid growth or merger, most organizations will move to tighten control by imposing constraints on individuals and/or reducing the freedom individuals have to make decisions about aspects of their life. In response to this, Cooper and Cartwright (1996, p. 80) proposed the continuum illustrated in Figure 8.1 to highlight the relationship between cultural types and the effect on the levels of autonomy or constraint that each culture type placed on individuals.

It seems reasonable to conclude therefore that organizational culture should change so as to reflect a culture where power is heightened and the culture of the major partner will prevail. This may cause adjustment of individual values as a result of higher levels of constraint being imposed by the direction in which the culture moves. Thus:

Hypothesis 4b: The organizational culture within each institution will change over time to reflect the culture of the major partner following a merger.

Hypothesis 4c: The change in organizational culture during merger activity will result in greater restraint on the individuals in the merging organizations.

CHANGE MANAGEMENT AND ACCULTURATION

According to Stahl and Voight (2008, see also Weber et al. 2009), integration efforts during the post-merger period are critical to success and performance. In this instance, acculturation would seem to be a key to managing cultural change. In this respect, Nahavandi and Malekzadeh (1988) proposed four methods of acculturation:

1. *Assimilation* is a unilateral process. Members of one group are willing to relinquish their culture as well as most of their organizational practices and systems. Following the merger, structural as well as cultural and behavioral assimilation will occur and one partner will cease to exist as a cultural entity.
2. *Integration* involves interaction and adaptation between the cultures of the merging partners and requires mutual contributions by both groups. It does not involve loss of cultural identity by either. This method leads to a degree of change in both groups' culture and practices with a flow of cultural elements between both.
3. *Separation* occurs when members of both cultures wish to preserve their culture and organizational system and resist any attempt to become assimilated with each other in any way or at any level. This means there will be minimal cultural exchange between the two groups, and each will function independently.
4. *Deculturation* occurs when members of one merging organization do not value their own culture and organizational practices and systems and do not want to be assimilated into the other organization. Deculturation involves losing cultural and psychological contact with both one's group and the other group and involves remaining an outcast to both.

Nahavandi and Malekzadeh (1988) note further that acculturation during mergers and acquisitions involves changes that occur as a result of contact between individuals of differing cultural origins (see also Schnapper, 1992). Cartwright and Cooper (1996) similarly report that unsatisfactory acculturation following a merger can have an adverse impact on organizational and human outcomes. In making an assessment of the culture of the merging partner, therefore, it seems that individuals take into account two factors: (1) the extent to which they value their existing culture and wish to preserve it, and (2) the extent to which individuals perceive the culture of the merging partner to be desirable enough to induce a move in culture.

Considering what happens when the partners wish to preserve their own culture and practices, the two modes of acculturation that apply are assimilation and separation. In assimilation, the major partner preserves its own culture and imposes it on the minor partner, while the minor partner relinquishes their culture and ceases to exist as a cultural entity. In separation, both parties attempt to maintain their pre-merger culture. Thus:

Hypothesis 5a: When merging partners wish to preserve their own culture and practices, assimilation and/or separation will be the preferred modes of acculturation.

In the instance when the partners do not wish to preserve their own culture and practices, the two modes of acculturation that apply are integration and deculturation. In integration, the merging partners forge a new and distinct culture. Thus, we expect:

Hypothesis 5b: When merging partners do not wish to preserve their own culture and practices, integration and/or deculturation will be the preferred modes of acculturation.

METHODS

Participants

Our study was conducted in the Australian tertiary education sector during the last decade of the twentieth century when there was a rash of mergers in the industry. The major partners were three large Australian universities located in a single metropolitan area. The minor partners were "Colleges of Advanced Education" (CAEs).[1] The mergers took place under the "Dawkins Reform" of Australian education, where universities and CAEs merged to become members of a single level of tertiary institution in the country (see DeAngelis 1992, for more detail of the Dawkins

Table 8.1   Samples (Ns and mean ages)

Institution	Survey 1	Survey 2	Survey 3
Mean Age	44.0	44.5	46.6
	N	N	N
Institution 1	83	66	52
Institution 2	60	44	37
Institution 3	44	37	31
Overall	187	147	120
Males	117	85	66
Major partner	96	72	56
Minor partner	91	75	64

reforms). In the instance of the three institutions included in this research, the CAEs became separate campuses of expanded universities. Thus, the term "cross-site analysis" in this chapter refers to the different campuses involved.

The three institutions included in this research were selected because of their geographical proximity to one another, number of merging partners involved, and the fundamental differences which existed between them in terms of size, orientation, length of existence, organizational philosophy and structure, and the manner in which each institution approached the merger/change process.[2] The sample used for analysis comprised academic faculty members from each of the campuses of the three institutions involved as shown in Table 8.1.

Measures

The survey instrument comprised four sections, as follows:

Section 1: Personal data and expectations
This section included personal and job-related information and respondents' expectations of the merger.

Section 2: Individual Values Survey
This comprised Schwartz and Bilsky's (1987, 1990) value survey, based on the Rokeach (1973) 36 item sort instrument. Schwartz (1992) expanded the list to 56 variables and converted the response format to a 9-point scale. The instrument was presented in two value lists. The first represents 30 'terminal' or end-state values such as wisdom, equality and pleasure. The second represents 26 'instrumental' values, or modes of behavior, such as obedience and independence.

Participants were required to ask themselves: What values are important to ME as guiding principles in MY life and what values are less important to me. They respond by rating different values in terms of their importance on a 9-point scale, -1 (opposed to my values), 0 (not important), 1,2 (unlabeled), 3 (important), 4,5 (unlabeled), 6 (very important) and 7 (of extreme importance).

Section 3: Organizational Culture Survey

To measure organizational culture, we adopted a 'type' approach (Ashkanasy et al. 2000a). Thus, we employed Harrison's (1975) instrument, which is based on the premise that there are four main types of organizational culture: power (as exercised by management), role (as defined and emphasized in the organization), task (in terms of the emphasis that is placed on tasks done in the organization), and person or self (in terms of the regard given to individuals in the work force). Similar to Ashkanasy and Holmes (1995), we asked respondents to rank the importance of the four types for each of 15 organizational issues and for three scenarios: existing, future and preferred (a total of 180 scores).

Section 4: Method of acculturation

In this section, we asked respondents to reply to items developed in accordance with the Nahavandi and Malekzadeh (1988) acculturation model, which includes four modes of acculturation discussed in the introduction to this chapter: Integration, assimilation, separation, and deculturation. In an additional question, we asked respondents to comment on which of the four methods of acculturation best resembled the process adopted by their institution.

Procedure

The survey was administered in pencil-and-paper format to the same group of participants at each campus of the three institutions on three occasions over four years (two-year intervals). All participants were assured that their responses were completely anonymous and confidential. Completed responses were returned via pre-paid mail.

In addition to the questionnaire administration, the first author conducted 60 interviews with participants. Interviewees comprised 22 from Institution 1 (12 from the major partner), 20 from Institution 2 (6 from the major partner), and 18 from Institution 3 (7 from the major partner). The purpose of the interviews was to ascertain participants' attitudes towards preservation of their cultures and practices. Participants were asked specifically to comment on the method of acculturation that had occurred (or was occurring) and to indicate whether they felt it was important in the merger process to preserve the existing culture and practices in their institution.

RESULTS

Reliability of Culture Measure

As a first step, we assessed the reliability and one-dimensional structure of the Harrison culture-type measure. To accomplish this, we calculated Cronbach's alpha for all the twelve dimensions by three survey administrations across each 15-item scale. Results in Table 8.2 provided alpha values ranging from 0.63 to 0.91 which, given the disparity of the subject matter covered in the items, suggest that the scales were tapping unitary constructs and were therefore adequate to use in our analysis.

Factor Analysis of the Values Survey

We used Principal Axis Factor analysis with Varimax rotation to factor analyse the 56 items in the Schwartz and Bilsky (1987, 1990) value survey

Table 8.2   Reliability coefficients for culture surveys

Survey	1 (N = 187)	2* (N = 146)	3* (N = 117)
Existing Culture			
Power	0.86	0.87	0.85
Role	0.82	0.63	0.81
Task	0.82	0.83	0.84
Person Support	0.89	0.83	0.88
Future Culture			
Power	0.88	0.87	0.86
Role	0.73	0.63	0.56
Task	0.83	0.83	0.86
Person Support	0.88	0.84	0.88
Preferred Culture			
Power	0.91	0.88	0.88
Role	0.67	0.53	0.64
Task	0.85	0.82	0.65
Person Support	0.85	0.82	0.84

Note: * Cases with incomplete data were omitted from the analysis.

Table 8.3   Alphas for factors extracted at Times 1, 2, and 3

Factor N[a]	Time 1 187	Time 2 147	Time 3 119
1	0.84	0.83	0.85
2	0.81	0.80	0.79
3	0.84	0.84	0.81
4	0.82	0.83	0.82
5	0.74	0.74	0.75
6	0.16	0.06	0.25
7	0.32	0.30	0.53

Note: [a] Cases with incomplete data omitted from analysis.

administered at Times 1, 2, and 3. Using Cattel's (1966) Scree Test, seven factors emerged. The percentage of total variance accounted for by these seven factors in each survey was Survey 1: 51.87 percent; Survey 2: 50.39 percent; and Survey 3: 52.86 percent. Comparison of the factor structures across surveys revealed that the items consistently loaded on the same factors in each survey administration. These sets of variables were then grouped into seven factors or domains (according to the Schwartz (1992) domains) and tested across the three surveys. Cronbach's alpha coefficients computed to test reliability of the factors constructed are listed above in Table 8.3.

Factors 6 and 7 failed to meet the threshold of .70 for reliability, and therefore were omitted from further consideration. The five factors retained were therefore identified as representative of individual values of the academics surveyed across the three institutions. We labeled the five factors as shown below.

- **Accomplishment:** This factor includes authority, influential, social recognition, successful, ambitious, wealth, varied life, exciting life and social power. It is a combination of Schwartz's (1992) power, achievement and stimulation motivational types of values. The defining goal of this value type is personal success, stimulation and the satisfaction of an individual need for social status and prestige through dominance and control over people and resources.
- **Freedom:** Factor 2 includes unity with nature, world of beauty, protecting the environment, broadminded, world peace, social justice, freedom, daring, creativity, wisdom, humble, curious, equality and inner harmony. It combines primarily Schwartz's (1992) universalism and self-direction motivational types of values. The motiv-

ational goal of universalism values can be derived from those survival needs of groups and individuals when people come into contact with those outside the extended primary group. The motivational goal of security values is derived from safety, harmony, stability of society, and relationships of self.

- **Maturity:** Items include honest, loyal, capable, healthy, self-respect, responsible, independent, mature love, select own goals and true friendship. This factor combines Schwartz's (1992) benevolence and self-direction motivational types of values.

- **Discipline of self:** This factor includes respect for elders, national security, clean, respect for tradition, polite, reciprocation of favors, obedient, protecting face, self-discipline, accepting life, social order and family security. It combines Schwartz's (1992) security, tradition and conformity value types. It focuses on tradition, norms and roles.

- **Inner peace:** The final factor includes spiritual life, religious, meaning to life, forgiving and helpful. It focuses on positive interaction in order to promote the flourishing of groups and achieve meaning by transcending reality.

Test of Hypothesis 1: Individuals and Their Values

The five value factors we identified in the factor analysis were used to test the level of congruence between the individual values of persons from merging partners (Hypothesis 1). To test this, we employed a two-way between-groups ANOVA to test that accomplishment, freedom, maturity, discipline of self, and inner peace, were congruent between the major versus minor organizational types or status (major versus minor partner) within each institution. Results of this analysis are given in Table 8.4.

As can be seen in Table 8.4, there was a significant main effect of institution on accomplishment, and a significant interaction for freedom. Simple effects analysis revealed that the main effect on accomplishment was the result of Institution 1 members valuing accomplishment less than in the other two institutions, where this value was undifferentiated. Post-hoc planned comparisons (Tukey) revealed that the interaction resulted from a significant difference in the freedom value across the major and minor partners in Institution 1, with freedom valued more highly in the minor than the major partner. There were no significant effects across partner status for Institutions 2 and 3.

In summary, Hypothesis 1 was supported for four of the five values insofar as there were no partner status differences within instructions on the values of accomplishment, maturity, discipline of self, and inner

*Table 8.4   Results of ANOVA tests for institution (A) and status
               (B: major vs. minor)*

Factor	Source	F
1. Accomplishment	Institution (A)	4.21*
	Status (B)	0.73
	A × B	1.94
2. Freedom	A	2.18
	B	0.02
	A × B	3.82*
3. Maturity	A	2.69
	B	0.66
	A × B	0.43
4. Discipline of Self	A	2.49
	B	0.97
	A × B	0.37
5. Inner Peace	A	0.83
	B	0.98
	A × B	0.15

Notes:
d.f. = 2122.
*p < 0.05.

peace. The exception occurred in Institution 1, where members of the minor partner valued freedom more than those in the major partner. Interestingly, Institution 1 was differentiated from the other institutions in that its members placed a higher value on accomplishment than did the others.

Test of Hypothesis 2: Organizational Cultures of Merging Partners

We sought here to assess the cultures of each institution, and in particular of the merging partners of each institution at the commencement of the merger. Mean scores and standard deviations for Survey 1 existing culture were calculated as shown in Table 8.5.

To test Hypothesis 2, we employed a three-way MANOVA with one repeated measures factor: Culture (the four culture types); and two between-subjects factors: Institution (three institutions) and partner status (major and minor). While the three-way interaction was not significant, $F_{(6468)} = 1.329$, $p = 0.260$, we found a significant two-way interaction of culture and status, $F_{(3468)} = 6.096$, $p = 0.003$). Post-hoc (Tukey) tests revealed this was caused by significantly different weightings

Table 8.5 Mean scores and standard deviations for existing culture type across institutions status at Times 1, 2, and 3

Time 1

	Status	Power Mean SD	Role Mean SD	Task Mean SD	Person Mean SD
1	Major	22.28 (7.84)	30.04 (5.53)	26.64 (6.46)	12.96 (8.67)
	Minor	30.32 (8.42)	28.44 (7.06)	20.20 (7.69)	10.16 (7.74)
	Total	26.30 (9.02)	29.24 (6.33)	23.42 (7.75)	11.56 (8.25)
2	Major	28.07 (7.01)	31.86 (6.06)	21.50 (4.52)	9.14 (6.27)
	Minor	30.55 (7.32)	32.00 (9.13)	20.95 (4.70)	8.80 (9.60)
	Total	29.53 (7.20)	31.94 (7.90)	21.18 (4.56)	8.94 (8.28)
3	Major	24.64 (14.51)	25.09 (12.52)	24.64 (9.76)	15.46 (12.09)
	Minor	29.86 (9.97)	31.75 (4.04)	20.38 (5.71)	8.06 (5.76)
	Total	27.74 (12.06)	29.04 (8.99)	22.11 (7.75)	11.07 (9.43)
All Inst	Major	24.42 (9.60)	29.46 (7.93)	24.76 (7.08)	12.44 (9.07)
	Minor	30.28 (8.39)	30.48 (7.30)	20.49 (6.24)	9.16 (7.89)
	All 3 Inst	27.64 (9.38)	30.02 (7.57)	22.41 (6.94)	10.64 (8.56)

Time 2

	Status	Power Mean SD	Role Mean SD	Task Mean SD	Person Mean SD
1	Major	20.44 (10.26)	29.08 (6.36)	27.44 (8.52)	16.00 (9.69)
	Minor	29.20 (8.07)	31.24 (3.44)	21.04 (6.35)	8.68 (5.28)
	Total	24.82 (10.15)	30.16 (5.18)	24.24 (8.11)	12.32 (8.57)
2	Major	32.57 (8.60)	30.71 (3.95)	18.50 (5.69)	8.07 (6.28)
	Minor	28.25 (9.42)	30.75 (4.84)	20.85 (6.19)	9.25 (7.09)
	Total	30.03 (9.21)	30.76 (4.43)	19.88 (6.02)	8.77 (6.70)
3	Major	27.18 (14.20)	31.18 (4.54)	22.46 (7.16)	9.18 (9.77)
	Minor	26.81 (8.85)	30.38 (4.60)	22.25 (6.39)	10.00 (5.87)
	Total	26.96 (11.08)	30.70 (4.51)	22.33 (6.58)	9.67 (7.53)

Table 8.5 (continued)

	Status	Time 2 Power Mean SD	Change across Time 1–3	Role Mean SD	Change across Time 1–3	Task Mean SD	Change across Time 1–3	Person Mean SD	Change across Time 1–3
All Inst	Major	25.32 (11.84)		30.00 (5.39)		23.84 (8.35)		12.28 (9.50)	
	Minor	28.26 (8.64)		30.85 (4.20)		21.30 (6.23)		9.20 (5.60)	
	Total	26.94 (10.26)		30.47 (4.77)		22.44 (7.34)		10.59 (7.88)	

	Status	Time 3 Power Mean SD	Change across Time 1–3	Role Mean SD	Change across Time 1–3	Task Mean SD	Change across Time 1–3	Person Mean SD	Change across Time 1–3
1	Major	27.72 (9.09)	←	29.12 (6.74)	→	23.56 (7.75)	→	11.60 (8.65)	→
	Minor	31.44 (6.81)	←	31.00 (3.61)	←	19.88 (5.46)	→	8.12 (5.40)	→
	Total	29.58 (8.17)	←	30.06 (5.43)	→	21.72 (6.89)	→	9.86 (7.35)	→
2	Major	31.07 (8.12)	←	28.36 (7.53)	→	19.71 (7.03)	→	11.36 (10.54)	←
	Minor	30.75 (7.19)	←	32.30 (5.13)	←	19.65 (3.98)	→	8.95 (8.14)	←
	Total	30.88 (7.47)	←	30.68 (6.43)	→	19.68 (5.35)	→	9.94 (9.13)	→
3	Major	26.36 (13.92)	←	31.55 (4.20)	→	24.18 (7.59)	←	10.46 (9.62)	←
	Minor	25.69 (9.85)	→	25.56 (10.96)	→	23.25 (9.00)	←	14.75 (9.93)	←
	Total	25.96 (11.43)	→	28.00 (9.22)	→	23.63 (8.31)	→	13.00 (9.85)	→
All Inst	Major	28.36 (10.03)	←	29.44 (6.50)	→	22.62 (7.60)	→	11.28 (9.23)	←
	Minor	29.71 (8.07)	→	30.00 (7.14)	→	20.69 (6.29)	←	10.13 (8.07)	←
	Total	29.10 (8.99)	←	29.75 (6.84)	→	21.56 (6.95)	→	10.64 (8.59)	→

Table 8.6   Mean and Standard Deviation on scores for treatment levels of effect of merger on individual values

Treatment Levels	1	2	3
Institution (A)	Inst1 1.12 (0.28)	Inst2 1.42 (0.81)	Inst3 1.29 (0.89)
Organizational Type (B)	Major 1.02 (0.73)	Minor 1.44 (0.86)	All 3 1.28 (0.70)
A × B Minor	Inst1 1.23 (0.35)	Inst2 1.57 (0.90)	Inst3 1.47 (1.15)
A × B Major	Inst1 1.00 (0.00)	Inst2 1.00 (0.00)	Inst3 1.05 (0.13)

assigned to the four different culture types by individuals across the major and minor merging partners. Pairwise comparisons using a Bonferroni adjustment found, in support of Hypothesis 2, that there were significant ($p < 0.05$) differences between the minor and major partners in terms of the culture dimensions of power, task/achievement, and person/support type cultures.

Test of Hypothesis 3: Changing Individual Values

In Hypothesis 3, we stated that individual values would adapt over time as a result of the merger activities of the institution. A within-person ANOVA was conducted to test whether the five value factors (accomplishment, freedom, maturity, discipline of self and inner peace) changed significantly over time. Results were Accomplishment F = 0.653, Freedom F = 0.234, Maturity F = 0.322, Discipline of Self F = 0.850, Inner Peace F = 1.522; all *ns* (df = 4267).

With respect to Hypothesis 3, the interviews with members of the merging institutions revealed the extent to which they felt there had been a change to their underlying values as a result of the merger process. Reference to the mean scores in Table 8.6 indicates that, across all three institutions, there was virtually no change to individual values. Respondents in the major partners reported 'no change', while some individuals in minor campuses reported 'very little change' to their individual values. Overall 94.5 percent of respondents reported very little or no change to their personal values over the time of the merger process. Hypothesis 3 was therefore not supported.

Test of Hypothesis 4a: Organizational Culture Change

Cartwright and Cooper (1996) suggest that, as the merger process unfolds, the merged organization is reframed and the distribution of power evolves over time. To test core change effects, we therefore undertook a MANOVA with two repeated measures factors: Time (Surveys 1 to 3) and culture (the four culture types); and one between-subject factor: Institution. Results were a marginally significant multivariate main effect for time, $F(12,642) = 1.539$, $p = 0.09$, but a strongly significant multivariate interaction of time and institution, ($F(3,321) = 4.911$, $p = 0.01$). To illustrate this effect, we have represented the direction of the change effects in the lower panel of Table 8.5.

As can be seem in Table 8.5, changes in culture type as assigned by respondents in the minor and major partners occurred in all three institutions across the three surveys. In Institution 1, power was the strongest culture type followed by role. Both power and role culture types increased as the merger progressed with a corresponding decline in both task and person/support culture types. The manner in which culture types were scores across Institution 2 shifted as a whole with power marginally, but not significantly, displacing role as the dominant culture type. In terms of the impact on the individual in the post-merger period, there was some improvement in the scores for *person/support* in Institution 2 across the whole institution. Institution 3 was interesting in a different way. In the major partner, scores indicate that power and role increased, but this was not the case in the minor partner, where scores on task and person/support culture types increased. Overall in Institution 3, and contrary to what we anticipated in Hypothesis 4b, the influence of the minor partner's culture type appears to have prevailed. Moreover, and despite an improvement in the scores for person/support culture type in two of the institutions, this culture type was still poorly rated in all three institutions in terms of the mean scores, and the rating across the three institutions declined. There was a similar decrease across institutions in the scores for *task/achievement.* Overall, therefore, Hypothesis 4a was supported insofar as the culture in each institution did change during the merger process, but the nature and extent of the change differed between the institutions.

Test of Hypothesis 4b: Culture Changes to Reflect the Culture of the Dominant Partner

In Hypothesis 4b, we anticipated that culture in the minor partners in the mergers would be influenced by that of the major partner. This was not what we found, however. As can be seen in Table 8.5, for two of the institutions (Institutions 1 and 2), it was the culture of the major partners that moved towards that of the minor partner. This was an unexpected finding, and is opposite of what we predicted based on the extant literature.

Test of Hypothesis 4c: Merger Activity and Restraint on Individuals

We based Hypothesis 4c on Cartwright and Cooper's (1996) contention that merging organizations tend to try to tighten control by imposing a greater level of constraint on individuals (Figure 8.1). The results in Table 8.5 support this idea. We found that all three institutions increased power culture type and decreased role, task/achievement and person/support culture types. In terms of the Cartwright and Cooper (1996) model, the mergers resulted in a shift to the right on the continuum, as we anticipated in Hypothesis 4c.

Examining the results for each institution, the move to constrain individuals was greatest in Institution 1, with an increase in both power and role and a decrease in task and person/support. Institution 2 also moved to a culture more dominated by power and therefore to greater constraint on individuals. There was some minor improvement in the person/support culture but, of the three institutions, Institution 2 still ranked lowest on this type with a mean score of 9.94 (out of a possible 30). Institution 3 was the only institution to move to the left of the continuum, granting greater autonomy to individuals with an increase in both task and person support and decreases in power and role.

Test of Hypotheses 5a and 5b: Method of Acculturation

Hypotheses 5a and 5b were that the method of acculturation (assimilation, integration, separation, or deculturation; Nahavandi and Malekzadeh 1988) would depend on whether the members of the merging institutions wished to preserve their own cultures and practices. Figure 8.2 illustrates the method of acculturation which occurred in each merger. To test for differences across the institutions we used a Chi-square test. Results were that there was a significant institution effect, Chi-square $= 21.34$, df $= 4$, $p < 0.01$, and a significant interaction, Chi-square $= 20.73$, df $= 4$, $p < 0.05$. Post-hoc analysis revealed further that Institution 2 members viewed the process as involving more integration than those in Institutions 1 or 3. Further analysis of differences for minor and major by institution, revealed no differences for Institution 1 or Institution 3. In summary, we found that there were differences between the three institutions in terms of the method of acculturation they adopted. We also found a difference between the minor and major partners in terms of views on method of acculturation, but only in Institution 2.

With respect to Hypotheses 5a and 5b, we relied on the results of the interviews with members of the merging institutions to determine the level

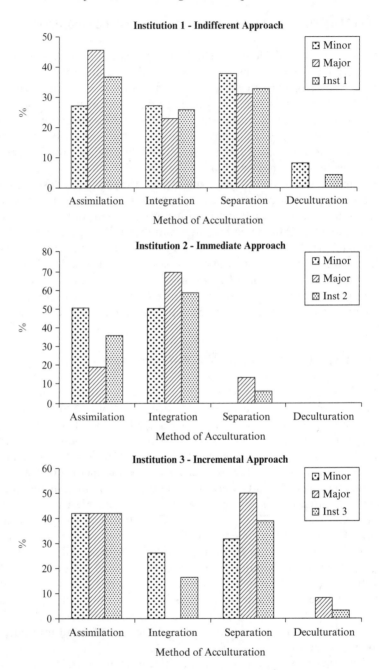

Figure 8.2   Method of acculturation adopted in each institution

at which members felt they wished to preserve their existing cultures and practices. The results of this are summarized as follows:

Institutions 1 and 3

Members of these institutions expressed strong views in the interviews that the existing cultures and practices in their respective organizations ought to be preserved after the merger. This was true both for the major and the minor partners in both instances.

As can be seen in Figure 8.2, and consistent with Hypothesis 5a, assimilation and separation were the perceived modes of acculturation. In Institution 1, 37 percent of respondents reported that assimilation had occurred; this view was more prevalent in the major partner. Thirty-three percent of individuals who responded opted for separation and there was little difference between the opinions of those in minor/major partners. Again, this appears to be largely because of the manner in which the merger was managed, in that action following the merger had been delayed, different sections of this organization were perceived to be at different stages, and some respondents still thought that independence would prevail.

In Institution 3, 42 percent of respondents thought that assimilation had occurred and there was no difference between minor and major partners. In addition, 26 percent of individuals in minor partners opted for integration. Thirty-nine percent of those who responded, however, opted for separation, and this view was more prevalent in major partners.

Institution 2

Members of Institution 2, unlike those in Institutions 1 and 3, expressed ambivalence as to whether the existing cultures and practices in their respective organizations ought to be preserved after the merger. Similar to Institutions 1 and 3, this view held regardless of whether the interviewees were from the major or the minor partners.

In support of Hypothesis 5b, we found that 58 percent of individuals in Institution 2 indicated the predominant method of acculturation had been integration. Moreover, 36 percent of respondents (mostly from the minor partner) indicated that assimilation had occurred. In other words, individuals from the minor partner of Institution 2 were more willing to relinquish their culture and to be merged into that of the major partner. Those that were not willing were integrated anyway, resulting in a new organizational identity. Also, in Institution 2 action following the merger had been swift so that, by the time of the last survey, integration appears to have occurred.

DISCUSSION

In summary of our findings, we found no evidence of any change in individual values. We did find, however, that there had been shifts in the cultures of the institutions during the period of the study, with two of the three institutions shifting towards a culture in which power was the dominant type, resulting in greater restraint placed on individuals. Surprisingly, in two institutions the culture of the major partner actually moved towards that of the minor partners.

We found support for both of our hypotheses regarding method of acculturation (assimilation, integration, separation and deculturation), although the method of acculturation varied. Based on our findings, we identified three methods of managing the merger process. We labeled these *immediate*, *incremental*, and *indifferent*. Despite the fact that all mergers were between similar organizations in the one industry (tertiary education), the different approaches adopted to manage the merger process in each institution had a greater influence on the perceived method of acculturation than did the degree of congruence between cultures and individual values.

With regard to limitations of the study, one of the major types of bias and misinformation which may arise in multi-level research is misspecification (that is, aggregation) of individual-level data to say something about another level (that is, the organization). Aggregation may add meaning, however, when the error component of the individual-level datum is reduced and reliability is improved by averaging those individual-level errors and biases that are random (Rousseau 1985).

As a means of data collection, questionnaire response rates may also be affected by negative or apathetic attitudes towards questionnaires particularly in large organizations. A further possible limitation may be the erosion in response rate for surveys two and three due to staff turnover. As indicated in Table 8.1, despite some attrition, 119 individuals responded to all three surveys across the six-year period of this study.

Time elapsed since the merger announcement was factored in because this variable might have influenced respondents' emotions and objectivity (Kitching 1967; Sales and Mirvis 1984). Since this is a longitudinal study, it is possible that the effects of the merger had been overtaken by economic factors which were now prevalent and may have influenced attitudes (for example, see Ashkanasy and Holmes 1995).

Finally, it should be noted that the present study was based on self-report measures and the variables for individual values and organizational culture were measured in the same survey using a similar method. Therefore there is a probability of method variance in that artifactual covariance between the two variables may lead to error when inferring substantive relationships which do not exist (Podsakoff and Organ 1986). In defense of our method, however, we argue that our study was longitudinal and the instruments measured ontologically different constructs.

Contributions to Theory

We contend that our research program extends organizational behavior research in six ways. First it is a longitudinal study and integrates what is known about organizational change more generally with cultural change in particular (Martin 2002). Second, it addresses a notable gap in the literature by highlighting the role of individual values in merger evoked cultural change. Third, it overcomes confusion about values in the literature by highlighting the fact that culture happens in organizations; individual values happen in individuals and they are not the same. Fourth, the research determines cultural differences between merging partners and uses four perspectives, assimilation, integration, separation and deculturation, to assess the cultural change process. Fifth, a multi-level approach to the study of mergers in organizations is adopted by (a) focusing on the effects, for both individual values and organizational culture, of mergers in the tertiary education sector, and (b) elaborating on the outcomes for individuals as a result of changes in organizational culture and the method of acculturation that occurs following a merger. Finally, the study gives voice to the perceptions and opinions of those who are most affected by the merger: individual faculty members at all levels of appointment, and highlights that different groups of individuals may perceive mergers differently with consequent implications for the way acculturation following the merger is viewed and the process is managed.

Contributions to Practice

Most mergers arise as a result of the need to rationalize, to increase efficiency, or to reduce costs. As Cartwright and Cooper (1996) observe, however, unless mergers are handled effectively, they usually fail to realize these objectives; and indeed, the reverse commonly occurs. Appointment of a skilled change management facilitator or 'champion' should occur at the start of any merger process.

Further, because mergers bring together two or more different groups of individuals, (even though they are often involved in the same sector or industry), an assessment of the values of individuals from merging partners should occur prior to the commencement of the merger. Given the findings of this study – indicating that the values of individuals are enduring and do not change despite outside influences such as a merger – cognizance of members' personal values will allow change to be framed so that individuals involved are able to maintain their values in the new organization post-merger.

The same argument follows for organizational culture. An assessment of the culture of the merging partners, and the extent of allegiance by individuals to their culture, should be undertaken at the commencement of the merger. This will determine the direction cultural change should take to assist in avoiding the tensions that occur when individual values are placed in conflict with the direction of organizational change.

Our findings also imply that, for a merger to be successful, congruence between individual values and the organizational cultures of merging partners' needs to exist. Our results indicate that, when there is dissonance between organizational members' values, such as accomplishment, freedom, maturity, discipline of self, and inner peace and the organizational culture type (power, role, task and person support) that results from the merger, unsatisfactory outcomes for individuals are a likely result. In addition, when there is lack of congruence between merging organizational cultures, conflict and a high level of dissatisfaction may occur for individuals. In addition to this, our findings suggest that, when insufficient emphasis is given to person support, espoused or otherwise, organizations tend to move toward a cultural emphasis on power and role.

Change managers should also be aware of the influence of minor/major parties in a merger situation, the direction in which the new organizational culture moves as a result of the merger, and the consequent level of constraint placed on individuals as a result. This study showed that organizational culture did move over time but it is not always the culture of the major partner in a merger situation which prevails in terms of the new organizational culture that develops, contrary to findings by Cartwright and Cooper (1996).

Merger partners need also: (1) to select carefully the method or process to be used to manage the merger and develop a new culture following the merger (method of acculturation); (2) to establish effective channels of communication which involve individuals at all levels of the organization; (3) to select willing partners first and move to more difficult partners after allowing more time for consultation and justification; and (4) to allow people to be 'changed' with dignity by acknowledging contributions and justifying the need for them personally to move on.

Implications for Future Research

The present research is one of the few longitudinal studies to emphasize the importance of individual values in combination with organizational culture in a merger process. Further studies need to be undertaken, however, to test the generalizability of our findings regarding the role individual values play in mergers in other industries.

Our work is also one of the few studies to analyse mergers in the tertiary education sector. Future research could examine whether the findings in this study are generalizable to other educational settings within and outside Australia. In addition, the population for this study was drawn from academic faculty. The study could be replicated to include other professional populations to enable comparisons to be drawn.

Future research might also include the effect of control variables such as organizational type (public versus private), organizational size, and financial status to shed light on factors that cause organizational cultures to move in the direction they do following a merger.

More work needs also to be done on the link between individual values and organizational culture type in terms of Harrison's (1975) existing and preferred scenario. In a merger situation, it might be possible to use the preferred scenario as a base to work towards to gain commitment.

The present study also determined cultural differences between merging partners and used four perspectives – assimilation, integration, separation and deculturation, to assess the acculturation process following change. It also identified that the method used to manage the changes associated with the merger (immediate, incremental, indifferent) had different outcomes for individuals and their perceptions about the method of acculturation that transpired. Further work needs to be done to test the three change methods we identified, namely, incremental, immediate and indifferent, in other merger situations to test if these can be generalized to other contexts.

Finally, a study of this nature could also be expanded to examine the issue of corporate governance and management; for example, to examine whether directors approach mergers in the best interests of shareholders in terms of outcomes for individuals involved in the merger and the consequent effect on organizational culture and performance.

CONCLUSIONS

Weber and Drori (2008) suggest that mergers and acquisitions present a unique context to examine the impact of organizational change on individuals, including perceptions of the new organization and its management and culture. Graves (1981) emphasized also that successful organizational outcomes are linked to successful individual outcomes. In our research, we found that an understanding of the culture type of both organizations and the values of individuals who are part of the merger process plays a crucial role in determining whether merging partners will change or acculturate. While collective individual values placed greater emphasis on higher order needs such as accomplishment, freedom, maturity, discipline of self and inner peace, at the organizational level power and role culture types dominated over task/achievement and person/support. Individual values therefore came to be at odds with what was occurring in the culture of the organization.

In addition, individual values endured despite merger activity. The merger did produce shifts in culture over time but these changes were not in the direction individuals preferred. Moreover, the strengthening of the power culture in most institutions resulted in a decrease in individual autonomy and an increase in the level of organizationally-imposed constraint. Conflict between the values of individuals and cultural orientations existed and tensions arose as a result.

Finally, we found that the method of acculturation evolved as a result of the manner in which the merger was managed (immediate approach, incremental approach, indifferent approach) rather than being a planned strategy with consequent implications in terms of outcomes for both individuals and the organizations involved.

NOTES

1. CAEs are the equivalent of English polytechnic colleges or 2-year colleges in the US.
2. Institution 1 adopted an approach to 'hasten slowly' and took some seven years after formalization of the merger before real change was invoked. At the time of writing the process is drawing to a close with the relocation of a major operational unit from one campus (major) to another (minor). Institution 2 viewed the merger as mutually beneficial to all parties and invoked changes quickly so that rationalization occurred; new structures were put in place, smaller campuses closed and staff moved. At the time of the study the process had well and truly been completed. Institution 3 viewed the merger as an opportunity to expand in a rational manner. An incremental approach was adopted in that merger; the most willing partners merged first and negotiations with other institutions then proceeded. At the time of this study, the process was ongoing.

REFERENCES

Amis, J., Slack, T. and Hinings, C.R. (2002). 'Values and organizational change'. *Journal of Applied Behavioral Science*, 38, 436–465.

Angwin, D. and Vaara, E. (2005). '"Connectivity" in merging organizations: beyond traditional cultural perspectives'. *Organization Studies*, 26, 1445–1453.

Ashkanasy, N.M. and Holmes, S. (1995). 'Perceptions of organizational ideology following merger: a longitudinal study of merging accounting firms'. *Accounting, Organizations and Society*, 20, 19–34.

Ashkanasy, N.M., Broadfoot, L. and Falkus, S. (2000a). 'Questionnaire measures of organizational culture'. In. N.M. Ashkanasy, C. Wilderom and M. Peterson. *Handbook of Organizational Culture and Climate*. Thousand Oaks, CA: Sage, pp. 131–146.

Ashkanasy, N.M., Wilderom, C.P.M. and Peterson, M.F. (2000b). 'Introduction'. In: N.M. Ashkanasy, C.P.M. Wilderom and M.F. Peterson (eds), *Handbook of Organizational Cultures and Climate*. Thousand Oaks, CA: Sage.

Ashkanasy, N.M., Wilderom, C.P.M. and Peterson, M.F. (2011). 'Introduction'. In N.M. Ashkanasy, C.E.P. Wilderom and M.F. Peterson (eds), *The Handbook of Organizational Culture and Climate, second edition*. Thousand Oaks, CA: Sage, pp. 3–10.

Bareil, C., Savoie, A. and Meunier, S. (2007). 'Patterns of discomfort with organizational change'. *Journal of Change Management*, 7, 13–24.

Cartwright, S. (2005). 'Mergers and acquisitions: an update and appraisal'. *International Review of Industrial and Organizational Psychology*, 20, 1–38.

Cartwright, S. and Cooper, C.L. (1992). *Mergers and Acquisitions: The Human Factor*. Oxford: Butterworth-Heinemann.

Cartwright, S. and Cooper, C.L. (1996). *Managing Mergers, Acquisitions and Strategic Alliances: Integrating People and Cultures*. Oxford: Butterworth-Heinemann.

Cartwright, S. and Schoenberg, R. (2006). 'Thirty years of mergers and acquisitions research: recent advances and future opportunities'. *British Journal of Management*, 17, S1–S5.

Cattell, R.B. (1966). 'The Scree Test for the number of factors'. *Multivariate Behavioral Research*, 1, 245–276.

DeAngelis, R. (1992). 'The Dawkins revolution'. *The Australian Higher Education Review*, **35** (1), 37–42.

Earley, P.C. and Mosakowski, E. (2000). 'Creating hybrid team cultures: an empirical test of transnational team functioning'. *Academy of Management Journal*, 43, 26–49.

Frontiera, J. (2010). 'Leadership and organizational culture transformation in professional sport'. *Journal of Leadership and Organizational Studies*, 17, 71–86.

Goffee, R. and Jones, G. (2001). 'Organizational culture: a sociological perspective'. In C.L. Cooper, S. Cartwright and P.C. Earley, *The International Handbook of Organizational Culture and Climate*. Chichester, UK: Wiley.

Graves, D. (1981). 'Individual reactions to a merger of two small firms of brokers in the re-insurance industry: a total population survey'. *Journal of Management Studies*, 18, 89–113.

Harrison, R. (1975). 'Diagnosing organization ideology'. In J. Jones and J. Pfeiffer (eds), *The 1975 Annual Handbook for Group Facilitators*. La Jolla, CA: University Associates, pp. 101–107.

Hinrichs, J.R. (1972). 'Value adaptation of new PhDs to academic and industrial environments: a comparative longitudinal study'. *Personnel Psychology*, 25, 545–565.

Kavanagh, M.H. and Ashkanasy, N.M. (2006). 'The impact of leadership and change management strategy on organizational culture and individual acceptance of change during a merger'. *British Journal of Management*, 17, S81–S103.

Kitching, J. (1967). 'Why do mergers miscarry?' *Harvard Business Review*, **45** (6), 88–101.

Korman, A.K., Rosenbloom, A.H. and Walsh, R.J. (1978). 'Increasing the people-organisation fit in mergers and acquisitions'. *Personnel Journal*, **55** (3), 54–59.

Lord, R. and Brown, D. (2001). 'Leadership, values, and subordinates; self-concept'. *The Leadership Quarterly*, 12, 133–152.

Louis, M.R. (1985). 'An investigator's guide to workplace culture'. In P.J. Frost, L.F. Moore, M.R. Louis, C.C. Lundberg and J. Martin (eds), *Organizational Culture*. Beverly Hills, CA: Sage.

Major, D.A. (2000). 'Effective newcomer socialization into high-performance organizational cultures'. In N.M. Ashkanasy, C.P.E. Wilderom and M.F. Peterson (eds), *Handbook of Organizational Culture and Climate.* Thousand Oaks, CA: Sage, pp. 117–129.

Martin, J. (1992). *Cultures in Organization.* New York: Oxford University Press.

Martin, J. (2002). *Organizational Culture Mapping the Terrain.* Beverly Hills, CA: Sage.

Meyerson, D. and Martin, J. (1987). 'Cultural change: an integration of three different views'. *Journal of Management Studies*, 24, 623–647.

Nahavandi, A. and Malekzadeh, A.R. (1988). 'Acculturation in mergers and acquisitions'. *Academy of Management Review*, 13, 79–90.

Podsakoff, P.M. and Organ, D. (1986). 'Self-reports in organizational research: problems and prospects'. *Journal of Management*, 12, 531–544.

Rokeach, M. (1969). 'Value systems in religion'. *Review of Religious Research*, 11, 3–23.

Rokeach, M. (1973). *The Nature of Human Values*, New York: The Free Press.

Rousseau, D.M. (1985). 'Issues of level in organizational research'. *Research in Organizational Behavior*, 7, 1–37.

Sagiv, L. and Schwartz, S.H. (1995). 'Value priorities and readiness for outgroup social contact'. *Journal of Personality and Social Psychology*, 69, 437–448.

Sales, A.S. and Mirvis, P.H. (1984). 'When cultures collide: issues in acquisitions'. In J.R. Kimberley and R.E. Quinn (eds), *Managing Organizational Transitions.* Homewood, IL: Irwin pp. 107–133.

Schein, E.H. (1992). *Organizational Culture and Leadership: A Dynamic View*, 2nd edition. San Francisco, CA: Jossey-Bass.

Schnapper, M. (1992). 'Multicultural/multinational teambuilding after international mergers and acquisitions'. In N. Bergemann and A.L.J. Sourisseoux (eds), *Interkulturelles Management.* Heidelberg, Germany: Physica, pp. S.269–S.283.

Schwartz, S.H. (1992). 'Universals in the content and structure of values: theoretical advances in empirical tests in 20 countries'. *Advances in Experimental Psychology*, 25, 1–65.

Schwartz, S.H. and Bilsky, W. (1987). 'Toward a universal psychological structure of human values'. *Journal of Personality and Social Psychology*, 53, 550–562.

Schwartz, S.H. and Bilsky, W. (1988). 'Universality in the structure of values: theoretical advances and empirical studies in 20 countries'. *Advances in Experimental Social Psychology*, 25, 1–65.

Schwartz, S.H. and Bilsky, W. (1990). 'Toward a theory of the universal content and structure of values: extensions and cross cultural replications'. *Journal of Personality and Social Psychology*, 58, 878–891.

Schwartz, S.H. and Boehnke, K. (2004). 'Evaluating the structure of human values with confirmatory factor analysis'. *Journal of Research in Personality*, 38, 230–255.

Stahl, G.K. and Voight, A. (2008). 'Do cultural differences matter in mergers and acquisitions? A tentative model for examination'. *Organization Science*, 19, 160–176.

Teerikangas, S. and Very, P. (2006). 'The culture-performance relationship in M&A: From yes/no to how'. *British Journal of Management*, 17, S31–S48.

Van Maanen, J. and Schein, E.H. (1979). 'Toward a theory of organizational socialization'. *Research in Organizational Behavior*, 1, 209–264.

Watzlawick, P., Weaklund, J. and Fisch, R. (1974). *Change.* New York: Norton.

Weber, Y. (1996). 'Corporate cultural fit and performance in mergers and acquisitions'. *Human Relations*, 49, 1181–1202.

Weber, Y. (2000). 'Measuring cultural fit in merger and acquisitions'. In N.M. Ashkanasy, C.P.E. Wilderom and M.F. Petereson (eds), *Handbook of Organizational Culture and Climate.* Thousand Oaks, CA: Sage, pp. 131–145.

Weber, Y. and Drori, I. (2008). 'The linkages between cultural differences, psychological states, and performance in international'. In C.L. Cooper and S. Finkelstein (eds), *Mergers and Acquisitions. Advances in mergers and acquisitions.* Bingley, UK: Emerald Group Publishing, vol. 7, pp. 119–142.

Weber, Y., Tarba, S.Y. and Reichel, A. (2009). 'International mergers and acquisitions performance revisited – the role of cultural distance and post-acquisition integration approach'. In S. Finkelstein and C.L. Cooper (eds), *Advances in Mergers and Acquisitions*. Bingley, UK: Emerald Group Publishing, vol. 8, pp. 1–17.

Weick, K.E. and Quinn, R.E. (1999). 'Organizational change and development'. *Annual Review of Psychology*, 50, 361–386.

Whiteley, A.M. (1995). *Managing Change: A Core Values Approach*. South Melbourne, Australia: Macmillan.

PART IV

NEW AND UNDER-EXPLORED CONTEXT AND PROCESS VARIABLES IN VARIOUS M&A STAGES

9 Facilitating mergers through management and organization of communication: an analysis of strategic communication in a cross-border merger

Anne-Marie Søderberg

INTRODUCTION

Mergers are extraordinarily complex organizational change processes. Pre-merger considerations about a good 'strategic fit' and 'cultural fit' between potential company partners have attracted much focus among both scholars and business consultants. During the past 10–15 years more attention has been directed to the integration phase, often driven by an interest to better understand why the performance of many mergers has been disappointing, and how it may be improved. Some scholars have tried to investigate how human resources and cultural differences are managed in integration processes (Hitt et al., 2001; Morosino, 1998; Pablo and Javidan, 2004; Stahl and Mendenhall, 2005). Other scholars have tried to identify socio-cultural issues (for example, Ailon-Souday and Kunda, 2003; Riad, 2006; Risberg, 1999; Søderberg and Vaara, 2003) that may explain why only few mergers turn out to be an undisputable success whereas more of them fail, or at least meet serious challenges in areas where top managers and decision makers were not prepared for them. Stahl and Voigt, 2008, who have studied a substantive body of recent research contributions on the role of culture in M&A, conclude that cultural differences not only create major obstacles to achieving integration benefits. Differences in culture may also be a source of value creation and learning if cultural diversity within an organization is acknowledged, communicated and managed professionally. Empirical studies of the role communication plays in post-merger integration processes are still scarce (Bastien, 1987; DiFonzo and Bordia, 1998; Dooley and Zimmermann, 2006; Schweiger and DeNisi, 1991); not to speak of studies of how cultural diversity is acknowledged, communicated and managed in mergers and acquisitions.

In this chapter particular attention is drawn to the importance of strategic communication in relation to international mergers and acquisitions.

By combining approaches from organizational communication and organization studies I look closer at how post-merger processes can be facilitated through management and organization of strategic communication to internal and external stakeholders. I draw on a longitudinal case study (Søderberg and Vaara, 2003) of a complex merger of four North European banks that led to the formation of the transnational corporation Nordea. However, the purpose of the analysis is not to focus on the unique features of the Nordea merger, but rather to exemplify how strategic communication to both internal and external audiences – as well as lack of strategic communication – impact post-merger change processes. Based on what the transnational corporation learnt from its strategic communication during the initial sociocultural integration process, I outline some implications for other merging companies involved in complex change processes.

In the analysis of empirical material collected from the Nordea case study, I address two research questions:

1. How did top managers through strategic communication seek to give sense to organizational change processes following the complex merger?
2. How did the establishment of a transnational department for identity and communications support and facilitate post-merger integration processes?

The chapter is structured as follows. First, I deal with top managers' role as change agents informing internal and external audiences about the new company's vision and value platform at the time when the transnational merger was publicly announced. Second, I look at whether top and middle managers played their expected role as strategic communicators giving sense to change processes following the complex merger. Third, I look further into culture building and internal branding initiatives to see how top management communicated the vision, mission and new corporate values of the transnational company, and how these attempts to create commitment among employees in the merging companies – facilitated by HR and communications staff – were received. Fourth, I deal with the formal organization of internal and external communication processes in the merging companies through the establishment of a transnational identity and communications department, in order to understand how this organization may support and facilitate strategic communication related to post-merger integration processes. In the concluding remarks, I highlight the benefits of adding a communication perspective to studies of post-merger integration processes. I call attention both to implications of the analyzed case for M&A practice and to implications for further M&A research of change-related strategic communication.

A CASE STUDY OF INTERNATIONAL MERGERS AND ACQUISITIONS

The transnational corporation, Nordea, was officially established in the year 2000 through cross-border mergers and acquisitions involving four banks and two insurance companies located in Finland, Sweden, Denmark and Norway (see Figure 9.1). In 1997 Swedish Nordbanken merged with Finnish Merita. In March 2000 Merita-Nordbanken merged with the Danish financial corporation Unidanmark, and in October 2000 the Norwegian Christiania Bank of Kredittkasse was acquired. Further acquisitions in Sweden, the Baltic countries and Poland have subsequently been accomplished.

Nordea has established its position in the market and is today the largest financial services group in the Nordic and Baltic Sea region with around 33,800 employees, 1400 bank branches and total assets of around EUR 580 billion.[1] Nordea is the player in the region who has made the most significant progress in terms of the integration of banking and insurance activities across national boundaries. Its financial performance has been more than satisfactory, even in a period of financial crises, and it was awarded 'Bank of the Year 2010' in Denmark, Sweden and Norway.

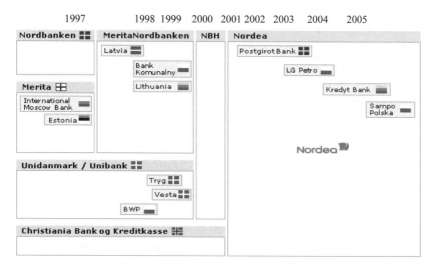

Figure 9.1   Nordea's history

A Nordic group of researchers[2] made participant observations, collected internal company documents and carried out in-depth narrative interviews in 2001 with 53 senior executives and key decision makers, representing different nationalities, business areas, staff functions, professions and power positions. The purpose of collecting their individual stories was to get different voices and perspectives on critical events and actions in relation to merger negotiations and the subsequent organizational change processes (Søderberg and Vaara, 2003, Søderberg, 2006; Vaara and Tienari, 2011). In 2002 and 2003, supplementary documents were collected, and interviews were conducted with top and middle managers in two corporate staff functions, Group HR and Group Identity and Communications, that is, two departments that were involved in and made responsible for culture-building and internal branding initiatives (Søderberg and Björkman, 2003; Björkman and Søderberg, 2006). Based on these field studies, I exemplify in the following sections how management and organization of strategic communication was used to facilitate the complex post-merger integration processes.

MANAGING FOUR MERGING COMPANIES THROUGH VARIOUS COMMUNICATION INITIATIVES

Prior to and during integration processes following a merger, managers must consider a number of issues involving communication of the changes to be made:

- What vision do we have for the merger of the organizations, and how can we communicate it to external and internal stakeholders?
- Which metaphors do we want to use in internal and external communications about the merger?
- Which meanings do managers and employees in the merging organizations assign to the merger and the new organization?
- How can a positive scenario of the future workplace be created, and how can employees' identification with the new organization be strengthened through managerial sensegiving of various actions and dialogue with those most deeply involved?
- How can conflicts and opposing interests between the merging organizations be handled through strategic communication? How can negative reactions such as skepticism, resistance and us-them-thinking among managers and employees be accommodated?

In the following sections I will look further into how top and middle managers in Nordea dealt with these issues, sometimes by themselves, sometimes assisted by HR and Communications staff members.

Communicating the Vision of the Merger

Corporate communications has in many ways been a major driver in the organizational change processes since the announcement of the trans-national merger of Unidanmark and Merita-Nordbanken in March 2000 at a press conference with a direct video-line switching linking the head-quarters in Copenhagen, Stockholm and Helsinki. A 'Merger Prospectus' justified the merger with statements like "The deregulation of financial services (. . .) and the formation of the European Economic and Monetary Union open opportunities for restructuring of the industry not only within countries, but also across national borders." Media interviews with key decision-makers also made use of a 'globalist' discourse (Vaara and Tienari, 2011) when legitimating the cross-border merger through empha-sis on the inevitability of a global restructuring of the financial services sector. The merger was 'naturalized' in media statements like "the wave of bank mergers continues. The trend towards larger units in European finan-cial services is ever more apparent" (Affärsvärlden, Sweden, 15 March 2000). Also future deals were anticipated: "The table is laid, Deutsche Bank! The expansion that Nordea has sought in the Nordic region is now complete, providing a good launch pad to the Baltics, Poland and maybe even Northern Germany" (Helsingin Sanomat, Finland, 17 October 2000) (quoted in Vaara and Tienari, 2011, p. 8).

This kind of sensegiving (Gioia and Chittipeddi, 1991) that framed the cross-border merger as a pioneering example of a global trend might also have served the function of drawing attention away from an alternative per-spective, a 'nationalist' view often evoked by each of the merger partners in the four countries. Within this perspective a key concern might be to protect 'national' interests when it comes to a distribution of managerial positions and centres of excellence, but also the handling of employment reductions, which are often affected by national differences in labor market legislation. Finally, decisions about which practices and systems borrowed from the four merger partners should be considered 'the best' and 'the standard' in the new transnational corporation could be viewed through a 'nationalist' lens.

Communicating Change through Actions

Strategic change communication is practiced not only with words, but also through non-verbal actions that carry symbolic significance and may cause an emotional stir: Who are chosen for top management positions? Are all managers assigned from one organization only, or is balance sought between the merging organizations in the distribution of managerial responsibility? In which location is the headquarters of the merged organizations located? What is the name of the new company? Which work procedures are made into 'best practice'? In making such decisions it is very important to display coherence in what managers say about for example a 'merger among equals', and how they (re)act.

An initiative that effectively promoted the idea of equality between the four merging organizations was the decision made by top management in Nordea that the new corporation would only have a 'virtual headquarter': Top managers would retain their offices in their home country organizations, but travel extensively in all the Nordic countries. Group executive meetings were to take place once a week either in Copenhagen, Helsinki, Oslo or Stockholm. However, this very time-consuming arrangement with a high symbolic impact was abandoned one and a half years after the cross-border merger, when it was decided to establish a corporate headquarters in Stockholm.

Another symbolic act after the merger deals was the decision to distribute power positions equally within Group Executive Management between representatives from the four Nordic countries. Some senior managers interpreted it positively as an attempt to strike a balance between 'rational decisions' and 'cultural equality'; other managers voiced critical comments to the 'balance of power' principle: "Democracy – if that is the right word – has been prioritized higher than competencies" and "To remain a good and effective and attractive bank in the future, a financial institution, we cannot base our decision on quotas" (Vaara and Tienari, 2003).

By referring to the consensus-oriented and often indecisive Nordic Council and the loss-making airline SAS, some managers tried to deconstruct this initiative as an effort to convincingly build a Nordic corporation. Disappointment could also be traced among those who did not get or maintain attractive managerial positions, which they considered themselves best qualified for. However, some managers emphasized that they understood very well the decisions made, and they accepted that symbolic expressions of the equality between the merging companies must be taken into consideration. But they comforted themselves that after a certain period, when "the honey moon phase is over" and "the hour of truth will come", they may well have another career change if those who were selected for top managerial positions did not perform according to the high expectations.

Managing Change through Framing

Among the many strategic communication initiatives taken in an early phase was also the launch of the new company name, Nordea, deriving from the words 'Nordic' and 'idea', and the new company logo, depicting a blue sail, said to allude to the sea that joins the countries around the Baltic Sea where the new transnational corporation operates. The company name and the corporate logo were presented in October 2000 to both internal and external audiences in advertisement campaigns in national newspapers and European business magazines, primarily with the purpose to increase knowledge about the Nordea corporation, but also to create more internal commitment through 'auto-communication', when organizational members read in external media about their own company.

Advertisement campaigns in European business magazines showed beautiful, but deserted Nordic landscapes. They also highlighted so-called 'Nordic ideas' (Nordic flexibility, Nordic freedom, Nordic individuality, Nordic opportunities and Nordic security); ideas that Nordea claimed were shared across national borders within the region where Nordea was going to be 'the Nordic champion'. These rather vague Nordic ideas about freedom, entrepreneurship, democracy, and equal opportunities probably had greater importance in the external positioning of the new Nordic corporation in an international context than as an internal unifying tool and an identity-constructing device.

Advertisement campaigns in North European newspapers illustrated the 'Nordic ideas' with pictures of products, designed in the respective countries of the four merger partners; for example, the classic egg-shaped chair, a functionalist style icon designed by the Danish architect Arne Jacobsen, or the famous and distinctive glass vase designed by the Finnish architect Alvar Aalto, both designers viewed as "individuals, entrepreneurs and (designers associated with) organizations who dare break new ground". The intent was once more to create pride and self-esteem among the employees in the four merging companies through national imagery, and to emphasize that each of the four merger partners contributed equally with good and sound 'Nordic ideas' (products and practices) to the new transnational corporation.

The corporate statement (vision, mission and corporate values) of the new corporation was in the first round negotiated among top managers and key decision makers from the four merging companies. They experienced the negotiation and formulation of a shared corporate statement as a useful process for making sure that they as key decision makers agreed on and were committed to a common understanding of the kind of organization that would be created through the merger, both in terms of its basic assumptions and cultural values, its internal functioning and its future direction. However, even though the efforts made to craft a joint values-based vision aimed at ensuring 'cultural compatibility', it did not seem to have any powerful effect on people in the merging organizations, at least in the short run.

Nordea's corporate statement – as of 2000 – consisted of a company vision: *to be valued as the leading financial services group in the Nordic and the Baltic financial markets with a substantial growth potential*, a mission: *making it possible (for ourselves and our customers)*, and three corporate values: *we create value, we are innovative,* and *we are empowering.* Not least the corporate values could be viewed as an example of conscious use of strategic ambiguity. According to Eisenberg (2006), strategic ambiguity may facilitate organizational change following a merger much better than communication with a high level of clarity and openness, because it makes it possible for various groups of internal and external stakeholders to choose their interpretation of top management's somewhat vague announcements. Moreover, it allows top management to keep open situations where they have not yet decided, nor are ready to make decisions that bind them long term. But the open question is how employees in the merging companies made sense (Weick, 1995) of the new corporate statement.

Scholars and consultants of merger management often recommend management to engage in a dialogue with employees in the merging companies and negotiate with them (Bastien, 1987; Schweiger and DeNisi, 2001). Dialogue and negotiation between managers and employees undoubtedly have a beneficial effect on employees' commitment and sensemaking. However, whereas employees often have an unfilled need for unequivocal, clear and concise communication, also of unpleasant consequences such as planned workforce reduction and reassignments to other localities, management may have a certain strategic interest in communicating ambiguous messages that are open to different interpretations. Explicit and accurate information on specific phases of the integration process is not always possible from the outset, nor is it always advantageous from a managerial perspective.

However, it is noticeable that in this initial phase of the Nordea merger employees were primarily 'told' about the new company vision, the mission and the corporate values. The corporate statement was presented to internal and external stakeholders on a new corporate website, and it was likewise presented to the employees in a new group internal magazine, *Nordic Ideas.* But the employees were not offered any opportunities for feedback to management, at least not in these media.

Sensegiving and Sensemaking of Organizational Changes

Members of an organization make sense of processes or activities in the organization by fitting them into an interpretative scheme or a system of meaning that has developed through experience and socialization. When organizations are altered in some drastic way, for example by a reorganization brought on by a merger, members often find that their existing interpreting schemes or frames of reference no longer suffice to make sense of new situations and to sort their own observations and the stories told into a coherent understanding of what is going on (Weick, 1995).

When organizational members are in need of new interpretation patterns, a CEO or other top managers can attempt to articulate or advocate their vision or preferred interpretive scheme, thus engaging in sensegiving processes (Gioia and Chittipeddi, 1991), influencing the sensemaking processes of both internal and external stakeholders. Sensegiving is different from sensemaking in that the person trying to *give* sense is attempting to influence other people to perceive and interpret certain actions and events in particular ways:

> 'sensemaking' has to do with meaning construction and reconstruction by the involved parties as they attempted to develop a meaningful framework for understanding the nature of the intended strategic change. 'Sensegiving' is concerned with the process of attempting to influence the sensemaking and meaning construction of others toward a preferred definition of organizational reality. (Gioia and Chittipeddi 1991: 442)

How did Nordea managers make sense of the organizational changes after the cross-border merger was announced, and how did they give sense to them? An analysis of interviews with 53 senior managers representing all four merger partners (Søderberg and Vaara, 2003) showed that these potential change agents did not speak univocally about the merger. They did not tell very much about their concerted efforts to bring the new transnational corporation forward. One and a half years after the merger there was still a lack of consensus, even at top management level, on how to interpret the vision and implement it.

In the stories told about the change processes, the senior managers fabricated very different plots about the merging organizations and about key actors inside the new corporation. They tended to cast themselves in the leading role as dynamic heroes seeking challenges and trying to solve emergent crises (Gabriel, 2000, pp. 73–77), whereas some of the merger partners were cast as either their allies or as their enemies or adversaries.

Nordea had articulated a vision to create a major Nordic financial corporation through ambitious plans for integration across national borders and business units. Statements referring to the merger processes drawing on an integration discourse can be found in most of the interviews with managers we conducted, as well as expressions of pride and commitment to bring the merger partners together and manage various integration projects. But the company vision was interpreted in different ways. The Danish merger partner, Unidanmark, created in the late 1990s a comprehensive financial business by merging retail banking and insurance and boosting asset management, and it became number two in the Danish financial market. The Danes shared a vision of Nordea as an institution with a broad portfolio of financial services. By contrast, the Swedish merger partner, Nordbanken, had succeeded in reconstructing a bank, which in the early 1990s was in severe crisis, by cutting it back to its core activities in retail banking. The Finnish merger partner, Merita, was number one in the Finnish market and at that time world leading in e-banking, and it wanted to push these services forward. With such very different experiences and backgrounds, it is understandable that the plots constructed by senior managers in the different countries and business areas also differed significantly.

Furthermore, many senior managers used their positioning as corporate heroes as a platform for expressing skepticism towards the other merger partners and even criticism of them. They more or less invented national differences in order to explain the existence of communication and cooperation problems across national borders (Vaara et al., 2003). Drawing on a reservoir of national stereotypes, they reproduced images of the nations and nationalities that could be seen as examples of 'banal nationalism' (Billig, 1995). Strong conflicts between the merger partners, particularly between Swedes and Danes, and to a certain extent also between Swedes and Finns, were articulated without any explicit questions from the interviewers about perceived national differences. Below are just a few examples of managerial sensemaking from an in-depth analysis of narrative interviews in 2001 with a Danish and a Swedish senior manager (Søderberg, 2006).

The Danish senior manager perceived Swedes as 'fundamentalist' and 'narrow-minded'. They 'think in silos', and they want to force a misplaced 'uniformity' upon everybody in the Nordic corporation, even though 'there is hardly any area where they perform better than the average, except short-term cost reductions'. The Danish manager also blamed the Swedes for speeding up the integration process before the decisions had been 'digested'.

The Swedish senior manager perceived Finns as hardworking people who always keep their promises and quickly implement joint decisions.

They were his allies and helpers in relation to the ambitious merger project:

> Swedish and Finnish bank directors get along very well. They support each other a lot, they work a lot . . . I think that Swedes and Finns feel that if you understand each other at the professional level, you also sort of trust each other. There is a kind of Japanese conception of honour in the Finnish mentality, which implies that you do not go back on previous agreements . . . As soon as the Danish directors enter the picture, the whole thing becomes more unpredictable.

In contrast to the Finns, the Danish merger partner was described in very negative terms and the Danish nation was depicted as being self-satisfied and isolationist:

> Denmark is parochial as hell . . . The Danes sit in their small communities with their small companies and feel no particular need for the rest of the world. It's no coincidence that they have chosen not to join the EMU, and they are reluctant to take on international commitments. This is also reflected in the internal culture in a corporation like ours. There is a very typical Danish attitude, even high up in the organisation: 'Aren't we okay as we are?'; 'why do we need to change that?'; and 'try to convince me!'.

Consequently, the Danish managers were regarded as 'unconstructive' and 'anti-authoritarian', displaying a behaviour which – from the Swedish manager's perspective – was totally incompatible with his vision of 'the Nordic Champion'.

Many senior managers also established and reinforced dichotomies between the different business areas (retail banking, asset management, insurance) involved in the merger, even though their main task was expected to be that of constructing a corporate identity of the new transnational corporation and giving sense to the complex integration processes they were spearheading. Instead of acting as committed change agents, the managers thus involved themselves in struggles over power with their merger partners from other nations and business areas.

The managers' stories about critical events in the intercultural collaboration were circulating in the merging organization and giving sense to specific actions. These stories brought with them a high risk of fragmenting the multinational matrix organization insofar as they contributed to establishing and upholding barriers between key people who were supposed to communicate and collaborate. Consequently, there was at this point in the merger process, one and a half years after the Nordic merger was publicly announced, a strong need to launch sociocultural integration initiatives.

Internal Branding through Framing

Frames are abstract notions that serve the purpose to organize social meanings and construct or modify particular interpretations of organizational events (Fairhurst and Sarr, 1996) and thereby try to direct other people's sensemaking and responses. Managers' framing of a merger involves the task of finding, for instance, strong and viable images/metaphors, stories and artifacts that connect the merger to everyday life in the organization and to offer interpretations that make people see events and actions in new ways and align their understanding and daily practices with the new organization's vision and mission and strengthen their organizational commitment. Therefore it is important if a merger is presented as a 'marriage of convenience' or rather as a merger between 'equal partners'. If top management aims at close integration of the merging companies, it is likewise important to avoid drawing on, for example, war metaphors and presenting the post-merger process as, for example, a 'battle for territory'.

In the Nordea merger extensive sociocultural integration was sought; therefore it was important to develop a new cultural platform with common values and common symbols to make the employees identify with the new company as an attractive community of practice. In such a context it may be advantageous to tell stories about what the new organization is, and what it stands for, showing the direction of the change and giving sense to it (Schultz et al., 2005; Weick, 1995). In order for managers to communicate the vision of the merger through images and storytelling, they are required to be very conscious about which assumptions about people and organizations are attached to the specific linguistic choices they make.

Many managers and employees will be inclined to consider organizational change processes in connection with a complex merger, such as the Nordea case, as something unpleasant and problematic. They may experience the changes as a threat, and as something that actually brings out insecurity and anxiety about the future. Any manager and employee involved in a merger sometimes have to reflect on questions such as: How is my position affected by the planned changes? Do I have to say goodbye to good colleagues and a familiar workplace? Will I lose influence, status and privileges? Am I sufficiently competent and capable of developing in line with the changed demands? These many questions reflecting insecurity and anxiety regarding what the future holds easily affect both managers' and employees' language use and their organizational images in a negative direction (Dooley and Zimmermann, 2006). In this regard managers as strategic communicators have much to learn from the techniques that are part of an 'appreciative inquiry' (Cooperrider and Whitney, 2005) where conscious efforts are made to 'frame' organizational changes in a positive way and put emphasis on new opportunities for future careers and for personal development of competencies.

In autumn 2001, it was decided to find new ways to guide Nordea employees' behaviour, create organizational identification with a new corporate brand, and mobilize support for the new corporate vision within the business areas and staff functions and at various locations in the Nordic region. An internal culture and branding process was initiated by top management and facilitated by staff members in the Group HR department and the Group Identity and Communications department. They were delegated responsibility for the execution of a process named 'From Words to Action' that took place from December 2001 to January 2002.

A booklet, *Making it Possible*, was produced for internal branding purposes and disseminated to all managers and employees in the transnational corporation. PowerPoint presentations were prepared to be used by the managers of different business units and staff functions in a top-down cascade process. The booklet – somewhat surprisingly – presented the new transnational organization as a community that not only had common goals, but was already sharing common values and practices. There were references to a 'Nordic character' and 'Nordic personality' and a 'Nordic way of thinking and acting':

> We have a Nordic foundation and we're proud of it. . . . Whenever we mention our Nordic character, it has nothing to do with our nationality. It is a question of cross-border cooperation. It is about learning from each other, sharing ideas . . . It is a question of welcoming diversity and respect for the Nordic heritage of freedom, equal opportunities and care for the environment. It's about our welfare and our strong belief in democracy. (op. cit., p.43)

These claims of a shared 'Nordic identity' were accompanied by aesthetic pictures of a Norwegian fjord, Finnish lakes, a Danish beech forest, and a Swedish, red-coloured wooden country house, and pictures of young, blond and blue-eyed Nordic people (Figure 9.2).

But the verbal and visual messages in the booklet were totally unrelated to the day-to-day experiences of Nordea employees and they did not say anything about what it means to be a pan-Nordic financial services group, compared to other banks and insurance companies operating in the Nordic countries.

The booklet *Making it Possible* can be seen as an example of conscious efforts to monitor and control processes of corporate identity formation and as a representation of the company's Nordic integration discourse emphasizing coherence and consistency across national borders and business areas. The managers, who had – for quite a while – been involved in power struggles across national borders, as demonstrated in the section above, were told that:

*Figure 9.2   Pictures of a young, blond and blue-eyed Nordic woman, a
Danish beech forest, and a Norwegian fjord*

> 'We are sufficiently similar to be able to cooperate and sufficiently dissimilar
> to inspire each other' (op. cit., p.19), and There is no contradiction between
> the ambition of creating a common culture and the aspiration to reach other
> goals as well. On the contrary, a common culture, which helps all managers and
> employees to move in the same direction, actually makes it easier to reach other
> goals' (op. cit., p.29).

The employees could read about a new corporate brand and their task as
'translators' of the new corporate vision, the mission and the set of corporate values into daily social practices:

> The combination of our Nordic way of thinking and our Nordic ideas is what
> distinguishes us from our competitors, and the same applies to our redefined
> offers in the financial services market: combining banking and insurance into
> financial partnership. Now all that remains is to fill these Nordic ideas with
> real substance. To provide superior service across our business areas and coun-
> tries through practical action, so our Nordic ideas become infused with such
> meaning to our customers that they identify with them and appreciate their real
> value. (op.cit., p.13)

In the foreword to *Making it Possible*, Nordea's CEO at that time stated
that the company vision and the strategic goal were to make the transnational corporation a larger player in the financial sector in the Nordic
and the Baltic region. The managers and employees were seen as those
who can help make the vision possible by 'living the corporate brand' (Ind,
2001) guided by Nordic ideas and a new corporate values statement.

The Group Identity and Communications department was in charge
of the production of the booklet in collaboration with a British advertisement agency. The HR managers in each business unit were given the
responsibility to plan the cascade process in more detail. In the present
stage of our knowledge about the ongoing power struggles within group
executive management and many senior managers' lack of responsibility

as change-agents, it was somewhat surprising that no challenges to the corporate identity and branding project were explicitly mentioned, and no obstacles were acknowledged, in the instructions made by the HR and Communications departments before the internal branding process was launched. Several of the HR managers, whom we interviewed, afterwards criticized the top-down approach, and they found the division of labor between Communications and HR problematic. The following interview statement gives an impression of how the cascade process was evaluated by some of the responsible HR managers:

> Top management initiated the branding process and made a promise to the employees about a continued dialogue. But they did not redeem it, and that is fatal. It is the way management loses trust capital in relation to the employees. The branding process was conducted as a top-down process, and top management did not show interest in getting any kind of feedback. The department Group Identity and Communications made it into an issue about how Nordea gets a new profile and thus differentiates itself from other companies. But they totally underestimated the big challenge concerning how to facilitate the employees' brand identification process. If we talk to our customers about what Nordea stands for, it is crucial that the Nordea employees get a feeling of what makes the difference. What is it they must do in a different way, because they are now working in Nordea and not any longer in Unidanmark, Nordbanken, Merita or CBK.

Another issue that truly undermined Nordea's efforts to introduce a new corporate culture and company brand was lack of strong support from the senior managers who were expected to give sense to this specific integration project. Top management articulated a 'One Company' discourse emphasizing that Nordea is or must become an integrated corporation. They had already argued for the need for merging, cooperating, and acquiring new and better competencies to secure growth in the internationalized financial services sector. But the harmonious perspective incorporated in the integrating and unifying discourse found in the booklet *Making it Possible* was seriously challenged by other voices and perspectives favoring local and national communities and identities. An HR manager told:

> NN (The CEO) was right when he decided to start this internal branding process, but he did not succeed in making the other managing directors responsible as partners in the cascade process.

Another middle manager confirmed this impression that – at least in some business areas – there was a lack of managerial support to the internal process:

Group Executive Management probably accepted all these fine words and the text in the brand book. But they did not mix their blood; they did not create a common understanding of the Nordic ideas and the common values. And if the top managers do not go through such a branding process themselves, they cannot implement the ideas behind.

An employee told in an interview that the exercise 'From Words to Action' took less than an hour at his workplace. The brand book was distributed by his manager, who then went through a series of pre-produced PowerPoint slides telling about Nordea's vision, mission, values and ideas. But there was no discussion of the presentation or any attempt to 'translate' the relatively abstract words and concepts into the department's own tasks.

However, we do not know how the brand book has been received and used in every part of the big Nordea corporation. It may somewhere have been welcomed as an initiative that could inspire practice in a way that some of the more abstract messages have been translated to local meanings that make good sense to a specific group of employees in a given organizational context. Or, conversely, some employees may have deconstructed the presented story, either because it did not meet their needs of sensegiving to the changes they witnessed in their working life, or because the story's inclusiveness obfuscated the divisions and potential antagonisms that can be found within every large corporation, Nordea included.

It was obvious that the new transnational corporation with the 'From Words to Action' exercise tried to shape interpretations of actual and future organizational events. But the vague images of the new organizational world discursively constructed through this branding exercise was, even though it was probably unintended, by many employees perceived as an – unsuccessful – attempt to impose a monological and unitary perception of the new transnational corporation.

A strong commitment to 'live the brand' (Ind, 2001, Schultz et al., 2005) and translate corporate values into shared standards and daily work practices rather occurs through dialogue, negotiation and struggles over meaning in which management and employees compete over various definitions of the organizational reality (Mumby, 2000: 595). According to internal HR surveys, Nordea's corporate values were accepted and understood throughout the organization. But, in hindsight it is obvious that this corporate culture and branding initiative did not succeed in generating a shared mindset among the many employees and developing a stronger commitment in the new corporate culture and the corporate brand. What was obviously lacking in this branding exercise was a more clear sense of direction (where are we coming from, and where are we heading?), as well as more compelling stories and more clear references to serious challenges to overcome through joint efforts. For a more in-depth critical analysis of this organization-wide branding process conceptualized and carried out as an internal marketing campaign, see Søderberg and Björkman, 2003.

Much has happened in Nordea since 2001–2003, when the field study of the initial phase of the complex post-merger integration was conducted. The company vision has changed from becoming a 'Nordic champion' to becoming a 'great European bank'. Also the corporate values decided on by the first group of top managers have been replaced by other values that seem to give more direction to daily activities. Among these values are 'One Nordea team', which is further elaborated on in four statements:

- *We team up to create value*
- *We work together across the organization*
- *We show trust and assume accountability*
- *We make rules and instructions clear and applicable.* (www.nordea.com)

Interaction between staff in Group HR and Group Identity and Communications was also intensified after the internal branding exercise analyzed above. More strategic approaches to both international human resource management and integrated communications were gradually developed. Job satisfaction has increased significantly and in 2010 Nordea was ranked as number 11 among the best large workplaces in Europe by the 'Great Place to Work Institute'. Also the Nordea brand has been established among both internal and external stakeholders. In 2011 Nordea was, for example, ranked as number 33 among 500 global banks by Brand Finance.

In the next section I will briefly describe how the complex organization of strategic communication in a new transnational department, Group Identity and Communications, has contributed substantively to increase the cohesiveness in the transnational corporation and enhance employees' trust and organizational commitment, and thereby also contributed to develop Nordea's corporate brand and reputation.

ORGANIZING STRATEGIC COMMUNICATION IN FOUR MERGING COMPANIES

The way communication is organized and managed after a merger carries important strategic and political dimensions (Cornelissen, 2004; Lewis, 2011). Previously, communication departments had very few explicit strategic tasks, and they were only to a small extent involved in the company's strategic thinking and actions. But many contemporary organizations are undergoing sweeping changes to accommodate to more competitive business conditions and to new responsibilities in relation to an increasing number of stakeholders. The changes related to the Nordea merger and the development of a transnational corporate communications department can thus serve as an example of how professional communicators in the early 2000s strived to integrate various communication activities at a horizontal level in order to make the merging companies speak with 'one voice', both to internal and external stakeholders in the many countries where the corporation operated. The description of the organizational development below is meant to give an impression of the complexity of communications management after a cross-border merger.

Communication activities in the four merging companies had been organized and operated in a more fragmented manner with disciplines such as public relations, advertising and marketing communications, branding, investor relations communication, HR-related communications and so on, separated into 'functional silos' within each company. One ambition for Nordea was to coordinate and streamline the various communication units, disciplines and activities into a single corporate communications department so that knowledge, experiences and skills could be more easily shared within the new transnational corporation. Another ambition was to integrate and coordinate internal and external communication in order to make the transnational corporation speak with 'one voice' and, if possible, act as 'one corpus', hence 'corporate communications'. A third ambition was to provide strategic input into decision-making at the corporate level and to devolve communication expertise to the business areas and staff functions. A fourth ambition was to coordinate and streamline communication plans and activities across national borders and languages, business areas and staff functions through face-to-face and virtual meetings and online knowledge-sharing between professionals working at different locations.

At the time of the cross-border merger in 2000, managers of the four companies' departments of communication were met with the expectation of gradually developing a transnational department. This so-called Group Identity and Communications (GIC) department was made co-responsible for strategic communication, including the corporate culture and branding exercise described above. But some communication tasks were at that point of time still located in other departments, for example in IT services, where people worked with a very demanding and time-consuming development of a transnational intranet and with a new corporate website.

The prevailing ambition was to centralize all communication competences and functions in GIC and at the same time strengthen the links between strategic communication and business perspectives. Attempts were made to coordinate and integrate for example HR-related internal communication and Internet-based job recruitment, but also to align internal communication of the new corporation's vision, mission and corporate values with the efforts made to position the company in relation to its external stakeholders, in order to pursue the ideas behind the corporate values and the ongoing corporate branding project.

Gradually, the transnational GIC department was established, and most of the professional communicators were located there; as were those who had responsibility for bridging the gap between communications and different business areas and staff functions. Figure 9.3 shows the organizational chart of the GIC department in 2005, five years after the quadruple cross-border merger took place. I will try to explain some of the ideas behind this departmental arrangement and the location of communications disciplines within the organizational hierarchy.

First a few words about the Group Translation section. Nordea is a multilingual organization, and that was – and still is – a challenge for communication across national borders (Vaara et al., 2005). After the merger in 2000 between Unidanmark and the Finnish-Swedish company Merita-Nordbanken, which had Swedish as shared company language, English was adopted as the new company language at management meetings in the headquarters and in the daily work in transnational staff functions and business areas; this decision affected the daily work of around 15–20 percent of Nordea's staff. Courses in English were offered to develop a higher level of linguistic proficiency among both managers and employees. However, the four Nordic languages, as well as Estonian, Latvian, Lithuanian, Polish and Russian, are still spoken in the local bank branches of Nordea and used in many documents written to specific local and national audiences.

One consequence of being a multilingual organization is that many texts, for example press releases, annual reports, websites, internal magazines and intranet instructions as well as many legal documents are published both in English, and in all the other languages in use within the transnational organization. A common terminology base in English is continuously developed, and many translators have been appointed by the GIC department to ensure a highly professional treatment of all kinds of linguistic issues in texts and presentations produced for different internal and external audiences.

'Communication partners' are employed by GIC, but they serve as advisors, sparring partners and sounding boards for the CEO, the business areas and for managers in different group functions such as HR, Legal

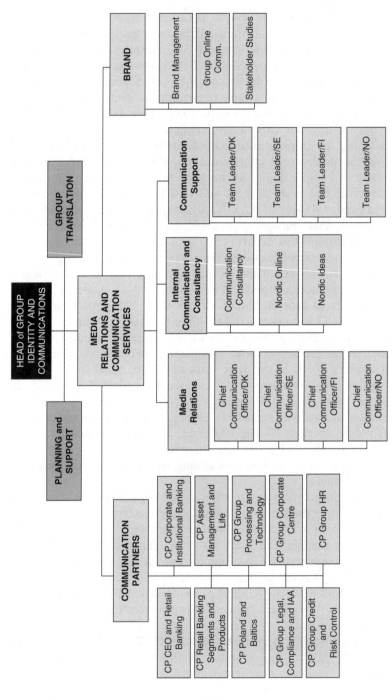

Figure 9.3   Nordea GIC: Organizational chart August 2005

Issues, Processing and Technology. The head of GIC serves as communication partner for Nordea's CEO, whereas other senior communications practitioners are strategic sparring partners for other senior executives. As high-level professional communicators they must be able to identify communication needs for the various business areas and group functions and translate these into communication activities that can reinforce the company's strategy and drive already planned communication activities.

Within the subgroup of media relations and communication services, the Chief Communication Officers provide communication support to the Country Senior Executives, that is, the spokesmen of Nordea Group Management in the four Nordic countries. They offer them general media training as well as training on specific critical issues, and they are responsible for the day-to-day media contact of these key personnel, but they are also involved in the maintenance and improvement of the company's media relations. They often work closely together with managers and employees in the different business areas and group functions, and roll out and drive certain company-wide communication concepts together with the 'Communication Partners'.

A support function divided into four country-based teams represents the communication department's production facility. The communication supporters' main tasks are to produce content for different channels, the intranet 'Nordic Online', the retail banking channel, and the internal magazine *Nordic Ideas*. They also support those responsible for media relations and assist the communication partners.

The main tasks of the group responsible for internal communication are to develop, measure and improve the internal communication structure and content, including the personnel magazine *Nordic Ideas*, the online channels and the line communication. Moreover this group is involved in the development and implementation of various communication tools as well as in communication training of middle managers to improve their line communication, so that they are able to fulfill the role as change agents and sensegivers.

A group of communication practitioners is responsible for maintaining and developing the Nordea corporate brand and for carrying out continuous stakeholder analysis to measure the company's reputation. Another group of communication practitioners is responsible for online communications technology for both internal and external audiences. They also take care of the company's use of external websites to support growth and sales and to help key stakeholders, including internal staff, consumers and the media, get a positive view of Nordea and increase its reputation.

The Group Identity and Communications department thus offers various tools to support and facilitate organizational change through strategic communication. Something that was obviously missing in the initial phases of the post-merger integration processes analyzed above.

CONCLUDING REMARKS

The Nordea merger is in many ways illuminating, and the empirical material collected in the longitudinal case study of integration processes is rich and can be used to show how many complex issues both managers and M&A scholars have to deal with. In this chapter I have focused on how communication can serve strategic purposes after a complex merger where one of many challenges is to embrace national, organizational and professional cultures in a transnational organization. In the following concluding remarks I highlight some of the benefits of adding a communication perspective to studies of post-merger integration processes and draw attention to the impact on practice and research of the communicative issues touched upon.

With examples from the initial phases of the sociocultural integration process in Nordea I tried to illuminate how difficult it is to create a new corporate culture that employees from merging companies feel attached to, and to launch a new corporate brand that employees are ready to live.

Observations and interviews conducted in relation to the corporate culture and branding process 'From Words to Action' clearly showed that a new culture cannot be imposed by top management and communicated top-down in a cascade process. A message to managers aiming at ambitious sociocultural integration between merging companies is that a new corporate culture does not exist, if it is not made sense of and discussed by those who should feel attached to and identify with it. Rather than focusing on abstract and ambiguous ideas and values, more efforts should be put into aligning ideas, values and norms around concrete organizational practices. Also reflections on perceived cultural differences between the merging companies should be included in a conscious development of a new culture.

Likewise, a new corporate brand does not emerge from a campaign where employees are told to follow certain directions and guidelines in a brand book and are treated as passive recipients. If the purpose is to enhance communication and collaboration between merging organizations and to strengthen commitment among employees to a corporate vision and mission, employees must be invited to dialogue and offered feedback opportunities. Culture- and brand-building processes following mergers and acquisitions must involve and empower employees as committed change implementers who enact the vision and mission of the new organization and translate suggested values and guiding principles into real-life experiences and daily practices at the workplace. In order to facilitate such processes strong linkages between corporate vision and strategy, integrated communications and HR management are crucial.

The complex Nordea merger is a case that helps us better understand how crucial it is that managers are ready to take on a role as strategic communicators in organizational change processes following a merger. Drawing on a globalist discourse, top management in Nordea convincingly gave sense to the merger to public media and other external stakeholders when they legitimated the move that led them to create a multinational corporation with ambitions to become 'the Nordic champion' within the financial services sector. However, the analysis of interviews with Nordea senior managers demonstrated problems that emerged in the initial phase of the sociocultural integration process, because some of these top managers involved themselves heavily in struggles for managerial power and positions with representatives of other nationalities, and cultivated a storytelling about the other merger partners based on 'nationalist' stereotypes. In this process they ran the risk of losing sight of the vision for the new transnational corporation, a vision that they were expected to give sense to and develop into new practices. It meant that they did not wholeheartedly play the expected role as change agents in relation to their subordinates in the merging companies and thus did not forcefully give sense to the organizational changes they spearheaded.

Therefore many middle managers missed a schema of interpretation that could have assisted them in their own framing and sensegiving of organizational changes in relation to their subordinates. This was a big issue since both research (DiFonzo and Bordia, 1998; Elving, 2005; Schuler et al., 2004) and practice tell us how important it is that – in particular – middle managers are able to keep an ongoing dialogue with their employees and update them about pending changes. This is important in order to decrease their insecurity and anxiety, so that they do not become incapable of action, or choose to leave the organization out of fear of being rejected at a later stage. But an ongoing dialogue is also crucial in order to offer employees a positive framing of the organizational changes they experience, to make them see opportunities for new tasks and/or new career opportunities, as opposed to loss of customary frames and procedures.

The Nordea case also illustrates the often underestimated need of assistance from professional communicators with a strategic perspective who can support and facilitate managerial efforts to integrate the merging companies. I have tried to shed light on the time-consuming and difficult process through which a transnational and multilingual department of identity and communications was gradually established and organized to serve strategic purposes, among other things. This department aimed at speaking with one voice internally and externally, and at the same time bridging national borders, business units and staff functions. I have emphasized that professional merger communication is not just matter of informing external audiences through press releases and preparing managers for media exposure or calming anxious employees and retaining key talents. It also comprises the development of an intranet that links employees in the merging companies, and setting up a corporate website that constantly updates external stakeholders about important steps in the establishment of the new organization and how its vision, mission and values can guide this development. Of utmost importance for successful post-merger integration is strategic communication support to different business areas and staff functions in order to strengthen the organizational links between communications, HR and business. In Nordea it was accomplished with so called 'communication partners' who were able to identify communication needs for various business areas and staff functions and translate these into communication activities that reinforced the company strategy.

This Nordea case study also has implications for future mergers and acquisitions research. It was planned as a study of sociocultural integration processes after international mergers and acquisitions. But along the way it was acknowledged that communicative issues were tightly integrated with the issues we initially had in focus. Therefore I collected more empirical material to be able to highlight both external and internal communication activities emerging from the mergers. With a position as professor of cross-cultural communication and management, it was particularly interesting for me also to follow the establishment and development of a transnational department for identity and communications. Future empirical studies may from the outset address merger communication as a research issue to be investigated further, both through interviews, participant observations and collection of documents produced in the merging companies' departments of communication, and with studies of how strategic communication in various ways may facilitate post-merger integration.

NOTES

1. Information from www.nordea.com, December 2010.
2. The case study was conducted by an interdisciplinary team of Nordic management researchers: Ingmar Björkman, Janne Tienari and Eero Vaara (Finland), Christine

Meyer and Tore Hundsnes (Norway), Annette Risberg (Sweden), and Anne-Marie Søderberg (Denmark).

REFERENCES

Ailon-Souday, G. and Kunda, G. (2003): 'The local selves of global workers: The social construction of national identity in the face of organizational globalization'. *Organization Studies*, **24** (7), 1073–1096.

Bastien, D.T. (1987): 'Common patterns of behavior and communication in corporate mergers and acquisitions'. *Human Resource Management*, 26, 17–33.

Billig, M. (1995): *Banal Nationalism*. Thousand Oaks, CA: Sage.

Björkman, I. and Søderberg, A.M. (2006): 'The HR function in large-scale mergers and acquisitions: The case of Nordea'. *Personnel Review*, **35** (6), 609–617.

Cooperrider, D.L. and Whitney, D.L. (2005): *Appreciative Inquiry. A Positive Revolution in Change*. San Francisco, CA: Berrett-Koehler.

Cornelissen, J. (2004): *Corporate Communications: Theory and Practice*. London: Sage.

DiFonzo, N. and Bordia, P. (1998): 'A tale of two corporations: managing uncertainty during organisational change'. *Human Resource Management*, **8** (2), 295–303.

Dooley, K.J. and Zimmerman, B.J. (2006): 'Merger as marriage: communication issues in postmerger integration'. In Risberg, A. (ed.): *Mergers and Acquisitions: A Critical Reader*. London: Routledge, pp. 215–230.

Eisenberg, E. (2006): *Strategic Ambiguities: Essays on Communication, Organization and Identity*. Thousand Oaks, CA: Sage.

Elving, W.J.L. (2005): 'The role of communication in organisational change'. *Corporate Communications: An International Journal*, **10** (2), 129–138.

Fairhurst, G.T. and Sarr, R.A. (1996): *The Art of Framing: Managing the Language of Leadership*. San Francisco, CA: Jossey-Bass.

Gabriel, Y. (2000): *Storytelling in Organizations: Facts, Fictions, and Fantasies*. New York: Oxford University Press.

Gioia, D.A. and Chittipeddi, K. (1991): 'Sensemaking and sensegiving in strategic change initiation'. *Strategic Management Journal*, **12** (6), 433–448.

Hitt, M.A.; Harrison, J.J. and Ireland, R.D. (2001): *Mergers and Acquisitions: A Guide to Creating Value for Stakeholders*. Oxford: Oxford University Press.

Ind, N. (2001): *Living the Brand*. London: Kogan Page.

Lewis, L.K. (2011): *Organizational Change. Creating Change through Strategic Communication*. Chichester: Wiley-Blackwell.

Morosino, P. (1998): *Managing Cultural Differences: Effective Strategy and Execution Across Cultures in Global Corporate Alliances*. New York: Pergamon.

Mumby, D.K. (2000): 'Power and politics'. In Jablin, F.M. and Putnam, L. (eds): *The New Handbook of Organizational Communication*. Thousand Oaks, CA: Sage, pp. 585–623.

Nordea Group (2002): *Making it Possible*. Brand book for internal company purposes.

Pablo, A.L. and Javidan, M. (eds) (2004): *Mergers and Acquisitions: Creating Integrative Knowledge*. Oxford: Blackwell.

Riad, S. (2006): 'The power of "organizational culture" as a discursive formation in merger integration'. *Organization Studies*, **26** (10), 1529–1554.

Risberg, A. (1999): *Ambiguities Thereafter. An Interpretive Approach to Acquisitions*. Lund, Sweden: Lund Studies in Economics and Management 46, The Institute of Economic Research, Lund University.

Schuler, R.S., Jackson, S.E. and Lou, Y. (2004): *Managing Human Resources in Cross-border Alliances*. London and New York: Routledge.

Schultz, M.; Antorini, Y.M. and Csaba, F. (eds) (2005): *Corporate Branding. Towards the Second Wave of Corporate Branding – Purpose/People/Process*. Copenhagen: Copenhagen Business School Press, pp. 181–216.

Schweiger, D.M. and DeNisi, A.S. (1991): 'Communication with employees following a merger: a longitudinal field experiment'. *Academy of Management Journal*, 34, 100–135.

Stahl, G.K. and Mendenhall, M. (eds) (2005): *Mergers and Acquisitions. Managing Culture and Human Resources.* Stanford, CA: Stanford University Press.

Stahl, G.K. and Voigt, A. (2008): 'Do cultural differences matter in mergers and acquisitions? A tentative model and examination', *Organization Science*, **19** (1), 160–176.

Søderberg, A-M. (2003): 'Sensegiving and sensemaking in an integration process: a narrative approach to the study of an international acquisition'. In Czarniawska, B. and Gagliardi, P. (eds): *Narratives We Organize By. Narrative approaches in organization studies.* Amsterdam/Philadelphia: John Benjamins, pp. 3–35.

Søderberg, A-M. (2006): 'Narrative interviewing and narrative analysis in a study of a cross-border merger', *Management International Review*, **46** (4), 1–20.

Søderberg, A-M. and Björkman, I. (2003): 'From words to action? – Socio-cultural integration initiatives in a cross-border merger'. In Søderberg, A-M. and Vaara, E. (eds): *Merging across Borders. People, Cultures and Politics.* Copenhagen: Copenhagen Business School Press, pp. 139–176.

Søderberg, A.-M. and Vaara, E. (eds) (2003): *Merging across Borders. People, Cultures and Politics.* Copenhagen: Copenhagen Business School Press.

Vaara, E. and Tienari, J. (2003): 'The "balance of power" principle. Nationality, politics and the distribution of organizational positions'. In Søderberg, A-M. and Vaara, E. (eds): *Merging across Borders. People, Cultures and Politics.* Copenhagen: Copenhagen Business School Press, pp. 87–110.

Vaara, E. and Tienari, J. (2011): 'On the narrative construction of multinational corporations'. *Organization Science*, **22** (2), 370–390.

Vaara, E; Tienari, J., Piekkari, R. and Säntti, R. (2005): 'Language and the circuits of power in a merging multinational corporation'. *Journal of Management Studies*, **42** (3), 595–623.

Weick, K.E. (1995): *Sensemaking in Organizations.* Thousand Oaks, CA: Sage Publications.

10 Determinants of top management retention in cross border acquisitions
Mohammad Faisal Ahammad, Keith W. Glaister, Yaakov Weber and Shlomo Yedidia Tarba

INTRODUCTION

Cross border mergers and acquisitions (M&A) are playing a progressively more important role in worldwide M&A activity both in terms of deal numbers and values (Bertrand and Zuniga, 2006). In parallel to this rise in activity, there has been increasing recognition of the poor performance of many cross border M&A (for example, Datta and Puia, 1995; Aw and Chatterjee, 2004). Recent research remains pessimistic over the success potential of cross border acquisition deals (for example, Moeller and Schlingemann, 2005). Problems with post-acquisition implementation are among the primary reasons given for this disappointing record (Olie, 1990; Haspeslagh and Jemison, 1991; Schweiger and Goulet, 2000, Child et al., 2001; Ranft and Lord, 2002).

Acquisition implementation problems often arise because of clashes of organizational cultures, systems, or strategies and because of the loss of key executives in the acquired firm. Academics trying to understand the reasons of the high failure rate focused on managerial attributes and human resource activities particularly during the integration phase (Vaara, 2002; Kiessling and Harvey, 2006; Fubini et al., 2007; Weber and Tarba, 2010; Weber et al., 2012a). The departure of an acquired firm's top managers, and the consequent loss of their knowledge and skills, is thought to be an important determinant of poor post-acquisition performance (Cannella and Hambrick, 1993; Gomes et al., 2011).

One of the critical aspects leading to success or failure of M&A, identified in numerous studies (Kummer, 2008), is people related. Many studies exploring M&A integration have reached the conclusion that retaining an effective top management team of the acquired entity after an M&A deal completion is a critical component of effective post-acquisition integration (Krug, 2009; Krug, 2003a; 2003b; Krug and Aguilera, 2005; Krug and Shill, 2008; Lubatkin et al., 1999). However, few firms appear to understand either the underlying causes of this turnover or how it should be managed. In this chapter, we examine the factors influencing top management retention in the context of cross border acquisitions. A deeper understanding of the employee retention techniques may help firms more effectively deal with employee turnover during the M&A integration process and can lead to the development of more effective top management teams.

Much of the prior research has used the theory of relative standing (Frank, 1986) to examine why top management turnover in acquired firms occurs (Ranft and Lord, 2000). The theory of relative standing primarily emphasizes the importance of non-financial incentives such as autonomy provided to the management of the acquired firm, commitment of the acquiring firm, and so on. However, financial incentives may substitute at least partially for many of these more intangible factors (Coff, 1997; Hambrick and Cannella, 1993). Financial incentives provide another form of indication of an employee's worth to an organization. The use of financial incentives to help achieve strategic and operational objectives has received some attention in the literature (Saura-Diaz and Gomez-Mejia, 1997). In the specific context of acquisitions, however, there is relatively little research on the use and efficacy of financial incentives as a mechanism to enhance retention (Ranft and Lord, 2000).

In order to explain the departure of top management teams, existing literature has used the relative standing theory (for example, Cannella and Hambrick, 1993) or market for corporate control theories (Walsh and Ellwood, 1991). Relatively few studies have investigated the determinants of top management retention by applying both the theory of relative standing and the financial incentives mechanism of retention. The purpose of this chapter is to explore the determinants of top management retention by applying relative standing theory and the financial incentive mechanism of retention in the context of cross border acquisitions. Specifically the objective is to assess the impact on top management retention by considering the autonomy of the acquired firm, the acquirer's commitment to the acquired organization, and financial incentives.

The chapter is structured as follows: the next section discusses the literature on employee retention in mergers and acquisitions. The following section develops the study's hypotheses. Section four presents the research methods employed in the study. In section five, the research findings and discussion are presented. Recommendations and conclusions are provided in the final section.

LITERATURE REVIEW AND HYPOTHESIS DEVELOPMENT

Cross border M&A represent a major organizational change, which generates employee uncertainty (Buono and Bowditch, 1989; Napier et al., 1989; Schweiger and DeNisi, 1991; Cartwright and Cooper, 1992) and this uncertainty results in negative attitudes and behavior amongst employees (see for example Buono and Bowditch, 1989; Bastien, 1987; Cartwright and Cooper, 1990) that will go on to affect acquisition performance and employee turnover (Krug and Hegarty, 2001; Paruchuri et al., 2006; Ranft, 2006; Schweiger and Goulet, 2000). Significant high rates of departure of acquired firms' top executives after acquisitions have generated considerable attention in the strategy literature (Bergh, 2001; Cannella and Hambrick, 1993; Davis and Nair, 2003; Hambrick and Cannella, 1993; Krug and Hegarty, 1997; Krug and Nigh, 1998; Very et al., 1997; Walsh, 1988, 1989; Walsh and Ellwood, 1991).

The prior research has mostly used the theory of relative standing (Frank, 1986) to help understand why turnover in acquired top management teams occurs. The theory of relative standing highlights the significance of the individual's feelings of status and worth relative to that of others in a proximate social setting. Researchers have argued that "some acquisitions result in extremely low relative standing for acquired executives – they feel inferior, the acquirers see them as inferior and themselves as superior, autonomy is removed, status is removed, and a climate of acrimony prevails" (Hambrick and Cannella, 1993: 733). The theory of relative standing predicts that executives of the acquired firm expect to be retained after an acquisition when they are given a greater degree of autonomy and a greater sense of status and importance in the newly merged firm. Appointing acquired executives to the newly merged firm's management team may help provide them with a positive sense of their status and worth in the new organization (Ranft and Lord, 2000). Likewise, other actions or symbols that indicate the significance of the acquisition to the acquiring firm, and that signal the commitment of the acquirer to the success of the acquisition, are likely to minimize the departure of key managers (Hambrick and Cannella, 1993).

In addition to the work by Hambrick and Cannella (1993), Walsh (1988, 1989) and Walsh and Ellwood (1991) also investigated top management turnover following acquisitions. These studies attempted to determine the underlying reasons for turnover but found that neither the relatedness of the acquisitions (Walsh, 1988), the degree of hostility of negotiating the acquisition deal (Walsh, 1989), nor the market for corporate control theories (Walsh and Ellwood, 1991) were able to explain high turnover rates.

Consequently, the theory of relative standing appears to offer the best explanation for top management turnover in acquired firms (Ranft and Lord, 2000).

Autonomy as a Determinant of Employee Retention

Autonomy refers to the strategic freedom to act, or the latitude of action that managers have when they formulate strategic activities, including implementation of organizational structure, determination of corporate development strategy and execution of technology transformations (Montanari, 1978; Takeuchi et al., 2008). Greater power granted to managers may lead to a better execution of quality standards, skills and expertise (Langfred and Moyer, 2004).

Limited empirical research exists on the relationship between autonomy and employee retention in the context of cross border acquisitions. However, managerial autonomy was investigated in the context of international joint ventures (IJVs). For instance, Newburry et al. (2003) suggested that the wider the scope of activity over which IJV has autonomy, the stronger is the autonomy–effectiveness relationship. Moreover, Grewal and Tansuhaj (2001) stated that task autonomy affects the psychological states of managers to adapt quickly to unanticipated market demands. For example, the use of upward influence to gain autonomy in an IJV is dependent upon the hierarchy of autonomy measures available to the IJV managers (Lyles and Reger, 1993). In an IJV context, managers may seek greater autonomy over their operations because freedom to maneuver should increase their likelihood of being able to deal with critical development issues without interference from their parent firm (Takeuchi et al., 2008).

Managerial autonomy can influence the acquired firm's intention to leave or stay. Hagedoorn and Hesen (2007) observed that managers with greater managerial discretion tend to be highly motivated and expend additional effort in pursuit of their strategic goals. The degree of autonomy given to the acquired firm increases the relative decision-making latitude of acquired managers' and employees. In the context of acquisitions, Cannella and Hambrick (1993) found that removal of autonomy from individuals during the first two years after the acquisition was associated with executive departure. Moreover, those acquired executives who were given status were less likely to leave. The negative impact of autonomy removal (Lubatkin et al., 1999; Chatterjee et al., 1992; Weber, 1996; Weber et al., 2011; Weber and Tarba, 2010; Weber and Tarba, 2011; Weber, Rachman-Moore, Tarba, 2012) was also confirmed in a European study by Very et al. (1997) who found that removal of autonomy from individuals accustomed to high levels of autonomy caused performance to deteriorate.

Prior research has identified autonomy removal as a characteristic of relative standing (Frank, 1986). This is a condition which contributes to the executives of the acquired firm feeling inferior relative to the acquiring firm executives, or the executives of the acquiring firm viewing them as superior. The implication of this research is that maintaining the relative standing of the executives of the acquired firm will enhance the retention of the acquired firm's executives (Schweiger and Goulet, 2000). In the context of acquisitions, appointing executives from the acquired firm to the newly merged firm's management team may help provide them with a positive sense of worth in the new organization (Ranft and Lord, 2000). Moreover, a greater degree of autonomy increases the relative decision-making latitude of managers and employees of the acquired firm. Greater autonomy provides incentives for employees of the acquired firm to stay with the firm because they are able to maintain greater control over their surroundings (Hambrick and Cannella, 1993; Huselid, 1995; Very et al., 1997). This is especially likely to be the case in acquisitions aimed at acquiring new skills and capabilities, because highly skilled professionals tend to desire or require relatively high levels of autonomy (Jelinek and Schoonhoven, 1995; Raelin, 1991). Based on the above argument, we propose the following hypothesis:

Hypothesis 1: Post-acquisition autonomy is positively associated with top management retention in the acquired firm.

Commitment as a Determinant of Employee Retention

Organizational support theory employs the social exchange perspective to explain employee–employer relationships (Loi et al., 2006). Eisenberger et al. (1986) developed perceived organizational support (POS) to understand employee–employer exchange relationships. POS refers to an individual's perception regarding the extent to which a firm values employees' contributions and cares about employees' well-being (that is, the degree to which the organization is committed to its employees) (Eisenberger et al., 1986). Thus, employees tend to seek a balance in their exchange associations with their organizations by having their attitudes and behaviors based on their employer's commitment to them individually (Eisenberger et al., 1990).

Enhanced POS makes employees feel compelled to care about the firm's well-being and to help the firm reach its objectives (Eisenberger et al., 2001). POS increases employees' effort-outcome expectancy, which makes employees believe that their efforts will be rewarded in the future (Eisenberger et al., 1986). Employees who perceive high POS tend to be strongly affiliated with and loyal to their organization (Loi et al., 2006).

Based on high effort-outcome expectancy and employees' willingness to maintain membership with the organization because of enhanced POS, Loi et al. (2006) further proposed that enhanced POS will lower employees' intention to leave the firm.

Managers act as organizational agents who are responsible for guiding and evaluating subordinates' performance. Therefore, an employee tends to view their managers' attitudes and behavior towards employees as indicative of the firm's support and commitment towards employees (Cho et al., 2009). In acquisitions without commitment to the task, managers would not be able to realize the synergistic benefits and hence will not enhance organizational performance (Weber 1996, Lubatkin et al., 1999). Moreover, if the top management team does not demonstrate high levels of commitment to the strategy chosen, then it would be extremely difficult to empower subordinates and create a sense of belonging in the new combined firm (Vasilaki and O'Regan, 2008).

In the context of acquisitions, evidence of the acquiring firm's commitment to the success of the acquisition is likely to increase feelings of importance among the acquired firm's managers and employees. Such commitment may be articulated through positive internal and external media emphasizing the importance of the skills and capabilities of the acquired firm to the newly combined firm (Ranft and Lord, 2000). This positive publicity may increase acquired employees' feelings of worth within the new firm. Other kinds of indication of the acquiring firm's commitment might include mechanisms such as greater resources for training and professional development for the acquired firm's managers and employees. Highly skilled employees are likely to value opportunities for continued learning, training, and other forms of personal development in order to further increase their expertise and skills (Coff, 1997; Huselid, 1995; Pfeffer, 1994). Investment in such opportunities by the acquiring firm demonstrates its commitment to the success of the acquisition. In line with the predictions of the theory of relative standing, these positive indications of commitment are likely to increase the likelihood of the acquired firm's employees remaining after the acquisition. This argument leads to the following hypothesis:

Hypothesis 2: The acquiring firm's post-acquisition commitment to the acquired firm is positively associated with top management retention in the acquired firm.

Financial Incentive as a Determinant of Employee Retention

Incentives or rewards are discussed frequently in the literature (Agarwal, 1998). An incentive can be extrinsic or intrinsic; it can be a cash reward such as a bonus or it can be recognition, such as naming a worker 'employee of the month'.

Rewards are very important for job satisfaction because they fulfill basic needs as well as help to attain higher level goals. Earnings are the way in which workers get to know how much they are gaining by dedicating their time, effort and skills in a job (Bokemeier and Lacy, 1986). Attractive remuneration packages are an important factor in retention because they fulfill financial and material desires as well as provide the means of indicating an employee's status and position of power in the organization. An organization's reward system can affect the performance of employees and their desire to remain employed (for example, Bamberger and Meshoulam, 2000, MacDuffie, 1995). However, prior research demonstrates that there is a great deal of inter-individual difference in understanding the significance of financial rewards for employee retention (Pfeffer, 1998; Woodruffe, 1999).

The primary focus of the theory of relative standing is on the importance of non-financial incentives for determining post-acquisition employee retention. However, financial incentives may substitute at least partially for many of these more intangible factors (Coff, 1997; Hambrick and Cannella, 1993). Financial incentives offer another form of signal of an employee's worth to an organization. The utilization of financial incentives to assist in achieving strategic and operational objectives has received some consideration in the literature (Saura-Diaz and Gomez-Mejia, 1997). For instance, in high-technology industries, the use of financial incentives to retain highly skilled workers is sometimes considered as a key component of employee retention strategies (Balkin and Gomez-Mejia, 1990).

In the specific context of acquisitions, there is relatively little research on the use and efficacy of financial incentives as a mechanism to enhance retention. The study by Ghosh and Ruland (1998) found that ownership sharing was a legitimate incentive to retain acquired top managers. They found that managers of an acquired firm are more likely to remain in the combined firm when they receive shares in the new firm as payment for their ownership interest in the acquired firm. In fact, the findings indicate that jobs were not retained, following payment with stock, in only 10 percent of the acquisitions. However, their study also indicates that acquiring managers, who value continued control of the acquiring company, prefer to pay cash to avoid diluting their existing holding. With regards to providing incentives, Schweiger and Goulet (2000) suggested that a conscious effort to integrate acquired management into the combined firm must be made by the acquirer and that the sharing of ownership control appears to be an incentive structure that aids in this process, by reducing acquired management turnover.

Some practitioner-oriented literature supports the use of short- and long-term incentives to "help keep valuable executives on board during the transition period and signal key executives that they have important roles to play in the organization going forward" (Ferracone, 1987: 61). Financial incentives used to retain employees in acquisitions can take several forms: (1) "stay put" bonuses, generally a large bonus payable after the expiration of a certain period of time; (2) long-term contracts with bonuses payable over a given period of time; (3) stock options that can be exercised over some period of time or after a future date; and (4) increased base salary and/or benefits (Ranft and Lord, 2000).

To retain valuable human capital, firms may need to share the wealth they help generate through some form of rent sharing, such as through various types of financial incentives. Sharing the profits generated by knowledge workers' valuable expertise and skills promotes retention by raising their compensation to a higher level relative to the general labor market, as well as by increasing their perceived status in the firm (Coff, 1997; Hambrick and Cannella, 1993). Economic rewards linked to key employees' continued employment within the newly merged firm, therefore, are likely to enhance the prospects that these employees will remain after the acquisition is completed. Such logic suggests the following hypothesis:

Hypothesis 3: The use of financial incentives is positively associated with top management retention in the acquired firm.

RESEARCH METHODS

Data Collection

The data were gathered via a cross-sectional survey using a self-administered questionnaire on a sample of UK firms that had acquired North American and European firms during the five-year period from 2000 through 2004 inclusive. The development of the questionnaire was guided by a review of previous mergers and acquisitions research (for example, Shanley, 1994; Ranft and Lord, 2000; Schoenberg, 2004).

A list of potential sample firms was generated from the Mergers and Acquisitions Database of Thomson One Banker. The Thomson One Banker database provides comprehensive secondary information about mergers and acquisitions including cross border deals. The sample includes those deals in which the acquirer bought a 100 percent equity stake in the acquired company. Based on the results of the website search and telephone enquiries, a list of key informants and potential survey participants was assembled. This resulted in a final sampling frame of 591 international acquirers.

In April 2007, 591 questionnaires each with a covering letter and return envelope were posted to potential survey participants (that is, UK acquiring firm managers). Efforts were made to identify the individual in the acquiring firm that was involved with the acquisition decision and implementation process. In order to provide motivation for accurate responses, the respondents were guaranteed anonymity and were promised a summary report of research findings if requested. After three reminders, 69 questionnaires were returned, of which 65 were fully completed and usable, effectively a response rate of 11 percent. Given the well-documented difficulties of obtaining questionnaire responses from executives (Harzing, 1997) and the decreasing rate of response from executives (Cycyota and Harrison, 2006), the study's response rate of 11 percent can be considered reasonable. This response rate is similar to that reported in other academic studies of executives. For instance, Graham and Harvey (2001) achieved a response rate of nearly 9 percent from CFOs, and Mukherjee et al., (2004) obtained an 11.8 percent response rate in a survey mailed to 636 CFOs who were involved in acquisitions management.

All of the respondents had been directly involved in managing the CBA process. An examination of the job titles revealed 12 Chief Executive Officers, 16 Finance Directors or Chief Financial Officers, 23 Business Development Directors, 8 Managing Directors, and 6 Executive Directors. The sample represents acquisition activity on two continents: North America and Europe. In North America, the acquired firms are from the USA and Canada (21 and 9 respectively). Europe is represented by 35 acquisitions.

Since the dependent variable (top management retention), the key independent variables (post-acquisition autonomy, acquirer's commitment and financial incentives), and the controls are based on data provided by a single individual, they may be affected by common method bias. This is unlikely, however, because the items measuring these variables are dissimilar in content. These constructs are measured through a large number of items, and top managers are familiar with them.

Using survey research to investigate past events requires respondents to recollect information. Potentially this exposed the study to retrospective bias, because some information may be lost or distorted over time. We adopted a research design and survey instrument intended to minimize retrospective bias. In order to assess potential retrospective bias, responses concerning acquisitions made in 2004 were compared to acquisitions made in 2000. The t-tests for mean differences in variables were calculated and evinced no statistically significant differences in means between responses concerning acquisitions made in 2000 compared to acquisitions made in 2004. These findings suggest that retrospective bias does not pose a problem for the study.

The possibility of non-response bias was checked by using two procedures (following Ranft and Lord, 2000). First, non-response bias was tested for by implementing a test comparing early and late respondents along a number of key descriptive variables. Differences between the two groups were not statistically significant, suggesting that non-response bias is not a major problem. Second, the possibility of non-response bias was checked by comparing respondent and non-respondent firms with respect to their relative size and primary sector of operation. The t-tests of mean difference were insignificant, confirming no systematic bias between the responding firms and non-responding firms.

Measurement of Key Variables

In general, the study adapted scales used by other researchers in the field of international business and strategy research. Three management researchers examined the survey instrument for both content and face validity. In addition, five managers from the acquiring firms participated in a pre-test of the survey. Following the pre-tests, slight wording and ordering modifications were made to improve the clarity and organization of the survey instrument.

Dependent Variables – Top Management Retention

The top management retention of the acquired firm was measured using an item adapted from Shanley (1994). First, respondents were asked to indicate the importance of retaining top management (1 = 'not important' to 5 = 'extremely important'). Respondents were also asked to indicate the extent to which the prior top management team of the acquired firm had been retained one year after acquisition, on a Likert-type scale anchored from 1 ('no retention') and 5 ('full retention'). A composite measure of top management retention was calculated by multiplying level of "importance" with extent of "retention".

Independent Variables

Post-acquisition autonomy of the acquired firm
The degree of organizational autonomy granted to the acquired company in the post-acquisition period was measured using an instrument adapted

from that previously utilized by Datta and Grant (1990) and Schoenberg (2004). Respondents were asked to indicate the locus of decision making (1 = acquiring firm; 2 = acquired company, 3 = jointly) for 18 separate operational and strategic decisions affecting the acquired firm (listed in Appendix 10.1). All of the eighteen decision items loaded strongly (>0.6) onto a single component. An aggregate measure of autonomy was calculated by averaging the factor scores on all the items. Results for this measure were compared with responses on the single-item measure developed by Hambrick and Cannella (1993) to assess "overall autonomy", which was also included in the survey. The two measures were highly correlated (r = 0.91, p < 0.001). The aggregate measure of autonomy was used in subsequent analysis.

Acquirer's commitment to the acquired firm

Acquirer commitment was measured using an instrument adapted from that previously utilized by Ranft and Lord (2000). The four items in this measure assessed various dimensions of the acquirer's corporate commitment to the success of the acquisition. First, respondents indicated to what extent they agreed or disagreed with the statement that the acquirer was visibly committed to making the acquisition a success (1 = strongly disagree; 5 = strongly agree). The remaining items assessed other potential indicators of commitment: support for continued training and development of the acquired firm's employees; support for travel and liaison between the acquired firm and the acquiring firm; the use of positive public relations. Factor analysis of the items extracted a single factor. An aggregate measure of commitment was calculated by averaging factor scores on the four items.

Financial incentives

The survey presented respondents with items assessing the use of four different types of financial incentives (following Ranft and Lord, 2000) that might be used to encourage employees to stay with a company. These items included (1) short-run incentives, (2) long-term contracts, (3) stock options, and (4) performance bonuses (Balkin and Gomez-Mejia, 1990; Gerhart and Milkovich, 1990). Respondents were asked to indicate on a five-point scale the extent to which each type of incentive was offered (1 = no extent; 5 = great extent). Factor analysis on these items (with varimax rotation) extracted two factors (with eigenvalues >1). The first factor consisted of short-run incentives and long-term contracts, that is, each linked to a specific time frame for retaining an employee. The second factor consisted of stock options and other types of bonuses, that is, linked directly to performance outcomes of the newly merged business. An overall score for each of the factors was calculated by averaging the scores for the items that loaded on each factor. Because each measure appeared to tap into a different type of financial incentive, both measures were used in subsequent analyses.

Control Variables

The control variables included are relative size of the acquired firm, acquisition relatedness and attitude of the acquired firm. The size differences between an acquiring firm and target firm can affect the top management turnover (Walsh, 1989). A very large firm is likely to have a supply of skilled managers to replace the managers in a smaller acquired firm. This would not be the case as the size differences between the acquiring and target firm reduces. Moreover, the managers in the smaller target firm may be less skillful when managing in a larger and perhaps more bureaucratic context. Consequently, target firm top management retention is likely to vary negatively with an increase in the size differences between the acquiring firm and target firm. Relative size was operationalized as the ratio of the sales turnover of the acquired firm to that of the acquiring firm at the time of the acquisition (following Krishnan et al., 1997, and Schoenberg, 2004).

Walsh (1988) suggested that top management turnover following a related merger or acquisition would be higher than the turnover following an unrelated merger or acquisition. He argued that the acquiring firm's management team is familiar with a target firm's business in a related merger or acquisition. Consequently, the acquiring company can afford to lose many of the target firm's managers. However, in an unrelated merger or acquisition, the acquiring firm might be dependent upon the target firm's managers and thus the management of the acquiring firm should be interested in retaining managers of the target firm (Walsh, 1989). Pitts (1976) suggested that in an unrelated merger or acquisition, the acquiring firm cannot afford to lose the product and market experience of the target firm's management. The acquisition was considered related if the acquirer and the acquired firm operated in the same industry, and not related if they operated in different industries. The respondents were asked to indicate the industry the acquiring firm was operating in as well as the industry of the target firm. To control for potential effects of relatedness, the relatedness of the acquired firm and the acquirer was coded '1'if 'related' acquisitions and '0' if 'not related' acquisitions.

Target firms' top managers that express open hostility to the prospect of a merger or acquisition are unlikely to remain in the target firm (Walsh, 1989). To control for the potential effect of the attitude of the target firms' management, the respondents were asked to indicate on a five-point scale (following Schoenberg, 2004) the attitude of the acquired firm's board towards the acquisition (1 = no resistance to being acquired; 5 = major resistance to being acquired).

FINDINGS AND DISCUSSION

The survey data were screened to check for outliers, out-of-range values, missing data, and assumptions of normality and homoscedasticity by examining univariate statistics and scatterplots of the residuals (Tabachnick and Fidell, 1996). Descriptive statistics and correlations for each of the variables used in the analyses are presented in Table 10.1.

Condition indices and variance inflation factors were analyzed for the model to assess any potential problems with multicollinearity (Tabachnick and Fidell, 1996). Multicollinearity is not a problem as the variance inflation factor scores (VIFs: 1.23–1.71) are well within the cutoff of 10 recommended by Neter et al. (1985). Moreover, the Durbin-Watson test statistic for autocorrelation of the residuals indicates no existence of autocorrelation (Durbin-Watson statistic = 2.033). The regression models are presented in Table 10.2.

Table 10.2 shows the results for two regression models: Model 1 contains only the control variables; Model 2 contains the control variables and the explanatory variables. For Model 2, the regression equation has a significant F value ($p < 0.01$). In terms of explanatory power, about 36 percent of the variation in top management retention is explained by the independent variables. The explanatory variables autonomy ($\beta = 0.586$, $p < 0.01$) and acquirer commitment ($\beta = 0.202$, $p < 0.10$) are positive and significant predictors of top management retention during post-acquisition integration, providing support for Hypotheses 1 and 2. The coefficients of the financial incentive variables are not significant, Hypothesis 3, therefore, is not supported. In addition, the control variable for relative size is negative and significantly related to top management retention ($\beta = -0.259$, $p < 0.05$). The other control variables, acquisition relatedness and attitude of the acquired firm, are not significant predictors of top management retention.

The results provide support for the positive influence of continued autonomy of the acquired organization on retention of the top management team. Past research indicates that granting autonomy to an acquired firm's managers increases their feelings of relative standing in the firm and, therefore, minimizes their tendency to leave. Consistent with the theory of relative standing and Hambrick and Cannella's (1993) findings for

Table 10.1   Descriptive statistics and Pearson's correlations

Variables	Mean	SD	1	2	3	4	5	6	7	8
Autonomy	1.89	0.71	1							
Acquirer commitment	3.87	0.91	0.16	1						
Financial incentive (time)	2.23	1.04	0.18	0.41**	1					
Financial incentive (performance)	3.08	1.24	0.20	0.13	0.21	1				
Acquisition relatedness	0/1 variable	n/a	−0.12	−0.26*	−0.22*	0.08	1			
Relative size	0.60	0.44	0.31**	0.10	0.12	0.12	0.07	1		
Attitude of acquired firm	1.33	0.74	−0.17	0.01	−0.03	−0.10	−0.13	−0.09	1	
Top management retention	3.55	1.37	0.41**	0.04	0.06	0.16	0.03	−0.05	−0.08	1

Notes:
N = 65; SD = Standard deviation; ** $p < 0.01$, * $p < 0.05$, *** $p < 0.10$; two-tailed test.

Table 10.2   Regression results: determinants of top management retention

Variables	Model 1	Model 2
Control variables		
Relative size	−0.027	−0.259**
Acquisition relatedness	0.111	0.103
Attitude of acquired firm	−0.093	−0.134
Explanatory variables		
Autonomy		0.586***
Acquirer commitment		0.202*
Financial incentive (time)		−0.085
Financial incentive (performance)		−0.022
Model		
R^2	0.040	0.359
Adjusted R^2	0.034	0.268
F-statistics	0.370	3.926***

Notes: N = 65; Standardized beta coefficients: significant at ***$p < 0.01$, **$p < 0.05$, *$p < 0.10$; the t-test on each regression coefficient is two-tailed. Model 1 represents regression with control variables and Model 2 represents regression with explanatory and control variables.

top executives, the data suggest that the 'preservation' (Haspeslagh and Jemison, 1991: 147) mode of acquisition implementation (that is, acquisitions requiring a high level of organizational autonomy and a low need for strategic interdependence) may be sometimes appropriate for acquisitions aiming to acquire knowledge-based resources in order to prevent the loss of key resources through personnel turnover.

Some researchers (for example, Ashkenas et al., 1998) have recommended relatively rapid and complete integration of acquisitions in order to increase the chances of acquisition success. For some types of acquisitions, implementation strategies based on quick integration may be appropriate. However, the positive significant finding for autonomy in this sample of cross border acquisitions suggests a more cautious consideration of such recommendations. Critical aspects of acquisition implementation strategies, such as levels of autonomy, should be informed more by the specific motivations and resources of the particular acquisition situation rather than by some general prescription for all acquisitions.

The acquirer's corporate commitment to the acquisition was also found to have a positive influence on the retention of the top management team. Indications of commitment to the success of the acquisition integration (for example, support for training and travel, and positive public relations on the part of the acquirer) appear to enhance acquired employees' comfort within, and commitment to, the newly combined organization. The finding is consistent with Ranft and Lord (2000) who found a significant positive association between the acquirer's commitment towards the acquisition and employee retention.

This study does not find any statistically significant relationship between financial incentives and top management retention. Neither financial incentives based on time spent with the firm following acquisition, nor financial incentives based on post-acquisition performance criteria, are effective determinants of top management retention in this sample of cross border acquisitions. The less economically related and more socially oriented issues associated with autonomy and commitments are found to be more important determinants of top management team retention than are financial incentives. This finding appears to support the contention of Ranft and Lord (2000: 315) who argued that "the broader social logic behind the theory of relative standing therefore appears to be a better predictor of employee retention than a theory simply based on direct, personal economic interests". Firms offer financial incentives in the expectations that employees will stay after the acquisition. However, it is critical that the acquiring firm understands the limitations of financial incentives in an M&A situation. Financial incentives are not sufficient to buy hard work or long-term loyalty (Erickson and Troy, 2008). The acquiring firm should regain employee trust and commitment, otherwise, once the incentives are paid, employees may be more likely to consider other employment opportunities. The amount of money paid to the employees as retention incentives might have only a short-term temporal impact if not renewed or extended. An alternative explanation is that top management that are worthy of financial incentives for retention, are likely to be in demand not just by the acquirer, but also by other firms that may offer even greater incentives for the top management team to leave.

Relative size (measured as the ratio of the sales turnover of the acquired firm to that of the acquiring firm) has a negative and significant relationship with the retention of the top management team. This tends to suggest that acquiring a relatively smaller firm can lead to a higher level of top management retention, and acquiring a relatively larger firm can lead to a lower level of top management retention.

SUMMARY AND CONCLUSIONS

In many M&A, one of the most valuable resources of the firm is the retention of the acquired firm's top management team and key employees (Gomes et al., 2011; Kiessling and Harvey, 2006; Weber and Tarba,

2011; Weber et al., 2012b). The firm's culture, strategy, and dynamics are dependent to a large extent on the top management team of the acquired firm (Pfeffer, 1981) and, for continued superior performance of a successful target firm, the top management team need to be retained (Finkelstein and Hambrick, 1996; Koch and McGrath, 1996).

This study contributes to the existing literature by assessing the determinants of top management team retention in cross border acquisitions in terms of the impact of autonomy given to the acquired firm, the acquirer's commitment to the acquired firm and financial incentives provided to employees. This has been attempted by very few prior studies. A particular distinguishing feature of this study is that it investigates the determinants of top management retention in cross border acquisitions by applying both the theory of relative standing and the financial incentive mechanism of retention. Identifying the factors leading to employee retention can help the managers of the acquiring firm to manage the target firm's top management team more effectively after an acquisition.

Three potential determinants of top management retention were examined: the autonomy granted to the acquired firm; corporate commitment to the acquisition; and financial incentives for employees. The regression results provide support for the positive influence of continued autonomy of the acquired firm on the retention of top management. Consistent with prior research, the finding indicates that granting autonomy to an acquired firm's managers is likely to increase their feelings of relative standing in the firm and, therefore, reduces the probability of them leaving. The acquirer's corporate commitment to the acquisition was also found to have a positive influence on the retention of the top management. Evidence of commitment on the part of the acquirer appears to enhance the acquired employees' comfort with, and commitment to, the newly combined firms. The significant finding for commitment is consistent with the theory of relative standing. No significant relationship between financial incentives and employee retention was found in the context of cross border acquisitions. Neither financial incentives based on time nor financial incentives based on post-acquisition performance criteria, were effective determinants of top management retention. The more socially oriented factors related to autonomy and commitment were found to be more important determinants of top management retention than the more economically related financial incentives.

We found that autonomy and commitment rather than financial incentive are more important determinants of employee retention in the context of cross border acquisitions. This is one of the major contributions of the chapter. Firms providing financial incentives expect that such incentives are sufficient to cause the target firm's employees to stay. However, financial incentives have limitations, as financial incentives alone cannot create long-term employee trust and motivate employees to stay (Erickson and Troy, 2008). An alternative explanation is that top management that are worthy of financial incentives for retention, are likely to be in demand not just by the acquirer, but also by other firms that may offer even greater incentives for the top management team and encourage them to leave (Ranft and Lord, 2000). The acquiring firm should instead provide the top management team of the acquired firm more decision-making power in the combined firm. By increasing the autonomy of the top management team in the newly merged firm and assimilating them into the new management team, the acquiring firm can increase their feelings of importance and status in the new organizational context. Moreover, expressions of commitment to the success of the cross border acquisition, such as support for training and travel on the part of the acquirer, appears to enhance the acquired firm's employees comfort within, and commitment to, the newly combined firm. Therefore, autonomy and commitment were found to influence employee retention more than those of financial incentives.

From the perspective of management practice, this study provides managers with some indication of where to focus their efforts and expend their resources in order to retain valuable human capital during cross border acquisition integration. A major contribution of the study is that the relatively direct approach of using financial incentives to encourage retention does not appear to be particularly effective. In contrast, other less tangible and more social factors may prove more significant determinants of retention. Rather than solely focusing on compensation issues, managers of the acquiring firms should pay increased attention to issues related to autonomy and commitment during acquisition integration. For instance, in order to enhance employee retention, firms should invest in training and development of the acquired firm. Employee training is an indication of management commitment to building a life-long relationship with the employees thereby influencing their turnover decisions.

The findings of the present study offer a useful basis for future empirical investigation of top management retention in cross border acquisitions. The findings relating to autonomy highlight a persistent dilemma when high levels of autonomy are granted to an acquired firm. With a high level of autonomy and consequently a low level of integration of the acquired and acquiring firms, it may be difficult for the resources and capabilities of the two firms to be transferred successfully, shared, and combined. Assuming that in many acquisition cases there are synergies to be realized through integration, the need to maintain a large degree of post-acquisition autonomy for the acquired firm (in order to retain employees) creates a serious challenge. How this tension can be managed successfully is a question for future research.

The impact of financial incentives on employee retention is worthy of further consideration in future research, especially given the apparent popularity of such incentives in many acquisition implementation plans. At least for some groups of employees, broader issues related to their relative standing ultimately may prove to be more important than financial incentives in determining whether they decide to remain with the acquired firm. A detailed comparison of the effects of economic incentives and social standing on post-acquisition employee retention would be a fruitful avenue for future research.

As with any research, this study has limitations. The study relies on data provided by managers in 65 UK firms, so the generalization of the findings may be limited. However, selecting acquiring firms from one country was a purposeful way of dealing with the otherwise high variability in the studied firms' backgrounds. It should be further recognized that the sample selection was also guided by pragmatic reasoning based on time and cost constraints.

REFERENCES

Agarwal, N.C. (1998) 'Reward systems: emerging trends and issues', *Canadian Psychology*, Vol. 39, No. 1, pp. 60–70.

Ashkenas, R.N., DeMonaco, L.J. and Francis, S.C. (1998) 'Making the deal real: How GE Capital integrates acquisitions', *Harvard Business Review*, Vol. 76, pp. 165–178.

Aw, M. and Chatterjee, R. (2004) 'The performance of UK firms acquiring large cross-border and domestic takeover targets', *Applied Financial Economics*, Vol. 14, pp. 337–349.

Balkin, D.B. and Gomez-Mejia, L.R. (1990) 'Matching compensation and organizational strategies', *Strategic Management Journal*, Vol. 11, pp. 153–169.

Bamberger, P. and Meshoulam, I. (2000) *Human Resource Strategy: Formulation, implementation, and impact*, Thousand Oaks, CA: Sage Publications.

Bastien, D.T. (1987) 'Common patterns of behavior and communication in corporate mergers and acquisitions', *Human Resource Management*, Vol. 26, No. 1, pp. 17–34.

Bergh, D.D. (2001) 'Executive retention and acquisition outcomes: A test of opposing views on the influence of organizational tenure', *Journal of Management*, Vol. 27, No. 5, pp. 603–622.

Bertrand, O. and Zuniga, M.P. (2006) 'R&D and M&A: Are cross-border M&A different? An investigation on OECD countries', *International Journal of Industrial Organization*, Vol. 24, pp. 401–423.

Bokemeier, J.L. and Lacy, W.B. (1986) 'Job values, rewards and work conditions as factors in job satisfaction among men and women', *The Sociological Quarterly*, Vol. 28, No. 2, pp. 189–204.

Buono, A.F. and Bowditch, J.L. (1989) *The Human Side of Mergers and Acquisitions – Managing Collisions Between People, Cultures and Organizations*, San Francisco, CA: Jossey-Bass.

Cannella, A.A. and Hambrick, D.C. (1993) 'Effects of executive departures on the performance of acquired firms', *Strategic Management Journal*, Vol. 14, pp. 137–152.

Cartwright, S. and Cooper, C.L. (1990) 'The impact of mergers and acquisitions on people at work: Existing research issues', *British Journal of Management*, Vol. 1, pp. 65–76.

Cartwright, S. and Cooper, C.L. (1992) *Managing Mergers, Acquisitions and Strategic Alliances – Integrating People and Cultures*, Oxford: Butterworth-Heinemann.

Cartwright, S. and Cooper, C.L. (1993) 'The role of culture compatibility in successful organisational marriage' *Academy of Management Executive*, Vol. 7, No. 2, pp. 57–70.

Child, J., Falkner, D. and Pitkethly, R. (2001) *The Management of International Acquisitions*, Oxford: Oxford University Press.

Cho, S., Johanson, M.M. and Guchait, P. (2009) 'Employees intent to leave: A comparison of determinants of intent to leave versus intent to stay', *International Journal of Hospitality Management*, Vol. 28, pp. 374–381.

Coff, R. (1997) 'Human assets and management dilemmas: Coping with hazards on the road to resource-based theory', *Academy of Management Review*, Vol. 22, pp. 374–402.

Cycyota, C.S. and Harrison, D.A. (2006) 'What (not) to expect when surveying executives: A meta-analysis of top managers' response rates and techniques over time', *Organizational Research Method*, Vol. 9, No. 2, pp. 133–160.

Datta, D. and Grant, J. (1990) 'Relationships between type of acquisition, the autonomy given to the acquired firm, and acquisition success: An empirical analysis', *Journal of Management*, Vol. 16, pp. 29–44.

Datta, D. and Puia, G. (1995) 'Cross-border acquisitions: an examination of the influence of relatedness and cultural fit on shareholder value creation in US acquiring firms', *Management International Review*, Vol. 35, pp. 337–359.

Davis, R. and Nair, A. (2003) 'A note on top management turnover in international acquisitions'. *Management International Review*, Vol. 43, No. 2, pp. 172–183.

Eisenberger, R., Huntington, R., Hutchison, S. and Sowa, D. (1986) 'Perceived organizational support', *Journal of Applied Psychology*, Vol. 71, pp. 500–507.

Eisenberger, R., Fasolo, P. and LaMastro, V.D. (1990) 'Perceived organizational support and employee diligence, commitment, and innovation', *Journal of Applied Psychology*, Vol. 75, No. 1, pp. 51–59.

Eisenberger, R., Armeli, S., Rexwinkel, B., Lynch, P.D. and Rhoades, L. (2001) 'Reciprocation of perceived organizational support', *Journal of Applied Psychology*, Vol. 86, No. 1, pp. 42–51.

Erickson, R.A. and Troy, K.S. (2008) 'Retention after a merger: Keeping your employees from "jumping ship" and your intellectual capital and client relationships "on board"'. Deloitte – M&A consultant services, Deloitte Consulting LLP.

Ferracone, R. (1987) 'Blending compensation plans of combining firms', *Mergers and Acquisitions*, Vol. 22, pp. 57–65.

Finkelstein, S. and Hambrick, D. (1996) *Strategic Leadership: Top Executives and their Effects on Organizations*, Minneapolis/St Paul, MN: West Publishing Company.

Frank, R.H. (1986) *Choosing the Right Pond: Human Behavior and the Quest for Status*, New York: Oxford University Press.

Fubini, D., Price, C. and Zollo, M. (2007) *Mergers: Leadership, Performance and Corporate Health*, New York: INSEAD Business Press.

Gerhart, B. and Milkovich, G.T. (1990) 'Organizational differences in managerial compensation and financial performance', *Academy of Management Journal*, Vol. 33, pp. 663–691.

Ghosh, A. and Ruland, W. (1998) 'Managerial ownership, the method of payment for acquisitions and executive job retention', *The Journal of Finance*, Vol. 53, No. 2, pp. 785–798.

Gomes, E., Weber, Y., Brown, C. and Tarba, S.Y. (2011) *Mergers, Acquisitions and Strategic Alliances: Understanding the Process*. New York and Basingstoke, UK: Palgrave Macmillan.

Graham, J.R. and Harvey, C.R. (2001) 'The theory and practice of corporate finance: Evidence from the field', *Journal of Financial Economics*, Vol. 60, No. 2, pp. 187–243.

Grewal, R. and Tansuhaj, P. (2001) 'Building organizational capabilities for managing economic crisis: The role of management orientation and strategic flexibility', *Journal of Marketing*, Vol. 65, pp. 67–80.

Hagedoorn, J. and Hesen, G. (2007) 'Contract law and the governance of inter-firm technology partnerships: An analysis of different modes of partnering and their contractual implications', *Journal of Management Studies*, Vol. 44, No. 3, pp. 342–366.

Hambrick, D.C. and Cannella, A.A. (1993) 'Relative standing: A framework for understanding departures of acquired executives', *Academy of Management Journal*, Vol. 36, pp. 733–762.

Harzing, A. (1997) 'Response rates in international mail surveys: Results of a 22 country study', *International Business Review*, Vol. 6, No. 6, pp. 641–665.

Haspeslagh, P.J. and Jemison, D.B. (1991) *Managing Acquisitions, Creating Value Through Corporate Renewal*, New York: The Free Press.

Huselid, M.A. (1995) 'The impact of human resource management practices on turnover, productivity, and corporate financial performance', *Academy of Management Journal*, Vol. 38, pp. 635–672.

Jelinek, M. and Schoonhoven, C.B. (1995) 'Organizational culture as a strategic advantage: Insights from high-technology firms', in L.R. Gomez-Mejia and M.W. Lawless (eds): *Implementation Management in High Technology*, Greenwich, CT: JAI Press.

Kiessling, T. and Harvey, M. (2006) 'The human resource management issues during an acquisition: the target firm's top management team and key managers', *International Journal of Human Resource Management*, Vol. 17, pp. 1307–1320.

Koch, M.J. and McGrath, R.G. (1996) 'Improving labor productivity: human resource management policies do matter', *Strategic Management Journal*, Vol. 17, pp. 335–354.

Krishnan, H., Miller, A. and Judge, W. (1997) 'Diversification and top management team complementarity: Is performance improved by merging similar or dissimilar teams', *Strategic Management Journal*, Vol. 18, pp. 361–374.

Krug, J.A. (2003a) 'Executive turnover in acquired firms: An analysis of resource-based theory and the upper echelon's perspective', *Journal of Management and Governance*, Vol. 7, pp. 117–143.

Krug, J.A. (2003b) 'Why do they keep leaving?' *Harvard Business Review* (February), pp. 14–15.

Krug, J.A. (2009) 'Brain drain: why top management bolts after M&As', *Journal of Business Strategy*, Vol. 30, No. 6, pp. 4–14.

Krug, J.A. and Aguilera, R.V. (2005) 'Top management team turnover in mergers and acquisitions', in Cooper, C. and Finkelstein, S. (eds), *Advances in Mergers and Acquisitions*, Volume I, New York: JAI Press.

Krug, J.A. and Hegarty, W.H. (1997) 'Post acquisition turnover among U.S. top management teams: an analysis of the effects of foreign vs. domestic acquisitions of U.S. targets', *Strategic Management Journal*, Vol. 18, No. 8, pp. 667–675.

Krug, J.A. and Hegarty, W.H. (2001) 'Predicting who stays and leaves after an acquisition: A study of top managers in multinational firms', *Strategic Management Journal*, Vol. 22, No. 2, pp. 185–196.

Krug, J.A. and Nigh, D. (1998) 'Top management departures in cross-border acquisitions: governance issues in an international context', *Journal of International Management*, Vol. 4, No. 4, pp. 267–287.

Krug, J.A. and Shill, W. (2008) 'The big exit: Executive churn in the wake of M&As', *Journal of Business Strategy*, Vol. 29 No. 4, pp. 15–21.

Kummer, C. (2008) 'Motivation and retention of key people in mergers and acquisitions', *Strategic HR Review*, Vol. 7, No. 6, pp. 5–10.

Langfred, C.W. and Moyer, N.A. (2004) 'Effects of task autonomy on performance: An extended model considering motivational, informational, and structural mechanisms', *Journal of Applied Psychology*, Vol. 89, No. 6, pp. 934–945.

Loi, R., Hang-yue, N. and Foley, S. (2006) 'Linking employees' justice perceptions to organizational commitment and intention to leave: the mediating role of perceived organizational support', *Journal of Occupational and Organizational Psychology*, Vol. 79, pp. 101–120.

Lubatkin, M., Schweiger, D. and Weber, Y. (1999) 'Top management turnover in related M&A's: An additional test of the theory of relative standing', *Journal of Management*, Vol. 25 No. 1, pp. 55–73.

Lyles, M.A. and Reger, R.K. (1993) 'Managing for autonomy in joint ventures: A longitudinal study of upward influence', *Journal of Management Studies*, Vol. 30, No. 3, pp. 383–404.

MacDuffie, J. (1995) 'Human resource bundles and manufacturing performance: Organizational logic and flexible production systems in the world auto industry', *Industrial and Labor Relations Review*, Vol. 48, pp. 197–221.

Moeller, S.B. and Schlingemann, F.P. (2005) 'Global diversification and bidder gains: A comparison between cross-border and domestic acquisition', *Journal of Banking and Finance*, Vol. 29, No. 3, pp. 533–564.

Montanari, J.R. (1978) 'Managerial discretion: An expanded model of organization choice', *Academy of Management Review*, Vol. 3, No. 2, pp. 231–241.

Mukherjee, T.K., Kiymaz, H. and Baker, H.K. (2004) 'Merger motives and target valuation: A survey of evidence from CFOs', *Journal of Applied Finance*, Vol. 14, No. 2, pp. 7–24.

Napier, N.K., Simmons, G. and Stratton, K. (1989) 'Communication during a merger: experience of two banks', *Human Resource Planning*, Vol. 12, No. 2, pp. 105–122.

Neter, J., Wasserman, W. and Kutner, M.H. (1985) *Applied Linear Statistical Models: Regression, analysis of variance, and experimental design*, Homewood, IL: Irwin.

Newburry, W., Zeira, Y. and Yeheskel, O. (2003) 'Autonomy and effectiveness of equity international joint ventures (IJVs) in China', *International Business Review*, Vol. 12, pp. 395–419.

Olie, R. (1990) 'Culture and integration problems in international mergers and acquisitions', *European Management Journal*, Vol. 8, No. 2, pp. 206–215.

Paruchuri, S., Nerkar, A. and Hambrick, D. (2006) 'Acquisition integration and productivity losses in technical core: disruption of inventors in acquired companies', *Organization Science*, Vol. 17, No. 5, pp. 545–562.

Pfeffer, J. (1981) *Power in Organizations*, London: Pitman.

Pfeffer, J. (1994) *Competitive Advantage through People: Unleashing the power of the work force*, Boston, MA: Harvard Business School Press.

Pfeffer, J. (1998) 'Six myths about pay', *Harvard Business Review*, Vol. 76, May/June, pp. 38–57.

Pitts, R.A. (1976) 'Diversification strategies and organizational policies of large diversified firms', *Journal of Economics and Business*, Vol. 28, pp. 181–188.

Raelin, J.A. (1991) *The Clash of Cultures: Managers managing professionals*, Boston, MA: Harvard Business School Press.

Ranft, A.L. (2006) 'Knowledge preservation and transfer during post-acquisition integration', in C.L. Cooper and S. Finkelstein (eds), *Advances in Mergers and Acquisitions*, Vol. 5, UK: Elsevier Ltd, pp. 51–67.

Ranft, A.L. and Lord, M.D. (2000) 'Acquiring new knowledge: The role of retaining human capital in acquisitions of high-tech firms', *The Journal of High Technology Management Research*, Vol. 11, No. 2, pp. 295–319.

Ranft, A.L. and Lord, M.D. (2002) 'Acquiring new technologies and capabilities: A grounded model of acquisition implementation', *Organisation Science*, Vol. 13, No. 4, pp. 420–441.

Saura-Diaz, M.D. and Gomez-Mejia, L.R. (1997) 'The effectiveness of organization-wide compensation strategies in technology intensive firms', *The Journal of High Technology Management Research*, Vol. 8, pp. 301–315.

Schoenberg, R. (2004) 'Dimensions of management style compatibility and cross-border acquisition outcome', in C. Cooper and S. Finkelstein (eds), *Advances in Mergers and Acquisitions*, Vol. 3, pp. 149–175.

Schweiger, D.M. and Denisi, A.S. (1991) 'Communication with employees following a merger: A longitudinal field experiment', *Academy of Management Journal*, Vol. 34, No. 1, pp. 110–135.

Schweiger, D.M. and Goulet, P.K. (2000) 'Integrating mergers and acquisitions: An international research review', in C. Cooper and A. Gregory (eds), *Advances in Mergers and Acquisitions*, Vol. 1, pp. 61–91.

Shanley, M.T. (1994) 'Determinants and consequences of post-acquisition change', in G. von Krogh, A. Sinatra, and H. Singh (eds), *The Management of Corporate Acquisitions*, London: Macmillan, pp. 391–413.

Tabachnick, B.G. and Fidell, L.S. (1996) *Using Multivariate Statistics*, New York: Harper Collins.

Takeuchi, R., Shay, J.P. and Li, J. (2008) 'When does decision autonomy increase expatriate managers' adjustment? An empirical test', *Academy of Management Journal*, Vol. 51, No. 1, pp. 45–60.

Vaara, E. (2002) 'On the discursive construction of success/failure in narratives of post-merger integration', *Organisational Studies*, Vol. 23, pp. 211–248.

Vasilaki, A. and O'Regan, N. (2008) 'Enhancing post-acquisition organisational performance: The role of the Top Management Team', *Team Performance Management*, Vol. 14, No. 3/4, pp. 134–145.

Very, P., Lubatkin, M., Calori, R. and Veiga, J. (1997) 'Relative standing and the performance of recently acquired European firms', *Strategic Management Journal*, Vol. 18, pp. 593–614.

Walsh, J.P. (1988) 'Top management turnover following mergers and acquisitions'. *Strategic Management Journal*, Vol. 9, pp. 173–183.

Walsh, J.P. (1989) 'Doing a deal: Merger and acquisition negotiations and their impact upon target company top management turnover', *Strategic Management Journal*, Vol. 10, pp. 307–322.

Walsh, J.P. and Ellwood, J.W. (1991) 'Mergers, acquisitions, and the pruning of managerial deadwood', *Strategic Management Journal*, Vol. 12, pp. 201–217.

Weber, Y. (1996) 'Corporate culture fit and performance in mergers and acquisitions', *Human Relations*, Vol. 49, No. 9, pp. 1181–1202.

Weber, Y.and Tarba, S.Y. (2010) 'Human resource practices and performance of mergers and acquisitions in Israel', *Human Resource Management Review*, Vol. 20, pp. 203–211.

Weber, Y. and Tarba, S.Y. (2011) 'Exploring culture clash in related mergers: Post-merger integration in the high-tech industry', *International Journal of Organizational Analysis*, Vol. 19, No. 3, pp. 202–221.

Weber, Y., Tarba, S.Y. and Reichel, A. (2011) 'International mergers and acquisitions performance: Acquirer nationality and integration approaches', *International Studies of Management & Organization*, Vol. 41, No. 3, pp. 9–24.

Weber, Y., Rachman-Moore, D. and Tarba, S.Y. (2012a), 'Human resource practices during post-merger conflict and merger performance', *International Journal of Cross-Cultural Management* (forthcoming).

Weber, Y., Tarba, S.Y. and Rozen-Bachar, Z. (2012b) 'The effects of culture clash on international mergers in the high-tech industry', *World Review of Entrepreneurship, Management and Sustainable Development*, Vol. 8, No. 1, pp. 103–118.

Woodruffe, C. (1999) *Winning the Talent War: A strategic approach to attracting, developing and retaining the best people*, Chichester, UK: John Wiley & Sons.

APPENDIX 10.1   ACTIVITIES ALONG WHICH THE AUTONOMY GIVEN TO THE ACQUIRED FIRM MANAGERS WAS MEASURED

Product/Market Decisions in the Acquired Firm

a)   Introducing a new product line/service.
b)   Discontinuing an existing product line/service.
c)   Expanding into new geographic markets.
d)   Deciding brand names.
e)   Change in distribution channels/outlet sites.
f)   Investing in major assets to expand capacity for existing product/ services.
g)   Determining Research and Development content.
h)   Determining Research and Development budget.

Operating Decisions in the Acquired Firm

i)   Purchasing important raw materials/services.
j)   Changing the selling price on a major product or service.
k)   Changing selling and marketing techniques.
l)   Changing level of expenditure for advertising and promotion.

Personnel/Administrative Decisions in the Acquired Firm

m)   Hiring, promoting, firing high level managers (board/one-below board).
n)   Hiring, promoting, firing lower level managers.
o)   Changing salary and fringe benefit levels for salaried personnel.
p)   Determining and changing budget plans.
q)   Changes in high level reporting relationships/organizational structure.
r)   Changes in lower level reporting relationships/organizational structure.

11 Grief and the management of mergers and acquisitions

Philippe Very, Emmanuel Metais and Pierre-Guy Hourquet

INTRODUCTION

The apparent high failure rate of mergers and acquisitions (M&A) has generated a huge amount of research seeking explanations for the performance of these strategic moves. However, as some authors have noted (King et al., 2004), there is a need for creativity in this area because research findings poorly explain the variance in acquisition performance. One area where a comprehensive framework is lacking is the study of the association between the nature of the deal and its performance. The nature of the deal refers to whether the acquisition is a friendly or a hostile one. Deals are classified as hostile when the target resists the intrusion of the potential acquirer, and generally involve the takeover of listed companies. Friendly transactions occur when the acquirer and the target negotiate and find a mutually satisfying agreement for transferring control of the target to the acquirer. In theory, one would expect value creation from this collaborative approach to acquisition to be easier than creating value from a hostile takeover. This assumption is not corroborated by M&A performance studies, however, as hostile bidders tend to outperform friendly acquisitions in the long run in terms of shareholder value creation (Sudarsanam and Mahate, 2006). This counterintuitive finding leads to the following research question: *why do hostile acquirers outperform friendly ones?*

Researchers in finance have tested diverse explanations for the superior performance of hostile bids with more or less success. They have analyzed the choice of acquisition target and the method of payment or costs associated with these strategic moves. However, no researchers have made an in-depth study of differences in the management of the acquisition process to our knowledge, a factor previously identified as influencing acquisition performance (Haspeslagh and Jemison, 1987). In this theoretical chapter, we investigate how the acquisition context is likely to impact on monitoring of the acquisition process. We compare two extreme contexts: hostile takeovers that we described above, and mergers of equals. In a merger of equals, both companies willingly agree to contribute approximately equal value to the newly merged firm (Zaheer et al., 2003). We investigate employee reactions that could threaten or impede integration in each case by combining the theory of grief (Hazen, 2008) with Hirschman's (1970) model of employee responses. Our findings lead us to develop a set of hypotheses that link the nature of the deal, integration management and acquisition outcomes. These hypotheses, if corroborated, can help us to understand why hostile deals are likely to outperform friendly ones.

NATURE OF THE DEAL AND PERFORMANCE

Prior research has looked at the possible link between the nature of the deal and the acquirer's subsequent performance.[1] The nature of the deal refers to whether the strategic move is friendly or hostile in nature. Hostile takeovers are resisted by the target management, while friendly acquisitions require initial agreement between the management of the two companies. Most studies comparing the long-term performance of friendly and hostile deals have been made in the US and the UK. Franks et al. (1991) examined US acquisitions concluded between 1975 and 1984. They showed that over a three-year post-acquisition period the CARs (Cumulative Abnormal Returns) of hostile acquirers were between 0.1 percent and 1.3 percent, while friendly acquirers experienced CARs of between −0.3 percent and 0.8 percent. However, the authors did not follow up by testing the significance of this difference. Studying 452 UK takeovers made between 1984 and 1992, Gregory (1997) also found that the hostile bidders' CARs were better than those of friendly acquirers over a two-year post-acquisition period although the differences were considered insignificant. Barnes (1998) reached the same conclusions for 412 acquisitions between 1987 and 1993. Examining 519 acquisitions of UK firms concluded between 1983 and 1995, Sudarsanam and Mahate (2006) measured financial performance over a three-year post-acquisition period and identified a statistically significant difference in favor of hostile acquirers.

All of these studies suggest that hostile bidders achieve better long-term financial performance than friendly acquirers, although evidence of a statistically significant difference has not been made systematically. Some authors nonetheless conclude that there is enough proof (Sudarsanam and Mahate, 2006) and that the real issue is to explain why acquirers' performance should depend on the nature of the deal.

An initial explanation for this finding was proposed by Morck et al. (1988), namely that hostile and friendly bidders pursue different objectives. Hostile acquirers look for underperforming targets; they replace or monitor the inefficient target managers in order to improve the organization's performance. Thus, hostile takeovers play a disciplinary role in the corporate control market. Friendly acquirers pursue a different motive: they look for synergetic gains that require cooperation with the target management. This explanation implies that each type of deal possesses its own source of value creation. Subsequent studies have failed to identify such a difference, however (Franks and Mayer, 1996; Kini et al., 2004).

The second explanation suggests differences in the method of payment: hostile acquirers pay in cash while friendly ones tend to exchange shares (Niden, 1993). This explanation has been corroborated (Gregory and Matatko, 2004), but researchers argue that only a small portion of performance variance is explained by this transactional variable (Sudarsanam and Mahate, 2006).

The third explanation put forward is based on the costs associated with such moves (Sudarsanam and Mahate, 2006). Hostile bidders must propose a high value premium if they want to convince the target board and shareholders to accept their offer, which is generally rejected. When target management calls for a white knight, it even obliges the hostile bidder to increase its offer or to abandon the idea. The situation is quite different in friendly acquisitions. When a company is approached in a friendly manner, its top management is likely to accept a lower offer because the acquisition is perceived as a positive opportunity. Moreover, following the acquisition, the management team may wish to negotiate their retention. Consequently, each move is characterized by its own specific costs that can destroy value: the cost of a hostile bid resides in the premium paid, while the cost of a friendly acquisition resides in the retention of the target management team, whatever its ability to optimize economic performance. According to Sudarsanam and Mahate (2006), it remains unclear which mechanism destroys more shareholder value.

In this study, we want to go a step further. Research in finance has identified various sources of costs pertaining to each type of acquisition, but has neglected other knowledge accumulated by researchers regarding strategy, strategy implementation and organizational behavior. We believe that the acquisitions process perspective, in particular, offers an additional explanation that can help enrich our understanding of acquisition performance. This perspective acknowledges that the management team in the post-acquisition integration phase influences the long-term performance of an acquisition (Haspeslagh and Jemison, 1991; Jemison and Sitkin, 1986; Larsson and Finkelstein, 1999). Merging two companies involves combining the acquired and the acquirer's organizations, people and resources in order to exploit synergies and create the economic value expected from the transaction. As we will see, the process perspective allows the nature of the transaction to be linked to achievement of the expected economic value. To explain this notion, we apply the theory of grief and analyse its impact on integration.

ACQUISITIONS AND THE THEORY OF GRIEF

Grief and its Impact on Organizations

Originally developed in psychology, the theory of grief explains the processes of grief and grief recovery following a loss like the death of a close family member. Grief is a "psychosocial response to loss" (Pine, 1989: 16), and includes the physical, emotional and social responses of the individual to a major loss (Hazen, 2008). It is primarily envisioned as a response to the death of a loved one. Grief has also been extended to reactions to other events, however, like the end of a close relationship or the forced abandonment of an important aspect of life (Archer, 1999; James and Friedman, 1988; Jeffreys, 1995).

The concept has thus been extended to the context of organizations giving rise to two streams of research, essentially conducted by researchers in organizational psychology. The first analyses how organizations deal with grieving employees who have experienced a personal loss (Bento, 1994; Hazen, 2008). The second considers grief as a reaction to events faced in the workplace: how employees react to job loss (Archer and Rhodes, 1993; Brewington et al., 2004), how they respond to downsizing (Devine et al., 2003; Kets de Vries and Balazs, 1997), how to solve conflicts (Evans and Tyler-Evans, 2002), how top managers react to business failure (Harris and Sutton, 1986; Shepherd, 2003; Zell, 2003), and how to manage succession of a family business (Pailot, 2000; 1999). Researchers have spoken of "collective grief in work organizations" to describe the reactions of groups of employees facing a major organizational change (Harris and Sutton, 1986; Zell, 2003). Zell (2003) compares major restructuring to the process of death and rebirth. Even some psychiatrists (Jeffreys, 1995) have remarked on the occurrence of grief resulting from organizational changes like mergers. Employees can feel grief when they are attached to their company, workplace or job environment (Archer, 1999). Attachment implies a bond or tie between the individual and an attachment figure: for example, another individual, a group or an organization (Bowlby, 1980).

The theory of grief stipulates that grief is a natural response to loss (James and Friedman, 1988) that is manifested through emotions like sadness, guilt and anger. For Sigmund Freud, grief is "an affective fixation upon something that is past" (Freud, 1935: 244). Grief externalizes the difficulty of cutting ties with the past. Grief as a reaction to organizational change manifests itself through reduced morale, loss of a common purpose, loss of enthusiasm, loss of confidence, and even loss of loyalty to the group (Evans and Tyler-Evans, 2002). Such grief also interferes with the attention given to processing information (Mogg et al., 1990; Shepherd, 2003; Wells and Matthews, 1994), and generates concentration problems, errors in judgment, injury and accidents (Hazen, 2008; James and Friedman, 1988).

The Process of Grief Recovery

In general, grief from the death of a loved one is resolved within a period of two to six months (Hazen, 2008; Maciejewski et al., 2007; Ringold et al., 2005), although as Shepherd (2003) noted, loss of a loved one can hardly be compared to the loss of job conditions or of a business. There are different levels of grief, the highest level being the loss of a loved one. Consequently, grief recovery from the loss of job conditions should not exceed a few days, weeks or months.

Grief recovery is both an individual process and a social one. Research on the individual process has identified a stage theory of grief (Kübler-Ross, 1969). According to Maciejewski et al. (2007), grieving individuals move through a five-stage process: disbelief, yearning, anger, depression, and acceptance. Research on the social aspects of grief has proposed a dual model: the grieving individual performs two processes: focusing on the withdrawal of the lost relationship and attending to other interests in life like learning new tasks or strengthening other relationships (Stroebe and Schut, 1999). Shepherd (2003) calls them respectively "loss orientation" and "restoration orientation". People often emphasize one of the two processes, but both are necessary for grief recovery. Stroebe and Schut (1999) argue that the dual process – oscillation between loss orientation and restoration orientation – shortens the healing time.

Grief and Acquisition Integration

The theory of grief has previously been used to study changes like downsizing or conflict situations in organizations. This theory can therefore be mobilized to study a specific instance of change: acquisitions. A study by Schweiger, Ivancevitch and Power (1987) compares an acquisition to a loss and speaks about a period of immediate grief. Marks and Mirvis (1986) evoke the mourning of a corporate death for target executives. Buono and Bowditch (1989) and Cartwright and Cooper (1990) speak about the employees' grieving process. Unfortunately, these authors cite the concept without further developments. None of their studies investigated the economic impact of grief, and most of them use the concept of grief as if it pertains to any type of acquisition. Of course, acquisitions share one common feature: they involve a change of ownership and control, followed by more or less change in the way the acquired firm is managed (Bower, 2001; Haspeslagh and Jemison, 1991). Applied to the context of acquisitions, the theory of grief helps to describe the reactions of the acquired firm's employees and management immediately after a deal has been made. The announcement of an acquisition creates individual uncertainty and ambiguity about the future (Buono and Bowditch, 1989; Haspeslagh and Jemison, 1991): What about my job? What about my working conditions? What about my salary and perks? Such individual reactions emerge systematically in acquisitions (Schweiger et al., 1987).

However, these uncertainties about the future do not mean that employees will systematically feel a loss of attachment toward their company. To understand the emergence of employees' grief, we need to identify the conditions in which they feel a loss of attachment. The nature of the deal (hostile/friendly), combined with integration actions, provides a framework for explaining feelings of loss.

GRIEF, INTEGRATION PROCESSES AND THE NATURE OF THE TRANSACTION

The nature of the deal can be defined as the target perception of friendship characterizing the intentions manifested by the acquirer. An attempt to take control of a company can be perceived as hostile when the acquirer is acting without any prior negotiation with its target. The most hostile moves take the form of hostile takeovers of listed companies that are resisted by target top management. In such instances, the board will often use poison pills or look for a white knight to fight off the undesired acquirer. When the battle ends with the victory of the hostile bidder, the deal is qualified as a hostile takeover. The 2004 takeover of Aventis by Sanofi in the pharmaceutical industry and the 2006 takeover of Arcelor by Mittal in the steel industry illustrate such hostile moves.

On the other side of the spectrum are friendly deals desired by both parties. One transaction presented as a love match is the so-called "merger of equals". A merger of equals is a friendly transaction where the transaction announcement states that each partner will contribute equal value to the newly merged firm (Zaheer et al., 2003; Wulf, 2004). Such deals are primarily motivated by the exploitation of synergies in order to improve the new company's competitive position, based on a more or less explicit win-win contract between the parties which psychologically ensures the equal importance of both firms in the value creation process and justifies the merger. Citicorp and Travelers group, Viacom and CBS, and Bell and GTE are examples of mergers of equals.

In the following section, we compare these two extreme cases – hostile takeovers and mergers of equals – to identify the conditions in which employees start mourning for their past organization. As we will see, another variable impacts on the linkage between the nature of the deal and grief: the integration process.

The integration process comprises two components: the human integration process and the task integration process (Birkinshaw et al., 2000). The human integration process is defined as the development of a shared sense of identity and positive attitude toward the new organization. Task integration deals with the transfer of capabilities and resource sharing. Stahl and Voigt (2008) have shown that these components interact to facilitate synergy realization, which itself influences acquisition performance.

The Occurrence of Grief in Hostile Deals

Hostile bidders "win the battle" when they succeed in taking control of their target. Employees in the acquired company will often then feel like losers. Thus, when the victory is announced, the employees instantly understand that they must mourn their former organization and that the "good old times" are over. Organizational identity – who we are – will not resist the sudden change of ownership. Grief theory stipulates that people's recovery and attitudinal change can occur only when mourning for the past is over (Shepherd, 2003; Stroebe and Schut, 1999). In the case of a hostile takeover, grief should logically occur immediately after the victory has been announced. Capitulation signifies compliance and obedience to a new owner who is expected to introduce change in work practices and organization.

Hence the following proposition:

P1. Employees from firms acquired by hostile bidders grieve for their former organization immediately after the deal is announced.

The Occurrence of Grief in Mergers of Equals

The CEO piloting a "merger of equals" announces to stakeholders that each company will make an equal contribution to future value creation. A promise has been made and economic success will be built on the combination of both partners' resources.

A merger of equals is considered as friendly by the top executives of both companies, but it can be argued that the rank-and-file may have a different initial perception. Whatever the situation, the top executives will generally make an effort to convince employees of the win-win nature of the deal when it is announced. Haspeslagh and Jemison (1991) stressed the importance of communication and the need to reassure employees early on in the process. The reasons for merging must be clearly communicated in order to dissipate uncertainty and anxiety. This phase, right after the announcement, called "setting the stage" by Haspeslagh and Jemison, or "the first hundred days" (Angwin, 2004), aims to sow the seeds for a common project. This means that the top-management must strive to persuade employees of the benefits of the merger. The human integration process begins at this point. As the message delivered in the event of a merger of equals is that each company will contribute equally, employees may reasonably assume that one important aspect of the project resides in their company strengths, in other words, their organization will be one of the pillars for future prosperity. They should not see it as a break with the past and therefore have no reason to feel a sense of loss; consequently, with appropriate communication, grief is unlikely to occur at the announcement of the merger of equals.

However, mergers of equals are projects which rely on the exploitation of synergies in order to create a new company whose value is intended to exceed the sum of both firms' intrinsic value prior to the merger. Consequently, such transactions require the transfer of capabilities and the sharing of resources that will allow the firm to benefit from the synergies identified. This involves implementing task integration. However, as they have not previously mourned their organization, task integration is likely to generate unease in employees' minds in both companies. For the employees, the nature and extent of change must not challenge the survival of the two formerly independent organizations that are now merging. Changes perceived as alterations to the 'old' organizational identity will only be accepted if they do not breach the psychological win-win contract.

As a consequence, top managers in a "merger of equals" face the tough dual challenge of exploiting synergies by introducing change, while simultaneously respecting the "win-win contract", in other words, maintaining the status quo. If change is imposed in order to deliver the expected synergies, employees may feel that the contract has been broken and will begin to grieve for their former organization.[2] If the board chooses to preserve the win-win contract, any changes must be analyzed and discussed according to the terms of the original contract before being introduced. These negotiated processes could even prevent the transfer of capabilities that are sources of synergy, thus hampering the expected acquisition performance. Thus, the occurrence of grief in the course of integration depends on integration management.

Hence the following propositions:

P2. Employees from firms involved in a "merger of equals" may grieve for their former organization throughout the integration process.

P3. In a "merger of equals", integration management influences the occurrence of grief in the course of integration. Grief is more likely to occur if integration is imposed by top management.

It is worth noting that the imposition of integration changes should not constitute an issue for employees in the context of hostile takeovers. As mentioned earlier, employees from the acquired firm know that the battle is lost and that changes are likely to be introduced by the new owner. Consequently, the acquirer is free to impose the intended plan for transferring capabilities and sharing resources.

Figure 11.1 illustrates the framework linking the nature of the deal, integration management and the occurrence of grief.

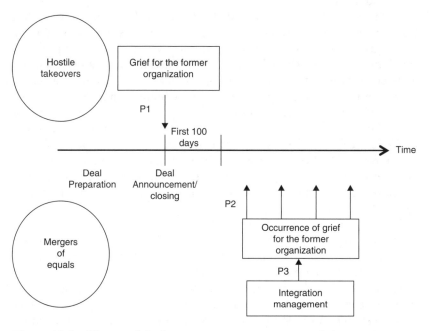

Figure 11.1   Nature of deal, integration management and the occurrence of grief

NATURE OF THE DEAL, GRIEF AND ACQUISITION PERFORMANCE

As mentioned earlier, the occurrence or non-occurrence of grief has an impact on acquisition performance. To explore this issue further, we first analyse the reactions of employees from acquired firms during integration, according to the occurrence of grief. We then study the impact of these reactions on acquisition performance.

From Grief to Employee Responses to Change

Psychological reactions at the time of a deal's announcement influence the behavior of employees over the following weeks, and the occurrence of grief will affect employee responses to the integration changes decided by the acquirer. Researchers have previously explored this causal relationship, analyzing the ways in which job satisfaction or dissatisfaction is linked to behaviors at work. Most studies have been based on the seminal work by Hirschman (1970) who investigated how employees respond to dissatisfying periods in their company. He identified three options: exit, voice and loyalty.

Exit means voluntary withdrawal from the job. The decision to leave is taken by an employee when he/she believes that the situation is unlikely to improve. The second option is called *voice*. Voice is a political response to job dissatisfaction. Hirschman (1970: 30) defined it as "any attempt at all to change rather than to escape from an objectionable state of affairs". *Voice* is a recuperative mechanism. Such attempts to change unfavorable job conditions are often attempted prior to choosing the *exit* solution (Steers and Mowday, 1981). The third alternative, *loyalty*, means that the employee decides to stay in the company even if they are suffering from a deteriorating situation. *Loyalty* is a reasoned calculation that supposes an expectation of improvement over time. The loyal employee remains silent, but hopes that "someone will act or something will happen" (Hirschman, 1970: 79).

Farrell (1983) enriched Hirschman's arguments with a fourth option: "neglect". *Neglect* refers to lax and disregardful behavior, as a consequence of job dissatisfaction. Employees remain within the organization but are inactive, inattentive and unattached to it.

The model embracing these four dimensions (Exit, Voice, Loyalty and Neglect) is generally called the EVLN model. We apply it to the context of acquisitions in order to analyse employees' responses to integration changes.

Acquisitions and Employee Responses to Change

The process perspective emphasizes integration management as a variable that influences long-term acquisition performance. In the following discussion, we assume that a fair price has been paid for a deal. In such conditions, long-term performance depends on the integration process that aims to facilitate delivery of the expected synergies (Stahl and Voigt, 2008), while at the same time avoiding value leakage (Csiszar and Schweiger, 1994). Value leakage essentially stems from the human issues raised by integration. The literature has numerous examples of acquisitions where employees strongly express their negative feelings (Buono and Bowditch, 1989; Cartwright and Cooper, 1990). Such anger can have many outcomes, as detailed in past research: employee departure, focus on internal problems and subsequent loss of clients, unwillingness to cooperate with partner's employees, difficulty in implementing synergies, and even sabotage or destruction of equipment in the worst cases. Value leakage generates additional integration costs due to absenteeism, low productivity, strikes, staff replacements, and so on. These costs may be incurred throughout the integration process and can threaten the fulfillment of economic expectations. Schweiger et al. (1987) identified sources of value leakage via interviews with individuals from acquired firms who remained with the acquirer and others who had left their jobs, either voluntarily or involuntarily. They identified five major concerns: loss of identity, lack of information and anxiety, obsession to survive, perception of lost talent, and family repercussions. Among those who were not laid off, some decided to stay (*loyalty* or *neglect* options) and others decided to leave (*exit* option). Unfortunately, while this study shows the diversity of employee responses, the authors did not link the chosen options to specific acquisition characteristics.

These findings invite us to distinguish two performance indicators:

- the ability to deliver synergies (value creation);
- additional integration costs (value leakage).

Combining these research findings with our analysis of grief in acquisitions, we apply the EVLN model to each extreme type of acquisition (that is, hostile takeover and merger of equals) and discuss the implications of our framework on our two performance indicators. It is worth noting that Bourantas and Nicandrou (1998) theoretically discuss the EVLN options in the context of mergers and acquisitions. They explore the variables that could influence the occurrence of the four options as a whole, but their work lacks overall precision as they simply list a number of variables that may or may not generate reactions. Nonetheless, the ideas developed below are partly based on their analysis.

Employee Reactions in Hostile Takeovers

Employees from an acquired firm involved in a hostile takeover are likely to mourn the past immediately as they know that the acquirer will impose changes. The dual model of grief recovery (Stroebe and Schut, 1999) involves withdrawal from the lost relationship ("loss orientation") and moving on to other interests ("restoration orientation"). The hostile take-over strategy provides a new purpose in life at work for the employee in the acquired firm. If the new project is perceived as a solution for healing the loss, the employee is likely to be satisfied with his/her new owner. If the acquirer's project is negatively perceived, the employee is liable to be dissatisfied.

The amount of time people need to recover from grief varies (Maciejewski et al., 2007). This difference is reflected in the EVLN model options that may be chosen by dissatisfied employees from firms acquired by hostile bidders: *exit*, *loyalty* or *neglect*. *Exit* is an option for employees with a "restoration orientation" of grief recovery or for those who have finished mourning the past. *Exit* will be chosen when the new organizational project fails to help them recover or does not provide an interesting purpose in life. In this case, they choose to leave the company, search-ing for new relationships that will help them to recover from their grief (Stroebe and Schut, 1999) or find a more satisfying job environment.

In specific job market conditions, dissatisfied employees can select the *loyalty* option. *Loyalty* refers to the decision to stay in the company when the situation is perceived as degenerating. *Loyalty* supposes an expect-ation of improvement over time. In hostile deals where employees feel like losers, they have no reason to believe that an improvement will occur. Thus, the only reason that might convince them to stay is the difficulty of finding comparable job opportunities outside the company. In such a case, they may perceive the change of ownership as the most attractive solution for them and are thus likely to become more or less satisfied with their new owner.

The third option is *neglect*. The *neglect* option may be selected by employees who are still in the grieving process, and particularly those who display a grief recovery "loss orientation". According to psychologists, when employees have not gotten over mourning the past, their negative emotions interfere with the attention they give to processing information (Mogg et al., 1990). The grievers have difficulty sleeping and concentrat-ing (Ringold et al., 2005) and these reactions characterize the *neglect* option that translates into inactive and inattentive behavior inside the organization.

Voice is unlikely to be an option in hostile contexts. Grief recovery involves cutting links with the past, and employees are therefore unlikely to complain about the loss of their former organization. Some stay because they adhere to the new project or because they are still in the grieving process. Others fail to adhere and prefer to leave.

To summarize, *exit*, *loyalty* and *neglect* are the options most frequently chosen by employees dissatisfied with the hostile deal. It is worth noting that these options are unlikely to last throughout the entire integration process. They characterize choices that can be made immediately after the announcement of a deal, during the grieving process or at its end. As no improvements over time are expected for dissatisfied people, the frequency of *exit* generally decreases as the integration process progresses. And *neglect* is no longer an option once the employee has ended the grieving process.

Employee Reactions in Mergers of Equals with Imposed Integration

In the case of mergers of equals, the theory of grief leads to a different set of options that can evolve throughout the integration process. The win-win contract implies that employees from acquired firms are optimistic at the time the deal is announced. Thus, at this stage of the integration process, the level of dissatisfaction can be said to be very low.

In keeping with our former arguments, grief is likely to occur over the course of integration, particularly when changes are imposed by the acquirer. Integration can be perceived as breaching the "win-win" contract and can lead to diverse reactions. Employees who are dissatisfied with the proposed integration change can choose the *exit* option, which means voluntary separation. They can also opt for *loyalty* if they think that the current state of affairs will improve. Another solution consists of fighting the dissatisfying proposals for change: thus, they choose the political option of *voice* in order to improve the state of affairs. This response occurs when employees fight to defend the interests of their former organization. *Voice* corresponds to the situation described earlier, when employees express their negative feelings strongly (Buono and Bowditch, 1989; Cartwright and Cooper, 1990). There is no reason for the *neglect* option to be chosen because this assumes that the person has started a grieving process. In short, dissatisfied employees involved in mergers of equals with imposed integration are likely to choose between *exit*, *voice* and *loyalty* during the process.

The occurrence of grief during integration assumes that employees no longer perceive any potential for improving the degenerating situation. Such perceptions are likely to emerge more or less rapidly in employees' minds. Employees will not all begin the grieving process at the same time. While some still expect or fight for improvements, others perceive the end of the psychological contract. Once they feel they have lost the game, employees will behave like "losers". As such, they are likely to choose from the set of options characterizing responses to hostile takeovers: *exit*, *loyalty* or *neglect*.

Employee Reactions in Mergers of Equals with Negotiated Integration

When the acquirer decides to compromise, integration will be negotiated by both parties until an agreement is reached. Consequently, there is no reason for grief, the proportion of dissatisfied employees from the target company is likely to be low and Hirschman's (1970) framework will not apply. As we said earlier, the decision to compromise reflects an attempt to associate employees from both firms around a common project. Thus, strong negative reactions are unlikely to emerge in a merger of equals with negotiated integration.

From Employee Responses to Acquisition Performance

The theoretical developments presented above showed that, depending on the occurrence of grief and the acquirer's management of integration, employee responses to integration change will differ between hostile take-overs and mergers of equals, and even among mergers of equals. Employee responses can also be linked to performance indicators: that is, ability to deliver synergies and extra costs of integration.

Hostile Takeovers, Employee Responses and Performance

Employees from firms acquired by hostile bidders use the *exit*, *loyalty* and *neglect* options at the start of the integration process. The *exit* response translates into the departure of employees. Researchers have highlighted the subsequent disruptive effect and the cost of hiring, selecting and train-ing new recruits (Mueller and Price, 1989; Sagie et al., 2002). High levels of employee turnover have been found to decrease organizational efficiency and to negatively impact on sales and profit (Kacmar et al., 2006). The turnover of top managers following acquisitions is higher for hostile deals than for friendly ones, as one might expect (Walsh, 1989). Turnover of the entire acquired firm's staff has not been extensively studied. We only know that if the first steps of the integration process are badly managed, it can lead to an employee exodus (Buono and Bowditch, 1989).

The *loyalty* response translates into silent behavior. The employee remains dissatisfied, but hopes that someone will act to improve the current state of affairs. This means that he/she is not motivated by the prevailing job conditions. This lack of motivation leads to absenteeism and low productivity (Harrison and Martocchio, 1998). Cartwright and Cooper (1990) effectively identified this type of increase in absenteeism among employees in acquisition situations.

The *neglect* option characterizes employees still involved in the grieving process, and particularly those adopting a loss orientation in grief recovery. Psychologists (Ringold et al., 2005) explain that employees in this situation are inactive, inattentive and make errors of judgment. They feel disconnected from the new organization and their lack of motivation favors absenteeism and decreased efficiency at work. In acquisition research, several authors have identified the risk of "merger standstill" right after the closing of a deal (Buono and Bowditch, 1989; Ivancevitch et al., 1987). Buono and Bowditch (1989) identified a possible decrease in productivity and operational effectiveness at this stage. Pritchett (1985) compares the behavior of employees in this phase to that of patients following clinical surgery. Patients' productivity and morale usually declines during the post-operative period, until they recover their physical and emotional strength. When we consider these findings overall, the *neglect* option may be considered as one cause of productivity decline in acquisitions.

In short, *exit*, *loyalty* and *neglect* options lead to loss of productivity and efficiency, and to an increase in recruitment costs. Consequently, employee reactions in hostile deals generate supplementary integration costs but do not force the acquirer to revise the initial economic forecasts.

Mergers of Equals with Imposed Integration, Employee Responses and Performance

According to our framework, employees in mergers of equals with imposed integration choose *exit*, *loyalty* or *voice* as soon as they become dissatisfied with the integration changes imposed by the acquirer. Earlier, we identified the negative consequences of *exit* and *loyalty* on company costs.

Voice reflects the employee actions for changing the prevailing situation. *Voice* is defined by Hirschman (1970) as a political response. Employees will use all means at their disposal to make decision-makers listen to them and take their demands into account. *Voice* creates costs associated with a lack of motivation and an unwillingness to cooperate with the partner's employees (Buono and Bowditch, 1989; Cartwright and Cooper, 1990, Ivancevitch et al., 1987).[3]

When the acquirer imposes change and *voice* does not produce the desired effect, employees are likely to start grieving for their former organization. Once the grieving process begins, employees select the *exit, loyalty* or *neglect* options that will raise recruitment costs and decrease organizational efficiency and productivity. Consequently, acquirers imposing integration in mergers of equals are liable to face an increase in costs during the integration process.

Mergers of Equals with Negotiated Integration, Employee Responses and Performance

The outcome is quite different when integration is negotiated in mergers of equals. The employees will exercise *exit, loyalty* and *voice* when the win-win contract is threatened, creating extra costs for the acquirer. Once a compromise has been found, the negative reactions should disappear with no additional costs. Compromising has another negative outcome, however. Negotiating integration means incorporating at least some of the acquired firm's employees' demands in the revised integration plan. This type of negotiation is likely to end up as a rational inefficient compromise. Rational inefficient compromises are agreements that are based on criteria different from efficiency optimization (Alemi et al., 1990; Kersten and Mallory, 1999; Prasnikar and Roth, 1992). Political scientists have shown that such political compromises are costly (Alesina, 1988; Dixit et al., 2000) as it means compromising on initial efficiency ambitions. Applied to the context of acquisitions, this reduces the chances of delivering the expected synergies because the compromise lowers ambitions in order to safeguard social peace. Even if the employees' become more committed, this will simply facilitate the achievement of the newly negotiated objectives. Consequently, the implementation of a merger of equals driven by a negotiated integration will hinder the ability to reach the transaction's initial economic objectives.

This leads us to formulate a number of hypotheses concerning the association between the nature of the deal, integration management and the achievement of economic acquisition objectives. These hypotheses are built on the following two conditions. First, as mentioned earlier, we assume that the transaction was made at a fair price (Sudarsanam and Mahate, 2006). Second, we also assume that the voluntary departure of employees is an issue: in some cases, such departures can serve the interests of an acquirer who plans to reduce the size of the staff through layoffs (Flanagan and O'Shaughnessy, 2005; Krishnan et al., 2007). This may apply if a source of value resides either in the improvement of the acquired firm's management (particularly in the case of hostile takeovers) or in the elimination of redundancies. Here we assume that the depart-ure of employees is a performance issue. It is also worth noting that the acquirer's economic performance is likely to evolve during the integration period: performance can be influenced by numerous factors like evolu-tions in the industry or other strategic moves made by the acquirer (Zollo and Meier, 2008). Our hypotheses are developed holding these factors constant.

P4. All things being equal, the nature of the deal and integration manage-ment influence acquisition performance.

P4a. All things being equal, immediately after the deal announcement, a hostile takeover is associated with extra integration costs.

P4b. All things being equal, in the course of integration, a merger of equals with imposed integration is associated with extra integration costs.

P4c. All things being equal, in the course of integration, a merger of equals with negotiated integration is associated with the inability to deliver the fore-casted synergies.

Figures 11.2, 11.3 and 11.4 illustrate our theoretical framework linking the nature of the deal, integration management and acquisition performance, respectively for hostile takeovers and mergers of equals.

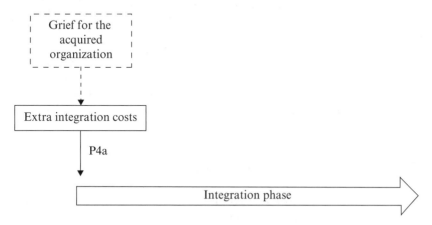

Figure 11.2   Grief and acquisition performance in hostile takeovers

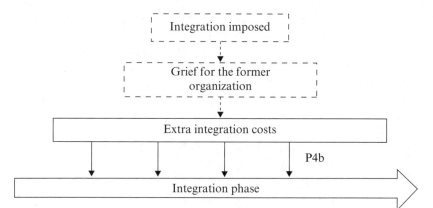

Figure 11.3   Grief and performance in mergers of equals with imposed integration

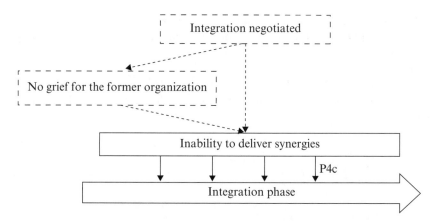

Figure 11.4   Grief and performance in mergers of equals with negotiated integration

DISCUSSION AND IMPLICATIONS

The grief-based theory of acquisition performance leads to three conclusions regarding the acquisition management process.

First, managing integration of hostile acquisitions is likely to be smoother than managing integration of mergers of equals. Hostile deals are characterized by the departure of employees and a drop in productivity and efficiency. In comparison, the scope of integration challenges faced in win-win deals is wider: these include more violent reactions from angry employees through the exercise of *voice*, and subsequent negotiation and resistance to change. *Voice* characterizes win-win deals. Therefore, while hostility is found in the pre-closing phase for hostile deals, mergers of equals can generate hostility in the post-closing phase.

Second, the acquirer's way of managing integration in mergers of equals is likely to generate human reactions that could negatively impact on acquisition performance. Integration is often conceived as a way to create value while resolving the issues that could contribute to value leakage (Csiszar and Schweiger, 1994). Our framework shows that the integration process management, whether imposed or negotiated, influences value leakage in such deals.

Third, our theory provides an indication of the location of the major sources of value creation within the overall acquisition process. Smoother integration of hostile deals leads one to postulate that integration is not the main challenge for value creation. As various researchers have argued (Morck et al., 1988), a major issue in hostile takeovers is determining the price to be paid for the target. Information about the target is scarce prior to the deal, as due diligence procedures cannot be implemented. Acquirers have to define a target price in a state of information asymmetry. Moreover, the target's defensive actions can force the acquirer to raise its price and create the risk of winner's curse (Sudarsanam and Mahate, 2006). As the price paid influences the ability to reach the economic acquisition object-ives, this is a key performance issue in hostile deals. Consequently, the creation of economic performance in hostile deals will primarily depend on the appropriate management of the pre-acquisition phase.

In mergers of equals, due diligence procedures can generally be imple-mented in order to reduce the problem of information asymmetry. Thus, firms are able to accumulate more knowledge about their partner that will help them to gauge synergies and firms' value. This knowledge helps deter-mine the maximum price that should be negotiated. Nonetheless, acqui-sition management has proved a problem in friendly deals where both parties negotiate. Acquirers have to manage the increasing momentum that characterizes this preparation and negotiation phase (Haspeslagh and Jemison, 1991). In addition to these research findings, our theoretical analysis indicates that integration in mergers of equals is a complex process involving serious challenges regarding delivery of the expected perform-ance. This leads us to deduce that the creation of economic performance in mergers of equals depends on the effective management of the whole acquisition process. These theoretical implications highlight the relevance of adopting a process view in future research on acquisition outcomes.

Our analysis of the negative consequences of employee reactions could give the impression that M&A cannot achieve economic performance whatever the nature of the deal. This is not true for at least four reasons:

- First, most extra integration costs can be broadly anticipated and integrated into the price calculations undertaken during the negotiation phase of the acquisition process. Since the 1980s, research has shown the almost systematic decrease in productivity and efficiency following an acquisition (Pritchett, 1985; Cartwright and Cooper, 1990). Accordingly, it can be reasonably assumed that experienced acquirers anticipate these extra costs. Thus, these costs should not prevent an acquirer from achieving the expected acquisition performance in hostile deals. This is also true for acquirers who impose integration in mergers of equals, although the impact of voice – prior to the grieving process – can be quite hard to predict.
- Second, employees' resistance in mergers of equals occurs if integration actions undertaken by top management are perceived as breaching the psychological "win-win contract". Mergers almost systematically induce transformational changes in the companies as their motivation lies in the emergence of the new group's new strategic direction (Buono and Bowditch, 1989). The partial or total integrity of the initial firms, as desired by its employees, cannot be preserved in most cases but there may be instances where the set of changes envisioned by each partner overlap perfectly. In such cases, the integration process can be monitored as planned and most employees will remain satisfied with the new project or even committed to it. Note that the literature has not yet identified such acquisitions.
- Third, in mergers of equals with imposed integration, our framework leads us to assume that performance achievement is associated with the capacity of the acquirer to provoke grief as early as possible in the integration phase. This paradoxical idea requires more exploration. If grief occurs at an early stage of integration, the period of *voice* and its unpredictable consequences will be shortened. Once the grieving is over, extra integration costs should only come into play early in the process, as is the case in hostile deals. Therefore, our framework advocates accompanying employees in their grieving process as early as possible.
- Fourth, we based our reflections on mergers of equals according to an integration management dichotomy, in other words, whether integration is imposed or negotiated. The reality can be much more nuanced: top managers can decide what is negotiable and what is

not. Ideally, what is negotiable should not prevent delivery of the main synergies. In other words, integration management is tricky and needs a subtle mix between the imposition of change and the search for agreement with the parties involved. However, what emerges from our analysis is that too much negotiation could threaten the economic outcomes of mergers.

CONCLUSION

King et al. (2004) showed that we know little about acquisition performance and called for a new way of thinking about acquisitions. The present theoretical study attempts to respond to this gap in theory. We chose to compare two extreme types of acquisition: mergers of equals and hostile takeovers, and applied the theory of grief, combined with the acquirer's mode of managing integration, to analyse employee reactions and their influence on acquisition performance. Our framework indicates that the construction of economic performance can be threatened in quite different ways when we compare the two types of acquisition. When a fair price has been paid for the target, delivering the expected synergies appears to be more challenging in mergers of equals than in hostile takeovers.

These arguments underline a paradox: from an economic perspective, integration of hostile deals is likely to go smoothly, while integration of mergers of equals can generate hostility. The honeymoon period in win-win mergers cannot last long due to the pressure to achieve economic performance. The atmosphere in both cases is likely to change after the deal closes: the losers stop fighting in hostile takeovers, and there is more tension and hostility between 'friends' during the integration phase of so-called mergers of equals.

Our analysis led us to formulate a set of propositions that can easily be tested in future research. It is worth noting that measurement tools exist for all the concepts included in the framework. Even the emergence of grief among employees and grief recovery can be evaluated (see for instance Ringold et al., 2005; Shepherd, 2003). A further avenue would be to analyse the occurrence and impact of grief in friendly acquisitions. We examined two extreme natures of transactions, but more investigation is needed to understand how our framework could be applied to deals of an intermediary nature.

The theory also has consequences on future M&A research. We know that sources of value creation are dependent on strategic objectives. In this chapter, we show that they are also likely to depend on the nature of the deal. This confirms the heterogeneity of the M&A market in several ways.

While most research considers this market as a whole, its heterogeneity calls for research that looks more closely at specific types of acquisitions. Researchers may, for instance, benefit from studying the integration of hostile takeovers, a type of deal almost exclusively studied in finance, but found to outperform friendly acquisitions.

NOTES

1. Recent work has shown that short-term measures of acquisition performance – like cumulative abnormal returns (CARs) around deal announcement – are not linked to long-term performance, but that integration process performance is associated with long-term performance (Zollo and Meier, 2008). In this chapter, we are interested in explaining variations in long-term performance and will not refer to short-term event window studies.
2. The feeling that the psychological contract is violated also depends on individual characteristics. Each employee has a specific level of attachment to the organization, and his/ her own perception of implicit mutual obligations. Therefore, over time in the context of a merger of equals, each employee develops his/her own perception that the contract is broken. This means that, in such a context, employees are likely to start their grieving process – if they start it – at different points of time in the course of integration.
3. If the situation degenerates too much, the consequences can be even worse: loss of clients, difficulty implementing synergies and so on (Very, 2004).

REFERENCES

Alemi, F., Fos, P. and Lacorte, W. 1990. 'A demonstration of methods for studying negotiations between physicians and health care managers'. *Decision Science*, 21: 633–641.

Alesina, A. 1988. 'Credibility and policy convergence in a two-party system with rational voters'. *American Economic Review*, 78: 796–805.

Angwin, D. 2004. 'Speed in M&A integration: the first 100 days'. *European Management Journal*, 22(4): 418–430.

Archer, J. 1999. *The Nature of Grief: The Evolution and Psychology of Reactions to Loss*. New York: Routledge.

Archer, J. and Rhodes, V. 1993. 'The grief process and job loss: a cross-sectional study'. *British Journal of Psychology*, 84(3): 395–411.

Barnes, P. 1998. 'Why do bidders do badly out of mergers? Some UK evidence'. *Journal of Business, Finance and Accounting*, 15: 45–49.

Bento, R.F. 1994. 'When the show must go on: disenfranchised grief in organizations'. *Journal of Managerial Psychology*, 9(6): 35–44.

Birkinshaw, J., Bresman, H. and Håkanson, L. 2000. 'Managing the post-acquisition integration process: how the human integration and task integration processes interact to foster value creation'. *Journal of Management Studies*, 37: 395–425.

Bourantas, D. and Nicandrou, I.I. 1998. 'Modelling post-acquisition employee behavior: typology and determining factors'. *Employee Relations*, 20: 73–91.

Bower, J.L. 2001. 'Not all M&A are alike . . . and that matters'. *Harvard Business Review*, 79(3): 93–101.

Bowlby, J. 1980. *Attachment and Loss. Vol. 3: Loss, Sadness and Depression*. New York: Basic Books.

Brewington, J.O., Nassar-McMillan, S.C., Flowers, C.P. and Furr, S.R. 2004. 'A preliminary investigation of factors associated with job loss grief'. *The Career Development Quarterly*, 53: 78–83.

Buono, A.F. and Bowditch, J.L. 1989. *The Human Side of Mergers and Acquisitions: Managing Collisions Between People, Cultures and Organizations*. San Francisco, CA: Jossey-Bass.

Cartwright, S. and Cooper, C.L. 1990. 'The impact of mergers and acquisitions on people at work: existing research and issues'. *British Journal of Management*, 1: 65–76.

Csiszar, E.N. and Schweiger, D.M. 1994. 'An integrative framework for creating value through acquisitions'. In H.E. Glass and B.N. Craven (eds), *Handbook of Business Strategy*. New York: Gohram & Lamont, pp. 93–115.

Devine, K., Reay, T., Stainton, L. and Collins-Nakai, R. 2003. 'Downsizing outcomes: better a victim than a survivor?' *Human Resource Management*, 42(2): 109–124.

Dixit, A., Grossman, G.M. and Gul, F. 2000. 'The dynamics of political compromise'. *Journal of Political Economy*, 108: 531–568.

Evans, M.J. and Tyler-Evans, M. 2002. 'Aspects of grief in conflict: re-visioning response to dispute'. *Conflict Resolution Quarterly*, 20: 83–97.

Farrell, D. 1983. 'Exit, voice, loyalty and neglect as responses to job dissatisfaction: a multi-dimensional scaling study'. *Academy of Management Journal*, 26: 596–607.

Flanagan, D.J. and O'Shaughnessy, K.C. 2005. 'The effect of layoffs on firm reputation'. *Journal of Management*, 31: 445–463.

Franks, J.R. and Mayer, C. 1996. 'Hostile takeovers and correction of managerial failure'. *Journal of Financial Economics*, 40: 163–181.

Franks, J.R., Harris, R.S. and Titman, S. 1991. 'The post-merger share price performance of acquiring firms'. *Journal of Financial Economics*, 29: 81–96.

Freud, S. 1935. *A General Introduction to Psychoanalysis*. New York: Liveright.

Gregory, A. 1997. 'An examination, of the long-run performance of UK acquiring firms'. *Journal of Business, Finance and Accounting*, 24: 971–1002.

Gregory, A. and Matatko, J. 2004. 'Biases in estimating long run abnormal returns and conditional measures of performance: the evidence on takeovers re-examined'. Working Paper 04/04, University of Exeter, UK.

Harris, S.G. and Sutton, R.L. 1986. 'Functions of parting ceremonies in dying organizations'. *Academy of Management Journal*, 29(1): 5–30.

Harrison, D. and Martocchio, J. 1998. 'Time for absenteeism: a 20-year review of origins, offshoots, and outcomes'. *Journal of Management*, 24(3): 305–350.

Haspeslagh, P.C. and Jemison, D.B. 1987. 'Acquisitions: myths and reality'. *Sloan Management Review*, 28(2): 53–58.

Haspeslagh, P.C. and Jemison, D.B. 1991. *Managing Acquisitions: Creating Value from Corporate Renewal*. New York: Free Press.

Hazen, M.A. 2008. 'Grief and the workplace'. *Academy of Management Perspectives*, 22(3): 78–86.

Hirschman, A.O. 1970. *Exit, Voice, and Loyalty: Responses to Decline in Firms, Organizations, and States*. Cambridge, MA: Harvard University Press.

Ivancevitch, J.M., Schweiger, D.M. and Power, F.R. 1987. 'Strategies for managing human resources during mergers and acquisitions'. *Human Resource Planning*, 10(1): 19–35.

James, J.W. and Friedman, R. 1988. *The Grief Recovery Outreach Program*. Los Angeles, CA: Grief Recovery Institute.

Jeffreys, J.S. 1995. *Coping with Workplace Change: Dealing with Loss and Grief*. Menlo Park, CA: Crisp Publications.

Jemison, D.B. and Sitkin, S.B. 1986. 'Corporate acquisitions: a process perspective'. *Academy of Management Review*, 11: 145–163.

Kacmar, K.M., Andrews, M.C., Van Rooy, D.L., Steilberg, R.C. and Cerrone, S. 2006. 'Sure everyone can be replaced . . . but at what cost? Turnover as a predictor of unit-level performance'. *Academy of Management Journal*, 49: 133–144.

Kersten, G.E. and Mallory, G.R. 1999. 'Rationale inefficient compromises in negotiation'. *Journal of Multi-Criteria Decision Analysis*, 8: 106–111.

Kets de Vries, M.F.R. and Balazs, K. 1997. 'The downside of downsizing'. *Human Relations*, 50(1): 11–50.

King, D.R., Dalton, D.R., Daily, C.M. and Covin, J.G. 2004. 'Meta-analyses of post-acquisition performance: indicators of unidentified moderators'. *Strategic Management Journal*, 25: 187–200.

Kini, O., Kracaw, W. and Mian, S. 2004. 'The nature and discipline of takeovers'. *Journal of Finance*, 59: 1511–1552.

Krishnan, H.A., Hitt, M.A. and Park, D. 2007. 'Acquisition premiums, subsequent work-force reductions and post-acquisition performance'. *Journal of Management Studies*, 44: 709–732.

Kübler-Ross, E. 1969. *On Death and Dying*. New York: MacMillan.

Larsson, R. and Finkelstein, S. 1999. 'Integrating strategic, organizational, and human resource perspectives on mergers and acquisitions: a case survey of synergy realization'. *Organization Science*, 10(1): 1–26.

Maciejewski, P.K., Zhang, B., Block, S.D. and Prigerson, H.G. 2007. 'An empirical examination of the stage theory of grief'. *The Journal of the American Medical Association*, 297: 716–723.

Marks, M.L. and Mirvis, P. 1986. 'The merger syndrome'. *Psychology Today*, October, 36–42.

Mogg, K., Matthews, A., Bird, C. and McGregor-Morris, R. 1990. 'Effects of stress and anxiety on the processing of threat stimuli'. *Journal of Personality and Social Psychology*, 59: 1230–1237.

Morck, R., Shleifer, A. and Vishny, R. 1988. 'Management ownership and market valuation: an empirical analysis'. *Journal of Financial Economics*, 20: 293–315.

Mueller, C.W. and Price, J.L. 1989. 'Some consequences of turnover: a work unit analysis'. *Human Relations*, 42: 389–402.

Niden, C.M. 1993. 'An empirical examination of whiteknight corporate takeovers: synergy and overbidding'. *Financial Management*, 22: 28–45.

Pailot, P. 1999. 'Freins psychologiques et transmission d'entreprise: un cadre d'analyse fondé sur la méthode biographique'. *Revue Internationale des PME*, 12(3): 9–32.

Pailot, P. 2000. 'De la difficulté de l'entrepreneur à quitter son entreprise'. In T. Verstraete (ed.), *Histoire d'entreprendre: les réalités de l'entrepreneuriat*. Paris, France: Ed. EMS, pp. 275–286.

Pine, V.R. 1989. 'Death, loss, and disenfranchised grief'. In K. Doka (ed.), *Disenfranchised Grief: Recognizing Hidden Sorrow*. Lexington, MA: D.C. Heath & Company Books, pp. 13–23.

Prasnikar, V. and Roth, A.E. 1992. 'Consideration of fairness and strategy: experimental data from sequential games'. *Quarterly Journal of Economics*, 107: 865–888.

Pritchett, P. 1985. *After the Merger: Managing the Shockwaves*. Homewood, IL: Dow Jones-Irwin.

Ringold, S., Lynm, C. and Glass, R.M. 2005. 'Grief'. *The Journal of the American Medical Association*, 293: 2686.

Sagie, A., Birati, A. and Tziner, A. 2002. 'Assessing the costs of behavioral and psychological withdrawal: new model and an empirical illustration'. *Applied Psychology*, 51: 67–89.

Schweiger, D.M., Ivancevitch, J.M. and Power, F.R. 1987. 'Executive actions for managing human resources before and after acquisition'. *Academy of Management Executive*, 1(2): 127–138.

Shepherd, D.A. 2003. 'Learning from business failure: propositions of grief recovery for the self-employed'. *Academy of Management Review*, 28: 318–328.

Stahl, G.K. and Voigt, A. 2008. 'Do cultural differences matter in mergers and acquisitions? A tentative model and examination'. *Organization Science*, 19(1): 160–176.

Steers, R.M. and Mowday, R.T. 1981. 'Employee turnover and post-decision accommodation process'. In L. Cummings and B. Staw (eds), *Research in Organizational Behavior*. Greenwich, CT: JAI Press, Vol. 3: 235–281.

Stroebe, M. and Schut, H. 1999. 'The dual process of coping with bereavement: rationale and description'. *Death Studies*, 23: 197–224.

Sudarsanam, S. and Mahate, A.A. 2006. 'Are friendly acquisitions too bad for shareholders and managers? Long-term value creation and top-management turnover in hostile and friendly acquirers'. *British Journal of Management*, 17: 7–30.

Very, P. 2004. *The Management of Mergers and Acquisitions*, Chichester, UK: Wiley.

Walsh, J.P. 1989. 'Doing a deal: merger and acquisition negotiations and their impact upon target company top management turnover'. *Strategic Management Journal*, 10(4): 307–322.

Wells, A. and Matthews, G. 1994. *Attention and Emotion: A Clinical Perspective*. Hove, UK: Lawrence Erlbaum Associates.

Wulf, J. 2004. 'Do CEOs in mergers trade power for premium? Evidence from "mergers of equals"'. *Journal of Law, Economics, and Organization*, 20(1): 60–101.

Zaheer, S., Schomaker, M. and Gene, M. 2003. 'Identity versus culture in mergers of equals'. *European Management Journal*, 21(2): 185–191.

Zell, D. 2003. 'Organizational change as a process of death, dying, and rebirth'. *Journal of Applied Behavioral Science*, 39: 73–96.

Zollo, M. and Meier, D. 2008. 'What is M&A performance?' *Academy of Management Perspectives*, 22(3): 55–77.

Index